CHILTON'S Repair and Tune-Up Guide

Corvette Stingray

1963-76

ILLUSTRATED

Prepared by the

Automotive Editorial Department

Chilton Book Company

Chilton Way

Radnor, Pa. 19089

215—687-8200

president and chief executive officer **WILLIAM A. BARBOUR;** executive vice president **RICHARD H. GROVES;** vice president and general manager **JOHN P. KUSHNERICK;** managing editor **JOHN H. WEISE, S.A.E.;** assistant managing editor **KERRY A. FREEMAN, S.A.E.;** technical editors **John G. Mohan, Ronald L. Sessions**

CHILTON BOOK COMPANY   RADNOR, PENNSYLVANIA

Library of Congress Cataloging in Publication Data

Chilton Book Company. Automotive Editorial Dept.
   Chilton's repair and tune-up guide, Corvette Stingray
1963–76.

   1. Corvette Stingray automobile. I. Title. II. Ti-
tle: Repair and tune-up guide, Corvette Stingray 1963–76.
TL215.C63C5   1975   629.28'7'22   75-40498
ISBN 0-8019-6321-4
ISBN 0-8019-6322-2 pbk.

ACKNOWLEDGMENT

Chilton Book Company thanks the Chevrolet Motor Division of
the General Motors Corporation for assistance in the production
of this book.

Information has been selected from Service and Overhaul man-
uals from 1963 through 1975.

Contents

Chapter 1

General Information and Maintenance

Introduction

The 1963 Corvette Stingray * is a complete departure from the Corvettes which preceded it. The body, frame, and front and rear suspensions are all of new design. Engines and transmissions are the only components that were shared with the older models. Stingray body styling evolved from the original William Mitchell Stingray sports/racing car which competed in 1959–60. Fiberglass bodywork was retained, but included a steel, reinforcing framework around the passenger compartment. The convertible model, with or without hardtop, was retained and a new body style added, the fastback coupe. Retractable headlights, rotated by two electric motors, were also a new feature for the Corvette.

The frame is a ladder type with five crossmembers. The wheelbase has been reduced from the 102 in. of previous models to a more compact 98 in., and the rear track shortened by 2 in. This, coupled with component relocation, resulted in a 48/52 percent front/rear weight distribution; a marked improvement over the 53 percent front weight bias of earlier model Corvettes. Overall body height was reduced by 2 in. Front and rear suspensions are both independent and newly designed for the Stingray. The short/long arm front suspension has the upper arm tilted at an angle of 9° for an anti-dive effect under braking. Steering knuckles pivot in ball joints, instead of the king pins and bushings of the early Corvettes. The fully independent rear suspension is sprung with a nine-leaf transverse spring. Universal-jointed axle driveshafts transmit power to the wheels. Steering gear is recirculating ball type and the linkage includes a hydraulic damper. Power steering and brakes both became optionally available for the first time on a Corvette. Brake drums were enlarged and the brakes were made self-adjusting. Air conditioning became optionally available in late 1963.

1964 saw detail body changes: functional passenger-compartment exhaust vents and elimination of the split rear window on the coupe, removal of the

* The model name Stingray, from 1963 through 1968, was spelled as two words, Sting Ray. From 1969, this one-word form is official.

non-functional vents on the hood, and new wheel covers. The Muncie four-speed transmission, introduced in mid-year 1963 to replace the Borg-Warner T-10, became the optional four-speed. The solid lifter engines received larger intake and exhaust valves, and horsepower increased from 340 to 365 and from 360 to 375 for the carburetted and fuel-injected engines respectively. Transistorized, breakerless ignition became optionally available on high performance engines in 1964.

In 1965, the big change was the introduction of four-wheel disc brakes. Braking power and fade resistance were greatly increased over the drum brakes. A flat hood replaced the 1964 hood which had twin indentations and other body changes included restyled wheel covers and functional exhaust vents behind the front wheels. A new version of the 327 cubic inch engine was introduced, the 350 horsepower, hydraulic-cam option. In midyear, a 396 cubic inch 425 horsepower engine was made available in the Corvette. 396 Corvettes were distinguished by the domed hood required for carburetor clearance. Cars equipped with the 396 received a larger front stabilizer bar and the addition of a rear stabilizer bar. Side-mounted exhausts with chambered mufflers joined the option list in 1965.

The 250, 365, and 375 horsepower engines were dropped in 1966. The 300 horsepower, 327 cubic inch engine became the standard power plant and the standard three-speed transmission was synchronized in all forward gears. The 396 was bored out to 427 cubic inches and offered in two versions, a 425 horsepower and a milder 390 horsepower model. A heavy-duty, four-speed transmission was introduced for use with the high performance 427. Body changes included a new, egg-crate grille, restyled wheel covers, and the addition of back-up lights.

1967 body styling changes included a hood scoop on 427 Stingrays, more subdued exhaust vents on the front fenders, and a center back-up light. Wheels were widened ½ inch to 6 inches and were slotted. The full wheel covers of former models were discarded for trim rings and center caps. The handbrake was changed to the pull-up type, and relocated to the center console. The 300, 350, and 390 horsepower engines remained the same for 1967. Three, two-barrel carburetors were added to the 390 horsepower engine to produce an additional engine rated at 400 horsepower. The same manifold and carburetors, plus aluminum cylinder heads, installed on the former 425 horsepower block gave a 435 horsepower rating.

For the 1968 Corvette, a completely redesigned body and interior were installed on a basically unchanged chassis. Many of the styling features of the new body had been previewed on the Mako Shark show car. Overall body width and height were reduced, while front and rear tread increased with the use of one inch wider wheels. The convertible model was retained and the fastback coupe was replaced with a hardtop model featuring removable roof panels and rear window. Headlights on 1968 and later cars are raised automatically, with vacuum power when the lights are switched on. Wide oval F70-15 tires replaced the 7.75-15 tires of previous years. The two-speed, Powerglide automatic transmission was superseded by the three-speed Turbo Hydra-Matic, a significant improvement for general driving and performance usage. Engines remained the same, except for the addition of the air-injection reactor pump to control exhaust emissions. Corvettes sold in California have been equipped with the A.I.R. system since 1966.

Body styling remained the same for 1969 except for the addition of a Stingray script above the engine exhaust vent. The doors were slightly reshaped, widening the cockpit by one inch at shoulder height. Wheel width was increased to 8 inches, which also increased front and rear tread. The anti-theft ignition, steering, and transmission lock were introduced in 1969, with the ignition switch mounted on the steering column. Side exhausts were offered for the first time on the new body in 1969. Headlight washers were now included in the standard equipment. The small block stroke was increased to give a displacement of 350 cubic inches; however, horsepower ratings remained the same. 427 engine options were the same as in 1968, except that the L88 430 horsepower model was available with a Turbo Hydra-Matic.

A new grille, larger parabolic reflector turn signals, and wheel well flares were added to the Stingray body for 1970. Cast metal grilles were added over the engine compartment exhaust vents and the tailpipe exits were made rectangular. The seats were redesigned, lowering them one inch for more headroom and making the headrests integral. The 427 stroke was increased for 1970 to give a displacement of 454 cubic inches. Triple, two-barrel carburetion was dropped from the big blocks in 1970. A 370 horsepower 350 cubic inch engine, the LT-1, was introduced to answer the need for a solid lifter, small block engine. The three-speed, manual transmission was discontinued in 1970, and the four-speed transmission and Positraction rear axle were made standard equipment.

Horsepower was decreased in 1971 through an across-the-board compression reduction. The 350 horsepower, hydraulic-cam version of the small block was deleted from the option list and a big block, mechanical-lifter engine was introduced. This engine, the LS6, produced 425 horsepower on regular gasoline.

1972 saw very few changes made to the Corvette. Rated horsepower was again down, due mostly to a new rating system which utilizes net instead of gross power outputs. The audio alarm anti-theft system is now a standard item, and the fiber optic light monitors have been discontinued. Only three engines are offered for 1972, two 350 cubic inch engines and one 454 cubic inch engine. There were no body changes, except for the addition of four new colors.

1973 saw the Corvette receive a new front end with a resilient body color bumper. The cool air induction hood covers the windshield wipers, allowing the wiper door and mechanism to be eliminated. New body mounts and extra soundproofing were also added for 1973. GR70-15 steel-belted radial tires are standard equipment. Two 350 cu in. engines were offered, but the optional L82 engine now had hydraulic lifters, replacing the solids available in 1972. The 454 Turbo-Jet was also available with a rating of 275 horsepower.

1974 was a year of very little change for the Corvette. A resilient rear section was added similar to the front system introduced in 1973. Three engines continued to be available, except in California where only the two 350s were available.

Changes to the 1975 Corvette include a catalytic reactor to reduce emissions, a fuel cell-type fuel tank, and the dropping of the 454 engine.

Only one Corvette body style was available for 1976, the convertible was dropped. The Turbo Hydra-Matic 350 replaced the 400 on the base engine. A partial steel underbody replaced the traditional fiberglass, which both improved body strength and heat protection from the exhaust system.

Corvettes have proven themselves in all types of automotive competition, and the Stingray has continued to bear the Corvette standard in many forms of racing. A Stingray coupe won the first race entered in October 1962 at Riverside Raceway. Since then, Corvettes have continued their winning ways in road racing in the SCCA A and B-Production classes. Corvettes have also taken numerous trophies in drag racing, in both the stock and modified classes. Sebring, Daytona, and Le Mans have witnessed many Corvette entries; Corvettes have placed well overall and succeeded in winning the GT class several times at these endurance races. The aerodynamic Stingray has also been utilized several times in setting Grand Touring class records during the Bonneville Speed Weeks. That racing improves the breed has certainly proved to be true in the case of the Corvette, with many race-proven pieces having become standard equipment or options on production Corvettes.

The intent of *Chilton's Repair and Tune-Up Guide for the Corvette Stingray* is to cover maintenance and repair procedures that the owner or average repair shop will be able to perform without special tools or equipment. Jobs which absolutely require special factory tools, such as automatic transmission overhaul, are best left to an authorized Chevrolet dealer. Corvette models manufactured from 1963 through 1976 are covered in this book. The tune-up and troubleshooting section is especially designed to enable the owner to diagnose and correct any minor problems before they become major repair jobs. A chapter is devoted to each operating system and includes repair and overhaul procedures.

Serial Number Identification

VEHICLE

The 1963 through 1967 Corvette vehicle serial number, body style, body trim number, and paint combination is located on the instrument panel reinforcing member directly under the glove compartment. The 1968 through 1976 vehicle

1963–67 vehicle serial number location

serial number plate is located on the top left of the instrument panel. The body number, trim, and paint number plate is located on the upper left-hand door hinge pillar. The vehicle serial number identifies the body style, model year, assembly plant (always S, for St. Louis), and production number.

ENGINE

All Corvette engine serial numbers are located on a pad between the water pump and the front of the right cylinder head. The first letter identifies the plant the engine was manufactured in and the numbers identify the date of production. The two or three-letter suffix identifies the engine type and equipment.

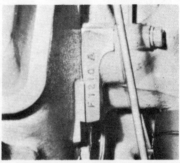

Engine serial number location

Interpreting the Serial Number

A typical vehicle serial number tag yields manufacturer's identity, vehicle type, model year, assembly plant and production unit number when broken down as shown in the following charts.

1963–71

Mfr Identity [1]	Body Style [2]	Model Year [3]	Assy Plant [4]	Unit No. [5]
1	5645	8	F	100025

[1] Manufacturer's identity number assigned to all Chevrolet built vehicles
[2] Model identification
[3] Last number of model year (1968)
[4] F-Flint
[5] Unit numbering will start at 100,001 at all plants

1972–76

Mfr Identity [1]	Series Code Letter [2]	Body Style [3]	Engine Model [4]	Model Year [5]	Assembly Plant [6]	Unit Number [7]
1	N	47	R	4	F	100025

[1] Manufacturer's identity number assigned to all Chevrolet built vehicles
[2] Model identification
[3] Model identification
[4] Engine code
[5] Last number of model year (1974)
[6] F-Flint
[7] Unit numbering will start at 000001 or 100,001 depending on the model

Engine Identification

1963–64
327 cubic inch engine

Manual transmission	RC
Manual transmission and high performance	RD
Special high performance	RE
Manual transmission and fuel injection	RF
Powerglide	SC
Powerglide and high performance	SD

1964
327 cubic inch engine

Manual transmission and A/C	RP
Manual transmission, high performance, A/C	RQ
Manual transmission, special high performance, A/C	RR
Manual transmission and transistor ignition	RT
Fuel injection and transistor ignition	RX
Manual transmission, transistor ignition, A/C	RU
Powerglide and A/C	SK
Powerglide, high performance, A/C	SL

1965
327 cubic inch engine

Manual transmission	HE
High performance	HF
Fuel injection	HG
Special high performance	HH
A/C	HI
High performance and A/C	HJ
Special high performance and A/C	HK
Transistor ignition	HL
Transistor ignition and A/C	HM
Fuel injection and transistor ignition	HN
Powerglide	HO
Powerglide and high performance	HP
Powerglide and A/C	HQ
Powerglide, high performance, A/C	HR
Special high performance and hydraulic lifters	HT
Special high performance, hydraulic lifters, A/C	HU
Special high performance, hydraulic lifters, transistor ignition	HV
Special high performance, hydraulic lifters, transistor ignition, A/C	HW

396 cubic inch engine

Special high performance	IF

1966
327 cubic inch engine

Manual transmission	HE
A.I.R.	HH
A.I.R. and Powerglide	HR
Special high performance and A.I.R.	HD
Powerglide	HO
Special high performance	HT
Power steering, special high performance, A.I.R.	HP
Special high performance, A/C, A.I.R.	KH

427 cubic inch engine

Special high performance and hydraulic lifters	IK
High performance	IL

A.I.R.	IM
Special high performance	IP
Powerglide	IQ
Powerglide and A.I.R.	IR

1967
327 cubic inch engine

Manual transmission	HE
A.I.R.	HH
A.I.R. and Powerglide	HR
Special high performance and A.I.R.	HD
Powerglide	HO
Special high performance	HT
Power steering, special high performance, A/C	HP
Special high performance, A/C, A.I.R.	KH

427 cubic inch engine

4-speed or Powerglide	IL
Triple carburetion	JC
A.I.R., special high performance, triple carburetion	JE
Heavy duty	IT
Aluminum heads	IU
A.I.R.	IM
A.I.R. and triple carburetion	JF
A.I.R. and aluminum heads	JH
Powerglide	IQ
Powerglide and triple carburetion	JD
A.I.R. and Powerglide	IR
A.I.R., triple carburetion, Powerglide	JG
A.I.R., special high performance, triple carburetion	JA

1968
327 cubic inch engine

Manual transmission	HE
Turbo Hydra-Matic	HO
Power steering and A/C	HP
Special high performance	HT

427 cubic inch engine

High performance	IL
High performance and triple carburetion	IM
High performance, triple carburetion, Turbo Hydra-Matic	IO
Turbo Hydra-Matic	IQ
Special high performance and triple carburetion	IR
High performance	IT
Special high performance, triple carburetion, aluminum heads	IU

1969
350 cubic inch engine

High performance	HW
High performance and A/C	HX
Manual transmission	HY
Turbo Hydra-Matic	HZ

427 cubic inch engine

High performance, Turbo Hydra-Matic	LL
High performance	LM
Triple carburetion, high performance, Turbo Hydra-Matic	LN
Heavy duty	LO
Aluminum heads	LP
Triple carburetion and high performance	LQ
Triple carburetion and special high performance	LR

Engine Identification (cont.)

1969
427 cubic inch engine

Triple carburetion, special high performance, heavy duty clutch	LU
Heavy duty and Turbo Hydra-Matic	LV
Triple carburetion, special high performance, Turbo Hydra-Matic	LX

1970
350 cubic inch engine

Manual transmission	CTL
Turbo Hydra-Matic	CTM
High performance	CTN
High performance and A/C	CTO
High performance and transistor ignition	CTP
High performance, transistor ignition, A/C	CTQ
Special high performance	CTR
Special high performance and transistor ignition	CTU
Special high performance, transistor ignition, 4-speed	CTV
High performance, 4-bbl carburetor, Turbo Hydra-Matic	CZN
High performance, 4-bbl carburetor, transistor ignition	CRI

454 cubic inch engine

High performance, 4-bbl carburetor, Turbo Hydra-Matic	CGW
High performance and 4-bbl	CZU
Heavy duty with 4-bbl	CZL
Heavy duty with 4-bbl and Turbo Hydra-Matic	CZN
High performance, 4-bbl, transistor ignition	CRI

1971
350 cubic inch engine

300 hp with 4-speed	CGS
350 hp with 4-speed	CGW, CGX
370 hp with 4-speed	CGZ, CGY
300 hp with Turbo Hydra-Matic	CGT

454 cubic inch engine

390 hp with Turbo Hydra-Matic	CPJ
390 hp with 4-speed	CPH
460 hp with 4-speed	CPK
460 hp with Turbo Hydra-Matic	CPL
450 hp with 4-speed	CPW
450 hp with Turbo Hydra-Matic	CPX

1972
350 cubic inch engine

200 hp with 4-speed	CKW
200 hp with 4-speed and NOX control (Calif.)	CDH
200 hp with Turbo Hydra-Matic	CKX
200 hp with Turbo Hydra-Matic and NOX control (Calif.)	CDJ
255 hp with 4-speed	CKY
255 hp with Turbo Hydra-Matic	CKZ
255 hp with 4-speed and A.I.R.	CRT
255 hp with Turbo Hydra-Matic and A.I.R.	CRS

454 cubic inch engine

270 hp with 4-speed	CPH
270 hp with Turbo Hydra-Matic	CPJ
270 hp	CSR, CSS

1973
350 cubic inch engine

190 hp with 4-speed	CKZ
190 hp with 4-speed (Calif.)	CLB
190 hp with Turbo Hydra-Matic	CLA
190 hp with Turbo Hydra-Matic (Calif.)	CLC
250 hp with 4-speed	CLR
250 hp with 4-speed (Calif.)	CLS
250 hp with Turbo Hydra-Matic	CLD
250 hp with Turbo Hydra-Matic (Calif.)	CLH

454 cubic inch engine

275 hp with 4-speed	CWM
275 hp with 4-speed (Calif.)	CWT
275 hp with Turbo Hydra-Matic	CWR
275 hp with Turbo Hydra-Matic (Calif.)	CWS

1974
350 cubic inch engine

195 hp with 4-speed	CKZ
195 hp with 4-speed (Calif.)	CLB
195 hp with Turbo Hydra-Matic	CLA
195 hp with Turbo Hydra-Matic (Calif.)	CLC
250 hp with 4-speed	CLR
250 hp with 4-speed (Calif.)	CLS
250 hp with Turbo Hydra-Matic	CLD
250 hp with Turbo Hydra-Matic (Calif.)	CLH

454 cubic inch engine

270 hp with 4-speed	CWM
270 hp with 4-speed (Calif.)	CWT
270 hp with Turbo Hydra-Matic	CWR
270 hp with Turbo Hydra-Matic (Calif.)	CWS

1975
350 cubic inch engine

195 hp with 4-speed	CRJ, CUA, CUB
195 hp with Turbo Hydra-Matic	CRK
250 hp with 4-speed	CRL, CUT, CUD
250 hp with Turbo Hydra-Matic	CRM

TRANSMISSION

The Borg-Warner T-10, 4-speed serial number is located on the rear face of the transmission case in the upper right corner. The Muncie 3-speed serial number is located on a boss above the filler plug.

Muncie 4-speed serial number location

Powerglide codes are stamped on the bottom of the oil pan. Serial numbers of 4-speed Muncie transmissions are located on the left-side cover flange of the case. Turbo Hydra-Matic serial numbers are found on the light blue plate on the right side of the transmission on 1968 models and on the upper left flange of the convertor housing opening on later models. The Borg-Warner T-16, 3-speed serial number is located on a boss at the right rear cover of the transmission extension. Transmission serial numbers give the plant and date of manufacture.

REAR AXLE

All Corvette Stingrays have the rear axle serial number located on the bottom surface of the carrier at the cover mounting flange. The two or three-letter prefix in the serial number identifies the rear-axle gear ratio.

Rear axle serial number location

Rear Axle Ratio Identification

Year	Prefix	Axle Ratio and Type
1963–64	CA	3.36 with 3-speed
	CJ	3.08 Positraction
	CB	3.36 Positraction
	CC	3.55 Positraction
	CD	3.70 Positraction
	CE	4.11 Positraction
	CF	4.56 Positraction
	CZ	3.08 with 4-speed
	CX	3.70 with 4-speed
1965	AK	3.36
	AL	3.08 Positraction
	AM	3.36 Positraction
	AN	3.55 Positraction
	AO	3.70 Positraction
	AP	4.11 Positraction
	AQ	4.56 Positraction
	AR	3.08
	AS	3.70 with 4-speed
	AT	3.08 Positraction with 396 engine

Year	Prefix	Axle Ratio and Type
1965	AU	3.36 Positraction with 396 engine
	AZ	3.55 Positraction with 396 engine
	FA	3.70 Positraction with 396 engine
	FB	4.11 Positraction with 396 engine
	FC	4.56 Positraction with 396 engine
1966	AK	3.36
	AL	3.08 Positraction
	AM	3.36 Positraction
	AN	3.55 Positraction
	AO	3.70 Positraction
	AP	4.11 Positraction
	AR	3.08 Positraction
	AS	3.70 with 4-speed
	AT	3.08 Positraction with 427 engine
	AU	3.36 Positraction with 427 engine
	AZ	3.55 Positraction with 427 engine
	FA	3.70 Positraction with 427 engine
	FB	4.11 Positraction with 427 engine
	FC	4.56 Positraction with 427 engine
1967	AK	3.36
	AL	3.08 Positraction
	AM	3.36 Positraction
	AN	3.55 Positraction
	AO	3.70 Positraction
	AP	4.11 Positraction
	AS	3.70 with 4-speed
	AT	3.08 Positraction with 427 engine
	AU	3.36 Positraction with 427 engine
	AZ	3.55 Positraction with 427 engine
	FA	3.70 Positraction with 427 engine
	FB	4.11 Positraction with 427 engine
	FC	4.56 Positraction with 427 engine
1968	AK	3.36
	AL	3.08 Positraction
	AM	3.36 Positraction
	AN	3.55 Positraction
	AO	3.70 Positraction
	AP	4.11 Positraction
	AS	3.70
	AT	3.08 Heavy duty Positraction
	AU	3.36 Heavy duy Positraction
	AV	3.08 Positraction
	AW	3.08 Heavy duty Positraction
1969	AK	3.36
	AL	3.08 Positraction
	AM	3.36 Positraction
	AN	3.55 Positraction
	AO	3.70 Positraction
	AP	4.11 Positraction
	AS	3.70
	AT	3.08 Heavy duty Positraction
	AU	3.36 Heavy duty Positraction
	AV	3.08
	AW	3.08 Heavy duty Positraction
	AY	2.73 Heavy duty Positraction
	AZ	3.55 Heavy duty Positraction
	FA	3.70 Heavy duty Positraction
	FB	4.11 Heavy duty Positraction
	FC	4.56 Positraction

Rear Axle Ratio Identification (cont.)

Year	Prefix	Axle Ratio and Type
1970	CAK	3.36
	CAL	3.08 Positraction
	CAM	3.36 Positraction
	CAN	3.55 Positraction
	CAO, CAS	3.70 Positraction with high performance 350 and close-ratio 4-speed
	CAP	4.11 Positraction
	CAT	3.08 Positraction
	CAU	3.36 Positraction
	CAV	3.08 Positraction
	CAW	3.08 Positraction with Turbo Hydra-Matic
	CAY	2.73 Positraction
	CAX	3.36 Positraction with Turbo Hydra-Matic
	CAZ	3.55 Positraction
	CFA	3.70 Positraction
	CFB	4.11 Positraction
	CFC	4.56 Positraction
	CLR	3.36 Positraction
1971	AA	3.55 Positraction
	AB	3.70 Positraction
	AC	4.11 Positraction
	AD	4.56 Positraction
	AW	3.08 Positraction
	AX, LR	3.36 Positraction
1972–76	AX, LR	3.36 Positraction
	AC	4.11 Positraction
	AB	3.70 Positraction
	AA	3.55 Positraction
	AW	3.08 Positraction
	AV	2.73 Positraction

Tools and Equipment

The following list is the basic requirement to perform most of the procedures described in this guide.

1. Sockets, to include a $^{13}/_{16}$ in. or $\frac{5}{8}$ in. spark plug socket. If possible, buy various length socket drive extensions.

2. Set of combination (one end open and one box) wrenches.

3. Spark plug wire gauge.

4. Flat feeler gauge for breaker points.

5. Slot and phillips head screwdriver.

6. Timing light, preferably a DC battery hook-up type.

7. Dwell/tachometer.

8. Torque wrench. This assures proper tightening of important fasteners and avoids costly thread stripping (too tight) or leaks (too loose).

9. Oil can filler spout. Much cleaner and neater than the old "punch the can with a screwdriver" trick.

10. Oil filter strap wrench. Makes removal of a tight filter much simpler. Never use to install filter.

11. Pair of channel lock pliers. Always handy to have.

12. Two sturdy jackstands—cinder blocks, bricks, and other makeshift supports are just not safe.

Routine Maintenance

AIR CLEANER

The air cleaner consists of a metal housing for a replaceable paper filter or permanent polyurethane element and the necessary hoses connecting it to the crankcase ventilation system. The air cleaner cover is held by a wing nut on all

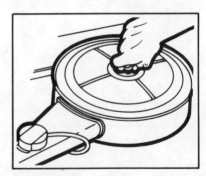

Unscrew the wing nut and remove the cover

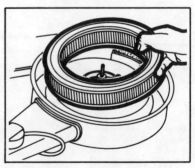

Remove and discard the old filter

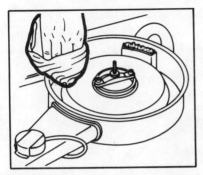

Using a clean rag or paper towel, wipe out the inside of the air cleaner

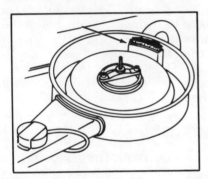

Check the small crankcase breather

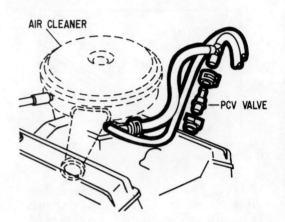

The PCV valve is located in the rocker arm cover on later models

models. If your Corvette is equipped with a paper element, it should be replaced once every 12,000 miles or 12 months, whichever comes first. Inspection and replacement should come more often when the car is operated under dusty conditions. To check the effectiveness of your paper element, remove the air cleaner assembly and, if the idle speed increases noticeably, the element is restricting airflow and should be replaced. Some high-performance models or cars equipped with optional air cleaners use a polyurethane element that must be removed, cleaned, and reoiled at 12,000 mile or 12 month intervals. Remove the filter and clean it in kerosene. Do not use paint thinner or a similar solvent and then squeeze it dry. Allow it to soak in SAE 30 oil and again squeeze it dry using a clean cloth to remove excess oil. Clean the inside of the air cleaner housing before reinstalling either type of filter.

POSITIVE CRANKCASE VENTILATION (PCV)

Once every 12,000 miles or 12 months, check the hoses and clean or replace them as necessary. At the same time,

clean or replace the ventilation filter located in the air cleaner housing on later models. The PCV valve should be replaced during this maintenance. The valve is screwed into the carburetor or located in the ventilation hose on 1963 models. 1964 and 1965 models are not equipped with a PCV valve, but use a metered orifice fitting instead. This is not replaced, as it is a permanent part of the system, but it should be cleaned with solvent as a part of regular maintenance. The valve is located in the hose or in the rocker cover on later models. PCV service has been lengthened to 24,000 miles or 24 months on 1972 and later models.

EVAPORATIVE EMISSIONS CONTROL SYSTEM

This system, standard since 1970, eliminates the release of unburned fuel vapors into the atmosphere. The only periodic maintenance required is an occasional check of the connecting lines of the system for kinks or other damage and deterioration. Lines should only be replaced with quality fuel line or special hose marked "evap." Every 12,000 miles or 12 months, the filter in the bottom of the carbon canister which is located in the engine compartment should be removed and replaced.

FLUID LEVEL CHECKS

Engine Oil

The engine oil level is checked with the dipstick, which is located at the left side of the engine block.

Oil dipstick marks

NOTE: *The oil should be checked before the engine is started or five minutes after the engine has been shut off. This gives the oil time to drain back to the oil pan and prevents an inaccurate oil level reading.*

Remove the dipstick from its tube, wipe it clean, and insert it back into the tube. Remove it again and observe the oil level. It should be maintained between the "full" and "add" marks without going above "full" or below "add."

CAUTION: *Do not overfill the crankcase. It may result in oil-fouled spark plugs or oil leaks caused by oil seal failure.*

Transmission Fluid

MANUAL TRANSMISSION

Remove the filler plug from the side of the transmission. The oil should be level with the bottom edge of the filler hole. This should be checked at least once every 6,000 miles and more often if any leakage or seepage is observed. Fill with SAE 80 or 90 multipurpose gear lubricant.

AUTOMATIC TRANSMISSION

Run the engine until it reaches normal operating temperature. Park the car on a level surface. With the transmission in Park and the engine idling, the fluid level on the dipstick should be between the "full" mark and ¼ inch below "full" mark. Replace the dipstick making sure that it is pushed fully into the filler tube.

CAUTION: *Do not overfill the automatic transmission. Use Dexron® or Type A automatic transmission fluid or any other equivalent fluid. One pint raises the level from "add" to "full."*

Brake Master Cylinder

Once every 6,000 miles or four months, check the brake fluid level in the master cylinder. The master cylinder is mounted on the firewall and is divided into two reservoirs and the fluid level in each reservoir must be maintained at ¼ inch below the top edge. Use only heavy-duty brake fluid (DOT 3 or 4), which is recommended for disc brake applications.

Coolant

Check the coolant level when the engine is cold. The level of coolant should be maintained 2 in. below the bottom of the filler neck, or the line on expansion tank-equipped models.

CAUTION: *Allow the engine to cool considerably and then add water while the engine is running.*

Rear Axle

STANDARD DIFFERENTIAL

The rear axle oil level should be checked when the chasis is lubricated. Remove the plug from the side of the housing. The lubricant level should be maintained at the bottom of the filler plug hole. When replacing oil, use SAE 80 or 90 multipurpose hypoid gear lubricant.

POSITRACTION DIFFERENTIAL

Lubricant level should be checked at each chassis lubrication and maintained at the bottom of the filler plug hole. Special Positraction oil must be used in this differential.

CAUTION: *Never use standard differential lubricant in a Positraction differential.*

Steering Gear

Check the lubricant by removing the center bolt on the side cover of the steering gear. Grease must be up to the level of this bolt hole.

Power Steering Reservoir

Maintain the proper fluid level as indicated on the cap of the reservoir. Check this level with the engine off and warm. Use GM power steering fluid or Dexron® automatic transmission fluid.

Battery

The electrolyte level in the battery should be checked about once every month and more often during hot weather or long trips. If the level is below the bottom of the split ring, distilled water should be added until the level reaches the ring.

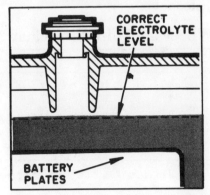

Correct battery electrolyte level

AIR CONDITIONING

This book contains no repair or maintenance procedures for the air conditioning system. It is recommended that any such repairs be left to the experts, whose personnel are well aware of the hazards and who have the proper equipment.

CAUTION: *The compressed refrigerant used in the air conditioning system expands into the atmosphere at a temperature of $-21.7°$ F or lower. This will freeze any surface, including your eyes, that it contacts. In addition, the refrigerant decomposes into a poisonous gas in the presence of flame. Do not open or disconnect any part of the air conditioning system.*

Sight Glass Check

You can safely make a few simple checks to determine if your air conditioning system needs service. The tests work best if the temperature is warm (about 70° F).

1. Place the automatic transmission in Park or the manual transmission in Neutral. Set the parking brake.

2. Run the engine at a fast idle (about 1,500 rpm) either with the help of a friend, or by temporarily readjusting the idle speed screw.

3. Set the controls for maximum cold with the blower on high.

4. Locate the sight glass in one of the system lines. Usually it is on the left alongside the top of the radiator.

5. If you see bubbles, the system must be recharged. Very likely there is a leak at some point.

6. If there are no bubbles, there is either no refrigerant at all or the system is fully charged. Feel the two hoses going to the belt-driven compressor. If they are both at the same temperature, the system is empty and must be recharged.

7. If one hose (high-pressure) is warm and the other (low-pressure) is cold, the system may be alright. However, you are probably making these tests because you think there is something wrong, so proceed to the next Step.

8. Have an assistant in the car turn the fan control on and off to operate the compressor clutch. Watch the sight glass.

9. If bubbles appear when the clutch is disengaged and disappear when it is engaged the system is properly charged.

10. If the refrigerant takes more than 45 seconds to bubble when the clutch is disengaged, the system is overcharged. This usually causes poor cooling at low speeds.

CAUTION: *If it is determined that the system has a leak, it should be corrected as soon as possible. Leaks may allow moisture to enter and cause a very expensive rust problem.*

NOTE: *Exercise the air conditioner for a few minutes, every two weeks or so, during the cold months. This avoids the possibility of the compressor seals drying out from lack of lubrication.*

DRIVE BELTS

Check the drive belts every 6,000 miles for evidence of wear such as cracking, fraying, and incorrect tension. Determine the belt tension at a point halfway between the pulleys by pressing on the belt with moderate thumb pressure. The belt should deflect about ¼ inch at this point. If the deflection is found to be too much or too little, loosen the mounting bolts and make the adjustments.

TIRES

Check the air pressure in your tires every few weeks. Make sure that the tires are cool, as you will get a false reading when the tires are heated because air pressure increases with temperature. A decal located on your glovebox door will tell you the proper tire pressure for the standard equipment tires. Naturally, when you replace tires you will want to get the correct tire pressures for the new ones from the dealer or manufacturer. It pays to buy a tire pressure gauge to keep in the car, since those at service stations are usually inaccurate or broken.

While you are checking the tire pressure, take a look at the tread. The tread should be wearing evenly across the tire. Excessive wear in the center of the tread indicates overinflation. Excessive wear on the outer edges indicates underinflation. An irregular wear pattern is usually a sign of incorrect front wheel alignment or wheel balance. A front end that is out of alignment will usually pull the car to one side of a flat road when the steering wheel is released. Incorrect wheel balance is usually accompanied by high speed vibration. Front wheels which are out of balance will produce vibration in the steering wheel, while unbalanced rear wheels will result in floor or trunk vibration.

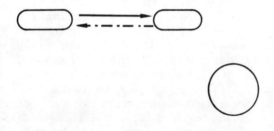

Use this rotation pattern for all tires, radial or non-radial

Rotating the tires every 6,000 miles or so will result in increased tread life. Use the correct pattern for your tire switching. Most automotive experts are in agreement that radial tires are better all around performers, giving prolonged wear and better handling. An added benefit which you should consider when purchasing tires is that radials have less rolling resistance and can give up to a 10% increase in fuel economy over a bias-ply tire.

Tires of different construction should never be mixed. Always replace tires in sets of four or five when switching tires types and never substitute a belted tire for a bias-ply, a radial for a belted tire, etc. an occasional pressure check and periodic rotation could make your tires last much longer than a neglected set and maintain the safety margin which was designed into them.

Wheel and Tire Size Chart

Year	Wheel Size	Tire Size
1963–64	15 x 5.5K①	6.70 x 15
1965–66	15 x 5.5K①	7.75 x 15
1967	15 x 6JK②	7.75 x 15
1968	15 x 7JK	F70 x 15
1969–72	15 x 8JJ	F70 x 15
1973–76	15 x 8JJ	GR70 x 15

① 15 x 6L aluminum knock-off wheel optionally available

② 15 x 6L aluminum bolt on wheel optionally available

Aluminum Wheels

An optional knock-off wheel was introduced with the 1963 Stingray. This wheel option consisted of 15 x 6L cast aluminum wheels, knock-off locking nuts, and wheel adapters. The latter bolt to the hub, using the existing wheel hub bolts. The flange of the adapter had five pins that fitted into corresponding holes in the optional wheels and located the wheel to the hub. The securing device was the single, center, knock-off nut.

Each Corvette delivered with the op-

Knock-off wheel adapter

tional, knock-off aluminum wheels, was equipped with a special knock-off hammer. Owners of these cars were urged to tighten the knock-off nut every 100 miles for the first 500 miles. The suggested method was to strike the ears of the nut eight hard blows.

For owners of these cars, the following maintenance suggestions are offered: exercise caution when using commercially available cleaners and use only those that will not react unfavorably with aluminum.

Inline fuel filter

Removing adapter pin

Should adapter pin replacement become necessary, remove the wheel and tire assembly and remove the adapter from the wheel hub. Select a socket of suitable size that will slip over the adapter pin. Position the socket over the back of the pin and clamp the entire assembly in a vise so that the socket acts as a spacer to receive the damaged pin. Tighten the vise and press the pin from the adapter. Position the replacement pin and start it into the hole by tapping lightly. Position the spacer socket on the opposite side and again clamp the assembly in the vise. Press the replacement pin into the adapter. Check to see that it seats firmly against its bore. Install the adapter and wheel.

FUEL FILTER

The filter in Carter WCFB, Rochester Quadrajet, Holley 2300, and Holley 4150

carburetors in located in the fuel inlet connection and should be replaced every 12,000 miles or sooner if engine flooding occurs. The Carter AFB uses an in-line filter, which should be replaced every 24,000 miles. The Rochester fuel injection unit also uses an in-line filter, which should be replaced every 15,000 miles.

To replace an in-line filter, disconnect the fitting at each end of the filter canister, discard the old filter, and install the replacement in the reverse order of removal.

To replace a fuel inlet filter:

1. Using an open-end wrench (preferably a line wrench), disconnect the fuel line connection from the larger fuel filter nut.

2. Remove the larger nut from the carburetor.

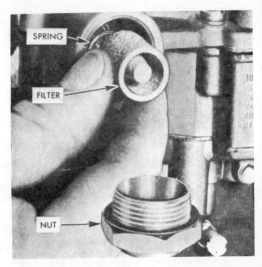

Most late models have this bronze fuel filter located behind the fuel fitting

3. Remove the filter element and spring from the carburetor.

4. Check the bronze element for dirt blockage by blowing on the cone end. If the element is good, air should pass through easily.

5. If the car has a paper element instead of a bronze element, check by blowing into the fuel inlet end. If air does not pass through easily replace the ele-

ment. Do not attempt to clean these elements.

6. Install the spring and then the element into the carburetor, making sure that the small end of the bronze cone is facing outward.

7. Install a new gasket on the large nut and tighten securely.

8. Insert the fuel line and tighten the nut with a line wrench.

Capacities & Pressures

Year	Model (cu in.)	Engine Crankcase Add 1 Qt for New Filter	Transmission Pts to Refill after Draining			Differential (pts)	Fuel Tank (gal)	Cooling System (qts)	Max Coolant Pressure (psi)
			Manual						
			3-spd	4-spd	Automatic				
1963	327	4	2	2.5	18	3.7	20	17	13
	327 HP	5	—	2.5	—	3.7	20	17	13
1964	327	4	2	2.5	18	3.7	20	17	13
	327 HP	5	—	2.5	—	3.7	20	17	13
1965	327	4	2	2.5	18	3.7	20	17	13
	327 HP	4	2	2.5	18	3.7	20	17	13
1966	327	4	3	3.0	18	3.7	20	19	15
	327 HP	5	—	3.0	—	3.7	20	19	15
	427	5	—	3.0	—	3.7	20	22	15
1967	327	4	3	3.0	19	3.7	20	19	15
	327 HP	5	—	3.0	—	3.7	20	19	15
	427	5	—	3.0	19	3.7	20	22	15
	427 HP	5	—	3.0	—	3.7	20	22	15
1968	327	4	3	3.0	22	3.7	20	15	15
	327 HP	4	—	3.0	—	3.7	20	15	15
	427	5	—	3.0	22	3.7	20	22	15
	427 HP	5	—	3.0	—	3.7	20	22	15
1969	350	4	3	3.0	—	4.0	20	—	15

Capacities & Pressures (cont.)

Year	Model (cu in.)	Engine Crankcase Add 1 Qt for New Filter	Transmission Pts to Refill after Draining			Differential (pts)	Fuel Tank (gal)	Cooling System (qts)	Max Coolant Pressure (psi)
			Manual						
			3-spd	4-spd	Automatic				
1969	350 HP	4	——	3.0	——	4.0	20	——	15
	427	5	——	3.0	——	4.0	20	——	15
	427 HP	5	——	3.0	——	4.0	20	——	15
1970	350	4	——	3.0	22	4.0	20	15	15
	350 HP	4	——	3.0	——	4.0	20	18	15
	454	5	——	3.0	22	4.0	20	22	15
	454 HP	5	——	3.0	22	4.0	20	22	15
1971	350	4	——	3.0	22	4.0	18	15	15
	350 HP	4	——	3.0	——	4.0	18	18	15
	454	5	——	3.0	22	4.0	18	22	15
	454 HP	5	——	3.0	22	4.0	18	20	15
1972	350	4	——	3.0	22	4.0	18	15	15
	350 HP	4	——	3.0	——	4.0	18	18	15
	454	5	——	3.0	22	4.0	18	22	15
1973	350	4	——	3.0	8 *	4.0	18	18	15
	454	5	——	3.0	8 *	4.0	18	24	15
1974	350	4	——	3.0	8 *	4.0	18	17	17
	454	5	——	3.0	8 *	4.0	18	22	23
1975–76	350	4	——	3.0	8 *	4.0	18	17	17

HP High performance engine
* Normal change does not include torque converter
—— Not applicable

BATTERY

The battery in 1963 through 1967 Corvettes is located on the right-side of the engine compartment behind the wheel well and under the radiator expansion tank. 1968 and later Corvettes have the battery located in the left-side well of the stowage compartment behind the seats. All Stingrays are equipped with a negative ground, twelve-volt battery.

In addition to routinely checking the electrolyte level of the battery, some other minor maintenance will keep your battery in peak starting condition. Two inexpensive battery tools, a hydometer and a post and cable cleaner, are available in most auto or hardware stores for about a dollar and more than earn back that small outlay. Besides checking the level of electrolyte, you should occasionally take a specific gravity reading to see what's going on inside the battery cells. Using your hydrometer, insert the tip into each cell and withdraw enough electrolyte to make the float ride freely. While holding the hydrometer straight up, take a reading. The specific gravity of a fully charged battery (at 80° F) is 1.270. Most commercially available hydrometers also have colored sections to save you reading the scale and these will clearly tell you your battery cell is (a) charged, (b) borderline—should be recharged, or (c) dead. Repeat the specific gravity for each cell.

NOTE: *Battery electrolyte or "acid" is very caustic and will dissolve skin and paintwork with equal relish, so be careful. Readings should be taken in as normal a room temperature atmosphere as possible. If the temperature varies from the 80° F standard above, add or subtract four (0.004) points for every 10° above (+) or below (−) the standard.*

The most completely charged battery will do you no good on a cold, rainy evening if the cables and posts are caked with corrosion. This is where your little wire brush cleaner comes in. Loosen and remove the cable clamps from the battery posts. Using the pointed end of the brush, give the inside surface of the clamp a good cleaning until it shines. Next, take the other end and place it over the post. Clean the post with a rotating motion until you achieve a shiny post. This done, install the clamps and re-tighten.

A slightly different procedure is used for 1972 and later models which are equipped with Delco side terminal batteries. The cable is cleaned in the same manner, but the internal threads in the battery can be cleaned with a special tool now available for that purpose. Exercise care when removing the cable retaining

bolts on side terminal batteries, as it is easy to strip them.

Keep the top of the battery clean, as a film of dirt can sometimes completely discharge a battery. A solution of baking soda and water may be used to clean the top surface, but be careful to flush this off with clear water and that none of the solution enters the filler holes.

Lubrication

OIL AND FUEL

Chevrolet recommends the use of a high quality, heavy-duty detergent oil having the proper viscosity for prevailing temperatures and an SE service rating. The SE rating will be printed on the top of the can. Under the classification system adopted by the American Petroleum Institute (API) in May, 1970, SE is the highest designation given for normal passenger car use. The S stands for passenger car and the second letter denotes a more specific application. SA oil, for instance, contains no additives and is suitable only for very light-duty. Oil designated MS may also be used, since this was the highest classification under the old API rating system. Pick your oil viscosity with regard to the anticipated temperatures during the period before your next oil change. Using the chart below, choose the oil viscosity for the lowest expected temperature. You will be assured of easy cold starting and sufficient engine protection.

Fuel should be selected for the brand and octane which performs without pinging. Find your exact engine model in the "General Engine Specifications" chart in Chapter 3. If the compression ratio is high than 9.0:1, you will have to use a premium gasoline. If your compression ratio is lower than 9.0:1, you can safely go with regular octane. Most 1971 and later models will operate successfully on regular if the car is properly tuned, especially as to correct ignition timing.

CAUTION: *It is absolutely imperative that only lead-free gasoline be used in 1975-76 models. Leaded fuel will render the catalytic converter ineffective.*

Oil Viscosity Selection Chart

	Anticipated Temperature Range	SAE Viscosity
Multi-grade	Above 32° F	10W—40 10W—50 20W—40 20W—50 10W—30
	May be used as low as — 10° F	10W—30 10W—40
	Consistently below 10° F	5W—20 5W—30
Single-grade	Above 32° F	30
	Temperature between + 32° F and — 10° F	10W

OIL CHANGES

The mileage figures given in your owner's manual are the Chevrolet recommended intervals for oil and filter changes assuming average driving. If your Corvette is being used under dusty, polluted, or off-road conditions, change the oil and filter sooner than specified. The same thing goes for cars driven in stop-and-go traffic or only for short distances.

Always drain the oil after the engine has been running long enough to bring it to operating temperature. Hot oil will flow easier and more contaminants will be removed along with the oil than if it were drained cold. You will need a large capacity drain pan, which you can purchase at any store which sells automotive parts. Another necessity is containers for the used oil. You will find that plastic bottles, such as those used for bleach or fabric softener, make excellent storage jugs. One ecologically desirable solution to the used oil disposal problem is to find a cooperative gas station owner who will allow you to dump your used oil into his tank. Another is to keep the oil for use around the house as a preservative on fences, railroad tie borders, etc.

Chevrolet recommends changing both the oil and filter during the first oil change and the filter every other oil change thereafter. For the small price of an oil filter, it's cheap insurance to re-

place the filter at every oil change. One of the larger filter manufacturers points out in its advertisements that not changing the filter leaves one quart of dirty oil in the engine. This claim is true and should be kept in mind when changing your oil.

Changing Your Oil

1. Run the engine until it reaches normal operating temperature.

2. Jack up the front of the car and support it on safety stands.

3. Slide a drain pan of at least 6 quarts capacity under the oil pan.

4. Loosen the drain plug. Turn the plug out by hand. By keeping an inward pressure on the plug as you unscrew it, oil won't escape past the threads and you can remove it without being burned by hot oil.

5. Allow the oil to drain completely and then install the drain plug. Don't overtighten the plug, or you'll be buying a new pan or a trick replacement plug for buggered threads.

6. Using a strap wrench, remove the oil filter. Keep in mind that it's holding about one quart of dirty, hot oil.

1963 through 1967 Corvettes use a cartridge type oil filter, and 1968 and later cars use the spin-off type. Adapters are available on the aftermarket to adapt the spin-off type to the 1963–67 cars.

7. Empty the old filter into the drain pan and dispose of the filter.

8. Using a clean rag, wipe off the filter adapter on the engine block. Be sure that the rag doesn't leave any lint which could clog an oil passage.

9. Coat the rubber gasket on the filter with fresh oil. Spin it onto the engine *by hand;* when the gasket touches the adapter surface give it another ½–¾ turn. No more, or you'll squash the gasket and it will leak.

Be sure to apply a thin film of oil to the rubber gasket before installation

10. Refill the engine with the correct amount of fresh oil. See the "Capacities" chart.

11. Crank the engine over several times and then start it. If the oil pressure gauge shows zero, shut the engine down and find out what's wrong.

12. If the oil pressure is OK and there are no leaks, shut the engine off and lower the car.

13. Wait a few minutes and check the oil level. Add oil, as necessary, to bring the level up to Full.

CHASSIS GREASING

Chassis greasing can be performed with a pressurized grease gun or it can be performed at home by using a hand-operated grease gun. Wipe the grease fit-tings clean before greasing in order to prevent the possibility of forcing any dirt into the component.

WHEEL BEARINGS

Once every 12 months or 12,000 miles, clean and repack wheel bearings with a wheel bearing grease. Use only enough grease to completely coat the rollers. Remove any excess grease from the exposed surface of the hub and seal.

It is important that wheel bearings be-properly adjusted after installation. Improperly adjusted wheel bearings can cause steering instability, front-end shimmy and wander, and increased tire wear. For complete adjustment procedures, see the "Wheel Bearing" section in Chapter 9.

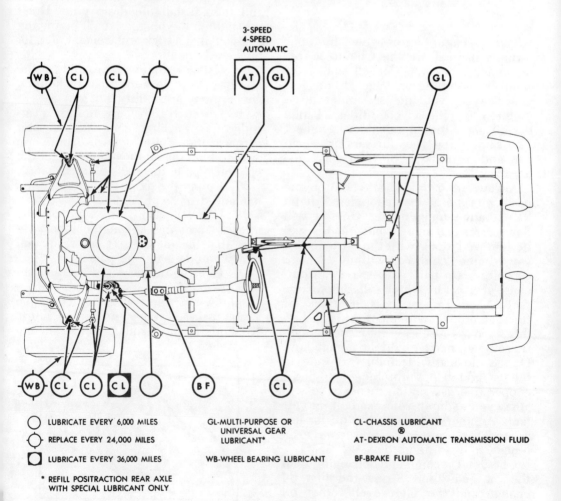

○ LUBRICATE EVERY 6,000 MILES

◇ REPLACE EVERY 24,000 MILES

▢ LUBRICATE EVERY 36,000 MILES

* REFILL POSITRACTION REAR AXLE WITH SPECIAL LUBRICANT ONLY

GL-MULTI-PURPOSE OR UNIVERSAL GEAR LUBRICANT*

WB-WHEEL BEARING LUBRICANT

CL-CHASSIS LUBRICANT

AT-DEXRON AUTOMATIC TRANSMISSION FLUID

BF-BRAKE FLUID

Lubrication points

Pushing, Towing, and Jump Starting

Corvettes equipped with either the Powerglide or Turbo Hydra-Matic automatic transmissions cannot be push-started. To push-start a Corvette that has either a three-speed or four-speed manual transmission, switch on the ignition, select the highest forward gear and keep the clutch pedal depressed until suitable speed has been provided by the pushing vehicle. When this speed, approximately 15 mph, is reached, slowly release the clutch to start the engine.

Corvettes may be towed at speeds up to 35 mph and distances not over 50 miles with the driveshaft in place, if no engine/drive-line damage is present. If engine/drive-line damage is known or suspected, the driveshaft should be disconnected before towing. Towing connections should not be made on bumpers, only on the spindle struts at the rear and the frame crossmember or lower control arm at the front.

When jump starting, be sure that the booster cables are properly connected. Do not use a booster battery with a higher rating than the discharged battery. Be careful to avoid causing sparks, as there is danger of explosion when connecting charged and discharged batteries.

Front towing point

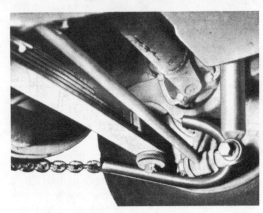

Rear towing point

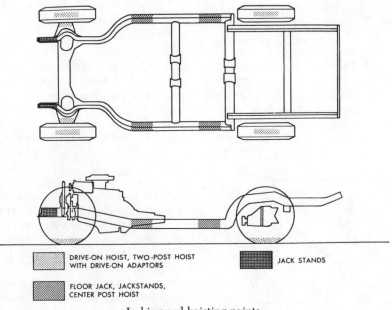

DRIVE-ON HOIST, TWO-POST HOIST WITH DRIVE-ON ADAPTORS

JACK STANDS

FLOOR JACK, JACKSTANDS, CENTER POST HOIST

Jacking and hoisting points

Chapter 2

Tune-Up and Troubleshooting

Tune-Up Procedures

SPARK PLUGS

In addition to performing their basic function of igniting the air-fuel mixture, spark plugs can also serve as very useful diagnostic tools. Once removed, compare your spark plugs with the samples in the "Troubleshooting" Section at the back of this chapter. Typical plug conditions are illustrated along with their causes and remedies. Plugs which exhibit only normal wear and deposits can be cleaned, gapped, and reinstalled. Before removing the spark plug leads, number the towers on the distributor cap with tape. Trace the No. 1 lead and then proceed in the firing order. Use the firing order illustrations in Chapter 3 if you get lost. This

Use a spark plug socket for removing and installing the plugs

prevents mix-ups when reinstalling the leads and also comes in handy when you're replacing wires or the distributor cap. Remove the spark plug shields on small block engines. Grasp each spark plug boot and pull it straight out.

Use a $^{13}/_{16}$ in. spark plug socket on all models through 1971. V8s from 1972 are equipped with tapered seat spark plugs which require a ⅝ in. socket. Install the spark plug socket on the plug's hex and remove it. If removal is difficult, loosen the plug only slightly and drip some light oil onto the threads. Allow the oil to penetrate and then unscrew the spark plug. Proceeding this way will prevent damaging the threads in the cylinder head. Be sure to keep the socket straight to avoid breaking the ceramic insulator. Inspect

Remove the spark plug wire by pulling on the boot, not the wire itself

Tune-Up Specifications

Year	Model	Spark Plugs Type	Gap (in.)	Distributor Point Dwell (deg)	Point Gap (in.)	Basic Ignition Timing (deg)	Cranking Compression (psi)	Valves Clearance (in.) Intake	Exhaust	Intake Opening (deg)	Idle Speed (rpm)	Normal Fuel Pressure (psi)
1963	250 hp	44	0.035	28–32	0.019	4B	160	①	①	32½B	475②	5¼–6½
	300 hp	44	0.035	28–32	0.019	8B	160	①	①	32½B	475②	5¼–6½
	340 hp	44	0.035	28–32	0.019	10B	150	0.008	0.018	35B	750	5¼–6½
	360 hp	44	0.035	28–32	0.019	10B	150	0.008	0.018	35B	850	5¼–6½
1964	250 hp	44	0.035	28–32	0.019	4B	160	①	①	32½B	500②	5¼–6½
	300 hp	44	0.035	28–32	0.019	8B	160	①	①	32½B	500②	5¼–6½
	365 hp	44	0.035	28–32	0.019	10B	150	0.030	0.030	60½B	800	5¼–6½
	375 hp	44	0.035	28–32	0.019	10B	150	0.030	0.030	60½B	800	5¼–6½
1965	250 hp	44	0.035	28–32	0.019	4B	160	①	①	32½B	500②	5¼–6½
	300 hp	44	0.035	28–32	0.019	8B	160	①	①	32½B	500②	5¼–6½
	350 hp	44	0.035	28–32	0.019	8B	150	①	①	54B	750	5¼–6½
	365 hp	44	0.035	28–32	0.019	12B	150	0.030	0.030	60½B	850	6½–7½
	375 hp	44	0.035	28–32	0.019	12B	150	0.030	0.030	60B	850	6½–7½
	425 hp	43N	0.035	28–32	0.019	10B	150	0.020	0.024	54B	800	7½
1966	300 hp	44	0.035	28–32	0.019	8B③	160	①	①	32½B	500②	6

Tune-Up Specifications (cont.)

Year	Model	Spark Plugs		Distributor		Basic Ignition Timing (deg)	Cranking Compression (psi)	Valves			Idle Speed (rpm)	Normal Fuel Pressure (psi)
		Type	Gap (in.)	Point Dwell (deg)	Point Gap (in.)			Clearance (in.) Intake	Exhaust	Intake Opening (deg)		
1966	350 hp	44	0.035	28–32	0.019	10B	150	[1]	[1]	54B	750	6
	390 hp	43N	0.035	28–32	0.019	4B	160	[1]	[1]	58B	600	6
	425 hp	43N	0.035	28–32	0.019	8B	150	0.020	0.024	54B	800	6
1967	300 hp	44	0.035	28–32	0.019	6B[4]	160	[1]	[1]	38B	500[5]	5–6½
	350 hp	44	0.035	28–32	0.019	10B	150	[1]	[1]	54B	700[5]	5–6½
	390 hp	43N	0.035	28–32	0.019	4B	160	[1]	[1]	56B	550[5]	5–6½
	400 hp	43N	0.035	28–32	0.019	4B	160	[1]	[1]	56B	550[5]	5–6½
	435 hp	43N	0.035	28–32	0.019	5B	150	0.024	0.028	44B	750[6]	5–6½
	430 hp	C42N	0.035	28–32	0.019	12B	150	0.022	0.024	54B	1000	5–6½
1968	300 hp	44	0.035	28–32	0.019	4B	160	[1]	[1]	28B	700[7]	5–6½
	350 hp	44	0.035	28–32	0.019	4B	150	[1]	[1]	54B	700[7]	5–6½
	390 hp	43N	0.035	28–32	0.019	4B	160	[1]	[1]	56B	700[7]	5–8½
	400 hp	43N	0.035	28–32	0.019	4B	160	[1]	[1]	56B	750[7]	5–8½
	435 hp	43N	0.035	28–32	0.019	4B	150	0.024	0.028	44B	750	5–8½
	430 hp	C42N	0.035	28–32	0.019	12B	150	0.022	0.024	62B	1000	5–8½

Year	hp											
1969	300 hp	R44	0.035	28–32	0.019	TDC⑧	160	①	①	28B	700⑦	5–6½
	350 hp	R44	0.035	28–32	0.019	4B	160	①	①	52B	750	5–6½
	390 hp	R43N	0.035	28–32	0.019	4B	160	①	①	56B	800⑦	5–8½
	400 hp	R43N	0.035	28–32	0.019	4B	160	①	①	56B	800⑦	5–8½
	435 hp	R43N	0.035	28–32	0.019	4B	160	0.024	0.024	44B	750	5–8½
	430 hp	C42N	0.035	28–32	0.019	12B	150	0.022	0.024	62B	1000	5–8½
1970	300 hp	R44	0.035	28–32	0.019	TDC⑧	160	①	①	28B	700⑦	5–6½
	350 hp	R44	0.035	28–32	0.019	4B	160	①	①	52B	750	5–6½
	370 hp	R43	0.035	Transistor Ignition		14B	190	0.024	0.030	43B	750	5–6½
	390 hp	R43T	0.035	28–32	0.019	6B	160	①	①	56B	700⑦	5–8½
	460 hp	R43T	0.035	Transistor Ignition		14B	150	0.024	0.028	62B	700	5–8½
1971	270 hp	R44TS	0.035	28–32	0.019	4B⑨	160	①	①	28B	600⑩	7½–9
	330 hp	R43TS	0.035	Transistor Ignition		8B⑪	150	0.024	0.030	43B	700	7½–9
	365 hp	R43TS	0.035	28–32	0.019	8B	160	①	①	56B	600	7½–9
	425 hp	R44	0.035	Transistor Ignition		8B	160	0.024	0.028	44B	700	7½–9
1972	200 hp	R44T	0.035	29–31	0.019	8B	160	①	①	28B	800⑦	7½–9

Tune-Up Specifications (cont.)

Year	Model	Spark Plugs		Distributor		Basic Ignition Timing (deg)	Cranking Compression (psi)	Valves			Idle Speed (rpm)	Normal Fuel Pressure (psi)
		Type	Gap (in.)	Point Dwell (deg)	Point Gap (in.)			Clearance (in.)		Intake Opening (deg)		
								Intake	Exhaust			
1972	255 hp	R44T	0.035	29–31	0.019	4B	150	0.024	0.030	43B	900	7½–9
	270 hp	R44T	0.035	28–30	0.019	8B	160	①	①	56B	750⑦	7½–9
1973	190 hp	R44T	0.035	29–31	0.019	12B	160	①	①	28B⑫	900⑦⑭	7½–9
	250 hp	R44T	0.035	29–31	0.019	8B	150	①	①	52B	900⑤⑭	7½–9
	270 hp	R44T	0.035	29–31	0.019	10B	160	①	①	55B	900⑦⑭	7½–9
1974	195 hp	R44T	0.035	29–31	0.019	8B⑬	160	①	①	28B⑫	900⑦	7½–9
	250 hp	R44T	0.035	29–31	0.019	8B	150	①	①	52B	900⑤	7½–9
	270 hp	R44T	0.035	29–31	0.019	10B	160	①	①	55B	800⑦	7½–9
1975–76	165 hp	R44TX	0.060	Electronic		6B	160	①	①	28B	800⑦	7½–9
	205 hp	R44TX	0.060	Electronic		12B	150	①	①	52B	900⑤	7½–9

① Hydraulic lifters—one turn down from zero lash
② 450 rpm auto trans
③ 2°A with auto trans
④ W/auto trans and A.I.R.—4°A
⑤ W/auto trans and A.I.R.—700 rpm
⑥ W/auto trans and A.I.R.—750 rpm
⑦ W/auto trans—600 rpm
⑧ W/auto trans—4°B
⑨ W/auto trans—8°B
⑩ W/auto trans—550 rpm
⑪ W/auto trans—12°B
⑫ California—44°B
⑬ California—4°B
⑭ 450 rpm with idle solenoid disconnected

NOTE: If specifications on the tune-up sticker under the hood differ from those given above, the sticker specifications take precedence.

the plugs using the "Troubleshooting" Section illustrations and then clean or discard them according to their condition.

Most new spark plugs come pregapped, but double check the setting or reset them if you desire a different gap. Recommended spark plug gap is given in the "Tune-Up Specifications" chart. Use a spark plug wire gauge for checking the

Use a wire feeler gauge to check spark plug gap

gap. The wire should pass through the electrodes with just a slight drag. Using the electrode bending tool on the end of the gauge, bend the side electrode to adjust the gap. Never attempt to adjust the center electrode. Lightly oil the threads of the replacement plug and install it. If you have a torque wrench, tighten the $^{13}/_{16}$ in. plugs to 20–25 ft lbs and $^{5}/_{8}$ in. plugs to 15 ft lbs. Be very careful not to overtighten the plug in the cylinder head.

NOTE: *Always replace the points and condenser as a unit. Uniset® points are available which combine the point set and condenser, greatly simplifying installation.*

BREAKER POINTS AND CONDENSER

Removal and Replacement

NOTE: *The optional magnetic pulse distributor and the HEI (High Energy Ignition) system used on some 1974 and all 1975–76 models requires no maintenance other than checking the condition of the cap and wires. There are no points to wear out or adjust.*

Point alignment is preset at the factory and requires no adjustment. Point sets using the push-in type wiring terminal should be used on those distributors equipped with an R.F.I. (radio frequency interference) shield (1970–74). Points

using a lockscrew type terminal may short out due to the shield contacting the screw.

1. Remove the distributor cap. Remove the ignition shield.
2. Remove the rotor.
3. If so equipped, remove the two-piece R.F.I. shield.
4. Loosen the two mounting screws and slide the contact point set from the breaker plate.

Remove the distributor cap by depressing the screw in the cap and rotating the latch away from the distributor (there are two latches)

5. Remove the primary and condenser leads from the terminal.
6. Loosen the condenser bracket screw and slide the condenser from the bracket.
7. Install the new point set and condenser and then tighten the mounting screws.

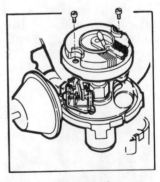

Rotor mounting—don't overtighten screws

8. Install the wires to the terminal so that they will not interfere with the cap, weight base, or breaker advance plate. Install the half of the R.F.I. shield which covers the points first.
9. Using a ⅛ in. allen wrench, make an initial point setting of 0.019 in.

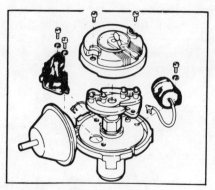

Point set and condenser mounting

10. The cam lubricator (if so equipped) must be replaced after 12 months or 12,000 miles. The end of the lubricator should be adjusted to just touch the cam lobes. Additional grease should not be applied to the lubricator.

11. Install the rotor. The two lugs on the bottom of the rotor are shaped differently, so that it can only be installed one way. Tighten the screws. Start the engine and check the point dwell and the ignition timing.

DWELL ANGLE

Dwell angle is the amount of time (measured in degrees of distributor cam rotation) that the contact points remain closed. Initial point gap (0.019 in.) determines dwell angle. If the points are too wide they open gradually and dwell angle (the time they remain closed) is small. This wide gap causes excessive arcing at the points and, because of this, point burning. This small dwell doesn't give the coil sufficient time to build up maximum energy and so coil output de-

creases. If the points are set too close, the dwell is increased but the points may bounce at higher speeds and the idle becomes rough and starting is made harder. The wider the point opening, the smaller the dwell and the smaller the gap, the larger the dwell. Adjusting the dwell by making the initial point gap setting with a feeler gauge is sufficient to get the car started but a finer adjustment should be made. A dwell meter is needed to check the adjustment.

1. Run the engine to normal operating temperatures and then let it idle.

2. Raise the adjusting window on the distributor cap and insert a 1/8 in. allen wrench into the adjusting screw.

3. Turn the adjusting screw until the specified dwell angle is obtained on the dwell meter.

HEI System Dwell/Tachometer Hookup

Connect one dwell/tach lead to the "TACH" terminal on the side of the distributor and the other to ground. Some tachometers must be connected to the "TACH" terminal and the battery positive terminal. Not all tachometers will operate correctly with the HEI system. Check with the manufacturer if there is any doubt.

CAUTION: *The "TACH" terminal should never be connected to ground.*

When hooking up a remote starter switch, disconnect the "BATT" terminal.

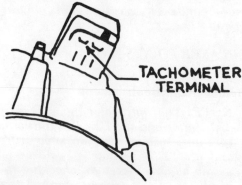

Hook up one dwell/tach lead to the tachometer terminal on the HEI system

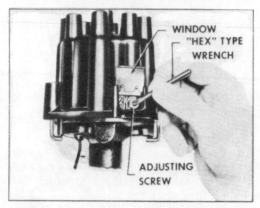

Adjusting point gap (dwell angle) with 1/8 in. allen wrench

IGNITION TIMING

Adjustment

1. Disconnect and plug the distributor vacuum advance hose.

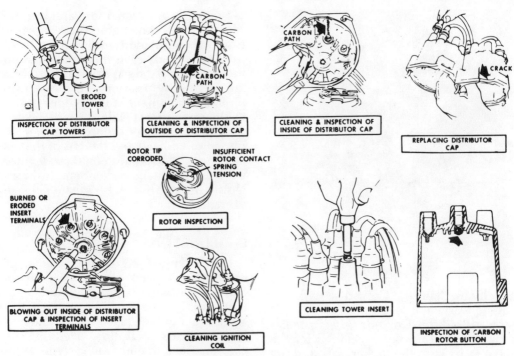

Distributor cap and rotor checkpoints

2. Start the engine and run it at idle speed.

3. Connect the timing light and, with the engine running at an idle, aim it at the timing tab on the front engine cover.

NOTE: *It may be necessary to clean off the tab and slash mark on the crankshaft pulley before proceeding any further. To further improve visibility, take a piece of chalk and fill in the slash mark on the crankshaft pulley. The "0" marking on the tab is TDC and all the BTDC (before top dead cen-*

Timing mark location

ter) settings are on the "before" (advance) side of the "0" or the "A" (advance) side of the "0." Later models are marked to indicate Before and After.

4. Loosen the distributor clamp bolt and turn the distributor until the slash on the crankshaft pulley lines up with the specified timing mark on the tab. Once the timing is correct, tighten the distributor clamp bolt and recheck the timing.

5. Turn off the engine, remove the timing light, and connect the vacuum advance hose.

VALVE LASH

Normalize the engine temperature by running it for approximately twenty minutes. Shut the engine off and remove the valve covers. Removal of the left valve cover on fuel-injection models requires that the air cleaner hose, air meter adapter, and pyrometer housing be removed first. Keep the screws and reinforcements together for ease of installation. After valve cover removal, torque the cylinder heads to specification. The use of oil stopper clips, readily available on the aftermarket, is highly recommended to prevent oil splatter. Restart the engine. Valve lash is set on both solid

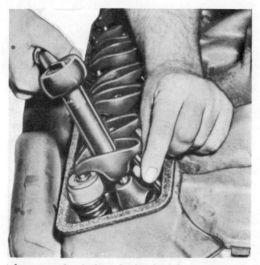

Adjusting valve lash on hydraulic lifter engine

and hydraulic-lifter Corvettes with the engine warm and idling.

On solid-lifter Corvettes, use a feeler gauge of the thickness specified for the valve lash. Turn the rocker arm stud nut until the correct lash is achieved. On Corvettes with hydraulic lifters, turn the rocker arm nut counterclockwise until the rocker arm starts to clatter. Reverse the direction and turn the rocker arm down slowly until the clatter just stops. This is the zero lash position. Turn the

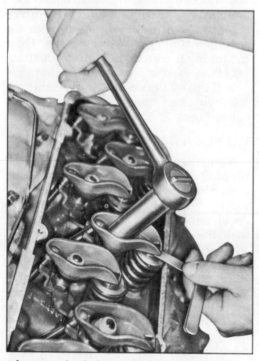

Adjusting valve lash on solid lifter engine

nut down ¼ additional turn and wait ten seconds until the engine runs smoothly. Continue with additional ¼ turns, waiting ten seconds each time, until the nut has been turned down one full turn from the zero lash position. This one turn, preload adjustment must be done slowly to allow the lifter to adjust itself and prevent possible interference between the intake valve head and the top of the piston. Such interference could cause internal engine damage and/or bent pushrods. Noisy lifters should be cleaned or replaced.

CARBURETOR

Idle mixture and speed adjustments are critical aspects of exhaust emission control. It is important that all tune-up instructions be carefully followed to ensure satisfactory engine performance and minimum exhaust pollution. The different combinations of emission systems application on the different engine models have resulted in a great variety of tune-up specifications. See the "Tune-Up Specifications" chart at the beginning of this chapter. Beginning in 1968, all models have a decal conspicuously placed in the engine compartment giving tune-up specifications.

When adjusting a carburetor with two idle mixture screws, adjust them alternately and evenly, unless otherwise stated.

In the following adjustment procedures the term "lean roll" means turning the mixture adjusting screws in (clockwise) from optimum setting to obtain an obvious drop in engine speed (usually 20 rpm).

1963–67 without A.I.R.

Adjust with air cleaner removed.

1. Connect a tachometer and vacuum gauge to the engine, then set the parking brake and shift the manual transmission into Neutral, automatic into Drive.
2. Turn the idle mixture screw(s) in until lightly seated, then back out 1½ turns.
3. With engine running, adjust the idle speed screw to obtain the specified rpm.
4. Adjust the idle mixture screw(s) to obtain the highest steady manifold vacuum at the specified speed. If necessary,

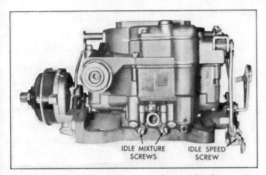

Carter WCFB idle mixture and speed adjustment screws

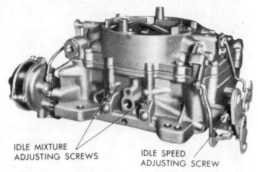

Carter AFB idle mixture and speed adjustment screws

reset the idle speed screw while adjusting mixture.

NOTE: *On air conditioned models, the air conditioner is turned on and the hot idle compensator valve is held closed while adjusting idle speed and mixture.*

5. Final adjustment should be made with the air cleaner installed.

6. Remove tachometer and vacuum gauge.

1966–67 with A.I.R.

Adjust with air cleaner removed.

1. Connect a tachometer to the engine, place manual transmission in Neutral, automatic in Drive.

2. Turn idle mixture screw(s) in until lightly seated, then back out 3 turns.

3. With engine running, adjust the idle speed screw to obtain the specified idle speed.

4. Adjust the idle mixture screw(s) in to "lean roll" position, then back them out (rich) ¼ turn. Readjust the idle speed screw to keep the engine at the specified idle speed while adjusting the mixture.

NOTE: *On air conditioned cars, turn the air conditioner off with 327 cu in.*

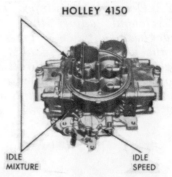

Holley 4150 idle mixture and speed adjustment screws

engines. Air conditioner must be on and hot idle compensator held closed with 427 cu in. engines.

5. Final adjustment should be made with the air cleaner installed.

6. Remove the tachometer.

1968–69

Adjust with air cleaner installed.

1. Turn the idle mixture screw(s) in until lightly seated, then back out 3 turns.

2. With engine at operating temperature, adjust idle speed screw to obtain specified rpm, manual transmission in Neutral and automatic in Drive.

NOTE: *On all 1968 models* except *350 H.P. 327 cu. in. with manual transmission, the air conditioner is turned* off. *On the above-mentioned vehicles the air conditioner is left* on. *On 1969 models, turn the air conditioner either on or off according to the instructions on the tune-up decal.*

3. Adjust one idle mixture screw to obtain the highest steady idle speed.

4. Adjust the idle speed screw to the speed specified on the tune-up decal.

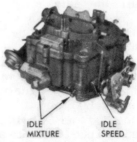

Rochester Quadrajet idle mixture and speed adjustment screws

NOTE: *On models equipped with an idle solenoid, adjust the solenoid plunger hex to obtain 600 rpm. Disconnect the wire at the solenoid to de-energize it, allowing the throttle lever to contact the carburetor idle speed screw. Adjust the carburetor idle screw to obtain 400 rpm.*

HOLLEY 2300C (PRIMARY)

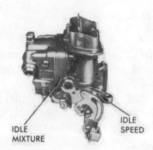

IDLE
MIXTURE

IDLE
SPEED

Holley 2300 idle mixture and speed adjustment screws

5. Adjust the mixture screw in to "lean roll" position, then back out (rich) ¼ turn.
6. Repeat Steps 3, 4 and 5 for the other idle mixture screw.
7. Readjust the idle speed screw to obtain final specified rpm, if necessary.

1970

Adjust with air cleaner installed.

If the vehicle is equipped with Evaporative Emission, disconnect the fuel tank line from the vapor canister while making the idle speed and mixture adjustments. Warm up the engine and leave it running while adjusting. The choke valve and, if applicable, air cleaner damper door should remain open. Leave the air conditioning off.

350 (300, 350 AND 370 H.P.) ENGINES

1. Adjust the idle mixture screws equally to obtain maximum idle speed.
2. On the 300 H.P. engine with manual transmission in Neutral adjust the idle speed screw to obtain 700 rpm. On the 300 H.P. engine with automatic transmission in Drive, adjust the idle speed screw to obtain 600 rpm.
3. On the 350 and 370 H.P. engines, adjust the idle speed screw to obtain 750 rpm with the manual transmission in Neutral.

454 (450 H.P.) ENGINE

1. Remove the air cleaner.
2. Disconnect the distributor vacuum hose at the distributor and plug the hose.
3. Adjust the mixture screws for maximum idle speed.
4. With manual transmission in Neutral, adjust the carburetor idle speed screw to obtain 750 rpm. With automatic transmission in Drive, adjust the carburetor idle speed screw to obtain 700 rpm.
5. Turn one idle mixture screw to obtain a 20 rpm drop in idle speed, then back the screw out ¼ turn. Repeat for the second idle mixture screw.
6. Repeat Step 4 above.
7. Reconnect the distributor vacuum hose and install the air cleaner.

454 (345 H.P.) AND 454 (390 H.P.) ENGINES

1. Disconnect the distributor vacuum hose at the distributor and plug the hose.
2. Turn the idle mixture screws in until they are lightly seated, then back them out 4 turns.
3. With automatic transmission in Drive, adjust the carburetor idle speed screw to obtain 630 rpm. Adjust the idle mixture screws in equally to obtain 600 rpm.
4. With manual transmission in Neutral, adjust the carburetor idle speed screw to obtain 700 rpm. Turn one of the mixture screws in until the engine speed drops to 400 rpm. Readjust the idle speed screw to obtain 700 rpm. Turn in the other mixture screw until the engine speed drops 40 rpm. Readjust the idle speed screw to obtain 700 rpm.
5. Reconnect the distributor vacuum hose.

1971

Adjust with air cleaner installed.

The following initial idle adjustments are part of the normal engine tune-up. There is a tune-up decal placed conspicuously in the engine compartment outlining the specific procedure and settings for each engine application. Follow all of the instructions when adjusting the idle. These tuning procedures are necessary to obtain the delicate balance of variables for the maintenance of both reliable engine

IDLE MIXTURE

SOLENOID SCREW

CARBURETOR (IDLE SPEED) SCREW

Holley 4150 (with idle solenoid) idle mixture and speed adjustment locations

performance and efficient exhaust emission control.

NOTE: *All engines except the 350 (330 H.P.) and 454 (425 H.P.) have limiter caps on the mixture-adjusting screws. The idle mixture is preset and the limiter caps installed at the factory in order to meet emission control standards. Do not remove these limiter caps unless all other possible causes of poor idle condition have been thoroughly checked out.*

The solenoid used on 1971 carburetors is different from the one used on earlier models. Combination Emission Control System (C.E.C. solenoid) valve regulates distributor vacuum as a function of transmission gear position.

CAUTION: *The C.E.C. solenoid is adjusted only after: 1) replacement of the solenoid, 2) major carburetor overhaul, or 3) after the throttle body is removed or replaced.*

All initial adjustments described below are made:

IDLE SPEED (SOLENOID) SCREW

Rochester Quadrajet (with idle solenoid) idle speed screw

1. With the engine warmed up and running.
2. With the choke fully open.
3. With the fuel tank gas cap removed.
4. With the vacuum hose disconnected at the distributor and plugged.

Be sure to reconnect the distributor vacuum hose and to connect the fuel tank to evaporative emission canister line or install the gas cap when idle adjustments are complete.

350 (4-BBL QUADRAJET) ENGINES

Adjust the carburetor idle speed screw (NOT the solenoid plunger) to obtain 600 rpm (manual transmission in Neutral with the air conditioner off) or 550 rpm (automatic transmission in Drive with the air conditioner on).

350 AND 454 (4-BBL HOLLEY) ENGINES

1. Adjust the carburetor idle speed screw (NOT the solenoid plunger) to obtain 700 rpm (manual transmission in Neutral or automatic transmission in Drive).

IDLE MIXTURE SCREWS

Rochester Quadrajet (with idle solenoid) idle mixture screws

2. Adjust the idle mixture screws alternately to obtain the maximum smooth idle speed.

3. Adjust one of the idle mixture screws to obtain a 20 rpm drop ("lean roll"), then back it out ¼ turn.

4. Repeat Step 4 above for the other idle mixture screw.

5. Readjust the carburetor idle speed screw to obtain 700 rpm if necessary.

454 (4-BBL QUADRAJET) ENGINES

Turn the air conditioner off. Adjust the carburetor idle speed screw (NOT the solenoid plunger) to obtain 600 rpm (manual transmission in Neutral or automatic transmission in Drive).

1972

NOTE: *All carburetors are equipped with idle limiter caps and idle mixture is preset at the factory and should not require adjustment.*

1. Remove the fuel filler cap but do not remove the vapor line.

2. Detach the distributor vacuum hose and plug the hose.

3. Set the parking brake and turn the air conditioner (if so equipped) off. On cars equipped with an automatic transmission, chock the wheels.

4. Allow the engine to reach normal operating temperature. Be sure that the choke is open.

5. If the car has an automatic transmission, set the selector in Drive. If the car has a manual transmission keep the transmission in Neutral.

6. Adjust the anti-dieseling solenoid to the *higher* of the two rpm figures given in the specifications.

CAUTION: *Do not turn the solenoid more than one complete turn unless the electrical lead is disconnected (solenoid deenergized).*

7. Disconnect the solenoid lead and set the idle speed to the *lower* of the two figures given in the specifications. Use the normal idle speed adjusting screw.

NOTE: *If no lower figure is given, adjust the idle to 450 rpm.*

8. Reconnect all of the wires and hoses which were disconnected in order to perform these adjustments.

1973

All models are equipped with idle limiter caps and idle solenoids. Disconnect the fuel tank line from the evaporative canister. The engine must be running at operating temperature, choke off, parking brake on, and rear wheels blocked. Disconnect the distributor vacuum hose and plug it. After adjustment, reconnect the vacuum and evaporative hoses.

FOUR-BARREL 350 AND 454 CU IN. V8s

1. Adjust the idle stop solenoid screw for 900 rpm on manual, 600 rpm on automatic.

2. Connect the distributor vacuum hose and position the fast idle cam follower on the top step of the fast idle cam (turn air conditioning off) and adjust the fast idle to 1300 rpm on manual transmission 350 engines; 1600 on manual 454 engines and all automatics (in Park).

OPTIONAL 350 CU IN. (L82) V8

1. Adjust the idle stop solenoid screw (air conditioning off) for a speed of 900 rpm on manual transmission; 700 rpm on automatic (in Drive).

2. Connect the distributor vacuum hose and position the fast idle cam follower on the top step of the cam (turn air conditioning off) and adjust the fast idle to 1300 rpm on manual; 1600 rpm on automatic.

1974

The same preconditions as for 1973 apply.

FOUR-BARREL 350 CU IN. V8

1. Turn the air conditioning off. Adjust the idle stop solenoid screw for 900 rpm on manual transmission models; 600 rpm on automatic (in Drive).

2. Connect the distributor vacuum hose. Position the fast idle cam follower on the top step of the fast idle cam and adjust the fast idle speed to 1300 rpm on manual; 1600 on automatic (in Park).

OPTIONAL 350 CU IN. (L82) V8

1. Turn the air conditioning off. Adjust the idle stop solenoid for 900 rpm on manual; 700 rpm on automatic (in Drive).

2. Connect the distributor vacuum hose. Position the fast idle cam follower on the top step of the cam and adjust the fast idle to 1300 rpm on manual; 1600 rpm on automatic (in Park).

454 CU IN. V8

1. Shut off the air conditioning. Adjust the idle stop solenoid screw for 800 rpm on manual; 600 rpm on automatic (in Drive).

2. Connect the distributor vacuum hose and position the fast idle cam follower on the top step of the cam and adjust the fast idle to 1600 rpm on manual; 1500 rpm on automatic (in Park).

1975–76

The same preconditions as for 1974 apply.

1. Turn the air conditioning off.
2. Disconnect the idle speed solenoid. Turn the idle speed screw to adjust for the lower of the two idle speeds specified on the underhood tune-up decal. Adjust automatic transmission cars in Drive with wheels blocked; manual transmission cars in Neutral.
3. Connect the idle speed solenoid. Open the throttle to extend the solenoid plunger.
4. Use the solenoid plunger to adjust the idle speed to the higher of the two speeds on the underhood tune-up decal.

THROTTLE LINKAGE ADJUSTMENT

All Models Except Three, Two-Barrel Carburetors

Adjust the length of the throttle linkage to ensure full opening of the throttle plates. Turn the threaded swivel at the throttle so that with the accelerator pedal fully depressed and the carburetor throttle valve fully open, the threaded swivel will freely enter into the throttle lever. The lever should then be turned two full turns to lengthen the control rod. Corvettes with cable-controlled throttles are adjusted as follows: block the accelerator pedal fully depressed, block the throttle lever fully open, and torque the cable clamp to 45 in lbs.

Three, Two-Barrel Carburetors

Loosen the cable clamp, then fully depress the accelerator pedal and fully open the throttle plate of the primary carburetor. Torque the cable clamp bolt to 45 in. lbs.

Bring the engine to operating temperature, set the idle to specifications, and turn it off. Bottom the clevis pin in the throttle slot of the primary carburetor and adjust the secondary closing rod of the rear carburetor so that it lacks ½ a rod diameter of being long enough to freely enter the rear secondary throttle hole. Connect the rod. Adjust the forward secondary rod so that it barely enters the throttle lever hole. Connect the rod and check the linkage operation to be sure the plates close completely.

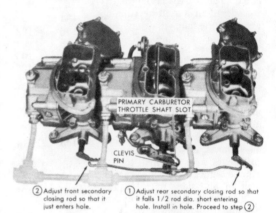

Three, two-barrel carburetor linkage adjustment

Engine Tune-Up

Engine tune-up is a procedure performed to restore engine performance, deteriorated due to normal wear and loss of adjustment. The three major areas considered in a routine tune-up are compression, ignition, and carburetion, although valve adjustment may be included.

A tune-up is performed in three steps: *analysis*, in which it is determined whether normal wear is responsible for performance loss, and which parts require replacement or service; *parts replacement or service*; and *adjustment*, in which engine adjustments are returned to original specifications. Since the advent of emission control equipment, precision adjustment has become increasingly critical, in order to maintain pollutant emission levels.

Analysis

The procedures below are used to indicate where adjustments, parts service or replacement are necessary within the realm of a normal tune-up. If, following these tests, all systems appear to be functioning properly, proceed to the Troubleshooting Section for further diagnosis.

—Remove all spark plugs, noting the cylinder in which they were installed. Remove the air cleaner, and position the throttle and choke in the full open position. Disconnect the coil high tension lead from the coil and the distributor cap. Insert a compression gauge into the spark plug port of each cylinder, in succession, and crank the engine with

Maxi. Press. Lbs. Sq. In.	Min. Press. Lbs. Sq. In.	Max. Press. Lbs. Sq. In.	Min. Press. Lbs. Sq. In.
134	101	188	141
136	102	190	142
138	104	192	144
140	105	194	145
142	107	196	147
146	110	198	148
148	111	200	150
150	113	202	151
152	114	204	153
154	115	206	154
156	117	208	156
158	118	210	157
160	120	212	158
162	121	214	160
164	123	216	162
166	124	218	163
168	126	220	165
170	127	222	166
172	129	224	168
174	131	226	169
176	132	228	171
178	133	230	172
180	135	232	174
182	136	234	175
184	138	236	177
186	140	238	178

Compression pressure limits
© Buick Div. G.M. Corp.)

the starter to obtain the highest possible reading. Record the readings, and compare the highest to the lowest on the compression pressure limit chart. If the difference exceeds the limits on the chart, or if all readings are excessively low, proceed to a wet compression check (see Troubleshooting Section).

—Evaluate the spark plugs according to the spark plug chart

in the Troubleshooting Section, and proceed as indicated in the chart.

—Remove the distributor cap, and inspect it inside and out for cracks and/or carbon tracks, and inside for excessive wear or burning of the rotor contacts. If any of these faults are evident, the cap must be replaced.

—Check the breaker points for burning, pitting or wear, and the contact heel resting on the distributor cam for excessive wear. If defects are noted, replace the entire breaker point set.

—Remove and inspect the rotor. If the contacts are burned or worn, or if the rotor is excessively loose on the distributor shaft (where applicable), the rotor must be replaced.

—Inspect the spark plug leads and the coil high tension lead for cracks or brittleness. If any of the wires appear defective, the entire set should be replaced.

—Check the air filter to ensure that it is functioning properly.

Parts Replacement and Service

The determination of whether to replace or service parts is at the mechanic's discretion; however, it is suggested that any parts in questionable condition be replaced rather than reused.

—Clean and regap, or replace, the spark plugs as needed. Lightly coat the threads with engine oil and install the plugs. CAUTION: *Do not over-torque taper-seat spark plugs, or plugs being installed in aluminum cylinder heads.*

—If the distributor cap is to be reused, clean the inside with a dry rag, and remove corrosion from the rotor contact points with fine emery cloth. Remove the spark plug wires one by one, and clean the wire ends and the inside of the towers. If the boots are loose, they should be replaced.

If the cap is to be replaced, transfer the wires one by one, cleaning the wire ends and replacing the boots if necessary.

—If the original points are to remain in service, clean them lightly with emery cloth, lubricate the contact heel with grease specifically designed for this purpose. Rotate the crankshaft until the heel rests on a high point of the distributor cam, and adjust the point gap to specifications.

When replacing the points, remove the original points and condenser, and wipe out the inside of the distributor housing with a clean, dry rag. Lightly lubricate the contact heel and pivot point, and install the points and condenser. Rotate the crankshaft until the heel rests on a high point of the distributor cam, and adjust the point gap to specifications. NOTE: *Always replace the condenser when changing the points.*

—If the rotor is to be reused, clean the contacts with solvent. Do not alter the spring tension of the rotor center contact. Install the rotor and the distributor cap.

—Replace the coil high tension lead and/or the spark plug leads as necessary.

—Clean the carburetor using a spray solvent (e.g., Gumout Spray). Remove the varnish from the throttle bores, and clean the linkage. Disconnect and plug the fuel line, and run the engine until it runs out of fuel. Partially fill the float chamber with solvent, and reconnect the fuel line. In extreme cases, the jets can be pressure flushed by inserting a rubber plug into the float vent, running the spray nozzle through it, and spraying the solvent until it squirts out of the venturi fuel dump.

—Clean and tighten all wiring connections in the primary electrical circuit.

Additional Services

The following services *should* be performed in conjunction with a routine tune-up to ensure efficient performance.

—Inspect the battery and fill to the proper level with distilled water. Remove the cable clamps, clean clamps and posts thoroughly, coat the posts lightly with petroleum jelly, reinstall and tighten.

—Inspect all belts, replace and/or adjust as necessary.

—Test the PCV valve (if so equipped), and clean or replace as indicated. Clean all crankcase ventilation hoses, or replace if cracked or hardened.

—Adjust the valves (if necessary) to manufacturer's specifications.

Adjustments

—Connect a dwell-tachometer between the distributor primary lead and ground. Remove the distributor cap and rotor (unless equipped with Delco externally adjustable distributor). With the ignition off, crank the engine with a remote starter switch and measure the point dwell angle. Adjust the dwell angle to specifications. NOTE: *Increasing the gap decreases the dwell angle and* *vice-versa.* Install the rotor and distributor cap.

—Connect a timing light according to the manufacturer's specifications. Identify the proper timing marks with chalk or paint. NOTE: *Luminescent (day-glo) paint is excellent for this purpose.* Start the engine, and run it until it reaches operating temperature. Disconnect and plug any distributor vacuum lines, and adjust idle to the speed required to adjust timing, according to specifications. Loosen the distributor clamp and adjust timing to specifications by rotating the distributor in the engine. NOTE: *To advance timing, rotate distributor opposite normal direction of rotor rotation, and vice-versa.*

—Synchronize the throttles and mixture of multiple carburetors (if so equipped) according to procedures given in the individual car sections.

—Adjust the idle speed, mixture, and idle quality, as specified in the car sections. Final idle adjustments should be made with the air cleaner installed. CAUTION: *Due to strict emission control requirements on 1969 and later models, special test equipment (CO meter, SUN Tester) may be necessary to properly adjust idle mixture to specifications.*

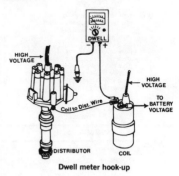

Dwell meter hook-up

Trouble-shooting

The following section is designed to aid in the rapid diagnosis of engine problems. The systematic format is used to diagnose problems ranging from engine starting difficulties to the need for engine overhaul. It is assumed that the user is equipped with basic hand tools and test equipment (tach-dwell meter, timing light, voltmeter, and ohmmeter).

Troubleshooting is divided into two sections. The first, *General Diagnosis*, is used to locate the problem area. In the second, *Specific Diagnosis*, the problem is systematically evaluated.

General Diagnosis

PROBLEM: Symptom	Begin diagnosis at Section Two, Number ——
Engine won't start:	
Starter doesn't turn	1.1, 2.1
Starter turns, engine doesn't	2.1
Starter turns engine very slowly	1.1, 2.4
Starter turns engine normally	3.1, 4.1
Starter turns engine very quickly	6.1
Engine fires intermittently	4.1
Engine fires consistently	5.1, 6.1
Engine runs poorly:	
Hard starting	3.1, 4.1, 5.1, 8.1
Rough idle	4.1, 5.1, 8.1
Stalling	3.1, 4.1, 5.1, 8.1
Engine dies at high speeds	4.1, 5.1
Hesitation (on acceleration from standing stop)	5.1, 8.1
Poor pickup	4.1, 5.1, 8.1
Lack of power	3.1, 4.1, 5.1, 8.1
Backfire through the carburetor	4.1, 8.1, 9.1
Backfire through the exhaust	4.1, 8.1, 9.1
Blue exhaust gases	6.1, 7.1
Black exhaust gases	5.1
Running on (after the ignition is shut off)	3.1, 8.1
Susceptible to moisture	4.1
Engine misfires under load	4.1, 7.1, 8.4, 9.1
Engine misfires at speed	4.1, 8.4
Engine misfires at idle	3.1, 4.1, 5.1, 7.1, 8.4

PROBLEM: Symptom	Probable Cause
Engine noises: ①	
Metallic grind while starting	Starter drive not engaging completely
Constant grind or rumble	*Starter drive not releasing, worn main bearings
Constant knock	Worn connecting rod bearings
Knock under load	Fuel octane too low, worn connecting rod bearings
Double knock	Loose piston pin
Metallic tap	*Collapsed or sticky valve lifter, excessive valve clearance, excessive end play in a rotating shaft
Scrape	*Fan belt contacting a stationary surface
Tick while starting	S.U. electric fuel pump (normal), starter brushes
Constant tick	*Generator brushes, shreaded fan belt
Squeal	*Improperly tensioned fan belt
Hiss or roar	*Steam escaping through a leak in the cooling system or the radiator overflow vent
Whistle	*Vacuum leak
Wheeze	Loose or cracked spark plug

①—It is extremely difficult to evaluate vehicle noises. While the above are general definitions of engine noises, those starred (*) should be considered as possibly originating elsewhere in the car. To aid diagnosis, the following list considers other potential sources of these sounds.

Metallic grind:
   Throwout bearing; transmission gears, bearings, or synchronizers; differential bearings, gears; something metallic in contact with brake drum or disc.
Metallic tap:
   U-joints; fan-to-radiator (or shroud) contact.
Scrape:
   Brake shoe or pad dragging; tire to body contact; suspension contacting undercarriage or exhaust; something non-metallic contacting brake shoe or drum.
Tick:
   Transmission gears; differential gears; lack of radio suppression; resonant vibration of body panels; windshield wiper motor or transmission; heater motor and blower.
Squeal:
   Brake shoe or pad not fully releasing; tires (excessive wear, uneven wear, improper inflation); front or rear wheel alignment (most commonly due to improper toe-in).
Hiss or whistle:
   Wind leaks (body or window); heater motor and blower fan.
Roar:
   Wheel bearings; wind leaks (body and window).

Specific Diagnosis

This section is arranged so that following each test, instructions are given to proceed to another, until a problem is diagnosed.

INDEX

Group		Topic
1	*	Battery
2	*	Cranking system
3	*	Primary electrical system
4	*	Secondary electrical system
5	*	Fuel system
6	*	Engine compression
7	**	Engine vacuum
8	**	Secondary electrical system
9	**	Valve train
10	**	Exhaust system
11	**	Cooling system
12	**	Engine lubrication

*—The engine need not be running.
**—The engine must be running.

SAMPLE SECTION

Test and Procedure	Results and Indications	Proceed to
4.1—Check for spark: Hold each spark plug wire approximately ¼″ from ground with gloves or a heavy, dry rag. Crank the engine and observe the spark.	→ If no spark is evident:	→ 4.2
	→ If spark is good in some cases:	→ 4.3
	→ If spark is good in all cases:	→ 4.6

DIAGNOSIS

1.1—Inspect the battery visually for case condition (corrosion, cracks) and water level.	If case is cracked, replace battery:	1.4
	If the case is intact, remove corrosion with a solution of baking soda and water (CAUTION: *do not get the solution into the battery*), and fill with water:	1.2
1.2—Check the battery cable connections: Insert a screwdriver between the battery post and the cable clamp. Turn the headlights on high beam, and observe them as the screwdriver is gently twisted to ensure good metal to metal contact. **Testing battery cable connections using a screwdriver**	If the lights brighten, remove and clean the clamp and post; coat the post with petroleum jelly, install and tighten the clamp:	1.4
	If no improvement is noted:	1.3

1.3—Test the state of charge of the battery using an individual cell tester or hydrometer.

Spec. Grav. Reading	Charged Condition
1.260-1.280	Fully Charged
1.230-1.250	Three Quarter Charged
1.200-1.220	One Half Charged
1.170-1.190	One Quarter Charged
1.140-1.160	Just About Flat
1.110-1.130	All The Way Down

State of battery charge

Electrolyte temperature (°F)	Specific gravity correction	
+120	+.016	
	+.012	
+100	+.008	ADD to reading
	+.004	
+80	no correction	
	−.004	
+60	−.008	
	−.012	
+40	−.016	
	−.020	
+20	−.024	SUBTRACT from reading
	−.028	
0	−.032	
	−.036	
−20	−.040	

The effect of temperature on the specific gravity of battery electrolyte

If indicated, charge the battery. NOTE: *If no obvious reason exists for the low state of charge (i.e., battery age, prolonged storage), the charging system should be tested:*   1.4

Test and Procedure	*Results and Indications*	*Proceed to*
1.4—Visually inspect battery cables for cracking, bad connection to ground, or bad connection to starter.	If necessary, tighten connections or replace the cables:	2.1

Tests in Group 2 are performed with coil high tension lead disconnected to prevent accidental starting.

Test and Procedure	*Results and Indications*	*Proceed to*
2.1—Test the starter motor and solenoid: Connect a jumper from the battery post of the solenoid (or relay) to the starter post of the solenoid (or relay).	If starter turns the engine normally:	2.2
	If the starter buzzes, or turns the engine very slowly:	2.4
	If no response, replace the solenoid (or relay).	3.1
	If the starter turns, but the engine doesn't, ensure that the flywheel ring gear is intact. If the gear is undamaged, replace the starter drive.	3.1
2.2—Determine whether ignition override switches are functioning properly (clutch start switch, neutral safety switch), by connecting a jumper across the switch(es), and turning the ignition switch to "start".	If starter operates, adjust or replace switch:	3.1
	If the starter doesn't operate:	2.3
2.3—Check the ignition switch "start" position: Connect a 12V test lamp between the starter post of the solenoid (or relay) and ground. Turn the ignition switch to the "start" position, and jiggle the key.	If the lamp doesn't light when the switch is turned, check the ignition switch for loose connections, cracked insulation, or broken wires. Repair or replace as necessary:	3.1
	If the lamp flickers when the key is jiggled, replace the ignition switch.	3.3

Checking the ignition switch "start" position

Test and Procedure	*Results and Indications*	*Proceed to*
2.4—Remove and bench test the starter, according to specifications in the car section.	If the starter does not meet specifications, repair or replace as needed:	3.1
	If the starter is operating properly:	2.5
2.5—Determine whether the engine can turn freely: Remove the spark plugs, and check for water in the cylinders. Check for water on the dipstick, or oil in the radiator. Attempt to turn the engine using an 18″ flex drive and socket on the crankshaft pulley nut or bolt.	If the engine will turn freely only with the spark plugs out, and hydrostatic lock (water in the cylinders) is ruled out, check valve timing:	9.2
	If engine will not turn freely, and it is known that the clutch and transmission are free, the engine must be disassembled for further evaluation:	Next Chapter

Tests and Procedures	Results and Indications	Proceed to
3.1—Check the ignition switch "on" position: Connect a jumper wire between the distributor side of the coil and ground, and a 12V test lamp between the switch side of the coil and ground. Remove the high tension lead from the coil. Turn the ignition switch on and jiggle the key.	If the lamp lights:	3.2
	If the lamp flickers when the key is jiggled, replace the ignition switch:	3.3
	If the lamp doesn't light, check for loose or open connections. If none are found, remove the ignition switch and check for continuity. If the switch is faulty, replace it:	3.3

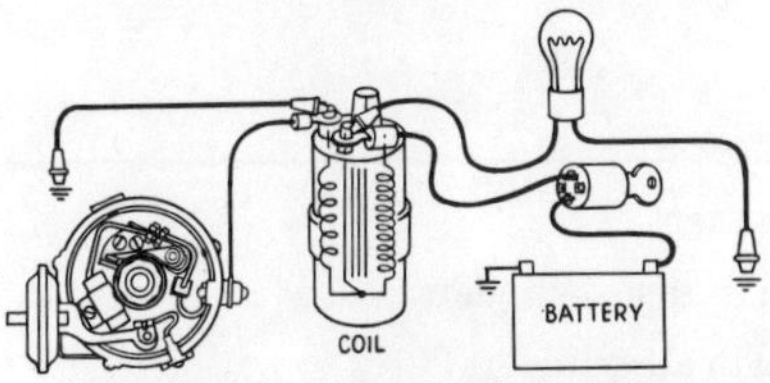

Checking the ignition switch "on" position

3.2—Check the ballast resistor or resistance wire for an open circuit, using an ohmmeter.	Replace the resistor or the resistance wire if the resistance is zero.	3.3
3.3—Visually inspect the breaker points for burning, pitting, or excessive wear. Gray coloring of the point contact surfaces is normal. Rotate the crankshaft until the contact heel rests on a high point of the distributor cam, and adjust the point gap to specifications.	If the breaker points are intact, clean the contact surfaces with fine emery cloth, and adjust the point gap to specifications. If pitted or worn, replace the points and condenser, and adjust the gap to specifications: NOTE: *Always lubricate the distributor cam according to manufacturer's recommendations when servicing the breaker points.*	3.4
3.4—Connect a dwell meter between the distributor primary lead and ground. Crank the engine and observe the point dwell angle.	If necessary, adjust the point dwell angle: NOTE: *Increasing the point gap decreases the dwell angle, and vice-versa.*	3.6
	If dwell meter shows little or no reading:	3.5

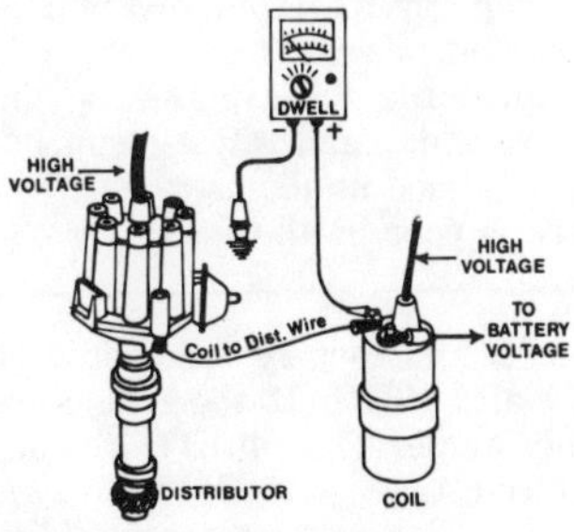

Dwell meter hook-up

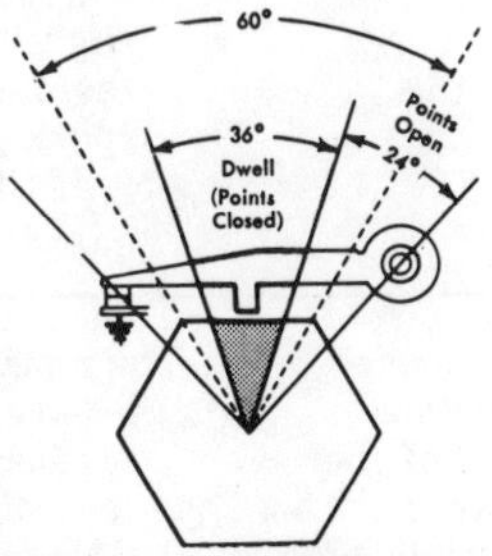

Dwell angle

3.5—Check the condenser for short: Connect an ohmmeter across the condenser body and the pigtail lead.	If any reading other than infinite resistance is noted, replace the condenser:	3.6

Checking the condenser for short

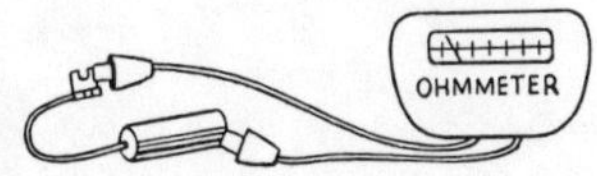

Test and Procedure	Results and Indications	Proceed to
3.6—Test the coil primary resistance: Connect an ohmmeter across the coil primary terminals, and read the resistance on the low scale. Note whether an external ballast resistor or resistance wire is utilized.	Coils utilizing ballast resistors or resistance wires should have approximately 1.0Ω resistance; coils with internal resistors should have approximately 4.0Ω resistance. If values far from the above are noted, replace the coil:	4.1

Testing the coil primary resistance

4.1—Check for spark: Hold each spark plug wire approximately $\frac{1}{4}''$ from ground with gloves or a heavy, dry rag. Crank the engine, and observe the spark.	If no spark is evident:	4.2
	If spark is good in some cylinders:	4.3
	If spark is good in all cylinders:	4.6

4.2—Check for spark at the coil high tension lead: Remove the coil high tension lead from the distributor and position it approximately $\frac{1}{4}''$ from ground. Crank the engine and observe spark. CAUTION: *This test should not be performed on cars equipped with transistorized ignition.*	If the spark is good and consistent:	4.3
	If the spark is good but intermittent, test the primary electrical system starting at 3.3:	3.3
	If the spark is weak or non-existent, replace the coil high tension lead, clean and tighten all connections and retest. If no improvement is noted:	4.4

4.3—Visually inspect the distributor cap and rotor for burned or corroded contacts, cracks, carbon tracks, or moisture. Also check the fit of the rotor on the distributor shaft (where applicable).	If moisture is present, dry thoroughly, and retest per 4.1:	4.1
	If burned or excessively corroded contacts, cracks, or carbon tracks are noted, replace the defective part(s) and retest per 4.1:	4.1

	If the rotor and cap appear intact, or are only slightly corroded, clean the contacts thoroughly (including the cap towers and spark plug wire ends) and retest per 4.1:
	    If the spark is good in all cases:
	    If the spark is poor in all cases:
		4.6
		4.5

4.4—Check the coil secondary resistance: Connect an ohmmeter across the distributor side of the coil and the coil tower. Read the resistance on the high scale of the ohmmeter.	The resistance of a satisfactory coil should be between $4K\Omega$ and $10K\Omega$. If the resistance is considerably higher (i.e., $40K\Omega$) replace the coil, and retest per 4.1: NOTE: *This does not apply to high performance coils.*	4.1

Testing the coil secondary resistance

Test and Procedure	Results and Indications	Proceed to
4.5—Visually inspect the spark plug wires for cracking or brittleness. Ensure that no two wires are positioned so as to cause induction firing (adjacent and parallel). Remove each wire, one by one, and check resistance with an ohmmeter.	Replace any cracked or brittle wires. If any of the wires are defective, replace the entire set. Replace any wires with excessive resistance (over 8000Ω per foot for suppression wire), and separate any wires that might cause induction firing.	4.6
4.6—Remove the spark plugs, noting the cylinders from which they were removed, and evaluate according to the chart below.	See below.	See below.

	Condition	Cause	Remedy	Proceed to
	Electrodes eroded, light brown deposits.	Normal wear. Normal wear is indicated by approximately .001″ wear per 1000 miles.	Clean and regap the spark plug if wear is not excessive: Replace the spark plug if excessively worn:	4.7
	Carbon fouling (black, dry, fluffy deposits).	If present on one or two plugs:		
		Faulty high tension lead(s).	Test the high tension leads:	4.5
		Burnt or sticking valve(s).	Check the valve train: (Clean and regap the plugs in either case.)	9.1
		If present on most or all plugs: Overly rich fuel mixture, due to restricted air filter, improper carburetor adjustment, improper choke or heat riser adjustment or operation.	Check the fuel system:	5.1
	Oil fouling (wet black deposits)	Worn engine components. NOTE: *Oil fouling may occur in new or recently rebuilt engines until broken in.*	Check engine vacuum and compression: Replace with new spark plug	6.1
	Lead fouling (gray, black, tan, or yellow deposits, which appear glazed or cinder-like).	Combustion by-products.	Clean and regap the plugs: (Use plugs of a different heat range if the problem recurs.)	4.7

	Condition	Cause	Remedy	Proceed to
	Gap bridging (deposits lodged between the electrodes).	Incomplete combustion, or transfer of deposits from the combustion chamber.	Replace the spark plugs:	4.7
	Overheating (burnt electrodes, and extremely white insulator with small black spots).	Ignition timing advanced too far.	Adjust timing to specifications:	8.2
		Overly lean fuel mixture.	Check the fuel system:	5.1
		Spark plugs not seated properly.	Clean spark plug seat and install a new gasket washer: (Replace the spark plugs in all cases.)	4.7
	Fused spot deposits on the insulator.	Combustion chamber blowby.	Clean and regap the spark plugs:	4.7
	Pre-ignition (melted or severely burned electrodes, blistered or cracked insulators, or metallic deposits on the insulator).	Incorrect spark plug heat range.	Replace with plugs of the proper heat range:	4.7
		Ignition timing advanced too far.	Adjust timing to specifications:	8.2
		Spark plugs not being cooled efficiently.	Clean the spark plug seat, and check the cooling system:	11.1
		Fuel mixture too lean.	Check the fuel system:	5.1
		Poor compression.	Check compression:	6.1
		Fuel grade too low.	Use higher octane fuel:	4.7

Test and Procedure	Results and Indications	Proceed to
4.7—Determine the static ignition timing: Using the flywheel or crankshaft pulley timing marks as a guide, locate top dead center on the *compression* stroke of the No. 1 cylinder. Remove the distributor cap.	Adjust the distributor so that the rotor points toward the No. 1 tower in the distributor cap, and the points are just opening:	4.8
4.8—Check coil polarity: Connect a voltmeter negative lead to the coil high tension lead, and the positive lead to ground (NOTE: *reverse the hook-up for positive ground cars*). Crank the engine momentarily. **Checking coil polarity**	If the voltmeter reads up-scale, the polarity is correct:	5.1
	If the voltmeter reads down-scale, reverse the coil polarity (switch the primary leads):	5.1

Test and Procedure	Results and Indications	Proceed to
5.1—Determine that the air filter is functioning efficiently: Hold paper elements up to a strong light, and attempt to see light through the filter.	Clean permanent air filters in gasoline (or manufacturer's recommendation), and allow to dry. Replace paper elements through which light cannot be seen:	5.2
5.2—Determine whether a flooding condition exists: Flooding is identified by a strong gasoline odor, and excessive gasoline present in the throttle bore(s) of the carburetor.	If flooding is not evident:	5.3
	If flooding is evident, permit the gasoline to dry for a few moments and restart. If flooding doesn't recur:	5.6
	If flooding is persistant:	5.5
5.3—Check that fuel is reaching the carburetor: Detach the fuel line at the carburetor inlet. Hold the end of the line in a cup (not styrofoam), and crank the engine.	If fuel flows smoothly:	5.6
	If fuel doesn't flow (NOTE: *Make sure that there is fuel in the tank*), or flows erratically:	5.4
5.4—Test the fuel pump: Disconnect all fuel lines from the fuel pump. Hold a finger over the input fitting, crank the engine (with electric pump, turn the ignition or pump on); and feel for suction.	If suction is evident, blow out the fuel line to the tank with low pressure compressed air until bubbling is heard from the fuel filler neck. Also blow out the carburetor fuel line (both ends disconnected):	5.6
	If no suction is evident, replace or repair the fuel pump:	5.6
	NOTE: *Repeated oil fouling of the spark plugs, or a no-start condition, could be the result of a ruptured vacuum booster pump diaphragm, through which oil or gasoline is being drawn into the intake manifold (where applicable).*	
5.5—Check the needle and seat: Tap the carburetor in the area of the needle and seat.	If flooding stops, a gasoline additive (e.g., Gumout) will often cure the problem:	5.6
	If flooding continues, check the fuel pump for excessive pressure at the carburetor (according to specifications). If the pressure is normal, the needle and seat must be removed and checked, and/or the float level adjusted:	5.6
5.6—Test the accelerator pump by looking into the throttle bores while operating the throttle.	If the accelerator pump appears to be operating normally:	5.7
	If the accelerator pump is not operating, the pump must be reconditioned. Where possible, service the pump with the carburetor(s) installed on the engine. If necessary, remove the carburetor. Prior to removal:	5.7
5.7—Determine whether the carburetor main fuel system is functioning: Spray a commercial starting fluid into the carburetor while attempting to start the engine.	If the engine starts, runs for a few seconds, and dies:	5.8
	If the engine doesn't start:	6.1

Test and Procedures	*Results and Indications*	*Proceed to*
5.8—Uncommon fuel system malfunctions: See below:	If the problem is solved:	6.1
	If the problem remains, remove and recondition the carburetor.	

Condition	*Indication*	*Test*	*Usual Weather Conditions*	*Remedy*
Vapor lock	Car will not restart shortly after running.	Cool the components of the fuel system until the engine starts.	Hot to very hot	Ensure that the exhaust manifold heat control valve is operating. Check with the vehicle manufacturer for the recommended solution to vapor lock on the model in question.
Carburetor icing	Car will not idle, stalls at low speeds.	Visually inspect the throttle plate area of the throttle bores for frost.	High humidity, 32-40° F.	Ensure that the exhaust manifold heat control valve is operating, and that the intake manifold heat riser is not blocked.
Water in the fuel	Engine sputters and stalls; may not start.	Pump a small amount of fuel into a glass jar. Allow to stand, and inspect for droplets or a layer of water.	High humidity, extreme temperature changes.	For droplets, use one or two cans of commercial gas dryer (Dry Gas) For a layer of water, the tank must be drained, and the fuel lines blown out with compressed air.

Test and Procedure	*Results and Indications*	*Proceed to*
6.1—Test engine compression: Remove all spark plugs. Insert a compression gauge into a spark plug port, crank the engine to obtain the maximum reading, and record.	If compression is within limits on all cylinders:	7.1
	If gauge reading is extremely low on all cylinders:	6.2
	If gauge reading is low on one or two cylinders:	6.2
	(If gauge readings are identical and low on two or more adjacent cylinders, the head gasket must be replaced.)	

Testing compression
(© Chevrolet Div. G.M. Corp.)

Compression pressure limits
(© Buick Div. G.M. Corp.)

Maxi. Press. Lbs. Sq. In.	*Min. Press. Lbs. Sq. In.*	*Maxi. Press. Lbs. Sq. In.*	*Min. Press. Lbs. Sq. In.*	*Max. Press. Lbs. Sq. In.*	*Min. Press. Lbs. Sq. In.*	*Max. Press. Lbs. Sq. In.*	*Min. Press. Lbs. Sq. In.*
134	101	162	121	188	141	214	160
136	102	164	123	190	142	216	162
138	104	166	124	192	144	218	163
140	105	168	126	194	145	220	165
142	107	170	127	196	147	222	166
146	110	172	129	198	148	224	168
148	111	174	131	200	150	226	169
150	113	176	132	202	151	228	171
152	114	178	133	204	153	230	172
154	115	180	135	206	154	232	174
156	117	182	136	208	156	234	175
158	118	184	138	210	157	236	177
160	120	186	140	212	158	238	178

Test and Procedure	Results and Indications	Proceed to
6.2—Test engine compression (wet): Squirt approximately 30 cc. of engine oil into each cylinder, and retest per 6.1.	If the readings improve, worn or cracked rings or broken pistons are indicated:	Next Chapter
	If the readings do not improve, burned or excessively carboned valves or a jumped timing chain are indicated:	7.1
	NOTE: *A jumped timing chain is often indicated by difficult cranking.*	
7.1—Perform a vacuum check of the engine: Attach a vacuum gauge to the intake manifold beyond the throttle plate. Start the engine, and observe the action of the needle over the range of engine speeds.	See below.	See below

	Reading	Indications	Proceed to
	Steady, from 17-22 in. Hg.	Normal.	8.1
	Low and steady.	Late ignition or valve timing, or low compression:	6.1
	Very low	Vacuum leak:	7.2
	Needle fluctuates as engine speed increases.	Ignition miss, blown cylinder head gasket, leaking valve or weak valve spring:	6.1, 8.3
	Gradual drop in reading at idle.	Excessive back pressure in the exhaust system:	10.1
	Intermittent fluctuation at idle.	Ignition miss, sticking valve:	8.3, 9.1
	Drifting needle.	Improper idle mixture adjustment, carburetors not synchronized (where applicable), or minor intake leak. Synchronize the carburetors, adjust the idle, and retest. If the condition persists:	7.2
	High and steady.	Early ignition timing:	8.2

Test and Procedure	*Results and Indications*	*Proceed to*
7.2—Attach a vacuum gauge per 7.1, and test for an intake manifold leak. Squirt a small amount of oil around the intake manifold gaskets, carburetor gaskets, plugs and fittings. Observe the action of the vacuum gauge.	If the reading improves, replace the indicated gasket, or seal the indicated fitting or plug: If the reading remains low:	8.1 7.3
7.3—Test all vacuum hoses and accessories for leaks as described in 7.2. Also check the carburetor body (dashpots, automatic choke mechanism, throttle shafts) for leaks in the same manner.	If the reading improves, service or replace the offending part(s): If the reading remains low:	8.1 6.1
8.1—Check the point dwell angle: Connect a dwell meter between the distributor primary wire and ground. Start the engine, and observe the dwell angle from idle to 3000 rpm.	If necessary, adjust the dwell angle. NOTE: *Increasing the point gap reduces the dwell angle and vice-versa.* If the dwell angle moves outside specifications as engine speed increases, the distributor should be removed and checked for cam accuracy, shaft end-play and concentricity, bushing wear, and adequate point arm tension (NOTE: *Most of these items may be checked with the distributor installed in the engine, using an oscilloscope*):	8.2
8.2—Connect a timing light (per manufacturer's recommendation) and check the dynamic ignition timing. Disconnect and plug the vacuum hose(s) to the distributor if specified, start the engine, and observe the timing marks at the specified engine speed.	If the timing is not correct, adjust to specifications by rotating the distributor in the engine: (Advance timing by rotating distributor opposite normal direction of rotor rotation, retard timing by rotating distributor in same direction as rotor rotation.)	8.3
8.3—Check the operation of the distributor advance mechanism(s): To test the mechanical advance, disconnect all but the mechanical advance, and observe the timing marks with a timing light as the engine speed is increased from idle. If the mark moves smoothly, without hesitation, it may be assumed that the mechanical advance is functioning properly. To test vacuum advance and/or retard systems, alternately crimp and release the vacuum line, and observe the timing mark for movement. If movement is noted, the system is operating.	If the systems are functioning: If the systems are not functioning, remove the distributor, and test on a distributor tester:	8.4 8.4
8.4—Locate an ignition miss: With the engine running, remove each spark plug wire, one by one, until one is found that doesn't cause the engine to roughen and slow down.	When the missing cylinder is identified:	4.1

Test and Procedure	Results and Indications	Proceed to
9.1—Evaluate the valve train: Remove the valve cover, and ensure that the valves are adjusted to specifications. A mechanic's stethoscope may be used to aid in the diagnosis of the valve train. By pushing the probe on or near push rods or rockers, valve noise often can be isolated. A timing light also may be used to diagnose valve problems. Connect the light according to manufacturer's recommendations, and start the engine. Vary the firing moment of the light by increasing the engine speed (and therefore the ignition advance), and moving the trigger from cylinder to cylinder. Observe the movement of each valve.	See below	See below

Observation	Probable Cause	Remedy	Proceed to
Metallic tap heard through the stethoscope.	Sticking hydraulic lifter or excessive valve clearance.	Adjust valve. If tap persists, remove and replace the lifter:	10.1
Metallic tap through the stethoscope, able to push the rocker arm (lifter side) down by hand.	Collapsed valve lifter.	Remove and replace the lifter:	10.1
Erratic, irregular motion of the valve stem.*	Sticking valve, burned valve.	Recondition the valve and/or valve guide:	Next Chapter
Eccentric motion of the pushrod at the rocker arm.*	Bent pushrod.	Replace the pushrod:	10.1
Valve retainer bounces as the valve closes.*	Weak valve spring or damper.	Remove and test the spring and damper. Replace if necessary:	10.1

*—When observed with a timing light.

Test and Procedure	Results and Indications	Proceed to
9.2—Check the valve timing: Locate top dead center of the No. 1 piston, and install a degree wheel or tape on the crankshaft pulley or damper with zero corresponding to an index mark on the engine. Rotate the crankshaft in its direction of rotation, and observe the opening of the No. 1 cylinder intake valve. The opening should correspond with the correct mark on the degree wheel according to specifications.	If the timing is not correct, the timing cover must be removed for further investigation:	

Test and Procedure	Results and Indications	Proceed to
10.1—Determine whether the exhaust manifold heat control valve is operating: Operate the valve by hand to determine whether it is free to move. If the valve is free, run the engine to operating temperature and observe the action of the valve, to ensure that it is opening.	If the valve sticks, spray it with a suitable solvent, open and close the valve to free it, and retest.	
	If the valve functions properly:	10.2
	If the valve does not free, or does not operate, replace the valve:	10.2
10.2—Ensure that there are no exhaust restrictions: Visually inspect the exhaust system for kinks, dents, or crushing. Also note that gasses are flowing freely from the tailpipe at all engine speeds, indicating no restriction in the muffler or resonator.	Replace any damaged portion of the system:	11.1
11.1—Visually inspect the fan belt for glazing, cracks, and fraying, and replace if necessary. Tighten the belt so that the longest span has approximately ½″ play at its midpoint under thumb pressure.	Replace or tighten the fan belt as necessary:	11.2

Checking the fan belt tension
(© Nissan Motor Co. Ltd.)

Test and Procedure	Results and Indications	Proceed to
11.2—Check the fluid level of the cooling system.	If full or slightly low, fill as necessary:	11.5
	If extremely low:	11.3
11.3—Visually inspect the external portions of the cooling system (radiator, radiator hoses, thermostat elbow, water pump seals, heater hoses, etc.) for leaks. If none are found, pressurize the cooling system to 14-15 psi.	If cooling system holds the pressure:	11.5
	If cooling system loses pressure rapidly, re-inspect external parts of the system for leaks under pressure. If none are found, check dipstick for coolant in crankcase. If no coolant is present, but pressure loss continues:	11.4
	If coolant is evident in crankcase, remove cylinder head(s), and check gasket(s). If gaskets are intact, block and cylinder head(s) should be checked for cracks or holes.	
	If the gasket(s) is blown, replace, and purge the crankcase of coolant:	12.6
	NOTE: Occasionally, due to atmospheric and driving conditions, condensation of water can occur in the crankcase. This causes the oil to appear milky white. To remedy, run the engine until hot, and change the oil and oil filter.	

Test and Procedure	Results and Indication	Proceed to
11.4—Check for combustion leaks into the cooling system: Pressurize the cooling system as above. Start the engine, and observe the pressure gauge. If the needle fluctuates, remove each spark plug wire, one by one, noting which cylinder(s) reduce or eliminate the fluctuation.	Cylinders which reduce or eliminate the fluctuation, when the spark plug wire is removed, are leaking into the cooling system. Replace the head gasket on the affected cylinder bank(s).	

Radiator pressure tester
(© American Motors Corp.)

Test and Procedure	Results and Indication	Proceed to
11.5—Check the radiator pressure cap: Attach a radiator pressure tester to the radiator cap (wet the seal prior to installation). Quickly pump up the pressure, noting the point at which the cap releases.	If the cap releases within ± 1 psi of the specified rating, it is operating properly:	11.6
	If the cap releases at more than ± 1 psi of the specified rating, it should be replaced:	11.6

Testing the radiator pressure cap
(© American Motors Corp.)

Test and Procedure	Results and Indication	Proceed to
11.6—Test the thermostat: Start the engine cold, remove the radiator cap, and insert a thermometer into the radiator. Allow the engine to idle. After a short while, there will be a sudden, rapid increase in coolant temperature. The temperature at which this sharp rise stops is the thermostat opening temperature.	If the thermostat opens at or about the specified temperature:	11.7
	If the temperature doesn't increase: (If the temperature increases slowly and gradually, replace the thermostat.)	11.7
11.7—Check the water pump: Remove the thermostat elbow and the thermostat, disconnect the coil high tension lead (to prevent starting), and crank the engine momentarily.	If coolant flows, replace the thermostat and retest per 11.6:	11.6
	If coolant doesn't flow, reverse flush the cooling system to alleviate any blockage that might exist. If system is not blocked, and coolant will not flow, recondition the water pump.	—
12.1—Check the oil pressure gauge or warning light: If the gauge shows low pressure, or the light is on, for no obvious reason, remove the oil pressure sender. Install an accurate oil pressure gauge and run the engine momentarily.	If oil pressure builds normally, run engine for a few moments to determine that it is functioning normally, and replace the sender.	—
	If the pressure remains low:	12.2
	If the pressure surges:	12.3
	If the oil pressure is zero:	12.3

Test and Procedure	Results and Indications	Proceed to
12.2—Visually inspect the oil: If the oil is watery or very thin, milky, or foamy, replace the oil and oil filter.	If the oil is normal:	12.3
	If after replacing oil the pressure remains low:	12.3
	If after replacing oil the pressure becomes normal:	—
12.3—Inspect the oil pressure relief valve and spring, to ensure that it is not sticking or stuck. Remove and thoroughly clean the valve, spring, and the valve body.	If the oil pressure improves:	—
	If no improvement is noted:	12.4

Oil pressure relief valve
(© British Leyland Motors)

Test and Procedure	Results and Indications	Proceed to
12.4—Check to ensure that the oil pump is not cavitating (sucking air instead of oil): See that the crankcase is neither over nor underfull, and that the pickup in the sump is in the proper position and free from sludge.	Fill or drain the crankcase to the proper capacity, and clean the pickup screen in solvent if necessary. If no improvement is noted:	12.5
12.5—Inspect the oil pump drive and the oil pump:	If the pump drive or the oil pump appear to be defective, service as necessary and retest per 12.1:	12.1
	If the pump drive and pump appear to be operating normally, the engine should be disassembled to determine where blockage exists:	Next Chapter
12.6—Purge the engine of ethylene glycol coolant: Completely drain the crankcase and the oil filter. Obtain a commercial butyl cellosolve base solvent, designated for this purpose, and follow the instructions precisely. Following this, install a new oil filter and refill the crankcase with the proper weight oil. The next oil and filter change should follow shortly thereafter (1000 miles).		

Chapter 3

Engine and Engine Rebuilding

Engine Electrical

DISTRIBUTOR

Removal and Installation

Remove the ignition shield covering the distributor and coil, and disconnect the tachometer drive cable and fuel injection drive from the distributor housing, if so equipped. Remove the primary coil wire or pick-up coil leads, and the distributor cap. Bring the engine to TDC, firing number one cylinder, and mark the rotor-to-distributor relationship. Remove the vacuum line and the hold-down clamp, and withdraw the distributor. As the distributor is removed, it will rotate the distributor shaft. Mark the new rotor-to-housing relation and set the rotor at that point when installing the distributor. When the distributor is seated, the rotation encountered during gear meshing should return the rotor to the original rotor-to-housing mark. Do not rotate the engine while the distributor is removed.

To install, position the rotor on the second reference mark that indicates the position of the rotor after its removal from the engine. Insert the distributor and replace the clamp; leaving it loose enough to turn the distributor for final timing.

Connect the distributor cap, primary coil wires, vacuum lines, and tachometer drive. Also connect the fuel injection pump drive-cables when applicable. Time engine and replace the ignition shields.

Disassembly and Assembly

BREAKER TYPE

Two screws secure the rotor. Remove these and the rotor. Remove the primary coil and condenser leads, point set and condenser. Remove the gear cover plate, then tap out the roll pin and remove the distributor shaft drive-gear. Note the number of shims used on the gear. Disconnect the advance weight springs, remove the weights and slide the cam from the mainshaft. Loosen the breaker plate clamp, expand it, and slide the plate from the housing. Reverse the procedure to reassemble.

BREAKERLESS TYPE

Remove the securing screws and withdraw the rotor. Remove the centrifugal weight springs and weights, and the tachometer drive gear. Tap out the roll pin and slide the distributor drive-gear from the distributor shaft. Remove the drive-shaft assembly, centrifugal weight sup-

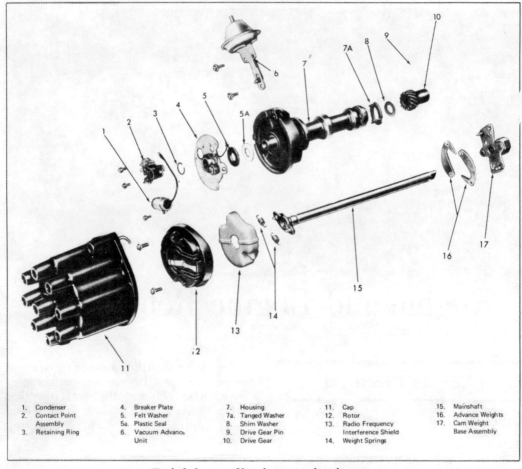

1. Condenser	4. Breaker Plate	7. Housing	11. Cap	15. Mainshaft
2. Contact Point Assembly	5. Felt Washer	7a. Tanged Washer	12. Rotor	16. Advance Weights
3. Retaining Ring	5a. Plastic Seal	8. Shim Washer	13. Radio Frequency	17. Cam Weight Base Assembly
	6. Vacuum Advance Unit	9. Drive Gear Pin	Interference Shield	
		10. Drive Gear	14. Weight Springs	

Exploded view of breaker point distributor

Distributor Specifications

NOTE: *The following specifications are given in degrees advance at crankshaft speed. Half degrees for distributor machine testing.*

Year	Model	Distributor Part Number	Centrifugal Advance			Vacuum Advance	
			Start Degrees @ rpm	Intermediate Degrees @ rpm	End Degrees @ rpm	Start Degrees @ in. Hg	End Degrees @ in. Hg
1963–64	All except fuel injection	1111024	0 @ 700	11 @ 1600	24 @ 4600	0 @ 8	15 @ 15.5
	Fuel injection	1111022	0 @ 700	11 @ 700	24 @ 4600	0 @ 8	15 @ 15.5
1965	Base engine	1111076	0 @ 750	15 @ 1500	26 @ 4100	0 @ 4	16.5 @ 8.2
	Special performance	1111069	0 @ 800	NA	24 @ 2350	0 @ 4	16.5 @ 8.2
	Fuel injection	1111070	0 @ 800	NA	24 @ 2350	0 @ 4	16.5 @ 8.2

Distributor Specifications (cont.)

NOTE: *The following specifications are given in degrees advance at crankshaft speed. Half degrees for distributor machine testing.*

Year	Model	Distributor Part Number	Centrifugal Advance			Vacuum Advance	
			Start Degrees @ rpm	Intermediate Degrees @ rpm	End Degrees @ rpm	Start Degrees @ in. Hg	End Degrees @ in. Hg
1965	Base engine	1111087	0 @ 750	15 @ 1500	30 @ 5100	0 @ 4	16.5 @ 8.2
	Special performance w/transistor ign	1111060	0 @ 800	NA	26 @ 2500	0 @ 4	16.5 @ 8.2
	F.I. w/transistor ign	1111064	0 @ 800	NA	26 @ 2500	0 @ 4	16.5 @ 8.2
1966	300 hp	1111194	0 @ 900	15 @ 1500	30 @ 5100	0 @ 6	15 @ 12
	350 hp	1111438	0 @ 950	20 @ 1800	30 @ 4700	0 @ 8	15 @ 15.5
	390 hp	1111293	0 @ 900	8 @ 1250	32 @ 5000	0 @ 7	12 @ 12
	350 hp w/transistor ign	1111441	0 @ 900	16.5 @ 1400	30 @ 4400	0 @ 8	15 @ 15.5
	390 hp w/transistor ign	1111294	0 @ 900	17 @ 2000	32 @ 5000	0 @ 7	12 @ 12
	425 hp	1111170	0 @ 900	17 @ 2000	32 @ 5000	0 @ 7	12 @ 12
1967–68	300 hp	1111194	0 @ 900	15 @ 1500	30 @ 5100	0 @ 6	15 @ 12
	350 hp	1111438	0 @ 950	20 @ 1800	30 @ 4700	0 @ 8	15 @ 15.5
	390 hp, 400 hp	1111293	0 @ 900	17 @ 2000	32 @ 5000	0 @ 7	12 @ 12
	435 hp	1111296	0 @ 900	NA	30 @ 3800	0 @ 8	15 @ 15.5
	430 hp L88	1111295	0 @ 1200	18 @ 1900	30 @ 5000	——	——
	350 hp w/transistor ign	1111441	0 @ 900	16.5 @ 1400	30 @ 4400	0 @ 8	15 @ 15.5
	390 hp, 400 hp	1111294	0 @ 900	17 @ 2000	32 @ 5000	0 @ 7	12 @ 12
1969	300 hp	1111490	0 @ 900	15 @ 1500	30 @ 5100	0 @ 8	19 @ 17
	350 hp	1111493	0 @ 1000	10 @ 1700	26 @ 5000	0 @ 7	15 @ 12
	390 hp, 400 hp	1111926	0 @ 900	17 @ 2000	26 @ 3800	0 @ 7	12 @ 12
	435 hp	1111928	0 @ 900	2 @ 1100	30 @ 3800	0 @ 8	15 @ 15.5
	430 hp L88	1111927	0 @ 1200	16 @ 1900	29 @ 5000	——	——
1970	300 hp	1111490	0 @ 900	15 @ 1500	30 @ 5100	0 @ 8	19 @ 17
	350 hp	1111493	0 @ 1150	10 @ 1700	26 @ 5000	0 @ 8	19 @ 17

Distributor Specifications (cont.)

NOTE: *The following specifications are given in degrees advance at crankshaft speed. Half degrees for distributor machine testing.*

Year	Model	Distributor Part Number	Centrifugal Advance			Vacuum Advance	
			Start Degrees @ rpm	Intermediate Degrees @ rpm	End Degrees @ rpm	Start Degrees @ in. Hg	End Degrees @ in. Hg
1970	370 hp	1111491	0 @ 1000	NA	26 @ 5000	0 @ 8	15 @ 15.5
	390 hp	1111464	0 @ 1085	17 @ 2100	22 @ 3200	0 @ 7	12 @ 12
	460 hp	1112026	0 @ 1000	NA	21 @ 2300	0 @ 7	12 @ 12
1971	270 hp	1112050	0 @ 1335	11 @ 2400	18 @ 4200	0 @ 8	15 @ 15.5
	330 hp	1112038	0 @ 1330	16 @ 2250	24 @ 5000	0 @ 8	15 @ 15.5
	365 hp	1112051	0 @ 1145	14 @ 2000	22 @ 3000	0 @ 8	20 @ 17
	425 hp w/manual trans	1112076	0 @ 1300	25 @ 2350	31 @ 6000	0 @ 7	12 @ 12
	425 hp w/auto trans	1112053	0 @ 1310	21 @ 2350	28 @ 5000	0 @ 7	12 @ 12
1972	200 hp	1112050	0 @ 1335	11 @ 2400	18 @ 4200	0 @ 8	15 @ 15.5
	255 hp	1112101	0 @ 1200	14 @ 2000	28 @ 5000	0 @ 8	15 @ 15.5
	270 hp	1112051	0 @ 1145	14 @ 2000	22 @ 3000	0 @ 8	20 @ 17
1973	190 hp	1112098	0 @ 1100	——	14 @ 4200	0 @ 6	15 @ 14
	250 hp	1112150	0 @ 1200	——	20 @ 5000	0 @ 6	15 @ 12
	270 hp	1112114	0 @ 1500	——	18 @ 4200	0 @ 6	20 @ 15
1974	195 hp	1112850	0 @ 1000	——	22 @ 4200	0 @ 4	14 @ 7.5–8.5
	195 hp	1112851	0 @ 1100	——	18 @ 4200	0 @ 4	14 @ 7.5–8.5
	250 hp	1112247	0 @ 1100	——	18 @ 4200	0 @ 7	15 @ 13–14
	250 hp	1112853	0 @ 1000	——	20 @ 5000	0 @ 4	14 @ 7.5–8.5
	270 hp	1112114	0 @ 1100	——	18 @ 4200	0 @ 7	20 @ 14.2–15.7
1975–76	165 hp	1112880	0 @ 1200	12 @ 2000	22 @ 4200	0 @ 4	18 @ 12
	165 hp	1112888	0 @ 1100	12 @ 1600	16 @ 4200	0 @ 4	18 @ 12
	205 hp	1112883	0 @ 1100	12 @ 1600	22 @ 4600	0 @ 4	15 @ 10

NA Not available
—— Not applicable

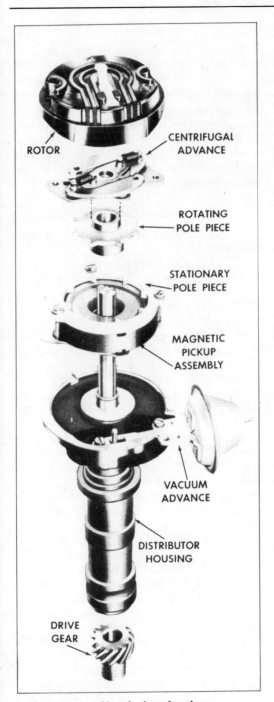

ROTOR

CENTRIFUGAL ADVANCE

ROTATING POLE PIECE

STATIONARY POLE PIECE

MAGNETIC PICKUP ASSEMBLY

VACUUM ADVANCE

DISTRIBUTOR HOUSING

DRIVE GEAR

Exploded view of breakerless distributor

HIGH ENERGY IGNITION (HEI) DISTRIBUTOR

The Delco-Remy High Energy Ignition (HEI) System is a breakerless, pulse triggered, transistor controlled, inductive discharge ignition system available as an option in 1974 and standard in 1975.

There are only nine external electrical connections; the ignition switch feed wire, and the eight spark plug leads. The ignition coil is located with the distributor cap, connecting directly to the rotor. The major difference between the HEI System and the Unit Ignition System is that the HEI System is a full 12 volt system, while the Unit Ignition System incorporates a resistance wire to limit the voltage to the coil except during periods of starter motor operation.

The magnetic pick-up assembly located inside the distributor contains a permanent magnet, a pole piece with internal teeth, and a pick-up coil. When the teeth of the rotating timer core and pole piece align, an induced voltage in the pick-up coil signals the electronic module to open the coil primary circuit. As the primary current decreases, a high voltage is induced in the secondary windings of the ignition coil, directing a spark through the rotor and high voltage leads to fire the spark plugs. The dwell period is automatically controlled by the electronic module and is increased with increasing engine rpm. The HEI System features a longer spark duration which is instrumental in firing lean and EGR diluted fuel/air mixtures. The condenser (capacitor) located within the HEI distributor is provided for noise (static) suppression purposes only and is not a regularly replaced ignition system component.

Component Replacement

IGNITION COIL

1. Disconnect the feed and module wire terminal connectors from the distributor cap.
2. Remove the ignition set retainer.
3. Remove the 4 coil cover-to-distributor cap screws and the coil cover.
4. Remove the 4 coil-to-distributor cap screws.
5. Using a blunt drift, press the coil

port, and timer core. Remove the pick-up coil-leads connector and the magnetic-core support-plate retaining ring. Remove the magnetic pick-up assembly from the housing as one unit. Remove the brass washer and felt gasket, and the vacuum advance unit. Reverse the procedure to reassemble.

wire spade terminals up out of distributor cap.

6. Lift the coil up out of the distributor cap.

7. Remove and clean the coil spring, rubber seal washer and coil cavity of the distributor cap.

8. Coat the rubber seal with a dielectric lubricant furnished in the replacement ignition coil package.

9. Reverse the above procedures to install.

DISTRIBUTOR CAP

1. Remove the feed and module wire terminal connectors from the distributor cap.

2. Remove the retainer and spark plug wires from the cap.

3. Depress and release the 4 distributor cap-to-housing retainers and lift off the cap assembly.

4. Remove the 4 coil cover screws and cover.

5. Using a finger or a blunt drift, push the spade terminals up out of the distributor cap.

6. Remove all 4 coil screws and lift the coil, coil spring and rubber seal washer out of the cap coil cavity.

7. Using a new distributor cap, reverse the above procedures to assemble being sure to clean and lubricate the rubber seal washer with dielectric lubricant.

ROTOR

1. Disconnect the feed and module wire connectors from the distributor.

2. Depress and release the 4 distributor cap to housing retainers and lift off the cap assembly.

3. Remove the two rotor attaching screws and rotor.

4. Reverse the above procedure to install.

VACUUM ADVANCE

1. Remove the distributor cap and rotor as previously described.

2. Disconnect the vacuum hose from the vacuum advance unit.

3. Remove the two vacuum advance retaining screws, pull the advance unit outward, rotate and disengage the operating rod from its tang.

4. Reverse the above procedure to install.

MODULE

1. Remove the distributor cap and rotor as previously described.

2. Disconnect the harness connector and pick-up coil spade connectors from the module.

3. Remove the two screws and module from the distributor housing.

4. Coat the bottom of the new module with dielectric lubricant. Reverse the above procedure to install.

Distributor Removal and Installation

1. Disconnect the ground cable from the battery.

2. Disconnect the feed and module terminal connectors from the distributor cap.

3. Disconnect the hose at the vacuum advance.

4. Depress and release the 4 distributor cap-to-housing retainers and lift off the cap assembly.

5. Using crayon or chalk, make locating marks on the rotor and module and on the distributor housing and engine for installation purposes.

6. Loosen and remove the distributor clamp bolt and clamp, and lift distributor out of the engine. Noting the relative position of the rotor and module alignment marks, make a second mark on the rotor to align it with the one mark on the module.

7. With a new O-ring on the distributor housing and the second mark on the rotor aligned with the mark on the module, install the distributor, taking care to align the mark on the housing with the one on the engine. It may be necessary to lift the distributor and turn the rotor slightly to align the gears and the oil pump driveshaft.

8. With the respective marks aligned, install the clamp and bolt finger-tight.

9. Install and secure the distributor cap.

10. Connect the feed and module connectors to the distributor cap.

11. Connect a timing light to the engine and plug the vacuum hose.

12. Connect the ground cable to the battery.

13. Start the engine and set the timing.

14. Turn the engine off and tighten the distributor clamp bolt. Disconnect the

Firing Order

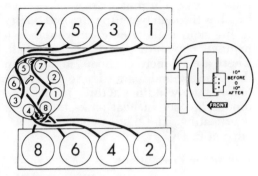

1963–74 except HEI

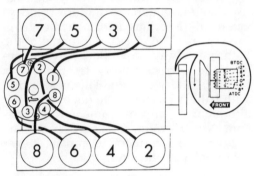

1974–76 HEI

timing light and unplug and connect the hose to the vacuum advance.

CHARGING SYSTEM

Isolation Checks

These are quick checks that will allow the tester to isolate the general source of charging circuit difficulty in either the alternator, regulator, or wiring harness. Once the defective component has been singled out, further checks and repairs may be made using the procedures given in the alternator or regulator sections. Make these checks after looking for obvious problems such as a weak battery or loose fan belt.

Start the engine and bring the idle to between 1500–2000 rpm. Turn off all accessories, lights, radio, etc., and then disconnect the battery ground cable. If the engine stops, it is safe to assume that the alternator is at fault. If, however, the engine continues to operate, the problem lies with either the regulator or wiring harness.

Having eliminated the alternator from

suspicion, the next step is to isolate the regulator from the harness and the easiest way is to substitute a known component. Remove the push-on wiring connector from the regulator and insert a regulator that is known to be good into the circuit, remembering to ground the regulator to the car. Idle the engine, remove the battery cable, and check the ammeter. If it indicates a dicharge condition, then the possible problem is an open resistor or a shorted, positive diode. If the ammeter continues to indicate a charge, then it is the regulator that is defective.

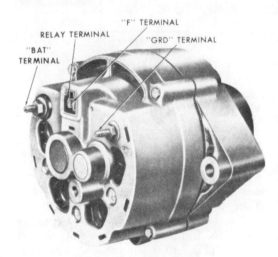

Alternator (with separate regulator) terminals

Alternator Tests

Prepare the alternator for testing by disconnecting the battery ground terminal, the BAT, light relay, field, and GRD leads from the alternator terminals.

Check the positive diodes by connecting an ohmmeter between the R and BAT terminals, and noting the lowest range on the ohmmeter scale. It should indicate very low resistance. Reversing the connections should result in an infinitely high resistance indication.

If the ohmmeter reads low or high in both directions, the diodes are defective. A low reading could also indicate a grounded stator.

To test for an open field, connect the ohmmeter between the F and GRD terminals and check the low range scale for a reading between 7 and 20 ohms. A zero indication or one of excessively high resistance suggests a faulty alternator.

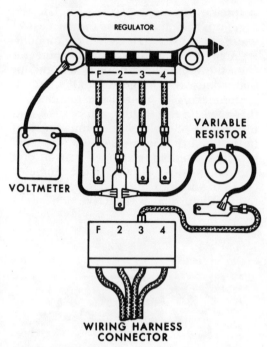

Field relay closing voltage check

Field Relay Tests

Fasten one voltmeter lead to the no. two regulator terminal and ground the other lead to the regulator. Idle the engine between 1500 and 2000 rpm. If the GEN lights still burns, and a volt reading of 3.5 to 6.5 is present, then the regulator field relay is faulty.

Accessory Circuit Resistance Tests

A resistor is connected to the ACC terminal ignition switch. To check for an open resistor, connect the voltmeter to the no. 4 connection of the wiring harness and ground the other voltmeter lead to the regulator. A zero reading, with the ignition switch turned to the ACC notch, indicates an open resistor. The resistance wire is an integral part of the ignition harness and carries a rating minimum of 10 ohms, 6.25 watts. The wire is not solderable and must be crimp-connected.

ALTERNATOR

The alternator used on Corvettes is a continuous-output Delcotron unit. It is comprised of two major components; a stator and a rotor. The stator has a laminated core that is attached to the frame of the alternator. A large number of wind-

ings cover the inside diameter of the stator and it is within this circle that the rotor turns. Current passes from two brushes through two slip rings and finally to the field coils which are wound in a manner concentric to the rotor shaft. There are six rectifier diodes mounted in the slip ring end frame. These are joined to the stator windings at three points. The diodes are set in heat sinks to prevent overheating. The diodes convert the AC current to DC.

Alternator Precautions

A few precautions should be observed when servicing an electrical system that uses an AC generator. Failure to do so can result in serious damage to the charging system. The negative terminal of the battery is always grounded. Always connect the correct battery terminals if a booster battery is used. This is also true with battery chargers. Do not operate the alternator on an open, uncontrolled circuit. Never ground or short across any regulator or alternator terminals. Never try to polarize the alternator.

Removal and Installation

1. Disconnect the negative cable from the battery, this will prevent damaging the alternator diodes.
2. Disconnect the battery (BAT), light relay, and ground (GRD) leads from their terminals on the alternator.
3. Disconnect the harness connector from the field terminals at the brush holder.
4. Loosen the pivot bolt at the bottom of the alternator and remove the brace bolt at the top. Slip off the drive belt and support the alternator.
5. Remove the pivot bolt and remove the alternator.
6. To install the alternator, reverse removal procedures. Tighten the fan belt to the correct tension.

Alternator Disassembly

Remove the pulley by positioning a box-end wrench over the pulley retaining nut and inserting a 5/16 in. allen wrench in the shaft to prevent it from turning. Unbolt the retaining nut and slide it off the pulley. Disconnect the battery ground strap to prevent diode damage and remove the generator. On the 6.2 in. perforated case generator, remove the blade-connector retaining nuts and remove the connectors. Slip the indictor light relay from the terminal post, then back out the retaining screws, and remove the brush holder. Leave the capacitor attached to the generator. Remove the four, long, case bolts and separate the end frame and rotor assembly from the stator assembly. Cover the slip ring and bearing with tape to prevent contamination.

Remove the rotor from the end frame. Extract the retainer plate screws and remove the retainer plate and the end frame bearing. Remove the three attaching screws and separate the stator from the end frame. Remove the heat sink.

Wash all metal parts with the exception of the stator and rotor assemblies. The rotor slip rings may be cleaned with 400 grain polishing cloth. It is a good idea to rotate the rotor while doing this to guard against rubbing flat spots on the slip rings. Maximum out-of-round tolerance for slip rings is 0.001 in. Remove as little metal as possible when truing on a lathe. Polish with 400 grain cloth and blow dry.

Tests

ROTOR

Attach one lead of a 110 volt test lamp or an ohmmeter to either slip ring, and the other lead to the rotor shaft or poles. A lighted test lamp or low ohmmeter

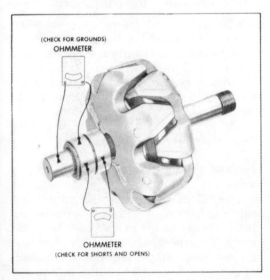

Rotor testing

reading indicates grounded field windings.

Attach the lamp or ohmmeter connections to each slip ring. The windings are open if the lamp fails to light or the ohmmeter reading is high.

Connect a 12 volt battery and an ammeter in series with the slip rings to check for shorts. The windings are shorted if the reading exceeds 1.5 amps. An ohmmeter may be substituted for the same check and will show a resistance reading of less than 6 ohms if the windings are shorted.

STATOR

Attach the test lamp or ohmmeter to the stator frame and one of the stator leads. A lighted lamp or low resistance reading indicates grounded windings.

Successively connect the test equipment between each pair of stator leads. Open windings will produce a high resistance and prevent the test lamp from lighting.

Shorts require special test equipment. If all other tests fail to locate the problem, it is more than likely a short in the stator.

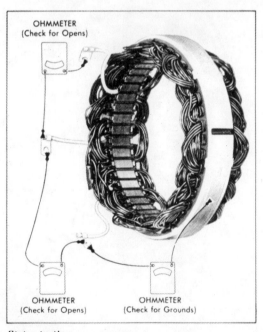

Stator testing

DIODE

The diodes may be checked for shorts or opens by using an ohmmeter or a 12 volt test lamp.

CAUTION: *Under no circumstances use a 110 volt test lamp.*

Use a 1½ volt cell ohmmeter that has been adjusted to the lowest range scale. Attach one lead to the heat sink and the other to the diode lead. A good diode will show a high and a low reading depending on the connection switch. Two low or two high readings signal a faulty diode. Check the other diodes in the same manner.

Check the end-frame mounted diodes by connecting one test lead to the frame and the other to the diode lead. Reverse the connection and check the readings. The same diagnosis is true here as for the heat sink diodes.

If an ohmmeter is not available, substitute a 12 volt test lamp. Connect and switch connections in the same fashion as with the ohmmeter. The lamp will light in only one direction. If it lights or fails to light in both directions, the diode is bad.

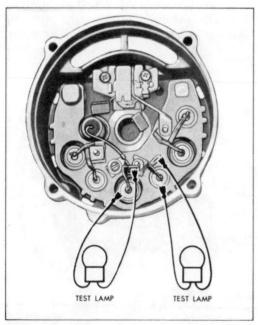

Diode check

Repairs

DIODE REPLACEMENT

Despite rumors to the contrary, the diodes may be replaced. It is not necessary to replace the entire generator assembly as some unscrupulous garage owners convinced their unwary cus-

tomers in the introductory days of the AC generator.

Two types of diodes, positive and negative, are used in the AC generator. The heat sink contains the positive diodes and these are marked with red. End frame diodes are the negative ones and they have black markings. Do not attempt to drive a diode from its bore or the other diodes may be damaged.

Support the end frame in an arbor press, select a suitable removal spacer, and press the diode from the frame. Use the same method to install a replacement diode.

To replace heat sink diodes, it is necessary to separate the heat sink from the end frame. Observe the stack-up closely to ensure correct reassembly of the BAT and GRD terminal bolts. Replace the diodes as described above, reassemble the bolt stack-ups and attach the heat sink to the end frame.

END FRAME REPLACEMENT

Install the brush holder on the replacement end frame, being careful to build up the parts stack properly. A pin or wire will hold the brushes in position until the unit has been completely assembled. Install the heat sink as previously described. Remove the brush holding pin or wire after the unit is assembled and allow the brushes to drop onto the slip rings.

BEARING REPLACEMENT

The drive end frame bearing is removed by detaching the retainer frame from the end plate and pressing the bearing out. Fill the bearing ¼ full with multipurpose grease; do not overfill. Press the bearing into the end frame. Install the retainer plate.

The slip ring end frame bearing of the 6 in. perforated-case generator is pressed off the rotor shaft. The replacement is pressed over the rotor shaft by using an arbor press.

The 5.5 in. aluminum Delcotron slip-ring end bearing is replaced by pressing it out from the inside of the case. To install the replacement, position a flat plate over the bearing and press it into the outside of the case. Press all bearings and diodes flush with their receptacles.

SLIP RING REPLACEMENT

Unsolder the field-to-slip ring connections and slide the rear bearing from the shaft. Attach a bearing puller and withdraw the slip ring from the shaft.

Start the replacement ring onto the shaft, with the slip ring and winding leads aligned. Align the slip ring lead that passes through the insulation with the winding lead that does not have a nylon insulator.

Press the aligned unit onto the shaft and position the slip ring $3^9/_{32}$ in. $\pm ^1/_{64}$ in., measured from the outside edge of the slip ring to the face of the stator nearest the pulley. Clip the excess lead material and solder the slip ring leads to the rotor winding connections. Use resin core solder.

Assembly

Attach the slip-ring end frame to the stator assembly and position the diode connectors above the diode, relay, and stator leads. Tighten the terminal nuts, then slide the front end frame over the rotor. Slide on the spacer, pulley, washer, and nut, and torque the shaft to 50–60 ft lbs. Attach the slip-ring end frame and stator to the rotor and drive end frame assembly and insert and tighten the thrubolts.

REGULATOR

There are two types of external regulators used on Corvettes, a standard, double-contact model and an optional, transistorized model. One transistor and two diodes are used in the optional volt-age regulator. The transistor assists the conventional voltage regulator in limiting voltage to a pre-set value. The diodes protect the system from transient voltages which may occur. Regulator tests and voltage adjustments may be made on the vehicle. Point cleaning and air gap adjustment must be made with the unit removed from the car.

Regulator Tests

REGULATOR CHECK—DOUBLE CONTACT REGULATOR

Disconnect the battery ground cable and insert a ¼ ohm resistor in the BAT terminal circuit. Separate the wiring harness connector at the regulator and attach a suitable adapter as shown in the accompanying illustration. Insert a 25 watt, 25 ohm variable resistor into the F circuit, then attach a voltmeter between the regulator no. 3 terminal and ground.

Run a jumper lead from the no. 3 regulator to the BAT terminal on the regulator. Finally, connect 1000 ohm impedance headphones between the F terminal on the regulator and ground. Check all connections and reconnect the battery cable.

The following comparison chart should be referred to during the checks:

Regulator Ambient Temperature F°	Regulator Normal Range Volts
65	13.9–15.0
85	13.8–14.8
105	13.7–14.6
125	13.5–14.4
145	13.4–14.2
165	13.2–14.0
185	13.1–13.9

OPEN RESISTOR AND DIODE CHECK— TRANSISTORIZED REGULATOR

An open resistor check is made by connecting the voltmeter between the F circuit and the regulator base plate. A reading of less than nine volts indicates that either the transistor or a regulator resistor is burned open.

A diode check necessitates removing the regulator from the vehicle and unsoldering the diode leads. Two diodes are exposed when the cover is removed; the suppression diode and the field dis-

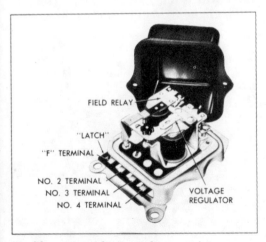

FIELD RELAY

"LATCH"

"F" TERMINAL

NO. 2 TERMINAL
NO. 3 TERMINAL
NO. 4 TERMINAL

VOLTAGE REGULATOR

Double-contact voltage regulator

charge diode. Attach an ohmmeter to the field discharge diode leads in the manner of the accompanying illustration. Reverse the connections and observe both readings. The diode is defective if both readings are less than two ohms or are infinitely high.

Subject the suppression diode to the same examination. Again, a normal diode will give a high and a low reading when the ohmmeter connections are reversed.

Test the diodes with the ohmmeter at 1½ volts and set on the lowest range scale. If diode replacement is necessary, keep in mind that excessive heat will damage the diode, and adjust the soldering time accordingly. Leave the ohmmeter connected as for the diode check if you desire to test for a shorted transistor, but do not start the engine.

With the cover off and the ignition on, open the voltage points and check the reading. A shorted transistor will cause a reading in excess of nine volts. Remove its attaching screws and unsolder the connections above the transistor to remove it.

Upper Contact Voltage Test— Double Contact Regulator

Turn all vehicle accessories off and close the variable resistor to the "no resistance" setting.

Attach a thermometer to the regulator cover then start the engine and set the idle at 1500 rpm. Let the engine idle for 15 minutes then cycle the generator by opening the variable resistor to "full resistance" and momentarily disconnecting and reconnecting the number four, wiring harness terminal lead. Finally, close the variable resistor to "no resistance."

Increase the idle speed to 2500 rpm and compare the ambient temperature and voltage readings with the comparison chart. At this time, the headphones should be emitting a steady buzz. Record the temperature and voltage settings as well as the desired settings but make no adjustments.

Lower Contact Voltage Test— Double Contact Regulator

Force the regulator to operate on the lower contact points by increasing the variable field resistance. As the transition from upper to lower points takes place,

the earphones will detect a drop in sound to a very weak signal then a return to normal. An accompanying change in voltmeter reading will occur.

Record the voltage setting of the lower contact points and compute the difference between the upper and lower contact point readings. The normal voltage difference should place the lower contact points 0.1 to 0.5 volts less than the uppers.

Compare the upper reading to the comparison chart. If the readings are not concurrent, the regulator must be adjusted.

Field Relay Test— Transistorized Regulator

Separate the wiring harness connector and connect a voltmeter between the R lead of the regulator and the regulator base plate. Insert a 50 ohm, variable resistor in the circuit between the regulator R lead and the wiring harness connector V receptacle. Open the resistor and switch off the ignition. Decrease the resistance slowly and observe the relay closing voltage. Bend the heel iron to adjust to specifications.

Voltage Adjustment

Double Contact Regulator

The regulator is adjusted when it is functioning on the upper contacts. First remove the regulator cover. To prevent accidental grounds, open the variable resistor to full resistance and disconnect the no. 4 regulator terminal lead. Reconnect the lead and close the resistor after the cover is off.

The large nylon nut adjusts the voltage

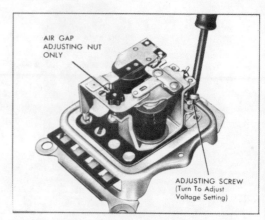

Double-contact voltage regulator adjustment

difference. Turn it clockwise to decrease the difference and counterclockwise to increase. If the correct voltage difference cannot be obtained, replace the regulator. Check the difference adjustment by noting the upper contact reading then increasing the variable field resistance and observing the lower contact voltage reading. As the operation changes from the upper to lower points, the headphones will emit a sound change from normal again. The lower points should show a voltage reading difference as previously specified.

Close the variable resistor, turn off all accessories, and observe the upper-contact voltage reading. Any change is due to the removal of the cover. At the beginning of the voltage tests, the actual voltage setting and the desired setting were recorded. Take the difference between the two figures and add or subtract them to the present voltage reading to derive the adjusted reading. If the adjusted reading is higher than the actual present voltage reading, turn the adjusting screw clockwise to increase the voltage. A lower adjusted voltage is reached by turning the adjusting screw counterclockwise.

Install the regulator cover and operate the engine for five minutes at 2500 rpm before checking the final voltage figures.

Transistorized Regulator

The regulator voltage changes in relation to the ambient temperature. This temperature is measured ¼ in. from the regulator cover. If a regulator setting change is needed, a check of the ambient temperature and a comparison with the accompanying chart will furnish the specified setting for the prevailing temperature.

Ambient Temperature vs. Regulator Voltage Setting

Regulator Ambient Temperature	Specified Voltage Range			
45° F	13.9	14.1	14.3	14.5
65° F	13.8	14.0	14.2	14.4
85° F	13.7	13.9	14.1	14.3
105° F	13.5	13.7	13.9	14.1
125° F	13.3	13.5	13.7	13.9
145° F	13.2	13.4	13.6	13.8
165° F	13.0	13.2	13.4	13.6

After selecting the desired voltage setting and checking the existing ambient temperature, disconnect the voltage regulator V lead from the wiring harness connector and run a jumper lead from the V lead to the BAT terminal of the generator. Connect a voltmeter from the V lead to the regulator ground plate. Insert an ammeter into the circuit by attaching one lead to the BAT terminal and the other to the horn relay.

Start the engine and run at 3000 rpm for 15 minutes. Generator output should be between 3 and 30 amps. Leave the cover installed. Stop the engine after 15 minutes and momentarily remove the jumper lead from the generator then reinstall. This cycles the generator. Start the engine and note the voltage setting with the engine at 3000 rpm.

Remove cover and turn the adjusting screw as required. Make the final setting with the screw being turned clockwise to ensure the removal of all slack and proper tensioning of the adjusting screw against the screwholder.

Cycle the generator after adjusting so that a valid final setting is achieved. Operate at 3000 rpm to verify adjustment. Should the generator output drop below 3 amps during the adjustment operation, turn on the accessories to force the required minimum ampere output.

Removal and Installation

1. Disconnect the negative cable from the battery.

2. Disconnect the wiring harness from the regulator.

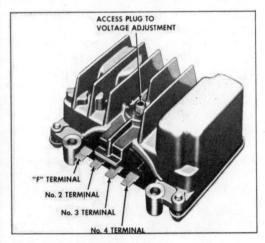

ACCESS PLUG TO
VOLTAGE ADJUSTMENT

"F" TERMINAL

No. 2 TERMINAL

No. 3 TERMINAL

No. 4 TERMINAL

Transistorized voltage regulator

3. Remove the mounting screws and remove the regulator.

4. Make sure that the regulator base rubber gasket is in place before installation.

5. Clean attaching area for proper grounding.

6. Install the regulator. Do not over-tighten the mounting screws, as this will cancel the cushioning effect of the rubber grommets.

7. Attach the wiring harness connector to the regulator.

8. Do not polarize the alternator. Connect the battery negative cable.

Contact Point Cleaning

DOUBLE CONTACT REGULATOR

A sooty point condition is normal and such points do not require cleaning. Unnecessary cleaning will reduce contact point life. Contacts on this regulator consist of a soft material which, if necessary, may be cleaned with crocus cloth or another fine abrasive. Wash the contacts with tri-chlorethylene after cleaning. Field relay contacts may be cleaned with a thin, fine-cut file. Only enough material to clean the points should be removed. Never use emery cloth to clean the contacts.

TRANSISTORIZED REGULATOR

The large contact point may be cleaned with a spoon or riffler file after loosening the upper contact support mounting screws. All oxidation should be removed, but it is not necessary to completely smooth the contact. The smaller contact does not oxidize and may be cleaned with a fine abrasive such as crocus cloth. Wash the contacts with tri-chorethylene after cleaning. Field relay contacts may be cleaned with a fine-cut file, remove only enough material to clean the points.

Point Opening and Air Gap Adjustment

DOUBLE CONTACT REGULATOR

The voltage regulator point opening is measured between the upper contacts while the lower contacts are touching. Adjustment may be made by bending the upper contact arm. Air gap is measured with a feeler gauge placed between the armature and core when the lower con-

tacts are touching. The nylon nut located on the contact support adjust the air gap.

Field relay point opening is checked as shown in figure. Carefully bend the armature stop for adjustment. Check the field relay air gap with the points just touching. The air gap rarely needs adjustment. As long as the point opening and closing voltages are within specifications, the relay will operate satisfactorily in spite of an air gap slightly out of the specified dimensions. The flat contact spring may be bent to make an adjustment.

TRANSISTORIZED REGULATOR

To adjust the voltage regulator air gap, push the armature (not the flat spring) down against a feeler gauge, and adjust the upper contact support so that the contacts align squarely and just touch when the contact support screws are tightened. The field relay unit air gap is checked with the points just touching. Carefully bend the flat contact support spring for adjustment. Field relay point opening is checked as shown in figure. Point opening very seldom needs adjustment. If air gap and closing voltage are within specifications, the relay will perform satisfactorily although point opening may be out of specifications.

INTEGRATED ALTERNATOR/REGULATOR

The Delcotron 10-SI combination alternator/regulator was used on some 1972 models and all later models. Removal and installation are similar to that for the standard alternator used before 1972. Testing procedures which differ are given below.

This system is an integrated AC generating system containing a built-in voltage regulator. Removal and replacement is essentially the same as for the standard AC generator.

The regulator is mounted inside the slip ring end frame. All regulator components are enclosed in an epoxy molding, and the regulator cannot be adjusted. Rotor and stator tests are the same as for the 5.5 Delcotron, covered previously.

Charging System Test— Low Charging Rate

1. After battery condition, drive belt tension, and wiring terminals and con-

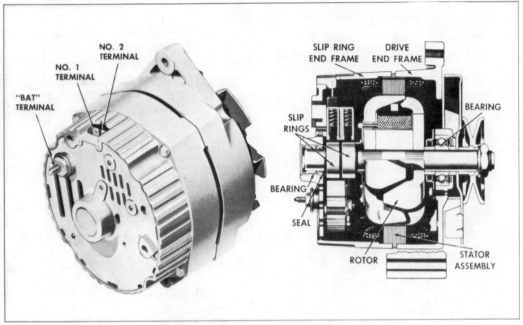

Integrated alternator/regulator

nections have been checked, charge the battery fully and perform the following test:

2. Connect a test voltmeter between the alternator BAT, terminal and ground, ignition switch on. Connect the voltmeter in turn to alternator terminals No. 1 and No. 2, the other voltmeter lead being grounded as before. A zero reading indicates an open circuit between the battery and each connection at the alternator. If this test discloses no faults in the wiring, proceed to Step 3.

Grounding field winding

3. Connect the test voltmeter to the alternator BAT terminal (the other test lead to ground), start the engine and run at 1,500–2,000 rpm with all lights and electrical accessories turned on. If the voltmeter reads 12.8 volts or greater, the alternator is good and no further checks need be made. If the voltmeter reads less than 12.8 volts, ground the field winding by inserting a screwdriver into the test hole in the end frame.

CAUTION: *Do not force the tab more than ¾ in. into the end frame.*

   a. If voltage increases to 13 volts or more, the regulator unit is defective;

   b. If voltage does not increase significantly, the generator is defective.

**Charging System Test—
High Charging Rate**

1. With the battery fully charged, connect a voltmeter between alternator terminal No. 2 and ground. If the reading is zero, No. 2 circuit from the battery is open.

2. If No. 2 circuit is OK, but an obvious overcharging condition still exists, proceed as follows:

   a. Remove the alternator and separate the end frames;

   b. Connect a low-range ohmmeter between the brush lead clip and the end frame (Test 1), then reverse the con-

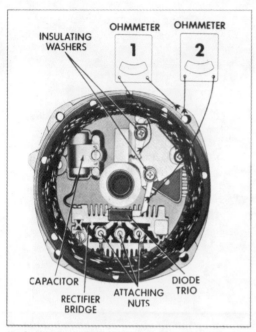

High charging rate test

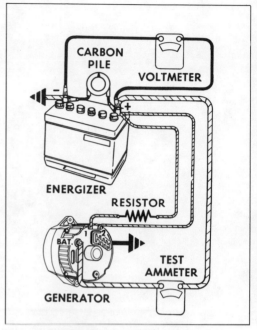

Alternator output test

nections. If both readings are zero, either the brush lead clip is grounded or the regulator is defective. A grounded brush lead clip can be due to damaged insulating sleeve or omission of the insulating washer.

Alternator Output Test

1. Connect a test voltmeter, ammeter, and a 10-ohm, 6-watt resistor into the charging circuit. Do not connect the carbon pile to the battery posts at this time.

2. Increase alternator speed and observe the voltmeter—if the voltage is uncontrolled with speed and increases to 16 volts or more, check for a grounded brush lead clip as previously covered. If a brush lead clip is not grounded, the voltage regulator is faulty and must be replaced.

3. Connect the carbon pile load to the battery terminals.

4. Operate the alternator at moderate speed and adjust the carbon pile to obtain maximum alternator output as indicated on the ammeter. If output is within 10% of rated output as stamped on the alternator frame, alternator is O.K. If output is not within specifications, ground the alternator field by inserting a screwdriver into the test hole in the end frame. If output now is within 10% of rating, replace the voltage regulator; if still not within specifications, check field winding, diode

trio, rectifier bridge and stator, as described later. Dissasembly of alternator up to and including Step 6 is necessary.

Disassembly and Assembly

1. Place alternator in a vise, clamped by the mounting flange only.

2. Remove the four through bolts and separate the slip ring end frame and stator assembly from the drive end and rotor assembly, using a screwdriver to pry the two sections apart. Use the slots provided for the purpose.

NOTE: *Scribe matchmarks on the parts to aid in assembly.*

3. Place a piece of tape over the slip ring end frame bearing to prevent entry of dirt; also tape shaft at slip ring end to prevent scratches.

4. Clean brushes, if they are to be reused, with trichloroethylene or carbon tetrachloride solvent. Use these solvents only in an adequately ventilated area.

5. Remove the stator lead nuts and separate the stator from the end frame.

6. Remove the screw that secures the diode trio and remove diode trio.

NOTE: *At this point, test the rotor, rectifier bridge, stator and diode trio if these tests are necessary.*

7. Remove the rectifier bridge hold-down screw and the BAT terminal screw, then disconnect condenser lead.

Remove rectifier bridge from end frame.

8. Remove the two securing screws and brush holder and regulator assemblies. Note the insulating sleeves over the screws.

9. Remove the retaining screw and condenser from the end frame.

10. Remove the slip ring end frame bearing, if it is to be replaced, using the procedure given later in this section.

11. Remove the pulley nut, washer, pulley, fan and spacer from the rotor shaft, using a $5/16$ in. allen key to hold the shaft while loosening the nut.

12. Remove rotor and spacers from drive end frame assembly.

13. Remove drive end frame bearing retainer plate, screws, plate, bearing, and slinger from end frame, if necessary.

14. To assemble, reverse order of disassembly. Pulley nut must be tightened to 40–50 ft. lbs.

Cleaning and Inspection

1. Clean all metal parts, except stator and rotor assemblies, in solvent.

2. Wipe off bearings and inspect them for pitting or roughness.

3. Inspect rotor slip rings for scoring. They may be cleaned with 400 grit sandpaper (not emery), rotating the rotor to make the rings concentric. Maximum out-of-true is 0.001 in. If slip rings are deeply scored, the entire rotor must be replaced as a unit.

4. Inspect brushes for wear; minimum length is ¼ in.

Diode Trio Initial Testing

1. Before removing this unit, connect an ohmmeter between the brush lead clip and the end frame. The lowest reading scale should be used for this test.

2. After taking a reading, reverse the lead connections. If the meter reads zero, the brush lead clip is probably grounded, due to omission of the insulating sleeve or insulating washer.

Diode Trio Removal

1. Remove the three nuts which secure the stator.

2. Remove stator.

3. Remove the screw which secures the diode trio lead clip, then remove diode trio.

NOTE: *The position of the insulating*

washer on the screw is critical; make sure that it is returned to the same position on reassembly.

Diode Trio Testing

1. Connect an ohmmeter, on lowest range, between the single brush connector and one stator lead connector.

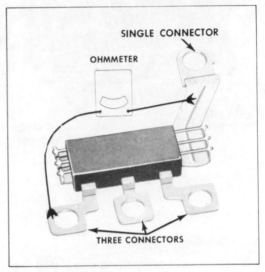

Diode trio check

2. Observe the reading, then reverse the meter leads. Repeat this test with each of the other two stator lead connectors. The readings on each of these tests should NOT be identical, there should be one low and one high reading for each test. If this is not the case, replace the diode trio.

CAUTION: *Do not use high voltage on the diode trio.*

Rectifier Bridge Testing

1. Connect an ohmmeter between the heat sink (ground) and the base of one of the three terminals. Then, reverse the meter leads and take a reading. If both readings are identical, the bridge is defective and must be replaced.

2. Repeat this test with the remaining two terminals, then between the INSULATED heat sink (as opposed to the GROUNDED heat sink in previous test) and each of the three terminals. As before, if any two readings are identical, on reversing the meter leads, the rectifier bridge must be replaced.

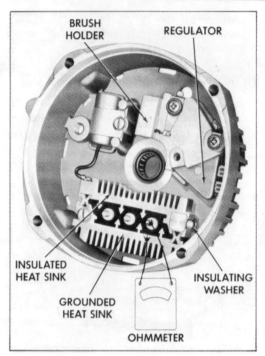

BRUSH HOLDER

REGULATOR

INSULATED HEAT SINK

GROUNDED HEAT SINK

INSULATING WASHER

OHMMETER

Rectifier bridge check

Rectifier Bridge Removal

1. Remove the attaching screw and the BAT terminal screw.

2. Disconnect the condenser lead.

3. Remove the rectifier bridge.

NOTE: *The insulator between the insulated heat sink and the end frame is extremely important to the operation of the unit. It must be replaced in exactly the same position on reassembly.*

CAUTION: *Do not use high voltage to test the rectifier bridge.*

Brush and/or Voltage Regulator Removal and Installation

1. Remove two brush holder screws and stator lead to strap nut and washer, brush holder screws and one of the diode trio lead strap attaching screws.

NOTE: *The insulating washers must be replaced in the same position on reassembly.*

2. Remove brush holder and brushes. The voltage regulator may also be removed at this time, if desired.

3. Brushes and brush springs must be free of corrosion and must be undamaged and completely free of oil or grease.

4. Insert spring and brushes into holder, noting whether they slide freely without binding. Insert wooden or plastic

toothpick into bottom hole in holder to retain brushes.

NOTE: *The brush holder is serviced as a unit; individual parts are not available.*

5. Reassemble in reverse order of disassembly.

Slip Ring End Frame Bearing and Seal Removal and Installation

1. With stator removed, press out bearing and seal, using a socket or similar tool that fits inside the end frame housing. Press from outside to inside, supporting the frame inside with a hollow cylinder (large, deep socket) to allow the seal and bearing to pass.

2. The bearings are sealed for life and permanently lubricated. If a bearing is dry, do not attempt to repack it, as it will throw off the grease and contaminate the inside of the generator.

3. Using a flat plate, press the new bearing from the outside toward the inside. A large vise is a handy press, but care must be exercised so that end frame is not distorted or cracked. Again, use a deep socket to support the inside of the end frame.

4. From inside the end frame, insert seal and press flush with housing.

5. Install stator and reconnect leads.

STARTING SYSTEM

The starting system consists of the starting motor, solenoid, and battery. The motor is comprised of a drive mechanism, an armature, brushes, field windings, and a frame. It has four pole shoes and four field shoes, one of which is shunted to the armature. A solenoid is attached to the starting motor frame and this controls the over-running clutch drive.

Starter Removal and Installation

1. Remove the positive cable from the battery to prevent accidental shorting. Remove the heat shield on big block models.

2. Disconnect the solenoid S, R, and battery leads. Mark these wires for correct replacement.

3. Loosen the supporting bracket bolt on the cylinder block and remove the stud nut and lockwasher on the front of the starter. Move the bracket out of the working area.

Alternator and Regulator Specifications

| Year | Alternator | | | | Regulator | | | | | |
	Model	Field Current Draw @ 12V	Output @ Generator RPM 2000	Output @ Generator RPM 5000	Model	Field Relay Air Gap (in.)	Field Relay Point Gap (in.)	Volts to Close	Regulator Air Gap (in.)	Regulator Point Gap (in.)	Volts at 125°
1963–64	1100628	1.9–2.3	27A	37A	1119512	0.015	0.030	2.3–3.7	0.067	0.014	13.5–14.4
1965–67	1100693	2.2–2.6	27A	37A	1119515	0.015	0.030	2.3–3.7	0.067	0.014	13.5–14.4
	1100696	2.2–2.6	29A	42A	1119515	0.015	0.030	2.3–3.7	0.067	0.014	13.5–14.4
1968	1100693	2.2–2.6	27A	37A	1119515	0.015	0.030	2.3–3.7	0.067	0.014	13.5–14.4
	1100794	2.2–2.6	27A	37A	1119515	0.015	0.030	2.3–3.7	0.067	0.014	13.5–14.4
	1100696	2.2–2.6	29A	42A	1119515	0.015	0.030	2.3–3.7	0.067	0.014	13.5–14.4
1969	1100696	2.2–2.6	27A	37A	1119515	0.015	0.030	2.3–3.7	0.067	0.014	13.5–14.4
1970	1100900	2.2–2.6	27A	37A	1119515	0.015	0.030	2.3–3.7	0.067	0.014	13.5–14.4
	1100901	2.2–2.6	27A	37A	1119515	0.015	0.030	2.3–3.7	0.067	0.014	13.5–14.4
1971–72	1100544	4–4.5	①	①	1119515	0.015	0.030	1.5–3.2	0.067	0.014	13.8–14.8
	1100543, 1100950	4–4.5	①	37A	1119515	0.015	0.030	1.5–3.2	0.067	0.014	13.8–14.8
	1100566	2.2–2.6	25A	35A	1119515	0.015	0.030	1.5–3.2	0.067	0.014	13.8–14.8
	1100843	2.2–2.6	—	58A	1119515	0.015	0.030	1.5–3.2	0.067	0.014	13.8–14.8
	1100917	2.8–3.2	—	59A	1119519	0.030	0.030	1.5–3.2	0.067	0.014	13.8–14.8

Alternator and Regulator Specifications (cont.)

| Year | Alternator | | | | Regulator | | | | | | |
	Model	Field Current Draw @ 12V	Output @ Generator RPM 2000	Output @ Generator RPM 5000	Model	Field Relay Air Gap (in.)	Field Relay Point Gap (in.)	Field Relay Volts to Close	Regulator Air Gap (in.)	Regulator Point Gap (in.)	Volts at 125°
1971–72	1100567	2.2–2.6	—	40A	1119515	0.015	0.030	1.5–3.2	0.067	0.014	13.8–14.8
	1100497	2.8–3.2	—	37A	Integrated with alternator						13.8–14.8
	1100934	2.8–3.2	—	37A	Integrated with alternator						13.8–14.8
1973–74	1100544	4.0–4.5	—	61A	Integrated with alternator						13.8–14.8
	1102353, 1100573, 1102346, 1100950	4.0–4.5	—	42A	Integrated with alternator						13.8–14.8
	1100934, 1100497	4.0–4.5	—	37A	Integrated with alternator						13.8–14.8
	1102354, 1100542	4.0–4.5	—	63A	Integrated with alternator						13.8–14.8
1975–76	1102483	4.0–4.5	—	37A	Integrated with alternator						13.8–14.8
	1100950	4.0–4.5	—	42A	Integrated with alternator						13.8–14.8

① Voltmeter not needed for cold output check. Load battery with carbon pile to obtain maximum output.

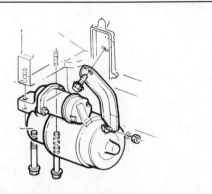

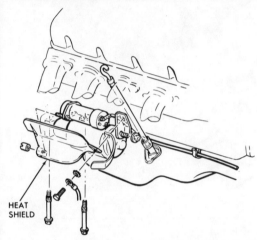

HEAT
SHIELD

Starter mounting—small block (top) and big block (bottom)

4. Loosen the mounting bolts while supporting the starter. Remove the mounting bolts and pull the starter out and down from the engine.

5. Reverse this procedure to install the starter.

Starting Motor Tests

A series of resistance checks may be made with the unit mounted on the vehicle. These require only a voltmeter. Connect the voltmeter between the positive post of the battery and the battery terminal of the solenoid. Ground the primary coil terminal to prevent the engine from starting, then crank the engine with the switch on.

Repeat the test; first with the voltmeter connected between the negative battery terminal and the starting motor housing, and finally with the voltmeter between the solenoid battery terminal and the solenoid motor terminal. A voltage drop in excess of 0.2 volts, indicates excessive resistance in the portion of the circuit being tested.

Solenoid Testing

Failure of the solenoid to retract may be due to an excessive voltage drop in the control circuit. Check this by connecting a voltmeter between the solenoid battery terminal and the solenoid switch terminal. A drop in excess of 3.5 volts indicates excessive resistance in the solenoid control circuit.

A voltage figure of less than 7.7 volts between the solenoid switch terminal and ground warrants checks of the solenoid current draw, starting motor pinion clearance, or for possible binding of the solenoid linkage.

Starter Disassembly

1. Disconnect the field coil connectors from the motor solenoid terminal.

2. Remove the thru-bolts.

3. Remove commutator end frame, field frame, and armature assembly from drive housing.

4. Remove the overrunning clutch from the armature shaft as follows:

   a. Slide the two-piece thrust collar off the end of the armature shaft.

   b. Slide a standard ½ in. pipe coupling or other spacer onto the shaft so that the end of the coupling butts against the edge of the retainer.

   c. Tap the end of the coupling with a hammer, driving retainer toward armature end of snap-ring.

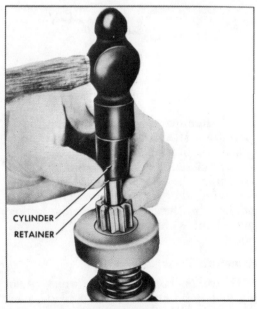

CYLINDER

RETAINER

Driving retainer off snap-ring

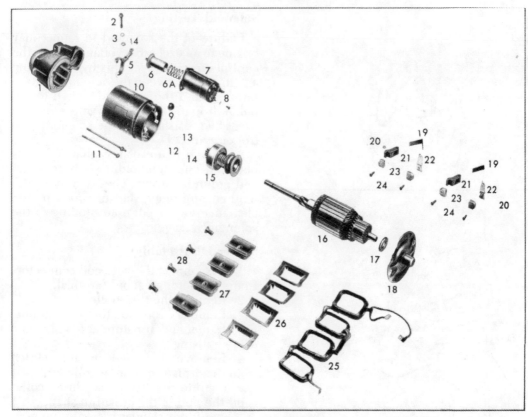

Exploded view of starter

1. Drive housing
2. Shift lever bolt
3. Shift lever nut and lockwasher
4. Pin
5. Shift lever
6. Solenoid plunger
6A. Solenoid return spring
7. Solenoid case
8. Screw and lockwasher
9. Grommet
10. Field frame
11. Through-bolts
12. Thrust collar
13. Snap-ring
14. Retainer

15. Overrunning clutch assembly
16. Armature
17. Braking washer
18. Commutator end frame
19. Brush springs
20. Washer
21. Insulated brush holders
22. Grounded brush holder
23. Brushes
24. Screws
25. Field coils
26. Insulators
27. Pole shoes
28. Screws

d. Remove snap-ring from its groove in the shaft using pliers. Slide retainer and clutch from armature shaft.

5. Disassemble brush assembly from field frame by releasing the V-spring and removing the support pin. The brush holders, brushes, and springs now can be pulled out as a unit and the leads disconnected.

Armature Tests

To test for shorts, place the armature on a growler and hold a hacksaw blade over the armature while rotating the armature.

A short will cause the saw blade to vibrate. Clean between the commutator cracks and repeat the test. Replace the armature if no improvement is noted.

To test for grounding, connect one test lamp lead to the armature core and the other to the commutator. A lighted lamp indicates a grounded armature and demands replacement.

Field Coil Tests

To test for an open circuit, attach a test lamp lead to each end of the field coils. An open circuit will prevent the lamp

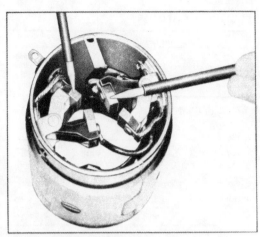

Testing for a grounded field coil

from lighting and will warrant replacement of the field coils.

To test for grounding, attach one test lead to the commutator bar and the other to the field frame. A grounded field coil will light the lamp. The shunt coil must be disconnected before making this check.

Starter Assembly

1. Install brushes into holders. Install solenoid, if so equipped.

2. Assemble insulated and grounded brush holder together using the V-spring and position the assembled unit on the support pin. Push holders and spring to bottom of support and rotate spring to engage the slot in support. Attach ground wire to grounded brush and field lead wire to insulated brush, then repeat for other brush sets.

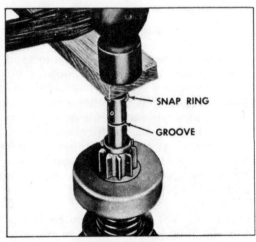

Forcing snap-ring over the armature shaft

3. Assemble overruning clutch to armature shaft as follows:

   a. Lubricate drive end of shaft with silicone lubricant.

   b. Slide clutch assembly onto shaft with pinion outward.

   c. Slide retainer onto shaft with cupped surface facing away from pinion.

   d. Stand armature up on a wood surface, commutator downwards. Position snap-ring on upper end of shaft and drive it onto shaft with a small block of wood and a hammer. Slide snap-ring into groove.

   e. Install thrust collar onto shaft with shoulder next to snap-ring.

   f. With retainer on one side of snapring and thrust collar on the other side, squeeze together with two sets of pliers until ring seats in retainer.

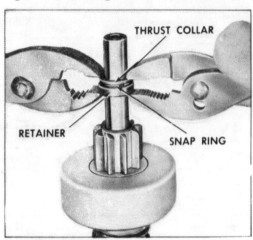

Forcing the snap-ring into the retainer

4. Lubricate drive end bushing with silicone lubricant, then slide armature and clutch assembly into place, at the same time engaging shift lever with clutch.

5. Position field frame over armature and apply sealer (silicone) between frame and solenoid case. Position frame against drive housing, making sure brushes are not damaged in the process.

6. Lubricate commutator end bushing with silicone lubricant, place a leather brake washer on the armature shaft and slide commutator end frame onto shaft. Install thru-bolts and tighten to 65 in. lbs.

7. Reconnect field coil connector /s to the solenoid motor terminal. Install solenoid mounting screws, if so equipped.

Battery and Starter Specifications

Year	Model	Battery Ampere Hour Capacity	Volts	Terminal Grounded	Lock Test Amps	Lock Test Volts	Lock Test Torque	No-Load Test Amps	No-Load Test Volts	No-Load Test rpm	Brush Spring Tension (oz)
1963–64	327 cu in.	61	12	Neg	330	3.5	——	65–100	10.6	3,600–5,100	35
1965–66	327 cu in.	61	12	Neg	330	3.5	——	83	10.6	4,350	35
	396, 427 cu in.	61	12	Neg	Not Recommended			83	10.6	4,350	35
1967	327 cu in.	61	12	Neg	Not Recommended			83	10.6	4,250	35
	427 cu in.	61	12	Neg	Not Recommended			85	10.6	9,900	35
1968	All Engines	62	12	Neg	Not Recommended			85	10.6	10,000	35
1969	All Engines	62	12	Neg	Not Recommended			85	9.0	10,000	35
1970	All Engines	62	12	Neg	Not Recommended			55–80	9.0	3,500–6,000	35
1971–72	350	62	12	Neg	Not Recommended			65–95	9.0	7,500–10,500	35
	454	76	12	Neg	Not Recommended			65–95	9.0	7,500–10,500	35
1973–74	350	①	12	Neg	Not Recommended			65–95	9.0	7,500–10,500	35
	454	②	12	Neg	Not Recommended			65–95	9.0	7,500–10,500	35
1975–76	350	①	12	Neg	Not Recommended			65–95	9.0	7,500–10,500	35

① Side terminal—cranking power 3,250 watts @ 0° F
② Side terminal—cranking power 3,750 watts @ 0° F

8. Check pinion clearance; it should be 0.010–0.140 in. Excessive clearance will force the replacement of worn parts since there is no method of adjusting the pinion.

Engine Mechanical

DESIGN

The success of the Corvette is largely due to the lengthy option lists that permit an owner to literally tailor his car to a specific type of driving or competition. For this reason, the engines that power the 1963–1976 models have been offered in five internal displacements and approximately 14 performance levels.

Induction systems for these engines are varied and range from a single, four-barrel configuration to three, two-barrels, and fuel injection.

The most common engine is the 327 cubic inch V8. It was offered from 1963 through 1968 and spanned a horsepower range of 250 to 375; the latter figure being obtained with fuel injection. The 327, in addition to fuel injection, has used the Carter WCFB and AFB, Holley, and Rochester Quadrajet carburetors.

The stroke of the 327 was lengthened in 1969 and this brought the displacement to 350 cu in. The 350 as found in the 1969 through 1976 Corvettes has been available in horsepower ratings from 165 to 370. It is offered with either a single, four-barrel Rochester or Holley carburetor. The 327 and 350 engines are collectively referred to as the small block Corvette engines.

The 327 engine was derived from the earlier 265 and 283 Corvette engines, but featured many improvements. The block was a completely new casting and provided stronger main bearing webs. The bottom ends of the cylinders were relieved to clear the longer stroke crankshaft. All 327 and 350 cubic inch engines, except base power plants, are equipped with forged crankshafts. Main bearing diameters were increased from 2.30 to 2.45 inches in 1968.

The large block engines were introduced to provide more torque and more flexible horsepower than the peakier small blocks. The cylinder block is quite conventional, the heads are where the innovation lies. Intake and exhaust valves are canted away from each other for optimum gas flow and port configuration. The seemingly strange angles at which the valves point gave rise to the nickname of "Porcupine" which was applied to these heads when they first appeared on NASCAR racing Chevrolets in 1963.

The large block Corvette engine was introduced in 1965 with an initial offering of 396 cubic inches and 425 hp. The 396 was enlarged to 427 cubic inches with a bore increase in 1966, although the top rated horsepower remained at 425. The 427, optional from 1966 through

1969, was offered in 390, 400, 425, 430, and 435 horsepower versions. Carburetors used on the large blocks included four-barrel Holley and Rochester carburetors and three, two-barrel carburetors. The 427 received a stroke increase in 1970 and became the 454. It reached its highest performance rating in 1970 with an output of 460 horsepower for the rare LS-7.

Generally speaking, the small and large block Corvette engines are of the same basic design. They feature eight cylinders arranged in a vee configuration. The cylinders are numbered front to rear with cylinders 1, 3, 5, and 7 on the left bank and 2, 4, 6, and 8 on the right, when viewed from the rear. Firing order for both engines is 1-8-4-3-6-5-7-2. Both the crankshaft and camshaft are supported by five bearings. Viewed from the front, crankshaft rotation is clockwise. Lubrication is full pressure, and a gear type oil pump feeds the system through a full flow oil filter. Both the oil pump and the distributor are driven by the camshaft. The main oil gallery pressurizes the bearings via the crankshaft and camshaft. The valve lifter oil gallery provides oil to the lifters which, in turn, feed the rocker arms through the hollow pushrods.

The standard bearer of Corvette high performance models was established, with the 1967 introduction of the 430 horsepower L-88 limited production option engine. This unit was furnished with a Tuft-rided and cross-drilled heavy duty crankshaft, magnafluxed and shotpeened connecting rods with $7/16$ inch connecting bolts, forged pistons with pop-up domes, and aluminum cylinder heads.

The peak of large block development was reached in 1969 with the ZL-1 engine. This was the basic L-88 engine but with an aluminum cylinder block.

General Engine Specifications

Year	Engine Displacement (cu in.)	Carburetor Type	Horsepower @ rpm ■	Torque @ rpm (ft lbs) ■	Bore and Stroke (in.)	Compression Ratio	Oil Pressure @ 2000 rpm
1963–64	327	4 bbl	250 @ 4400	350 @ 2800	4.00 x 3.25	10.5 : 1	45
	327	4 bbl	300 @ 5000	360 @ 2800	4.00 x 3.25	10.5 : 1	45

General Engine Specifications (cont.)

Year	Engine Displacement (cu in.)	Carburetor Type	Horsepower @ rpm ■	Torque @ rpm (ft lbs) ■	Bore and Stroke (in.)	Compression Ratio	Oil Pressure @ 2000 rpm
1963	327	4 bbl	340 @ 6000	344 @ 4000	4.00 x 3.25	11.25 : 1	45
	327	Fuel Inj	360 @ 6000	352 @ 5000	4.00 x 3.25	11.25 : 1	45
1964	327	4 bbl	365 @ 6200	360 @ 3600	4.00 x 3.25	11.0 : 1	45
	327	Fuel Inj	375 @ 6200	350 @ 4000	4.00 x 3.25	11.0 : 1	45
1965	327	4 bbl	250 @ 4400	350 @ 2800	4.00 x 3.25	10.5 : 1	45
	327	4 bbl	300 @ 5000	360 @ 3200	4.00 x 3.25	10.5 : 1	45
	327	4 bbl	350 @ 5800	360 @ 3800	4.00 x 3.25	11.0 : 1	45
	327	4 bbl	375 @ 6200	350 @ 4000	4.00 x 3.25	11.0 : 1	45
	327	Fuel Inj	365 @ 6200	350 @ 4600	4.00 x 3.25	11.0 : 1	45
	396	4 bbl	425 @ 6400	415 @ 4000	4.094 x 3.760	11.0 : 1	45
1966	327	4 bbl	300 @ 5000	360 @ 3200	4.00 x 3.25	10.5 : 1	45
	327	4 bbl	350 @ 5800	360 @ 3600	4.00 x 3.25	11.0 : 1	45
	427	4 bbl	390 @ 5200	460 @ 3600	4.25 x 3.76	10.25 : 1	60
	427	4 bbl	425 @ 5600	460 @ 4000	4.25 x 3.76	11.0 : 1	60
1967–68	327	4 bbl	300 @ 5000	360 @ 3400	4.00 x 3.25	10.0 : 1	45
	327	4 bbl	350 @ 5800	360 @ 3600	4.00 x 3.25	11.0 : 1	45
	427	4 bbl	390 @ 5400	460 @ 3600	4.25 x 3.76	10.25 : 1	65
	427	3–2 bbl	400 @ 5400	460 @ 3600	4.25 x 3.76	10.25 : 1	65
	427	3–2 bbl	435 @ 5800	460 @ 4000	4.25 x 3.76	11.0 : 1	65
	427①	4 bbl	430 @ 5200	450 @ 4400	4.25 x 3.76	12.0 : 1	65
1969	350	4 bbl	300 @ 4800	380 @ 3200	4.00 x 3.48	10.25 : 1	45
	350	4 bbl	350 @ 5600	380 @ 3200	4.00 x 3.48	11.0 : 1	45
	427	4 bbl	390 @ 5400	460 @ 3600	4.25 x 3.76	10.25 : 1	65
	427	3–2 bbl	400 @ 5400	460 @ 3600	4.25 x 3.76	10.25 : 1	65

General Engine Specifications (cont.)

Year	Engine Displacement (cu in.)	Carburetor Type	Horsepower @ rpm ■	Torque @ rpm (ft lbs) ■	Bore and Stroke (in.)	Compression Ratio	Oil Pressure @ 2000 rpm
1969	427	3–2 bbl	435 @ 5800	460 @ 4000	4.25 x 3.76	11.0 : 1	65
	427①	4 bbl	430 @ 5200	450 @ 4400	4.25 x 3.76	12.0 : 1	65
1970	350	4 bbl	300 @ 4800	380 @ 3200	4.00 x 3.48	10.25 : 1	40
	350	4 bbl	350 @ 5600	380 @ 3600	4.00 x 3.48	11.0 : 1	40
	350	4 bbl	370 @ 6000	380 @ 4000	4.00 x 3.48	11.0 : 1	40
	454	4 bbl	390 @ 4800	500 @ 3400	4.251 x 4.000	10.25 : 1	40
	454	4 bbl	460 @ 5600	490 @ 3000	4.251 x 4.000	11.25 : 1	40
1971	350	4 bbl	270 @ 4800	360 @ 3200	4.00 x 3.48	8.5 : 1	40
	350	4 bbl	330 @ 5600	360 @ 4000	4.00 x 3.48	9.0 : 1	40
	454	4 bbl	365 @ 4800	465 @ 3200	4.251 x 4.000	8.5 : 1	40
	454	4 bbl	425 @ 5600	475 @ 4000	4.251 x 4.000	8.5 : 1	40
1972	350	4 bbl	200 @ 4400	300 @ 2800	4.00 x 3.48	8.5 : 1	40
	350	4 bbl	255 @ 5600	280 @ 4000	4.00 x 3.48	9.0 : 1	40
	454	4 bbl	270 @ 4000②	390 @ 3200	4.251 x 4.000	8.5 : 1	40
1973	350	4 bbl	190 @ 4400	270 @ 2800	4.000 x 3.480	8.5 : 1	40
	350	4 bbl	250 @ 5200	285 @ 4000	4.000 x 3.480	9.0 : 1	40
	454	4 bbl	275 @ 4400	395 @ 2800	4.251 x 4.000	8.25 : 1	40
1974	350	4 bbl	195 @ 4400	275 @ 2800	4.000 x 3.480	8.5 : 1	40
	350	4 bbl	250 @ 5200	285 @ 4000	4.000 x 3.480	9.0 : 1	40
	454	4 bbl	270 @ 4400	380 @ 2800	4.251 x 4.000	8.25 : 1	40
1975–76	350	4 bbl	165 @ 3800	255 @ 2400	4.000 x 3.480	8.5 : 1	40
	350	4 bbl	205 @ 4800	255 @ 3600	4.000 x 3.480	9.0 : 1	40

■ Beginning 1972, horsepower and torque are SAE net figures. They are measured at the rear of the transmission with all accessories installed and operating. Since the figures vary when a given engine is installed in different models, some are representative rather than exact.
① Limited production engine L88, for special purposes
② Not available in California

Valve Specifications

Year	Engine Displacement (cu in.)	Seat Angle (deg)	Face Angle (deg)	Spring Test Pressure (lbs @ in.)	Spring Installed Height (in.)	STEM TO GUIDE Clearance (in.)		STEM Diameter (in.)	
						Intake	Exhaust	Intake	Exhaust
1963–64	327	46	45	175 @ 1.26	1.66	0.0010–0.0027	0.0016–0.0033	0.3404–0.3417	0.3410–0.3417
	327 (High Perf)	46	45	175 @ 1.26	1.66	0.0010–0.0027	0.0016–0.0033	0.3404–0.3417	0.3410–0.3417
1965–66	327	46	45	175 @ 1.26	1.66	0.0010–0.0027	0.0016–0.0033	0.3404–0.3417	0.3410–0.3417
	327 (350 hp)	46	45	175 @ 1.26	1.66	0.0010–0.0027	0.0016–0.0033	0.3410–0.3417	0.3410–0.3417
	327 (fuel inj)	46	45	175 @ 1.26	1.66	0.0010–0.0027	0.0016–0.0033	0.3410–0.3417	0.3410–0.3417
	396	46	45	315 @ 1.38	1⅞	0.0005–0.0024	0.0012–0.0029	0.3715–0.3722	0.3713–0.3720
	427	46	45	315 @ 1.38	1.88	0.0010–0.0027	0.0015–0.0032	0.3715–0.3722	0.3713–0.3720
	427 (425 hp)	46	45	315 @ 1.38	1.88	0.0010–0.0027	0.0015–0.0032	0.3715–0.3722	0.3713–0.3720
1967	327 (300 hp)	46	45	200 @ 1.25	1-21/32	0.0010–0.0027	0.0015–0.0032	0.3410–0.3417	0.3410–0.3417
	327 (350 hp)	46	45	200 @ 1.25	1-21/32	0.0010–0.0027	0.0015–0.0032	0.3410–0.3417	0.3410–0.3417
	427 (390, 400 hp)	46	45			0.0010–0.0027	0.0015–0.0032	0.3715–0.3722	0.3713–0.3720
	427 (435 hp)	46	45	315 @ 1.38	1⅞	0.0010–0.0027	0.0015–0.0032	0.3715–0.3722	0.3713–0.3720
1968	327 (exc 350 hp)	46	45	198 @ 1.25	1.70	0.0010–0.0027	0.0017–0.0027	0.3410–0.3417	0.3410–0.3417
	327 (350 hp)	46	45	198 @ 1.25	1.70	0.0010–0.0027	0.0017–0.0027	0.3410–0.3417	0.3410–0.3417
	427 (exc 435 hp)	46	45	315 @ 1.38	1.88	0.0010–0.0027	0.0015–0.0032	0.3715–0.3722	0.3713–0.3722

Year	Engine								
1968	427 (435 hp)	46	45	315 @ 1.38	1.88	0.0010–0.0027	0.0015–0.0032	0.3715–0.3722	0.3713–0.3722
1969	350	46	45	200 @ 1.25	1.70	0.0010–0.0027	0.0010–0.0027	0.3410–0.3417	0.3410–0.3417
	350 (350 hp)	46	45	200 @ 1.25	1.70	0.0010–0.0027	0.0010–0.0027	0.3410–0.3417	0.3410–0.3417
	427 (390 400 hp)	46	45	312 @ 1.38	1.88	0.0010–0.0027	0.0010–0.0027	0.3715–0.3722	0.3713–0.3722
	427 (435 hp)	46	45	312 @ 1.38	1.88	0.0010–0.0027	0.0010–0.0027	0.3715–0.3722	0.3713–0.3722
1970	350	46	45	80 @ 1.70	1 23/32	0.0010–0.0037	0.0010–0.0047	0.3414	0.3414
	454	46	45	75 @ 1.88①	1 7/8	0.0010–0.0037	0.0010–0.0047	0.3718	0.3718
	454②	46	45	75 @ 1.88③	1 7/8	0.0010–0.0037	0.0010–0.0047	0.3718	0.3718
1971	350	46	45	80 @ 1.70	1 23/32	0.0010–0.0037	0.0010–0.0047	0.3414	0.3414
	454	46	45	75 @ 1.88①	1 7/8	0.0010–0.0037	0.0010–0.0047	0.3719	0.3717
1972	350	46	45	80 @ 1.70	1 23/32	0.0010–0.0037	0.0010–0.0047	0.3414	0.3414
	454	46	45	75 @ 1.88①	1 7/8	0.0010–0.0037	0.0010–0.0047	0.3719	0.3717
1973	350	46	45	80 @ 1.70④	1 23/32	0.0010–0.0027	0.0010–0.0027	0.3414	0.3414
	454	46	45	80 @ 1.88	1 7/8	0.0010–0.0027	0.0010–0.0027	0.3719	0.3717
1974	350	46	45	80 @ 1.70④	1 23/32	0.0010–0.0027	0.0010–0.0027	0.3414	0.3414
	454	46	45	80 @ 1.88	1 7/8	0.0010–0.0027	0.0010–0.0027	0.3719	0.3717
1975–76	350	46	45	80 @ 1.70④	1 23/32	0.0010–0.0027	0.0010–0.0027	0.3414	0.3414

① Inner spring 30 @ 1.78
② 460 hp
③ Inner spring 41 @ 1.78
④ Intake given; 80 @ 1.61 for exhaust spring

Crankshaft and Connecting Rod Specifications

All measurements are given in in.

Year	Engine	CRANKSHAFT				CONNECTING ROD		
		Main Brg Journal Dia	Main Brg Oil Clearance	Shaft End-Play	Thrust on No.	Journal Diameter	Oil Clearance	Side Clearance
1963–65	All	2.2978–2.2988	0.0008–0.0034	0.002–0.006	5	1.999–2.000	0.0007–0.0028	0.0017–0.0038
1966–67	All 327 cu in.	2.2978–2.2988	0.0008–0.0034	0.002–0.006	5	1.999–2.000	0.0007–0.0028	0.009–0.013
1966–67 1968	390 hp 400 hp	2.7481–2.7490	0.0013–0.0025	0.006–0.010	5	2.199–2.200	0.0009–0.0025	0.015–0.021
1966 1967 1968	425 hp 430 hp 435 hp	2.7481–2.7490	0.0013–0.0025	0.006–0.010	5	2.198–2.199	0.0014–0.0030	0.019–0.025
1968	327 cu in.	2.4484–2.4493	0.0008–0.0034	0.002–0.006	5	2.099–2.100	0.0007–0.0028	0.009–0.013
1969	350 cu in.	2.4474–2.4488	no. 1–2–3–4 0.0008–0.0020 no. 5 0.0018–0.0034	0.003–0.011	5	2.099–2.100	0.0007–0.0028	0.009–0.013
1969	390 & 400 hp	no. 1–2–3–4 2.7481–2.7490 no. 5 2.7478–2.7488	no. 1–2–3–4 0.0013–0.0025 no. 5 0.0015–0.0031	0.006–0.010	5	2.199–2.200	0.0009–0.0025	0.015–0.021
1967–69	L88	no. 1–2–3–4 2.7418–2.7490 no. 5 2.7478–2.7488	no. 1–2–3–4 0.0013–0.0025 no. 5 0.0015–0.0031	0.006–0.010	5	2.1985–2.1995	0.0014–0.0030	0.019–0.025
1969	435 hp	no. 1–4 2.7481–2.7490 no. 5 2.7478–2.7488	no. 1–2–3–4 0.0013–0.0025 no. 5 0.0015–0.0031	0.006–0.010	5	2.1985–2.1995	0.0014–0.0030	0.019–0.025

Year	Engine							
1970	350	2.4484–2.4493③	0.0003–0.0015④	0.002–0.006	5	2.0990–2.1000	0.0007–0.0028	0.008–0.014
	454	2.7485–2.7494①	0.0013–0.0025⑥	0.006–0.010	5	2.1990–2.2000	0.0009–0.0025	0.015–0.021
	454 (460 hp)	2.7481–2.7490②	0.0013–0.0025⑦	0.006–0.010	5	2.1985–2.1995	0.0014–0.0030	0.019–0.025
1971	350	2.4484–2.4493③	0.0008–0.0020⑤	0.002–0.006	5	2.0990–2.1000	0.0013–0.0035	0.008–0.014
	350 (330 hp)	2.4484–2.4493③	0.0013–0.0025⑨	0.002–0.006	5	2.0990–2.1000	0.0013–0.0035	0.008–0.014
	454 (365 hp)	2.7485–2.7494⑪	0.0013–0.0025⑥	0.006–0.010	5	2.1990–2.2000	0.0009–0.0025	0.015–0.021
	454 (425 hp)	2.7481–2.7490②	0.0013–0.0025⑦	0.006–0.010	5	2.1985–2.1995	0.0009–0.0025	0.019–0.025
1972	350	2.4484–2.4493⑧	0.0008–0.0020⑤	0.002–0.006	5	2.0990–2.1000	0.0013–0.0035	0.008–0.014
	350 (255 hp)	2.4484–2.4493⑧	0.0013–0.0025⑨	0.002–0.006	5	2.0990–2.1000	0.0013–0.0035	0.008–0.014
	454 (270 hp)	2.7485–2.7494⑪	0.0013–0.0025⑥	0.006–0.010	5	2.1990–2.2000	0.0009–0.0025	0.015–0.021
1973–74	350	2.4502⑫	0.0013–0.0025⑨	0.002–0.006	5	2.0990–2.1000	0.0013–0.0035	0.008–0.014
	454	2.7504⑬	0.0007–0.0019⑩	0.006–0.010	5	2.1990–2.2000	0.0009–0.0025	0.015–0.021
1975–76	350	2.4502⑫	0.0013–0.0025⑨	0.002–0.007	5	2.0990–2.1000	0.0013–0.0035	0.008–0.014

① Nos. 3, 4 —2.7481–2.7490; No. 5 —2.7478–2.7488
② No. 5 —2.7478–2.7488
③ No. 5 —2.4479–2.4488
④ Nos. 2, 3, 4 —0.0006–0.0018; No. 5 —0.0008–0.0023
⑤ Nos. 2, 3, 4 —0.0011–0.0023; No. 5 —0.0017–0.0033
⑥ No. 5 —0.0024–0.0040
⑦ No. 5 —0.0029–0.0045
⑧ Nos. 2, 3, 4 —2.4481–2.4490; No. 5 —2.4479–2.4488
⑨ No. 5 —0.0023–0.0033; with auto. trans. No. 1 —0.0019–0.0031
⑩ Nos. 2, 3, 4 —0.0013–0.0025; No. 5 —0.0019–0.0035
⑪ Nos. 2, 3, 4 —2.7481–2.7490; No. 5 —2.7478–2.7488
⑫ No. 5 —2.4508
⑬ Nos. 1, 5 —2.7499

Piston Clearance

Year	Engine Displacement (cu in.)	Advertised Horsepower	Piston-to-Bore Clearance (in.) ●	Year	Engine Displacement (cu in.)	Advertised Horsepower	Piston-to-Bore Clearance (in.) ●
1963–76	327	All	0.0005–0.0025	1963–76	427	430	0.0058–0.0080
	350	165, 190, 250, 300	0.0007–0.0027			435	0.0040–0.0065
		350	0.0020–0.0036		454	245, 275	0.0018–0.0035
		245, 370	0.0036–0.0061			345	0.0024–0.0049
	396	425	0.0036–0.0065			360	0.0024–0.0049
	427	390	0.0024–0.0045			390	0.0024–0.0049
		400	0.0024–0.0045			450	0.0040–0.0065

● Service range—minimum to maximum

Ring Gap

All measurements are given in inches

Year	Engine Displacement (cu in.)	Top Compression	Bottom Compression
1963–68	327	0.013–0.023	0.013–0.025
1969–71	350	0.010–0.020①	0.013–0.025①
1965–74	396, 427, 454	0.010–0.020	0.010–0.020
1973–76	350	0.010–0.020	0.013–0.025②

① 250, 300 hp 350 cu in.
   Top—0.013–0.023
   2nd—0.013–0.025
② 250, 255 hp 350 cu in.—0.013–0.023

Year	Engine Displacement (cu in.)	Oil Control
1963–74	All engines except 396, 427	0.015–0.055
	396, 427	0.010–0.030
1975–76	350	0.015–0.055

Torque Specifications
All readings are given in ft lbs

Year	Engine Displacement (cu in.)	Cylinder Head Bolts	Rod Bearing Bolts	Main Bearing Bolts	Crankshaft Balancer Bolt	Flywheel-To-Crankshaft Bolts	Manifold	
							Intake	Exhaust
1963–67	327	60–70	35	80	60⑤	60	30	18–22
1968–76	327, 350	60–70	45	75②	60⑤	60	30	18–22
1965	396	80	50	115	85	65	30	20
1966–76	427, 454	80①	50④	100③	85	65	30	20

① Aluminum heads—short bolts 65; long bolts 75
② Engines with 4-bolt mains—outer bolts 65
③ Engines with 4-bolt mains—short bolts 95; long bolts 105
④ $\frac{7}{16}$ rod bolts—70
⑤ Where applicable

Ring Side Clearance
All measurements are given in inches

Year	Engine Displacement (cu in.)	Top Compression	Bottom Compression
1963–68	327	0.0012–0.0032①	0.0012–0.0027①
1969	350	0.0012–0.0032	0.0012–0.0027
1970–76	350	0.0012–0.0032	0.0012–0.0027
1965	396	0.0017–0.0032	0.0017–0.0032
1967–69	427	0.0017–0.0032	0.0017–0.0032
1971–76	454	0.0017–0.0032	0.0017–0.0032

① 250, 275 hp 327 cu in.
  Top—0.0012–0.0027
  2nd—0.0012–0.0032

Year	Engine Displacement (cu in.)	Oil Control
1963–68	327	0.000–0.005
1969–76	350	0.000–0.005
1965	396	0.0005–0.0065
1967–69	427	0.0005–0.0065
1970–76	454	0.0005–0.0065

ENGINE REMOVAL AND REPLACEMENT

This procedure is basically the same for all engines regardless of size and model year. Certain pieces of optional equipment require minor specific changes but the overall operation remains the same.

1. The engine may be removed separately from the transmission, through the top of the engine compartment. Begin by draining the cooling system and the engine crankcase. If a suitable plug is not available for the propeller shaft opening after the shaft has been removed, then drain the transmission.

2. Disconnect the battery cables from the battery terminals and remove the air cleaner and ignition shields. Remember to cover the carburetor.

3. Disconnect wiring at the alternator, temperature sending unit, oil pressure switch, primary coil lead, and CEC solenoid when applicable. Also disconnect the engine ground wires and the accelerator rod at the bellcrank.

4. Disconnect the power brake hose at the carburetor end when applicable. Disconnect the tachometer drive cable at the distributor and the throttle valve if so equipped. Scribe the hood hinge locations on the support brackets and remove the hood.

5. Remove the radiator shroud and radiator, then the fan and fan assembly. If the car is equipped with power steering, remove the pump mounting bolts and push the pump into the vacant radiator opening. An alternate method is to disconnect the pump lines and plug both ends.

6. Remove the heater hose from the clip at the alternator bracket, then disconnect the hose from the engine connections and move back for extra clearance. Remove the rocker arm covers and place the vehicle on jack stands.

7. Remove the center head bolt on each head, and install the lift tool to the engine. Unhook the distributor cap and move it forward. Cover the distributor with a clean cloth.

8. Remove the propeller shaft and disconnect the speedometer cable. Disconnect the exhaust pipes at the manifold flanges. On cars equipped with large block engines, the front stud on each manifold must be removed before the exhaust pipes can be removed.

9. Disconnect the wire leads at the starter solenoid. Remove the gas tank line at the fuel pump and plug the line to prevent fuel siphoning.

10. Block the clutch pedal in the return position and remove the clutch cross-shaft. Remove the oil filter and oil cooler lines if so equipped. Remove the starting motor. If the Corvette is equipped with a manual transmission, remove the flywheel cover plate. If equipped with an automatic transmission, remove the converter underpan.

11. Remove the front engine mount thru-bolts. Support the transmission with a floor jack and remove the transmission-to-engine bolts. If the car has Powerglide, remove the converter-to-flywheel bolts and install the converter holding bracket to the transmission.

12. Move the engine forward and upward as needed to clear the engine compartment.

13. Replacement is the reversal of this procedure.

DISASSEMBLY AND ASSEMBLY

1. Secure the engine on stand or table. Remove the alternator and the ignition shields that cover the spark plugs. Disconnect the fuel lines, spark advance line, crankcase ventilation line, and A.I.R. system when applicable. Remove the carburetor(s) or fuel injector.

2. Remove the distributor cap, spark plug wires, and spark plugs. Loosen the securing clamp and remove the distributor. Be sure to keep the capless distributor wrapped in a clean cloth. Remove the coil.

3. Remove the water pump and thermostat housing and extract the thermostat. Remove the intake and exhaust manifolds. Remove the rocker arms and withdraw the pushrods and valve lifters. Keep the pushrods, rocker arms, and lifters in the order that they are removed, so as not to interfere with established wear patterns when they are reassembled.

4. Remove the cylinder heads, being careful not to scratch or gouge the sealing surfaces. Remove the fuel pump and fuel

pump pushrod. Use a gear puller to remove the crankshaft damper. Remove the oil pan and the oil pan baffle on high performance engines. Remove the timing chain cover and the crankshaft oil slinger.

5. Remove the camshaft sprocket. The sprocket is a light, press fit on the camshaft and if it remains on the shaft after the removal of its retaining bolts, tap the sprocket lightly with a plastic hammer to facilitate its removal. Remove the timing chain with the sprocket. Use a gear puller to remove the crankshaft sprocket.

6. Remove the camshaft with special care. All of the bearing journals are the same size so be careful not to damage them during removal. Remove the oil pump, screen assembly, and extension shaft from the rear main bearing.

7. Check the connecting rods for correct cylinder identification, the rods and caps are marked to prevent their interchange. When rods and caps are adequately identified, remove the caps. Check cylinder bores for ridges and remove any existing ridges before attempting to remove the piston and rod assemblies.

8. Loosen the clutch cover bolts slowly and evenly to remove pressure from the springs and prevent distortion of the cover. When tension is released, remove the clutch pressure plate and driven disc. Remove the flywheel from the crankshaft.

9. Check the numbering of the main bearing caps and remove them. Lift the crankshaft from the upper bearing halves.

10. To assemble, first install the rear main seal. Position and lubricate replacement main bearing halves in the block and install the crankshaft. Position the main caps and replacement bearings and torque to specifications.

11. Attach the flywheel so that complementing dowel holes in flywheel and crankshaft are in alignment. Install automatic transmission flywheels with the converter attaching pads facing the transmission. Place a wood block between the block and crankshaft to prevent the shaft from turning. Torque the flywheel bolts to 60 ft lbs on 327/350 engines and 65 ft lbs for 396/427/454 powerplants.

12. Install the piston and connecting rod assemblies. Install the oil pump,

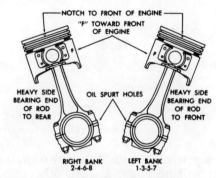

Correct piston/connecting rod positioning for 327 and 350 cu in. engines

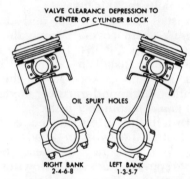

Correct piston/connecting rod positioning for 396, 427, and 454 cu in. engines

screen and extension. Torque the bolts to 65 ft lbs.

13. Lubricate and install the camshaft. Install the crankshaft sprocket and rotate until the timing mark on the sprocket is vertically nearest the camshaft. Hang the timing chain on the camshaft sprocket and rotate the camshaft so that when the

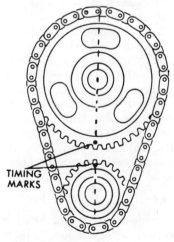

Timing mark alignment

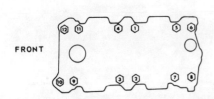
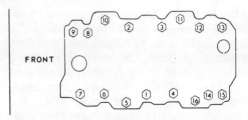

Intake manifold tightening sequence (small block V8, left; big block V8, right)

sprocket is placed on it, the two timing marks will be opposite each other. Slip the chain over the crankshaft so that the timing marks are kept in alignment and install the camshaft sprocket. Torque its securing bolts to 20 ft lbs.

14. Install the oil slinger and attach the timing chain cover. Torque the attaching bolts to 7 ft lbs. Install the torsional damper. Install the front and rear oil pan seals and gaskets. Install the oil pan baffle (high performance models), and oil pan. Tighten to 7 ft lbs.

15. Install the lifters in the correct bores. Install the cylinder heads using new gaskets. Torque the head bolts evenly to specifications and following the correct tightening sequence. Replace the pushrods in the correct bores, and install the rocker arm assemblies. Install the intake manifold gaskets and seals. Install the intake manifold and torque the bolts in sequence.

16. Replace the thermostat and thermostat housing. Tighten the attaching bolts to 30 ft lbs. Attach the water pump and torque the bolts to 30 ft lbs. Install the distributor, mount the coil and connect the electrical leads. Install the spark plugs and tighten to 25 ft lbs. Replace the distributor cap and spark plug wires.

17. Install the carburetor(s) or fuel injection unit. Insert the fuel pump push rod and fuel pump. Torque the bolts to 9 ft lbs. Install the exhaust manifolds and torque their center bolts 25–35 ft lbs; outer bolts with French locks, 20 ft lbs.

18. Lubricate the pilot bushing on manual transmission cars and install the driven disc and pressure plate so that corresponding X marks align. Tighten bolts evenly to 35 ft lbs.

CYLINDER HEAD SERVICING

Disassemble the cylinder head with a valve spring compressor. Place the valves, springs, and retainers in a rack to

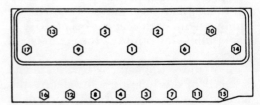

Small block V8 cylinder head bolt tightening sequence

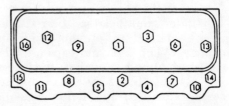

Big block V8 cylinder head bolt tightening sequence

prevent them from mixing. Use a drill-driven wire brush to clean carbon from the combustion chambers and ports. Check for cracks or corrosion. Clean the valves on a buffing wheel and inspect for cracked or burned faces or damaged stems.

Use a dial indicator to check for excessive valve stem-to-bore clearance. Mount the indicator on the valve-cover gasket rail and position the indicator pick-up so that lateral movement of the valve stem will be detected. Insert test valve, align indicator, and drop valve $1/16$ in. from its seat. Move the stem sideways and note the reading of the dial indicator. Replace valve stems that exceed specifications. Check valve spring tension against specifications chart. Replace springs that are not within 10 lbs of the specified loads.

Assemble the valve springs for 327/350 engines in the following manner: Position the valve spring shim, valve spring, damper, valve shield, and valve cap over the valve stem. Compress the spring and install the oil seal in the stem's lower groove. Check to see that the seal is not

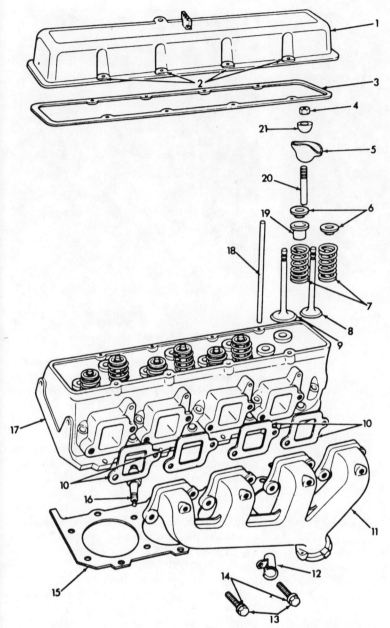

1. Valve cover
2. Screw reinforcements
3. Gasket
4. Adjusting nut
5. Rocker arm
6. Valve spring retainer
7. Valve spring
8. Exhaust valve
9. Intake valve
10. Gasket
11. Exhaust manifold
12. Spark plug shield
13. Bolt
14. Washer
15. Head gasket
16. Spark plug
17. Cylinder head
18. Pushrod
19. Spring shield
20. Rocker arm stud
21. Rocker arm ball

Exploded view of big block cylinder head

twisted. Install the two locks on the stem and release the spring tension. Check for proper assembly.

To assemble the large block valves, place the valve spring shim on the spring seat and install the oil seal over the valve and guide. Position the valve spring, damper, and valve cap over the valve stem. Compress the spring and install the stem locks. Release the spring tension and check for proper assembly.

Check the installed valve spring height and install a $1/16$ in. shim if height exceeds specifications. Do not shim a spring to a height under specifications.

Replace the cylinder head as follows: Carefully clean the mating surfaces and position the replacement head gasket. Be sure that the head bolts and bolt holes in the head are free of dirt and grease or inaccurate torque readings will result.

If the gasket is made of steel, coat both sides with aluminum paint or spray-on copper sealer. Do not use a sealer if the

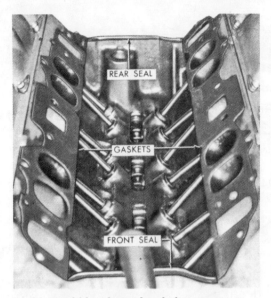

Intake manifold gasket and seal placement

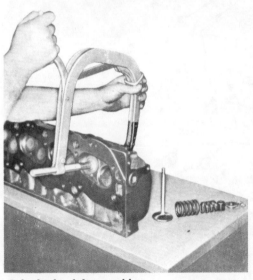

Cylinder head disassembly

Checking valve stem-to-bore clearance

gasket is a composition steel/asbestos type. Lay the cylinder head in place and install the head bolts, finger-tight. Tighten the headbolts to 65 ft lbs for the small block and 80 ft lbs for the large block. Tighten in even stages and according to the correct torquing sequence.

When the cylinder head has been removed or the valve train disturbed, a preliminary valve adjustment will be required. To do this, on engines with hydraulic lifters, bring the engine to top dead center and firing on the number one cylinder. Make the adjustment by loosening the adjusting nut until there is move-

ment in the pushrod, then tighten until movement ceases. This is best determined by trying to rotate the pushrod while tightening the nut. This is the zero lash position. Tighten the adjusting nut one additional turn. This preloads the hydraulic lifter plunger in the center of its travel and completes the adjustment.

With the engine positioned at TDC on no. 1 cylinder, adjust the following valves:

Intake—1, 2, 5, 7   Exhaust—1, 3, 4, 8

Rotate the engine one revolution and again stop at TDC. Cylinder no. 6 is now on the firing stroke. Adjust:

Intake—3, 4, 6, 8   Exhaust—2, 5, 6, 7

Adjust mechanical valve lifters as follows: Rotate the engine to TDC. This condition is identified by a static valve condition of number one cylinder during the final stages of the manual engine rotation. Movement of the valves indicates that the engine's firing stroke is on no. 6 cylinder.

With engine at TDC, adjust the following valves to feeler gauge specifications.

Intake—2, 7   Exhaust—4, 8

Rotate the engine ½ revolution (clockwise) and adjust:

Intake—1, 8   Exhaust—3, 6

Rotate the engine another ½ revolution, bringing the engine to TDC, no. 6 cylinder. Adjust:

Intake—3, 4   Exhaust—5, 7
 Rotate the engine ½ revolution. Adjust:
Intake—5, 6   Exhaust—1, 2
 Warm the engine and readjust to specifications as described in Chapter 2.

CRANKSHAFT SERVICING

Crankshaft servicing literally makes or breaks any engine; especially a high performance one such as the Corvette.

The most critical maintenance operation is the replacement of the crankshaft main bearings. These bearings are of the precision insert design and do not require adjustment through shims. They are offered in undersizes of 0.001 in., 0.002 in., 0.009 in., 0.010 in., 0.020 in., and 0.030 in.

Despite the advent of these inserts and accompanying precision machine work, it does happen that sizing mistakes are made and no crankshaft should be installed in a block without checking clearances. One of the simplest means of doing so is to use plastigage. This is a wax-like plastic material that is formed into precision threads. It will compress evenly between two surfaces, without damage, and when measured, will indicate the actual clearance. Certain precautions should be observed, however, and the following method should be used for accuracy.

It is easiest to check bearing clearance with the engine removed from the car and the block inverted. This ensures that the crank is resting against the upper bearing shells. If plastigage is to be used on an engine still in the vehicle, it will be necessary to support the crankshaft at both ends so that clearance between the crankshaft and the upper bearing shells is eliminated.

For demonstration purposes, assume that the engine is inverted on a work stand. Position the replacement upper bearing halves in the block and carefully lay the crank in place. Both the upper and lower bearing halves must be free of oil for the test. Beginning with the rear main bearing, cut a piece of plastigage sufficient to span the width of the crankshaft journal when placed in line with the longitudinal axis of the crankshaft.

Position the rear main bearing cap, with bearing half in place, into its proper placement. Insert the main bearing bolts

Checking main bearing clearance with Plastigage®

and, with a torque wrench, evenly tighten them to specifications. Do not rotate the crankshaft with the plastigage between the journal and bearing. If this happens, the plastic thread will smear and reveal nothing.

When the correct torque has been achieved, loosen the bolts and carefully remove the bearing cap. The plastigage will be found either on the journal or the bearing surface. Regardless of its location, measure the compressed width of the plastic against the gauge printed on the packaging envelope. The flattened width will indicate the actual clearance between the bearing and the journal. Clearances beyond specifications will require bearing substitution and/or crankshaft grinding. Repeat the procedure for the remaining bearings. If the flattened plastigage tapers either in the middle or at the ends, or exhibits any unusual patterns, it indicates that something is amiss and a close check with a micrometer is called for before continuing assembly.

When all the bearings have been satisfactorily checked, remove the plastigage and check the crankshaft for excessive drag by rotating it. Finally, check the crankshaft end-play. Force the crankshaft toward the front of the block and measure the clearance between the crankshaft and the front of the rear main bearing with a feeler gauge. Replace the bearing if it exceeds specifications.

With all clearances checked, the crankshaft is ready for placement in the block. Begin by installing the rear main seal halves in the rear main bearing cap and cylinder block grooves. The seal is correctly installed when the lips face the front of the engine. Lubricate these lips but keep oil off the mating surfaces. Insert the main bearing halves in the block and the bearing caps and lubricate the bearing surfaces with clean engine oil. Carefully lay the crankshaft in place.

Coat the mating surfaces of the rear main bearing and the block with a thin layer of oil sealing compound. Keep the sealer off the crankshaft and seal lips. Position the main bearing caps with their arrows aimed at the front of the block. Torque the front four bearings to specifications. Tighten the rear main bearing cap bolts to 12 ft lbs and tap the crankshaft first backward then forward, using a soft hammer. This aligns the rear main bearing and crankshaft thrust surfaces. Complete the installation by torquing all main bearing caps to specifications.

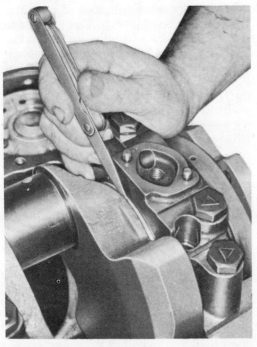

Checking crankshaft end-play

CONNECTING RODS AND BEARINGS

The method of checking connecting rod bearing clearance is basically the same as for the crankshaft. Exercise the same precautionary steps to protect the connecting rod journals from damage and do not rotate the connecting rod on the journal with plastigage in place. To aid accuracy, pull the connecting rod up snug against the journal so that all clearance will be reflected in the bearing cap.

To remove the piston and rod assemblies from the block, force the piston downward in the block and use a ridge cutter to remove the ridge from the top of the cylinder. This done, carefully remove the assemblies. It is a good idea to place a rag in the cylinder, during the cutting operation so that loose chips will be caught. Also, when removing the bearing caps, slip pieces of rubber hose over the connecting rod bolts so they will not scratch the connecting rod journal when they exit the cylinder block.

It is cheap insurance to replace connecting rod bolts if the engine has seen extended service or is used for competition. Use a ring compressor to prevent the rings from catching on the block during reassembly. Lubricate the inside of the compressor liberally. Position the piston/rod assembly in the cylinder. They are correctly positioned with the connecting rod bearing tang slots are opposite the camshaft.

Be sure that the rod bolts are protected by tape or scrap pieces of hose to prevent damaging the rod journals. Use a wood mallet handle and lightly tap the piston into the cylinder. Attach the rod caps and torque the rod bolts to specification.

PISTONS, PINS, AND RINGS

Corvette pistons are made of aluminum alloy and should not be exposed to careless treatment. Never use a wire brush to clean these pistons. Use cleaning solvent to remove varnish or carbon. Clean the ring grooves with a groove cleaner tool. Be sure the oil holes in the grooves are clear. Check for cracks, scuff marks, etc., and replace any piston that is suspect. Check the piston skirt measurement with a micrometer and compare to specifications.

Piston pins are matched to an individual piston and should be replaced with the piston as a set, not separately. Clean the pin with solvent and with a micrometer, check the pin external size and the piston pin bore size. Replace both if wear tolerance exceeds the specifications by 0.001 in.

Two compression rings and an oil ring assembly are used on Corvette pistons. The compression rings are marked on their top side and should always be assembled to the piston with this mark upward. Before assembling the rings to the piston, they should be fitted to their individual cylinder bore. To do this, place a compression ring in its cylinder and press it into the cylinder about ¼ inch above normal ring travel. A piston may be used to keep the ring even in the bore. If the gap between the ring ends exceeds tolerances, replace it, or, if the gap is too small, carefully widen the gap with a file. Repeat this procedure until rings are matched to their bores. Now check for ring/piston interference by placing the outer edge of the compression rings in their respective grooves and rolling them around the piston. Investigate any interference.

To install rings on a piston, first slip the oil control ring spacer into its groove and secure its tang in an oil hole. Butt the ends of the spacer together and install the lower spacer ring with its gap installed

according to the enclosed chart. Install the upper ring in the same manner, then check the assembly for binding. Install the second compression ring expander and then the ring. The second ring is identified by a chamfer or step on its lower edge. Be sure the gap is correctly spaced. Install the top compression ring. This ring has its chamfer on its upper edge and is chrome faced.

Corvette rings are furnished in oversizes of 0.020 in., 0.030 in., and 0.040 in.

CAMSHAFT REMOVAL AND REPLACEMENT

Remove the radiator and shroud. Remove the fan and fan pulley. Use a gear puller to remove the harmonic balancer. Remove the oil pan, water pump, and the timing chain cover.

On top of the engine, remove the battery cables, carburetor(s)/fuel injection unit, distributor shielding, and distributor. Be sure to mark the distributor so that it will not be necessary to retime the engine.

When the intake manifold has been cleared of obstructions, remove it to expose the valve lifters. Cover the open area and remove the fuel pump and push rod.

Remove the rocker arm covers and rocker arms and withdraw the pushrods and lifters. Keep the pushrods and lifters in order so that they can be returned to their original positions. Remove the grille, timing chain, and camshaft

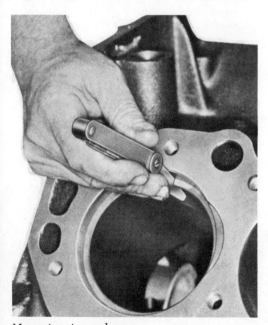
Measuring ring end-gap

Camshaft removal

sprocket. Loosen the engine side mount through bolts and jack up the front of the engine slightly. This is necessary for the camshaft to clear the radiator brace. Run two ⁵/₁₆–18 x 4 in. bolts into the camshaft bolt holes and carefully remove the camshaft from the engine. Do not rotate the crankshaft until the camshaft has been replaced and the sprocket and chain correctly installed and aligned. Alignment procedures are the same as those in the engine assembly section.

Reverse the operation to complete the replacement. Lubricate the cam and lifters with E.O.S. additive before installation. Make an initial and final valve adjustment as previously described.

VALVE LIFTERS

Two types of lifters are employed in the Corvette engine: mechanical and hydraulic. Mechanical lifters require no maintenance and in fact should not be disassembled. Wash the lifter in solvent, then dry and clear its oil holes with compressed air. If the lifter is scored or damaged, replace it. If the bottom of the lifter is scored, it is a good idea to check the corresponding camshaft lobe for damage. Whenever a lifter is replaced, E.O.S. additive should be used for a reasonable break-in period.

There are two hydraulic lifters available for Corvette engines. Their principles are the same and they are interchangeable as a unit but their parts are not interchangeable. They are simply identified as types A and B.

To disassemble either, depress the plunger with a pushrod and remove the pushrod retainer seat with a thin screwdriver blade. If the lifter is an A type, remove the pushrod seat and the metering valve. If a B, take out the seat and the inertia valve assembly. Pull out the plunger, check valve assembly and plunger spring. Pry the ball retainer loose and shake out the check valve and a spring.

Wash the disassembled lifter in solvent and replace the entire unit if damage or excessive wear is evident.

To assemble the lifter, invert the plunger and place the check ball over the hole in the plunger's end. Position the

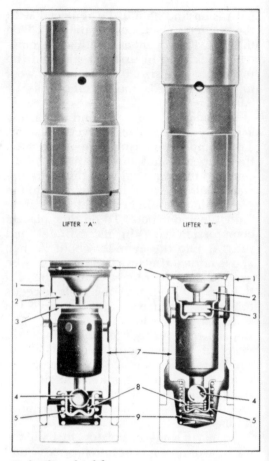

Hydraulic valve lifters

1. Lifter body
2. Pushrod seat
3. Metering valve (lifter A)
   Intertia valve (lifter B)
4. Check ball
5. Check ball retainer
6. Pushrod seat retainer
7. Plunger
8. Check ball spring
9. Plunger spring

check ball spring inside the ball so that the spring contacts the ball. Press-fit the retainer into the plunger. Place the plunger spring over the retainer, then slip the lifter body over the entire assembly. Make sure that the oil feed holes in the plunger and lifter body align.

Now turn the lifter over and fill it with SAE 10 oil. Depress the plunger with an ⅛ in. drift pin until the plunger seats and the oil holes are lined up. Slip the end of a ¹/₁₆ in. drift through the aligned oil holes to secure the plunger.

Withdraw the ⅛ in. drift pin and continue filling the assembly with oil. Refit the pushrod seat and metering valve assembly on A types, and the seat and inertia valve assembly on B types.

Engine Lubrication

OIL PAN

Removal and Installation

1. Disconnect the battery and remove the dipstick and its tube.
2. Raise the car and support the front on stands.
3. Remove the starter and flywheel shield.
4. Disconnect the steering idler arm and lower it out of the way.
5. Remove the oil pan and discard the side gaskets and end seals.
6. On high performance engines, the oil splash shield must be removed before further operations can be carried out.
7. Glue the side gaskets and end seals to the oil pan.
8. Install the pan on the engine and tighten the bolts in a criss-cross pattern. Do not overtighten these bolts.

REAR MAIN OIL SEAL

Replacement

The rear main bearing seal may be replaced without removing the crankshaft. Both upper and lower seals must be replaced at the same time.

1. Remove the oil pan and oil pump.
2. Remove the rear main bearing cap, and pry the seal out from the bottom with a small screwdriver.
3. Remove the upper seal with a small hammer and a brass pin punch. Tap on one end of the seal until the opposite end can be gripped with pliers.
4. Clean the bearing cap and crankshaft.
5. Coat the lips and bead of the seal with a light engine oil. Do not get oil on the seal ends.
6. Insert the new seal into the bearing cap, rolling it into place with your finger and thumb. Press lightly on the seal, so that the seal tangs on the cap don't cut the bead on the back of the seal.
7. Lubricate the lip of the new oil seal and slowly push it into place while turning the crankshaft. Make sure that the seal tangs don't cut the bead on the back of the seal.

8. Install the main bearing cap and torque to specifications.

OIL PUMP

The oil pump is a two-piece housing containing a pressure regulator valve and the two pump gears. It is driven by the distributor shaft, which is in turn driven off the camshaft.

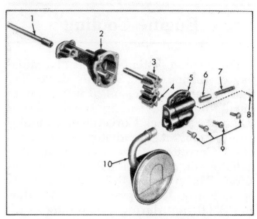

Exploded view of small block oil pump

1. Shaft extension
2. Pump body
3. Drive gear and shaft
4. Idler gear
5. Pump cover
6. Pressure regulator valve
7. Pressure regulator spring
8. Retaining pin
9. Screws
10. Pickup screen and pipe

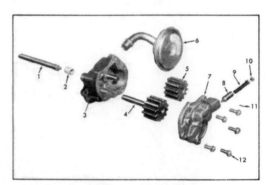

Exploded view of big block oil pump

1. Shaft extension
2. Shaft coupling
3. Pump body
4. Drive gear and shaft
5. Idler gear
6. Pickup screen and pipe
7. Pump cover
8. Pressure regulator valve
9. Pressure regulator spring
10. Washer
11. Retaining pin
12. Screws

Removal and Installation

1. Remove the oil pan.

2. Remove the oil pump-to-rear main bearing cap bolt. Remove the pump and the extension shaft.

3. Installation is the reverse of removal.

Engine Cooling

The cooling system consists of a radiator, expansion tank, viscous drive fan, thermostat, and mechanical water pump. Small block and certain special-performance large block Corvettes use an aluminum cross-flow radiator. Most large block Corvettes utilize a larger capacity radiator of conventional copper-brass alloy. The viscous drive fan restricts operation at 1500 rpm in cold weather and 3500 rpm during warmer temperatures. This fan requires less horsepower to drive during high rpm operation and reduces under-hood noise.

Corvettes equipped with aluminum radiators demand certain precautions during normal operation and maintenance. Caution is advised when removing and replacing the filler cap, to avoid denting or scratching the sealing surfaces of the filler neck. Do not use replacement filler caps that use brass in their construction. Extended use will damage the radiator and necessitate extensive repair or replacement. The same precautionary measure should be taken with replacement drain cocks. A ⅛ in. cast iron plug may be substituted only for an extremely short period of time. Use only antifreezes and cleaners that are recommended for aluminum cooling systems.

RADIATOR

Removal and Installation

1963–68

1. Drain the radiator and cylinder block.

2. Remove upper and lower hoses and expansion tank hose.

3. Remove radiator shroud(s).

4. Remove retaining clamps and care-

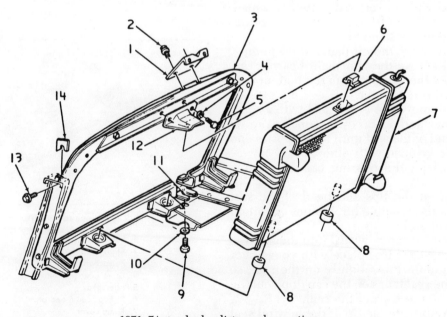

1971–74 standard radiator and mounting

1. Bracket	6. Upper cushion	11. Shim
2. Screw	7. Radiator	12. Bracket
3. Support	8. Cushion	13. Screw
4. Washer	9. Bolt	14. Shim
5. Bolt	10. Washer	

fully pull radiator up and out of vehicle.

5. Reverse this procedure to install the radiator. Be sure that the two rubber cushions are correctly seated under the radiator before tightening.

6. Refill the cooling system and check for leaks.

1969–74

1. Drain the radiator.

2. Raise the hood and insert a bolt in the hole of the hood support. Remove the hood.

3. Remove the radiator inlet and outlet hoses and, if applicable, the transmission coolant hoses.

4. If applicable, remove the supply tank hose at the radiator connection.

5. Remove the shroud to radiator support bracket screws (the L88 engine does not have a fan shroud).

6. Remove the shroud to radiator baffle bracket screws and let the shroud rest on the fan.

7. Remove the radiator upper support bracket screws and carefully lift the radiator from the car.

8. Install in the reverse order of removal.

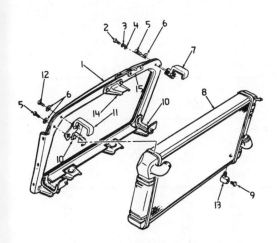

1971 heavy-duty 454 radiator and mounting

1. Support	9. Plug
2. Bolt	10. Insulator
3. Washer	11. Plate
4. Washer	12. Bolt
5. Bolt	13. Elbow
6. Washer	14. Bracket
7. Plate	15. Bracket
8. Radiator	

1975–76

1. Drain the radiator and disconnect the battery ground cable. Disconnect cooler lines on automatic transmission models.

2. Remove the hood. This is a two-man job.

3. Remove the radiator support brackets attached to the fan shroud.

4. Remove the two front hood hinge bolts.

5. From inside the wheel well, remove the six radiator side support bolts.

6. Remove the two bottom radiator support bolts and the center brace.

7. Pull the radiator support forward and use a clamp to retain it to the right hood hinge.

8. Disconnect the two radiator hoses and the overflow hose.

9. Carefully lift the radiator out of the car.

10. If replacing the radiator, remove the shrouds and mount them on the new unit.

11. Installation is the reverse of removal.

WATER PUMP

Removal and Installation

1. Drain the radiator.

2. Remove the fan.

3. Loosen the alternator mounting, rotate the alternator, and remove the fan belt. Remove power steering belt, A.I.R. belt, and idler belt, if so equipped.

4. Disconnect radiator and heater hoses.

5. Remove the water pump retaining bolts and remove the pump.

6. Reverse this procedure to install.

THERMOSTAT

Removal and Installation

1. Drain enough coolant from the radiator to bring the level below the thermostat.

2. Remove the two bolts retaining the water neck to the manifold.

3. Lift the water neck (with radiator hose attached) and remove the thermostat.

4. Reverse this procedure to install, using a new gasket.

Engine Rebuilding

This section describes, in detail, the procedures involved in rebuilding a typical engine. The procedures specifically refer to an inline engine, however, they are basically identical to those used in rebuilding engines of nearly all design and configurations. Procedures for servicing atypical engines (i.e., horizontally opposed) are described in the appropriate section, although in most cases, cylinder head reconditioning procedures described in this chapter will apply.

The section is divided into two sections. The first, Cylinder Head Reconditioning, assumes that the cylinder head is removed from the engine, all manifolds are removed, and the cylinder head is on a workbench. The camshaft should be removed from overhead cam cylinder heads. The second section, Cylinder Block Reconditioning, covers the block, pistons, connecting rods and crankshaft. It is assumed that the engine is mounted on a work stand, and the cylinder head and all accessories are removed.

Procedures are identified as follows:

Unmarked—Basic procedures that must be performed in order to successfully complete the rebuilding process.

Starred (*)—Procedures that should be performed to ensure maximum performance and engine life.

Double starred (**)—Procedures that may be performed to increase engine performance and reliability. These procedures are usually reserved for extremely heavy-duty or competition usage.

In many cases, a choice of methods is also provided. Methods are identified in the same manner as procedures. The choice of method for a procedure is at the discretion of the user.

The tools required for the basic rebuilding procedure should, with minor exceptions, be those

TORQUE (ft. lbs.)*

U.S.

Bolt Diameter (inches)	Bolt Grade (SAE)				Wrench Size (inches)	
	1 and 2	5	6	8	Bolt	Nut
1/4	5	7	10	10.5	3/8	7/16
5/16	9	14	19	22	1/2	9/16
3/8	15	25	34	37	9/16	5/8
7/16	24	40	55	60	5/8	3/4
1/2	37	60	85	92	3/4	13/16
9/16	53	88	120	132	7/8	7/8
5/8	74	120	167	180	15/16	1
3/4	120	200	280	296	1-1/8	1-1/8
7/8	190	302	440	473	1-5/16	1-5/16
1	282	466	660	714	1-1/2	1-1/2

Metric

Bolt Diameter (mm)	Bolt Grade				Wrench Size (mm) Bolt and Nut
	5D	8G	10K	12K	
6	5	6	8	10	10
8	10	16	22	27	14
10	19	31	40	49	17
12	34	54	70	86	19
14	55	89	117	137	22
16	83	132	175	208	24
18	111	182	236	283	27
22	182	284	394	464	32
24	261	419	570	689	36

*—Torque values are for lightly oiled bolts. CAUTION: Bolts threaded into aluminum require much less torque.

General Torque Specifications

96

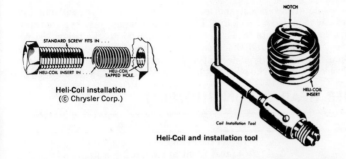

Heli-Coil installation
(© Chrysler Corp.)

Heli-Coil and installation tool

Heli-Coil Insert			Drill	Tap	Insert. Tool	Extract-ing Tool
Thread Size	Part No.	Insert Length (In.)	Size		Part No.	Part No.	Part No.
1/2 -20	1185-4	3/8	17/64 (.266)	4 CPB	528-4N	1227-6
5/16-18	1185-5	15/32	Q (.332)	5 CPB	528-5N	1227-6
3/8 -16	1185-6	9/16	X (.397)	6 CPB	528-6N	1227-6
7/16-14	1185-7	21/32	29/64 (.453)	7 CPB	528-7N	1227-16
1/2 -13	1185-8	3/4	33/64 (.516)	8 CPB	528-8N	1227-16

Heli-Coil Specifications

included in a mechanic's tool kit. An accurate torque wrench, and a dial indicator (reading in thousandths) mounted on a universal base should be available. Bolts and nuts with no torque specification should be tightened according to size (see chart). Special tools, where required, all are readily available from the major tool suppliers (i.e., Craftsman, Snap-On, K-D). The services of a competent automotive machine shop must also be readily available.

When assembling the engine, any parts that will be in frictional contact must be pre-lubricated, to provide protection on initial start-up. Vortex Pre-Lube, STP, or any product specifically formulated for this purpose may be used. NOTE: *Do not use engine oil.* Where semi-permanent (locked but removable) installation of bolts or nuts is desired, threads should be cleaned and coated with Loctite. Studs may be permanently installed using Loctite Stud and Bearing Mount.

Aluminum has become increasingly popular for use in engines, due to its low weight and excellent heat transfer characteristics. The following precautions

must be observed when handling aluminum engine parts:
—Never hot-tank aluminum parts.
—Remove all aluminum parts (identification tags, etc.) from engine parts before hot-tanking (otherwise they will be removed during the process).
—Always coat threads lightly with engine oil or anti-seize compounds before installation, to prevent seizure.
—Never over-torque bolts or spark plugs in aluminum threads. Should stripping occur, threads can be restored according to the following procedure, using Heli-Coil thread inserts:

Tap drill the hole with the stripped threads to the specified size (see chart). Using the specified tap (NOTE: *Heli-Coil tap sizes refer to the size thread being replaced, rather than the actual tap size*), tap the hole for the Heli-Coil. Place the insert on the proper installation tool (see chart). Apply pressure on the insert while winding it clockwise into the hole, until the top of the insert is one turn below the surface. Remove the installation tool, and break the installation tang from the bottom of the in-

sert by moving it up and down. If the Heli-Coil must be removed, tap the removal tool firmly into the hole, so that it engages the top thread, and turn the tool counter-clockwise to extract the insert.

Snapped bolts or studs may be removed, using a stud extractor (unthreaded) or Vise-Grip pliers (threaded). Penetrating oil (e.g., Liquid Wrench) will often aid in breaking frozen threads. In cases where the stud or bolt is flush with, or below the surface, proceed as follows:

Drill a hole in the broken stud or bolt, approximately 1/2 its diameter. Select a screw extractor (e.g., Easy-Out) of the proper size, and tap it into the stud or bolt. Turn the extractor counter-clockwise to remove the stud or bolt.

Magnaflux and Zyglo are inspection techniques used to locate material flaws, such as stress cracks. Magnafluxing coats the part with fine magnetic particles, and subjects the part to a magnetic field. Cracks cause breaks

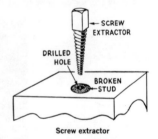

Screw extractor

in the magnetic field, which are outlined by the particles. Since Magnaflux is a magnetic process, it is applicable only to ferrous materials. The Zyglo process coats the material with a fluorescent dye penetrant, and then subjects it to blacklight inspection, under which cracks glow bright-

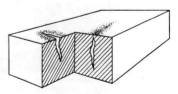

Magnaflux indication of cracks

ly. Parts made of any material may be tested using Zyglo. While Magnaflux and Zyglo are excellent for general inspection, and locating hidden defects, specific checks of suspected cracks may be made at lower cost and more readily using spot check dye. The dye is sprayed onto the suspected area, wiped off, and the area is then sprayed with a developer. Cracks then will show up brightly. Spot check dyes will only indicate surface cracks; therefore, structural cracks below the surface may escape detection. When questionable, the part should be tested using Magnaflux or Zyglo.

CYLINDER HEAD RECONDITIONING

Procedure	Method
Identify the valves: 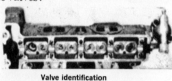 Valve identification (© SAAB)	Invert the cylinder head, and number the valve faces front to rear, using a permanent felt-tip marker.
Remove the rocker arms:	Remove the rocker arms with shaft(s) or balls and nuts. Wire the sets of rockers, balls and nuts together, and identify according to the corresponding valve.
Remove the valves and springs:	Using an appropriate valve spring compressor (depending on the configuration of the cylinder head), compress the valve springs. Lift out the keepers with needlenose pliers, release the compressor, and remove the valve, spring, and spring retainer.
Check the valve stem-to-guide clearance:  Checking the valve stem-to-guide clearance (© American Motors Corp.)	Clean the valve stem with lacquer thinner or a similar solvent to remove all gum and varnish. Clean the valve guides using solvent and an expanding wire-type valve guide cleaner. Mount a dial indicator so that the stem is at 90° to the valve stem, as close to the valve guide as possible. Move the valve off its seat, and measure the valve guide-to-stem clearance by moving the stem back and forth to actuate the dial indicator. Measure the valve stems using a micrometer, and compare to specifications, to determine whether stem or guide wear is responsible for excessive clearance.
De-carbon the cylinder head and valves:  Removing carbon from the cylinder head (© Chevrolet Div. G.M. Corp.)	Chip carbon away from the valve heads, combustion chambers, and ports, using a chisel made of hardwood. Remove the remaining deposits with a stiff wire brush. NOTE: *Ensure that the deposits are actually removed, rather than burnished.*

Procedure	Method
Hot-tank the cylinder head:	Have the cylinder head hot-tanked to remove grease, corrosion, and scale from the water passages. NOTE: *In the case of overhead cam cylinder heads, consult the operator to determine whether the camshaft bearings will be damaged by the caustic solution.*
Degrease the remaining cylinder head parts:	Using solvent (i.e., Gunk), clean the rockers, rocker shaft(s) (where applicable), rocker balls and nuts, springs, spring retainers, and keepers. Do not remove the protective coating from the springs.
Check the cylinder head for warpage:  **Checking the cylinder head for warpage** (© Ford Motor Co.)	Place a straight-edge across the gasket surface of the cylinder head. Using feeler gauges, determine the clearance at the center of the straight-edge. Measure across both diagonals, along the longitudinal centerline, and across the cylinder head at several points. If warpage exceeds .003″ in a 6″ span, or .006″ over the total length, the cylinder head must be resurfaced. NOTE: *If warpage exceeds the manufacturers maximum tolerance for material removal, the cylinder head must be replaced.* When milling the cylinder heads of V-type engines, the intake manifold mounting position is altered, and must be corrected by milling the manifold flange a proportionate amount.
** Porting and gasket matching:  **Marking the cylinder head for gasket matching** (© Petersen Publishing Co.)  **Port configuration before and after gasket matching** (© Petersen Publishing Co.)	** Coat the manifold flanges of the cylinder head with Prussian blue dye. Glue intake and exhaust gaskets to the cylinder head in their installed position using rubber cement and scribe the outline of the ports on the manifold flanges. Remove the gaskets. Using a small cutter in a hand-held power tool (i.e., Dremel Moto-Tool), gradually taper the walls of the port out to the scribed outline of the gasket. Further enlargement of the ports should include the removal of sharp edges and radiusing of sharp corners. Do not alter the valve guides. NOTE: *The most efficient port configuration is determined only by extensive testing. Therefore, it is best to consult someone experienced with the head in question to determine the optimum alterations.*

Procedure	*Method*

** Polish the ports:

Relieved and polished ports
(© Petersen Publishing Co.)

Polished combustion chamber
(© Petersen Publishing Co.)

** Using a grinding stone with the above mentioned tool, polish the walls of the intake and exhaust ports, and combustion chamber. Use progressively finer stones until all surface imperfections are removed. NOTE: *Through testing, it has been determined that a smooth surface is more effective than a mirror polished surface in intake ports, and vice-versa in exhaust ports.*

---

* Knurling the valve guides:

Cut-away view of a knurled valve guide
(© Petersen Publishing Co.)

* Valve guides which are not excessively worn or distorted may, in some cases, be knurled rather than replaced. Knurling is a process in which metal is displaced and raised, thereby reducing clearance. Knurling also provides excellent oil control. The possibility of knurling rather than replacing valve guides should be discussed with a machinist.

Replacing the valve guides: NOTE: *Valve guides should only be replaced if damaged or if an oversize valve stem is not available.*

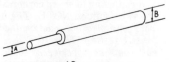

A-VALVE GUIDE I.D.
B-SLIGHTLY SMALLER THAN VALVE GUIDE O.D.

Valve guide removal tool

WASHERS

A-VALVE GUIDE I.D.
B-LARGER THAN THE VALVE GUIDE O.D.

Valve guide installation tool (with washers used during installation)

Depending on the type of cylinder head, valve guides may be pressed, hammered, or shrunk in. In cases where the guides are shrunk into the head, replacement should be left to an equipped machine shop. In other cases, the guides are replaced as follows: Press or tap the valve guides out of the head using a stepped drift (see illustration). Determine the height above the boss that the guide must extend, and obtain a stack of washers, their I.D. similar to the guide's O.D., of that height. Place the stack of washers on the guide, and insert the guide into the boss. NOTE: *Valve guides are often tapered or beveled for installation.* Using the stepped installation tool (see illustration), press or tap the guides into position. Ream the guides according to the size of the valve stem.

Procedure	*Method*
Replacing valve seat inserts:	Replacement of valve seat inserts which are worn beyond resurfacing or broken, if feasible, must be done by a machine shop.
Resurfacing (grinding) the valve face:  **Grinding a valve** (© Subaru) 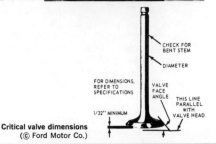 **Critical valve dimensions** (© Ford Motor Co.)	Using a valve grinder, resurface the valves according to specifications. CAUTION: *Valve face angle is not always identical to valve seat angle.* A minimum margin of 1/32″ should remain after grinding the valve. The valve stem tip should also be squared and resurfaced, by placing the stem in the V-block of the grinder, and turning it while pressing lightly against the grinding wheel.
Resurfacing the valve seats using reamers:  **Reaming the valve seat** (© S.p.A. Fiat) **Valve seat width and centering** (© Ford Motor Co.)	Select a reamer of the correct seat angle, slightly larger than the diameter of the valve seat, and assemble it with a pilot of the correct size. Install the pilot into the valve guide, and using steady pressure, turn the reamer clockwise. CAUTION: *Do not turn the reamer counter-clockwise.* Remove only as much material as necessary to clean the seat. Check the concentricity of the seat (see below). If the dye method is not used, coat the valve face with Prussian blue dye, install and rotate it on the valve seat. Using the dye marked area as a centering guide, center and narrow the valve seat to specifications with correction cutters. NOTE: *When no specifications are available, minimum seat width for exhaust valves should be 5/64″, intake valves 1/16″.* After making correction cuts, check the position of the valve seat on the valve face using Prussian blue dye.
* Resurfacing the valve seats using a grinder:  **Grinding a valve seat** (© Subaru)	Select a pilot of the correct size, and a coarse stone of the correct seat angle. Lubricate the pilot if necessary, and install the tool in the valve guide. Move the stone on and off the seat at approximately two cycles per second, until all flaws are removed from the seat. Install a fine stone, and finish the seat. Center and narrow the seat using correction stones, as described above.

Procedure	Method
Checking the valve seat concentricity: 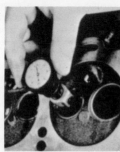 **Checking the valve seat concentricity using a dial gauge** (© American Motors Corp.)	Coat the valve face with Prussian blue dye, install the valve, and rotate it on the valve seat. If the entire seat becomes coated, and the valve is known to be concentric, the seat is concentric.
	* Install the dial gauge pilot into the guide, and rest the arm on the valve seat. Zero the gauge, and rotate the arm around the seat. Run-out should not exceed .002″.
* Lapping the valves: NOTE: *Valve lapping is done to ensure efficient sealing of resurfaced valves and seats. Valve lapping alone is not recommended for use as a resurfacing procedure.*  **Hand lapping the valves**  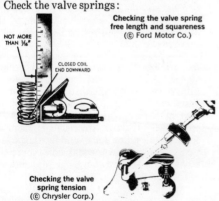 HAND DRILL / ROD / SUCTION CUP **Home made mechanical valve lapping tool**	* Invert the cylinder head, lightly lubricate the valve stems, and install the valves in the head as numbered. Coat valve seats with fine grinding compound, and attach the lapping tool suction cup to a valve head (NOTE: *Moisten the suction cup*). Rotate the tool between the palms, changing position and lifting the tool often to prevent grooving. Lap the valve until a smooth, polished seat is evident. Remove the valve and tool, and rinse away all traces of grinding compound.
	** Fasten a suction cup to a piece of drill rod, and mount the rod in a hand drill. Proceed as above, using the hand drill as a lapping tool. CAUTION: *Due to the higher speeds involved when using the hand drill, care must be exercised to avoid grooving the seat.* Lift the tool and change direction of rotation often.
Check the valve springs: **Checking the valve spring free length and squareness** (© Ford Motor Co.) NOT MORE THAN 1/16″ CLOSED COIL END DOWNWARD **Checking the valve spring tension** (© Chrysler Corp.)	Place the spring on a flat surface next to a square. Measure the height of the spring, and rotate it against the edge of the square to measure distortion. If spring height varies (by comparison) by more than 1/16″ or if distortion exceeds 1/16″, replace the spring.
	** In addition to evaluating the spring as above, test the spring pressure at the installed and compressed (installed height minus valve lift) height using a valve spring tester. Springs used on small displacement engines (up to 3 liters) should be ± 1 lb. of all other springs in either position. A tolerance of ± 5 lbs. is permissible on larger engines.

Procedure	Method
* Install valve stem seals:  **Valve stem seal installation** (© Ford Motor Co.) SEAL	* Due to the pressure differential that exists at the ends of the intake valve guides (atmospheric pressure above, manifold vacuum below), oil is drawn through the valve guides into the intake port. This has been alleviated somewhat since the addition of positive crankcase ventilation, which lowers the pressure above the guides. Several types of valve stem seals are available to reduce blow-by. Certain seals simply slip over the stem and guide boss, while others require that the boss be machined. Recently, Teflon guide seals have become popular. Consult a parts supplier or machinist concerning availability and suggested usages. NOTE: *When installing seals, ensure that a small amount of oil is able to pass the seal to lubricate the valve guides; otherwise, excessive wear may result.*
Install the valves:	Lubricate the valve stems, and install the valves in the cylinder head as numbered. Lubricate and position the seals (if used, see above) and the valve springs. Install the spring retainers, compress the springs, and insert the keys using needlenose pliers or a tool designed for this purpose. NOTE: *Retain the keys with wheel bearing grease during installation.*
Checking valve spring installed height: 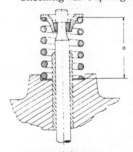  **Valve spring installed height dimension** (© Porsche) **Measuring valve spring installed height** (© Petersen Publishing Co.)	Measure the distance between the spring pad and the lower edge of the spring retainer, and compare to specifications. If the installed height is incorrect, add shim washers between the spring pad and the spring. CAUTION: *Use only washers designed for this purpose.*
** CC'ing the combustion chambers:	** Invert the cylinder head and place a bead of sealer around a combustion chamber. Install an apparatus designed for this purpose (burette mounted on a clear plate; see illustration) over the combustion chamber, and fill with the specified fluid to an even mark on the burette. Record the burette reading, and fill the combustion chamber with fluid. (NOTE: *A hole drilled in the plate will permit air to escape*). Subtract the burette reading, with the combustion chamber filled, from the previous reading, to determine combustion chamber volume in cc's. Duplicate this procedure in all combustion

Procedure	Method

CC'ing the combustion chamber
(© Petersen Publishing Co.)

chambers on the cylinder head, and compare the readings. The volume of all combustion chambers should be made equal to that of the largest. Combustion chamber volume may be increased in two ways. When only a small change is required (usually), a small cutter or coarse stone may be used to remove material from the combustion chamber. NOTE: *Check volume frequently.* Remove material over a wide area, so as not to change the configuration of the combustion chamber. When a larger change is required, the valve seat may be sunk (lowered into the head). NOTE: *When altering valve seat, remember to compensate for the change in spring installed height.*

Inspect the rocker arms, balls, studs, and nuts (where applicable):

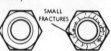

Stress cracks in rocker nuts
(© Ford Motor Co.)

Visually inspect the rocker arms, balls, studs, and nuts for cracks, galling, burning, scoring, or wear. If all parts are intact, liberally lubricate the rocker arms and balls, and install them on the cylinder head. If wear is noted on a rocker arm at the point of valve contact, grind it smooth and square, removing as little material as possible. Replace the rocker arm if excessively worn. If a rocker stud shows signs of wear, it must be replaced (see below). If a rocker nut shows stress cracks, replace it. If an exhaust ball is galled or burned, substitute the intake ball from the same cylinder (if it is intact), and install a new intake ball. NOTE: *Avoid using new rocker balls on exhaust valves.*

Replacing rocker studs:

Reaming the stud bore for oversize rocker studs
(© Buick Div. G.M. Corp.)

Extracting a pressed in rocker stud
(© Buick Div. G.M. Corp.)

In order to remove a threaded stud, lock two nuts on the stud, and unscrew the stud using the lower nut. Coat the lower threads of the new stud with Loctite, and install.

Two alternative methods are available for replacing pressed in studs. Remove the damaged stud using a stack of washers and a nut (see illustration). In the first, the boss is reamed .005-.006″ oversize, and an oversize stud pressed in. Control the stud extension over the boss using washers, in the same manner as valve guides. Before installing the stud, coat it with white lead and grease. To retain the stud more positively, drill a hole through the stud and boss, and install a roll pin. In the second method, the boss is tapped, and a threaded stud installed. Retain the stud using Loctite Stud and Bearing Mount.

Procedure	Method
Inspect the rocker shaft(s) and rocker arms (where applicable):  Disassembled rocker shaft parts arranged for inspection (© American Motors Corp.) 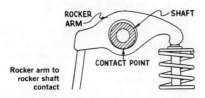 ROCKER ARM — SHAFT CONTACT POINT Rocker arm to rocker shaft contact	Remove rocker arms, springs and washers from rocker shaft. NOTE: *Lay out parts in the order they are removed.* Inspect rocker arms for pitting or wear on the valve contact point, or excessive bushing wear. Bushings need only be replaced if wear is excessive, because the rocker arm normally contacts the shaft at one point only. Grind the valve contact point of rocker arm smooth if necessary, removing as little material as possible. If excessive material must be removed to smooth and square the arm, it should be replaced. Clean out all oil holes and passages in rocker shaft. If shaft is grooved or worn, replace it. Lubricate and assemble the rocker shaft.
Inspect the camshaft bushings and the camshaft (overhead cam engines):	See next section.
Inspect the pushrods:	Remove the pushrods, and, if hollow, clean out the oil passages using fine wire. Roll each pushrod over a piece of clean glass. If a distinct clicking sound is heard as the pushrod rolls, the rod is bent, and must be replaced.
	* The length of all pushrods must be equal. Measure the length of the pushrods, compare to specifications, and replace as necessary.
Inspect the valve lifters: 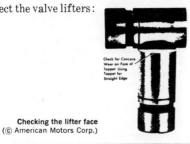 Check for Concave Wear on Face of Tappet Using Tappet for Straight Edge Checking the lifter face (© American Motors Corp.)	Remove lifters from their bores, and remove gum and varnish, using solvent. Clean walls of lifter bores. Check lifters for concave wear as illustrated. If face is worn concave, replace lifter, and carefully inspect the camshaft. Lightly lubricate lifter and insert it into its bore. If play is excessive, an oversize lifter must be installed (where possible). Consult a machinist concerning feasibility. If play is satisfactory, remove, lubricate, and reinstall the lifter.
* Testing hydraulic lifter leak down:  Lock Ring Plunger Cap Push Rod Socket Metering Disc Plunger Valve Seat Valve Valve Spring Valve Retainer Plunger Return Spring Tappet Body Exploded view of a typical hydraulic lifter (© American Motors Corp.)	Submerge lifter in a container of kerosene. Chuck a used pushrod or its equivalent into a drill press. Position container of kerosene so pushrod acts on the lifter plunger. Pump lifter with the drill press, until resistance increases. Pump several more times to bleed any air out of lifter. Apply very firm, constant pressure to the lifter, and observe rate at which fluid bleeds out of lifter. If the fluid bleeds very quickly (less than 15 seconds), lifter is defective. If the time exceeds 60 seconds, lifter is sticking. In either case, recondition or replace lifter. If lifter is operating properly (leak down time 15-60 seconds), lubricate and install it.

CYLINDER BLOCK RECONDITIONING

Procedure	*Method*

Checking the main bearing clearance:

Plastigage installed on main bearing journal
(© Chevrolet Div. G.M. Corp.)

Measuring Plastigage to determine
main bearing clearance
(© Chevrolet Div. G.M. Corp.)

Causes of bearing failure
(© Ford Motor Co.)

Invert engine, and remove cap from the bearing to be checked. Using a clean, dry rag, thoroughly clean all oil from crankshaft journal and bearing insert. NOTE: *Plastigage is soluble in oil; therefore, oil on the journal or bearing could result in erroneous readings.* Place a piece of Plastigage along the full length of journal, reinstall cap, and torque to specifications. Remove bearing cap, and determine bearing clearance by comparing width of Plastigage to the scale on Plastigage envelope. Journal taper is determined by comparing width of the Plastigage strip near its ends. Rotate crankshaft 90° and retest, to determine journal eccentricity. NOTE: *Do not rotate crankshaft with Plastigage installed.* If bearing insert and journal appear intact, and are within tolerances, no further main bearing service is required. If bearing or journal appear defective, cause of failure should be determined before replacement.

* Remove crankshaft from block (see below). Measure the main bearing journals at each end twice (90° apart) using a micrometer, to determine diameter, journal taper and eccentricity. If journals are within tolerances, reinstall bearing caps at their specified torque. Using a telescope gauge and micrometer, measure bearing I.D. parallel to piston axis and at 30° on each side of piston axis. Subtract journal O.D. from bearing I.D. to determine oil clearance. If crankshaft journals appear defective, or do not meet tolerances, there is no need to measure bearings; for the crankshaft will require grinding and/or undersize bearings will be required. If bearing appears defective, cause for failure should be determined prior to replacement.

Checking the connecting rod bearing clearance:

Plastigage installed on connecting rod
bearing journal
(© Chevrolet Div. G.M. Corp.)

Connecting rod bearing clearance is checked in the same manner as main bearing clearance, using Plastigage. Before removing the crankshaft, connecting rod side clearance also should be measured and recorded.

* Checking connecting rod bearing clearance, using a micrometer, is identical to checking main bearing clearance. If no other service

Procedure	Method

Measuring Plastigage to determine
connecting rod bearing clearance
(© Chevrolet Div. G.M. Corp.)

is required, the piston and rod assemblies need not be removed.

Removing the crankshaft:

Connecting rod matching marks
(© Ford Motor Co.)

Using a punch, mark the corresponding main bearing caps and saddles according to position (i.e., one punch on the front main cap and saddle, two on the second, three on the third, etc.). Using number stamps, identify the corresponding connecting rods and caps, according to cylinder (if no numbers are present). Remove the main and connecting rod caps, and place sleeves of plastic tubing over the connecting rod bolts, to protect the journals as the crankshaft is removed. Lift the crankshaft out of the block.

Remove the ridge from the top of the cylinder:

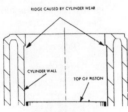

RIDGE CAUSED BY CYLINDER WEAR

CYLINDER WALL   TOP OF PISTON

Cylinder bore ridge
(© Pontiac Div. G.M. Corp.)

In order to facilitate removal of the piston and connecting rod, the ridge at the top of the cylinder (unworn area; see illustration) must be removed. Place the piston at the bottom of the bore, and cover it with a rag. Cut the ridge away using a ridge reamer, exercising extreme care to avoid cutting too deeply. Remove the rag, and remove cuttings that remain on the piston. CAUTION: *If the ridge is not removed, and new rings are installed, damage to rings will result.*

Removing the piston and connecting rod:

Removing the piston
(© SAAB)

Invert the engine, and push the pistons and connecting rods out of the cylinders. If necessary, tap the connecting rod boss with a wooden hammer handle, to force the piston out. CAUTION: *Do not attempt to force the piston past the cylinder ridge* (see above).

Procedure	Method
Service the crankshaft:	Ensure that all oil holes and passages in the crankshaft are open and free of sludge. If necessary, have the crankshaft ground to the largest possible undersize.
	** Have the crankshaft Magnafluxed, to locate stress cracks. Consult a machinist concerning additional service procedures, such as surface hardening (e.g., nitriding, Tuftriding) to improve wear characteristics, cross drilling and chamfering the oil holes to improve lubrication, and balancing.
Removing freeze plugs:	Drill a hole in the center of the freeze plugs, and pry them out using a screwdriver or drift.
Remove the oil gallery plugs:	Threaded plugs should be removed using an appropriate (usually square) wrench. To remove soft, pressed in plugs, drill a hole in the plug, and thread in a sheet metal screw. Pull the plug out by the screw using pliers.
Hot-tank the block:	Have the block hot-tanked to remove grease, corrosion, and scale from the water jackets. NOTE: *Consult the operator to determine whether the camshaft bearings will be damaged during the hot-tank process.*
Check the block for cracks:	Visually inspect the block for cracks or chips. The most common locations are as follows: Adjacent to freeze plugs. Between the cylinders and water jackets. Adjacent to the main bearing saddles. At the extreme bottom of the cylinders. Check only suspected cracks using spot check dye (see introduction). If a crack is located, consult a machinist concerning possible repairs.
	** Magnaflux the block to locate hidden cracks. If cracks are located, consult a machinist about feasibility of repair.
Install the oil gallery plugs and freeze plugs:	Coat freeze plugs with sealer and tap into position using a piece of pipe, slightly smaller than the plug, as a driver. To ensure retention, stake the edges of the plugs. Coat threaded oil gallery plugs with sealer and install. Drive replacement soft plugs into block using a large drift as a driver.
	* Rather than reinstalling lead plugs, drill and tap the holes, and install threaded plugs.

Procedure	Method

Check the bore diameter and surface:

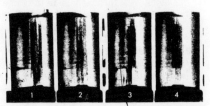

1, 2, 3 Piston skirt seizure resulted in this pattern. Engine
must be rebored

4. Piston skirt and oil ring
seizure caused this damage.
Engine must be rebored

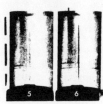

5, 6 Score marks caused by a
split piston skirt. Damage is
not serious enough to warrant
reboring

7. Ring seized longitudinally,
causing a score mark
1 3/16″ wide, on the land
side of the piston groove.
The honing pattern is de-
stroyed and the cylinder
must be rebored

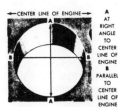

8. Result of oil ring seizure.
Engine must be rebored

9. Oil ring seizure here was not
serious enough to warrant
reboring. The honing
marks are still visible

Cylinder wall damage
(© Daimler-Benz A.G.)

Visually inspect the cylinder bores for roughness, scoring, or scuffing. If evident, the cylinder bore must be bored or honed oversize
to eliminate imperfections, and the smallest
possible oversize piston used. The new pistons should be given to the machinist with
the block, so that the cylinders can be bored
or honed exactly to the piston size (plus
clearance). If no flaws are evident, measure
the bore diameter using a telescope gauge
and micrometer, or dial gauge, parallel and
perpendicular to the engine centerline, at
the top (below the ridge) and bottom of the
bore. Subtract the bottom measurements
from the top to determine taper, and the
parallel to the centerline measurements
from the perpendicular measurements to
determine eccentricity. If the measurements
are not within specifications, the cylinder
must be bored or honed, and an oversize piston installed. If the measurements are within specifications the cylinder may be used
as is, with only finish honing (see below).
NOTE: *Prior to submitting the block for
boring, perform the following operation(s).*

Cylinder bore measuring
positions
(© Ford Motor Co.)

Measuring the cylinder bore
with a telescope gauge
(© Buick Div. G.M. Corp.)

Determining the cylinder bore
by measuring the telescope
gauge with a micrometer
(© Buick Div. G.M. Corp.)

Measuring the cylinder bore
with a dial gauge
(© Chevrolet Div. G.M. Corp.)

Procedure	Method
Check the block deck for warpage:	Using a straightedge and feeler gauges, check the block deck for warpage in the same manner that the cylinder head is checked (see Cylinder Head Reconditioning). If warpage exceeds specifications, have the deck resurfaced. NOTE: *In certain cases a specification for total material removal (Cylinder head and block deck) is provided. This specification must not be exceeded.*
* Check the deck height:	The deck height is the distance from the crankshaft centerline to the block deck. To measure, invert the engine, and install the crankshaft, retaining it with the center main cap. Measure the distance from the crankshaft journal to the block deck, parallel to the cylinder centerline. Measure the diameter of the end (front and rear) main journals, parallel to the centerline of the cylinders, divide the diameter in half, and subtract it from the previous measurement. The results of the front and rear measurements should be identical. If the difference exceeds .005", the deck height should be corrected. NOTE: *Block deck height and warpage should be corrected concurrently.*
Check the cylinder block bearing alignment:  **Checking main bearing saddle alignment** (© Petersen Publishing Co.)	Remove the upper bearing inserts. Place a straightedge in the bearing saddles along the centerline of the crankshaft. If clearance exists between the straightedge and the center saddle, the block must be align-bored.
Clean and inspect the pistons and connecting rods:  Piston ring expander **Removing the piston rings** (© Subaru)	Using a ring expander, remove the rings from the piston. Remove the retaining rings (if so equipped) and remove piston pin. NOTE: *If the piston pin must be pressed out, determine the proper method and use the proper tools; otherwise the piston will distort.* Clean the ring grooves using an appropriate tool, exercising care to avoid cutting too deeply. Thoroughly clean all carbon and varnish from the piston with solvent. CAUTION: *Do not use a wire brush or caustic solvent on pistons.* Inspect the pistons for scuffing, scoring, cracks, pitting, or excessive ring groove wear. If wear is evident, the piston must be replaced. Check the connecting rod length by measuring the rod from the inside of the large end to the inside of the small end using calipers (see

Procedure	Method

Cleaning the piston ring grooves
(© Ford Motor Co.)

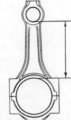

Connecting rod
length checking
dimension

illustration). All connecting rods should be equal length. Replace any rod that differs from the others in the engine.

* Have the connecting rod alignment checked in an alignment fixture by a machinist. Replace any twisted or bent rods.

* Magnaflux the connecting rods to locate stress cracks. If cracks are found, replace the connecting rod.

Fit the pistons to the cylinders:

Measuring the cylinder
with a telescope gauge
for piston fitting
(© Buick Div.
G.M. Corp.)

Measuring the piston
for fitting
(© Buick Div.
G.M. Corp.)

Using a telescope gauge and micrometer, or a dial gauge, measure the cylinder bore diameter perpendicular to the piston pin, $2\frac{1}{2}''$ below the deck. Measure the piston perpendicular to its pin on the skirt. The difference between the two measurements is the piston clearance. If the clearance is within specifications or slightly below (after boring or honing), finish honing is all that is required. If the clearance is excessive, try to obtain a slightly larger piston to bring clearance within specifications. Where this is not possible, obtain the first oversize piston, and hone (or if necessary, bore) the cylinder to size.

Assemble the pistons and connecting rods:

Installing piston pin lock rings
(© Nissan Motor Co., Ltd.)

Inspect piston pin, connecting rod small end bushing, and piston bore for galling, scoring, or excessive wear. If evident, replace defective part(s). Measure the I.D. of the piston boss and connecting rod small end, and the O.D. of the piston pin. If within specifications, assemble piston pin and rod. CAUTION: *If piston pin must be pressed in, determine the proper method and use the proper tools; otherwise the piston will distort.* Install the lock rings; ensure that they seat properly. If the parts are not within specifications, determine the service method for the type of engine. In some cases, piston and pin are serviced as an assembly when either is defective. Others specify reaming the piston and connecting rods for an oversize pin. If the connecting rod bushing is worn, it may in many cases be replaced. Reaming the piston and replacing the rod bushing are machine shop operations.

Procedure	*Method*

Clean and inspect the camshaft:

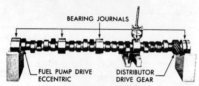

BEARING JOURNALS

FUEL PUMP DRIVE ECCENTRIC   DISTRIBUTOR DRIVE GEAR

Checking the camshaft for straightness
(© Chevrolet Motor Div. G.M. Corp.)

Camshaft lobe measurement
(© Ford Motor Co.)

Degrease the camshaft, using solvent, and clean out all oil holes. Visually inspect cam lobes and bearing journals for excessive wear. If a lobe is questionable, check all lobes as indicated below. If a journal or lobe is worn, the camshaft must be reground or replaced. NOTE: *If a journal is worn, there is a good chance that the bushings are worn.* If lobes and journals appear intact, place the front and rear journals in V-blocks, and rest a dial indicator on the center journal. Rotate the camshaft to check straightness. If deviation exceeds .001″, replace the camshaft.

* Check the camshaft lobes with a micrometer, by measuring the lobes from the nose to base and again at 90° (see illustration). The lift is determined by subtracting the second measurement from the first. If all exhaust lobes and all intake lobes are not identical, the camshaft must be reground or replaced.

Replace the camshaft bearings:

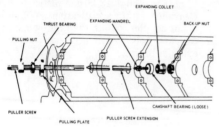

EXPANDING COLLET

THRUST BEARING   EXPANDING MANDREL   BACK-UP NUT

PULLING NUT

PULLER SCREW   CAMSHAFT BEARING (LOOSE)

PULLING PLATE   PULLER SCREW EXTENSION

Camshaft removal and installation tool (typical)
(© Ford Motor Co.)

If excessive wear is indicated, or if the engine is being completely rebuilt, camshaft bearings should be replaced as follows: Drive the camshaft rear plug from the block. Assemble the removal puller with its shoulder on the bearing to be removed. Gradually tighten the puller nut until bearing is removed. Remove remaining bearings, leaving the front and rear for last. To remove front and rear bearings, reverse position of the tool, so as to pull the bearings in toward the center of the block. Leave the tool in this position, pilot the new front and rear bearings on the installer, and pull them into position. Return the tool to its original position and pull remaining bearings into position. NOTE: *Ensure that oil holes align when installing bearings.* Replace camshaft rear plug, and stake it into position to aid retention.

Finish hone the cylinders:

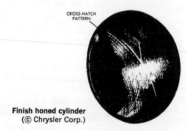

CROSS-HATCH PATTERN

Finish honed cylinder
(© Chrysler Corp.)

Chuck a flexible drive hone into a power drill, and insert it into the cylinder. Start the hone, and move it up and down in the cylinder at a rate which will produce approximately a 60° cross-hatch pattern (see illustration). NOTE: *Do not extend the hone below the cylinder bore.* After developing the pattern, remove the hone and recheck piston fit. Wash the cylinders with a detergent and water solution to remove abrasive dust, dry, and wipe several times with a rag soaked in engine oil.

Procedure	Method
Check piston ring end-gap:  **Checking ring end-gap** (© Chevrolet Motor Div. G.M. Corp.)	Compress the piston rings to be used in a cylinder, one at a time, into that cylinder, and press them approximately 1″ below the deck with an inverted piston. Using feeler gauges, measure the ring end-gap, and compare to specifications. Pull the ring out of the cylinder and file the ends with a fine file to obtain proper clearance. CAUTION: *If inadequate ring end-gap is utilized, ring breakage will result.*
Install the piston rings: 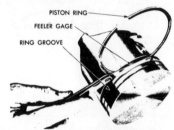 **Checking ring side clearance** (© Chrysler Corp.) 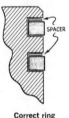 CORRECT INCORRECT Correct ring Piston groove depth spacer installation	Inspect the ring grooves in the piston for excessive wear or taper. If necessary, recut the groove(s) for use with an overwidth ring or a standard ring and spacer. If the groove is worn uniformly, overwidth rings, or standard rings and spacers may be installed without recutting. Roll the outside of the ring around the groove to check for burrs or deposits. If any are found, remove with a fine file. Hold the ring in the groove, and measure side clearance. If necessary, correct as indicated above. NOTE: *Always install any additional spacers above the piston ring.* The ring groove must be deep enough to allow the ring to seat below the lands (see illustration). In many cases, a "go-no-go" depth gauge will be provided with the piston rings. Shallow grooves may be corrected by recutting, while deep grooves require some type of filler or expander behind the piston. Consult the piston ring supplier concerning the suggested method. Install the rings on the piston, lowest ring first, using a ring expander. NOTE: *Position the ring markings as specified by the manufacturer (see car section).*
Install the camshaft:	Liberally lubricate the camshaft lobes and journals, and slide the camshaft into the block. CAUTION: *Exercise extreme care to avoid damaging the bearings when inserting the camshaft.* Install and tighten the camshaft thrust plate retaining bolts.
Check camshaft end-play:  **Checking camshaft end-play with a feeler gauge** (© Ford Motor Co.)	Using feeler gauges, determine whether the clearance between the camshaft boss (or gear) and backing plate is within specifications. Install shims behind the thrust plate, or reposition the camshaft gear and retest end-play.

Procedure	Method

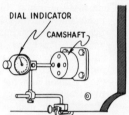

Checking camshaft end-play with a dial indicator

* Mount a dial indicator stand so that the stem of the dial indicator rests on the nose of the camshaft, parallel to the camshaft axis. Push the camshaft as far in as possible and zero the gauge. Move the camshaft outward to determine the amount of camshaft end-play. If the end-play is not within tolerance, install shims behind the thrust plate, or reposition the camshaft gear and retest.

Install the rear main seal (where applicable):

Seating the rear main seal
(© Buick Div. G.M. Corp.)

Position the block with the bearing saddles facing upward. Lay the rear main seal in its groove and press it lightly into its seat. Place a piece of pipe the same diameter as the crankshaft journal into the saddle, and firmly seat the seal. Hold the pipe in position, and trim the ends of the seal flush if required.

Install the crankshaft:

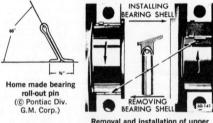

Home made bearing roll-out pin
(© Pontiac Div. G.M. Corp.)

Removal and installation of upper bearing insert using a roll-out pin
(© Buick Div. G.M. Corp.)

Thoroughly clean the main bearing saddles and caps. Place the upper halves of the bearing inserts on the saddles and press into position. NOTE: *Ensure that the oil holes align.* Press the corresponding bearing inserts into the main bearing caps. Lubricate the upper main bearings, and lay the crankshaft in position. Place a strip of Plastigage on each of the crankshaft journals, install the main caps, and torque to specifications. Remove the main caps, and compare the Plastigage to the scale on the Plastigage envelope. If clearances are within tolerances, remove the Plastigage, turn the crankshaft 90°, wipe off all oil and retest. If all clearances are correct, remove all Plastigage, thoroughly

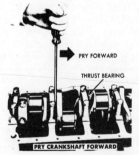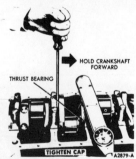

Aligning the thrust bearing
(© Ford Motor Co.)

Procedure	Method
	lubricate the main caps and bearing journals, and install the main caps. If clearances are not within tolerance, the upper bearing inserts may be removed, without removing the crankshaft, using a bearing roll out pin (see illustration). Roll in a bearing that will provide proper clearance, and retest. Torque all main caps, excluding the thrust bearing cap, to specifications. Tighten the thrust bearing cap finger tight. To properly align the thrust bearing, pry the crankshaft the extent of its axial travel several times, the last movement held toward the front of the engine, and torque the thrust bearing cap to specifications. Determine the crankshaft end-play (see below), and bring within tolerance with thrust washers.
Measure crankshaft end-play:  Checking crankshaft end-play with a dial indicator (© Ford Motor Co.)  Checking crankshaft end-play with a feeler gauge (© Chevrolet Div. (G.M. Corp.)	Mount a dial indicator stand on the front of the block, with the dial indicator stem resting on the nose of the crankshaft, parallel to the crankshaft axis. Pry the crankshaft the extent of its travel rearward, and zero the indicator. Pry the crankshaft forward and record crankshaft end-play. NOTE: *Crankshaft end-play also may be measured at the thrust bearing, using feeler gauges* (see illustration). 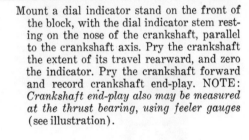
Install the pistons:	Press the upper connecting rod bearing halves into the connecting rods, and the lower halves into the connecting rod caps. Position the piston ring gaps according to specifications (see car section), and lubricate the pistons. Install a ring compresser on a piston, and press two long (8″) pieces of plastic tubing over the rod bolts. Using the plastic tubes as a guide, press the pistons into the bores and onto the crankshaft with a wooden hammer handle. After seating the rod on the crankshaft journal, remove the tubes and install the cap finger tight. Install the remaining pistons in the same man-

Procedure	*Method*
 **Tubing used as guide when installing a piston** (© Oldsmobile Div. G.M. Corp.) 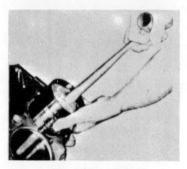 **Installing a piston** (© Chevrolet Div. G.M. Corp.)	ner. Invert the engine and check the bearing clearance at two points (90° apart) on each journal with Plastigage. NOTE: *Do not turn the crankshaft with Plastigage installed.* If clearance is within tolerances, remove *all* Plastigage, thoroughly lubricate the journals, and torque the rod caps to specifications. If clearance is not within specifications, install different thickness bearing inserts and recheck. CAUTION: *Never shim or file the connecting rods or caps.* Always install plastic tube sleeves over the rod bolts when the caps are not installed, to protect the crankshaft journals.
Check connecting rod side clearance:  **Checking connecting rod side clearance** (© Chevrolet Div. G.M. Corp.)	Determine the clearance between the sides of the connecting rods and the crankshaft, using feeler gauges. If clearance is below the minimum tolerance, the rod may be machined to provide adequate clearance. If clearance is excessive, substitute an unworn rod, and recheck. If clearance is still outside specifications, the crankshaft must be welded and reground, or replaced.
Inspect the timing chain:	Visually inspect the timing chain for broken or loose links, and replace the chain if any are found. If the chain will flex sideways, it must be replaced. Install the timing chain as specified. NOTE: *If the original timing chain is to be reused, install it in its original position.*

Procedure	*Method*
Check timing gear backlash and runout:	Mount a dial indicator with its stem resting on a tooth of the camshaft gear (as illustrated). Rotate the gear until all slack is removed, and zero the indicator. Rotate the gear in the opposite direction until slack is removed, and record gear backlash. Mount the indicator with its stem resting on the edge of the camshaft gear, parallel to the axis of the camshaft. Zero the indicator, and turn the camshaft gear one full turn, recording the runout. If either backlash or runout exceed specifications, replace the worn gear(s).

Checking camshaft gear backlash
(© Chevrolet Div. G.M. Corp.)

Checking camshaft gear runout
(© Chevrolet Div. G.M. Corp.)

Completing the Rebuilding Process

Following the above procedures, complete the rebuilding process as follows:

Fill the oil pump with oil, to prevent cavitating (sucking air) on initial engine start up. Install the oil pump and the pickup tube on the engine. Coat the oil pan gasket as necessary, and install the gasket and the oil pan. Mount the flywheel and the crankshaft vibrational damper or pulley on the crankshaft. NOTE: *Always use new bolts when installing the flywheel.* Inspect the clutch shaft pilot bushing in the crankshaft. If the bushing is excessively worn, remove it with an expanding puller and a slide hammer, and tap a new bushing into place.

Position the engine, cylinder head side up. Lubricate the lifters, and install them into their bores. Install the cylinder head, and torque it as specified in the car section. Insert the pushrods (where applicable), and install the rocker shaft(s) (if so equipped) or position the rocker arms on the pushrods. If solid lifters are utilized, adjust the valves to the "cold" specifications.

Mount the intake and exhaust manifolds, the carburetor(s), the distributor and spark plugs. Adjust the point gap and the static ignition timing. Mount all accessories and install the engine in the car. Fill the radiator with coolant, and the crankcase with high quality engine oil.

Break-in Procedure

Start the engine, and allow it to run at low speed for a few minutes, while checking for leaks. Stop the engine, check the oil level, and fill as necessary. Restart the engine, and fill the cooling system to capacity. Check the point dwell angle and adjust the ignition timing and the valves. Run the engine at low to medium speed (800-2500 rpm) for approximately ½ hour, and retorque the cylinder head bolts. Road test the car, and check again for leaks.

Follow the manufacturer's recommended engine break-in procedure and maintenance schedule for new engines.

Chapter 4

Emission Controls and Fuel System

Emission Controls

POSITIVE CRANKCASE VENTILATION

In this system, crankcase vapors are drawn into the intake manifold and burned as part of the engine combustion.

The "closed positive" system draws clean air from the carburetor air cleaner. The ventilation flow is regulated by a PCV valve located in the valve cover. Maintenance is covered in Chapter 1.

AIR INJECTION REACTOR

The A.I.R. system injects compressed air into the exhaust system, close enough to the exhaust valves to continue the burning of the normally unburned segment of the exhaust gases. To do this it employs an air injection pump and a system of hoses, valves, tubes, etc., neces-

Typical PCV system components

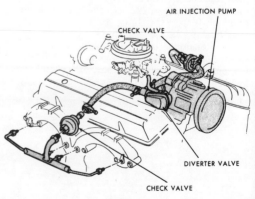

Typical 350 cu in. engine A.I.R. system components

sary to carry the compressed air from the pump to the exhaust manifolds. Carburetors and distributors for A.I.R. engines have specific modifications to adapt them to the air injection system; these components should not be interchanged with those intended for use on engines that do not have the system.

A diverter valve is used to prevent backfiring. The valve senses sudden increases in manifold vacuum and ceases the injection of air during fuel-rich periods. During coasting, this valve diverts the entire air flow through the muffler and during high engines speeds, expels it through a relief valve. Check valves in the system prevent exhaust gases from entering the pump.

On models with catalytic converters, it is not necessary to inject the air close to the exhaust valves. For this reason, not all models are equipped with manifolds on the exhaust manifolds for air injection as in previous years. Instead, one large pipe is used to inject air into the exhaust pipe ahead of the converter. Some models use part of the old system, but utilize only two or three of the injection nozzles on the exhaust manifold.

Air Pump Removal and Installation

1. Disconnect the air hoses at the pump.
2. Hold the pump pulley from turning and loosen the pulley bolts.
3. Loosen the pump mounting bolt and adjustment bracket bolt. Remove the drive belt.
4. Remove the mounting bolts and then remove the pump.
5. Install the pump using a reverse of the removal procedure.

EVAPORATIVE EMISSION CONTROL

Introduced on California cars in 1970, and nationwide in 1971, this system reduces the amount of escaping gasoline vapors. Float bowl emissions are controlled by internal carburetor modifications. Redesigned bowl vents, reduced bowl capacity, heat shields, and improved intake manifold-to-carburetor insulation serve to reduce vapor loss into the atmosphere. The venting of fuel tank vapors into the air has been stopped. Fuel vapors are now directed through lines to a canister containing an activated charcoal filter. Unburned vapors are trapped here until the engine is started. When the engine is running, the canister is purged by air drawn in by manifold vacuum. The air and fuel vapors are then directed into the engine to be burned. This system is designed to reduce fuel vapor emission. The canister filter should be replaced every 12 months or 12,000 miles. To replace the filter, proceed as follows:

The filter is located in the bottom of the

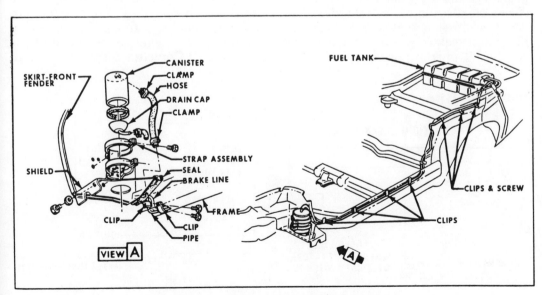

Evaporative emission control system components

canister. Pull out the old filter and work the new filter into place. It may be necessary, on earlier models, to remove the bottom of the canister for access.

ANTI-DIESELING SOLENOID

Some models may have an idle speed solenoid on the carburetor. All 1972–74 models have idle solenoids. Due to the leaner carburetor settings required for emission control, the engine may have a tendency to "diesel" or "run-on" after the ignition is turned off. The carburetor solenoid, energized when the ignition is on, maintains the normal idle speed. When the ignition is turned off, the solenoid is de-energized and permits the throttle valves to fully close, thus preventing run-on. For adjustment of carburetors with idle solenoids see Carburetor Adjustments.

TRANSMISSION CONTROLLED SPARK

Introduced in 1970, this system controls exhaust emissions by eliminating vacuum advance in the lower forward gears.

1970

The 1970 system consists of a transmission switch, solenoid vacuum switch, time delay relay, and a thermostatic water temperature switch. The solenoid vacuum switch is energized in the lower gears via the transmission switch and closes off distributor vacuum. The two-way transmission switch is activated by the shifter shaft on manual transmissions, and by oil pressure on automatic trans-

missions. The switch deenergizes the solenoid in high gear, the plunger extends and uncovers the vacuum port, and the distributor receives full vacuum. The temperature switch overrides the system when engine temperature is below 63° or above 232°. This allows vacuum advance in all gears. A time delay relay opens 15 seconds after the ignition is switched on. Full vacuum advance during this delay eliminates the possibility of stalling.

1971

The 1971 system is similar, except that the vacuum solenoid (now called a Combination Emissions Control solenoid) serves two functions. One function is 'to control distributor vacuum; the added function is to act as a deceleration throttle stop in high gear. This cuts down on emissions when the vehicle is coming to a stop in high gear. The CEC solenoid is controlled by a temperature switch, a transmission switch, and a 20 second time delay relay. This system also contains a reversing relay, which energizes the solenoid when the transmission switch, temperature switch or time delay completes the CEC circuit to ground. This system is directly opposite the 1970 system in operation. The 1970 vacuum solenoid was normally open to allow vacuum advance and when energized, closed to block vacuum. The 1971 system is normally closed blocking vacuum advance and when energized, opens to allow vacuum advance. The temperature switch completes the CEC circuit to ground when engine temperature is below 82°. Corvettes also have a high

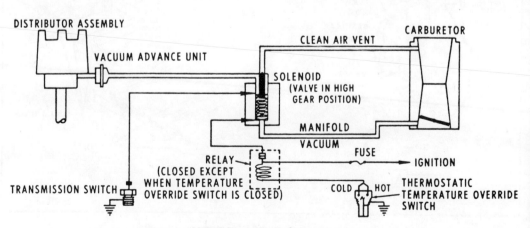

1970 TCS system schematic

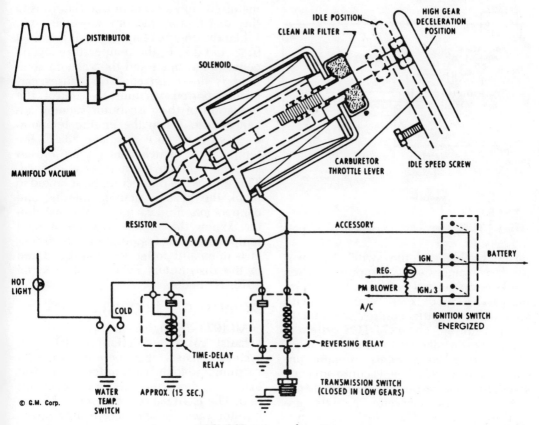

1971 TCS system schematic

temperature terminal on the switch to complete the CEC circuit when coolant temperature reaches 232°. The time delay relay allows vacuum advance (and raised idle speed) for 20 seconds after the ignition key is turned to the "on" position. Models with an automatic transmission and air conditioning also have a solid state timing device which engages the air conditioning compressor for three seconds after the ignition key is turned to the "off" position to prevent the engine from running-on. Two throttle settings are necessary; one for curb idle and one for emission control on coast. Both settings are described in the tune-up chapter.

1972–74

A vacuum advance solenoid similar to that used in 1970 is used. The CEC valve is not used. This relay is normally closed to block vacuum and opens when energized to allow vacuum advance. The solenoid controls distributor vacuum advance and performs no throttle position-

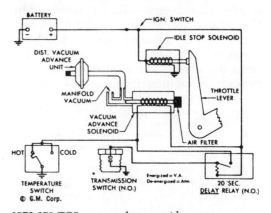

1972 350 TCS system—hot override on

ing function. The 1973–74 TCS system differs from the 1972 system in three ways. The 23 second upshift delay has been replaced by a 20 second starting relay. This relay closes to complete the TCS circuit and open the TCS solenoid, allowing vacuum advance, for 20 seconds after the key is turned to the "on" position. The operating temperature of the temperature override switch has been

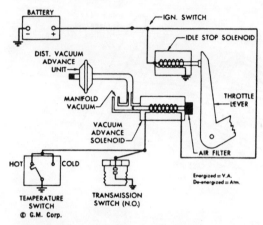

1972 454 TCS system—hot override on

raised to 93°, and the switch that was used to engage the A/C compressor when the key was turned "off" has been eliminated. All models are equipped with an electric throttle control solenoid to prevent run-on. The 1974 TCS system is used only on manual transmission models. System components remain unchanged from 1973. The vacuum advance solenoid is located on the coil bracket.

All 1973–74 Corvette models are equipped with a Thermo-Override system instead of the normal TCS system. This system consists of a three-position temperature switch, which is mounted in the right cylinder head and a two-position vacuum advance solenoid. Three vacuum lines are connected to the solenoid, a ported vacuum line from the carburetor, a vacuum line from the intake

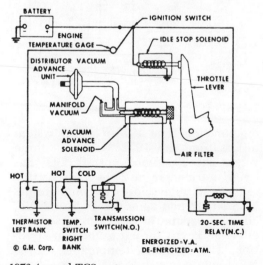

1973 4-speed TCS system

manifold, and a vacuum line that runs to the distributor vacuum advance unit. When the engine temperature is between 92°F and 232°F, the temperature switch contacts are open and the vacuum solenoid is de-energized. This causes carburetor-ported vacuum to control the operation of the distributor vacuum advance unit. When the engine temperature is below 93°F or above 232°F, the temperature switch contacts are closed and the vacuum solenoid is energized. This moves the plunger in the solenoid to block the ported vacuum opening and connect manifold vacuum to the distributor. When the engine reaches normal temperature, the temperature switch contacts open and ported vacuum is restored to the distributor. TCS is not used on 1975–76 models.

EXHAUST GAS RECIRCULATION

All 1973–76 engines are equipped with exhaust gas recirculation (EGR). This system consists of a metering valve, a vacuum line to the carburetor, and cast-in exhaust gas passages in the intake manifold. The EGR valve is controlled by carburetor vacuum, and accordingly opens and closes to admit exhaust gases into the fuel/air mixture. The exhaust gases lower the combustion temperature, and reduce the amount of oxides of nitrogen (NO_x) produced. The valve is closed at idle and wide open throttle, but is open between the two extreme throttle positions.

As the car accelerates, the carburetor throttle plate uncovers the vacuum port for the EGR valve. At 3–5 in. Hg, the EGR valve opens and then some of the exhaust gases are allowed to flow into the

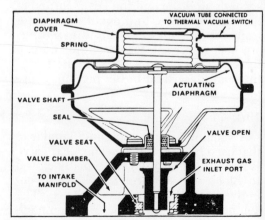

EGR valve cross-section

air/fuel mixture to lower the combustion temperature. At full-throttle the valve closes again.

EGR Valve Removal and Installation

1. Detach the vacuum line from the EGR valve.

2. Unfasten the two bolts which attach the valve to the manifold. Withdraw the valve.

3. Installation is the reverse of removal. Always use a new gasket between the valve and the manifold.

EARLY FUEL EVAPORATION SYSTEM

1975–76 models are equipped with this system to reduce engine warm-up time, improve driveability, and reduce emissions. On start-up, a vacuum motor acts to close a heat valve in the exhaust manifold which causes exhaust gases to enter the intake manifold heat riser passages. Incoming fuel mixture is then heated and more complete fuel evaporation is provided during warm-up.

CATALYTIC CONVERTER

All 1975–76 models are equipped with a catalytic converter. The converter is located midway in the exhaust system. Stainless steel exhaust pipes are used ahead of the converter. The converter is stainless steel with an aluminized steel cover and a ceramic felt blanket to insulate the converter from the floorpan. The catalyst pellet bed inside the converter

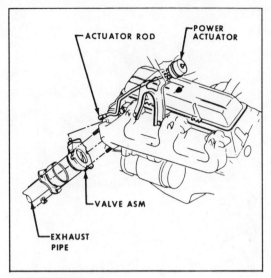

350 V8 EFE system

consists of noble metals which cause a reaction that converts hydrocarbons and carbon monoxide into water and carbon dioxide.

Fuel System

FUEL PUMP

The Corvette fuel pump is a diaphragm type, actuated by an eccentric on the engine camshaft. A pushrod connects the camshaft eccentric and the fuel pump

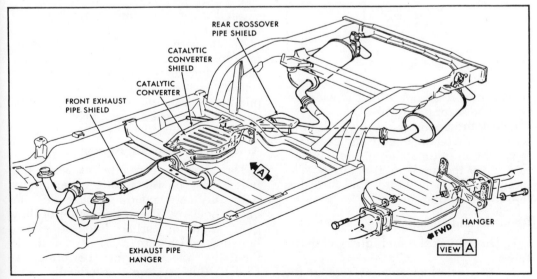

1975 Corvette exhaust system showing catalytic converter

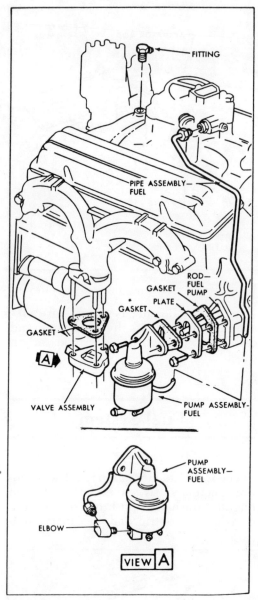

FITTING

PIPE ASSEMBLY—
FUEL

ROD—
GASKET   FUEL
PUMP
PLATE
GASKET

GASKET

[A]

VALVE ASSEMBLY

PUMP ASSEMBLY—
FUEL

PUMP
ASSEMBLY—
FUEL

ELBOW

VIEW [A]

1974 350 fuel pump mounting

rocker arm. A rubber gasket is used between the mating surfaces.

Check the operation of the fuel pump with the unit on the engine and gas in the tank. The inlet (or suction) line transfers fuel from the tank to the pump. The pump outlet (or pressure) line furnishes fuel to the carburetor(s).

Removal and Installation

1. Disconnect the fuel inlet and outlet lines.

2. On small block engines, remove the upper bolt from the right front mounting

boss. Insert a longer bolt (⅜–16 x 2 in.) in this hole to hold the fuel pump pushrod.

3. Remove the fuel pump mounting bolts and remove the fuel pump. The pushrod may be retained in position on large block engines with either mechanical fingers or heavy grease.

4. Install the fuel pump using a reverse procedure and check for leaks.

CARTER WCFB CARBURETOR

The Carter WCFB is the standard carburetor on 1963–1965 Corvettes.

Functionally, it is two, dual carburetors mounted in a single housing and is comprised of four basic components: choke housing, top cover, main body, and throttle flange. The metering rods, accelerator pump, and choke are located in the primary side of the carburetor body. It has the five conventional systems: float, low speed, high speed, accelerator pump, and choke.

Idle Speed and Mixture Adjustments

Idle speed and mixture adjustments are best accomplished using a tachometer and vacuum gauge. Make this adjustment with the air cleaner installed.

Bring the engine to operating temperature, check to see that the choke is fully off, and adjust the idle-speed adjustment screw to give 475 rpm (450 on automatic transmissions in Drive range). Adjust the idle-mixture adjustment screws separately until peak vacuum and rpm are indicated on the vacuum gauge and tachometer.

An alternative method is to set the idle-mixture screws lean to a beginning, rough idle, then back screws out (enrichen) ¼ turn. Never bottom the idle-mixture adjustment screws or possible damage to the needle seat may result.

Automatic Choke Adjustment

The choke is correctly set when the index mark on the plastic cover aligns with the corresponding mark on the choke housing. The introduction of dirt, gum, water or carbon into the choke housing or vacuum passage can detrimentally affect engine performance. Check this system periodically and clean if necessary.

Intermediate Choke Rod Adjustment

The intermediate choke rod adjustment requires the removal of the choke coil housing assembly, gasket, and baffle plate. Open the choke valve and position a 0.026 in. wire gauge between the bottom of the slot in the piston and the top of the slot in the choke piston housing. Seat the choke piston on the gauge. The measurement between the top of the choke valve and the air horn divider should be 0.096 in. Adjustment is made by bending the intermediate choke rod.

Float Adjustment

To make the float adjustment, remove the top cover then disassemble and reassemble the floats without the cover gasket. Make the lateral adjustment by placing the ¼ in. float gauge (supplied in the carburetor overhaul kit) under the center of the secondary float so that the notched portion of the gauge fits over the edge of the casting. Bend the floats until their sides just clear the vertical uprights of the gauge. Repeat the adjustment on the primary float using either the ⅛ in. float gauge or a ⅛ in. drill bit.

The vertical adjustment is correct when the floats just clear the horizontal bar of the gauges when the gauges are positioned as described above. The required clearance between the top of the floats and the bowl cover is ⅛ in. on the primary floats and ¼ in. on the secondary floats.

Float drop measurement must be made with the top cover gasket removed. Measure between the lowest point of the floats and the bottom of the top cover. This should be 2 in. for both primary and secondary floats. Adjust the accelerator pump by backing off the idle-speed adjustment screw and positioning the float-drop adjustment gauge (supplied in re-

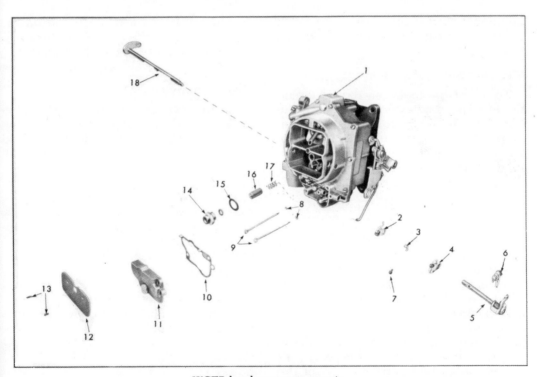

WCFB bowl cover upper parts

1. Bowl cover	6. Choke shaft lever	13. Choke valve screw
2. Metering rod arm	7. Vent arm screw	14. Inlet fitting nut
3. Vent arm	8. Metering rod discs	15. Filter gaskets
4. Pump operating arm and link	9. Metering rods	16. Filter
5. Pump countershaft assembly	10. Dust cover gasket	17. Filter spring
	11. Dust cover	18. Choke valve shaft
	12. Choke valve	

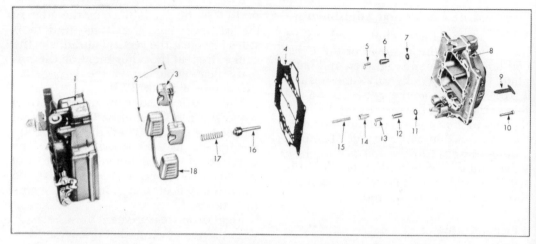

WCFB lower bowl cover parts

1. Carburetor body	8. Bowl cover	14. Vacuum piston
2. Float hinge pins	9. Vacuum piston link	15. Vacuum piston spring
3. Secondary float	10. Bowl cover attaching	16. Pump plunger assembly
4. Bowl cover gasket	screw	17. Pump plunger return spring
5. Secondary float needle	11. Needle seat gasket	18. Primary float
6. Secondary float needle seat	12. Primary float needle seat	
7. Needle seat gasket	13. Primary float needle	

building kits) on the dust cover boot. Bend the top flat of the pump arm so that it is parallel to the gauge.

Metering Rod Adjustment

To adjust the metering rods, back off the idle-speed adjusting screw until the throttle valves are fully seated, then loosen the screw in the metering arm. Depress the metering rod arm upward until it just touches the hanger. Secure the arm with the set screw.

Unloader and Secondary Throttle Lever Adjustment

Make the unloader adjustment with the throttle valves wide open. Measure between the inboard edge of the choke valve and the center wall of the top cover. Bend the unloader tang to obtain a 3/16 in. clearance.

Turn the carburetor upside down to adjust the secondary throttle lever. With the primary valves wide open, the secondary valves should be within 4° to 7° of the wide open position. Bend the connector rod at its upper angle until actuation of the throttle linkage fully opens the primary valves. Bend the tang on the secondary throttle dog so that with the primary throttle valves open, the secondary throttle-to-bore angle will be 5½°. There

should be 0.017 in.–0.022 in. clearance between the positive closing shoes on the primary and secondary throttle levers with the throttle valves closed.

Disassembly and Assembly

1. Remove the carburetor from the engine but do not drain the fuel in the bowl. Tap the filter nut lightly with a hammer then remove the inlet nut and gasket and lift out the filter.

2. Disconnect the choke connector rod, intermediate choke rod, and throttle rod. Remove the metering-rod dust cover and vapor vent arm. Loosen the pump operating arm and metering-rod arm securing screws, and withdraw the countershaft.

3. Remove the metering rod arm and link. Turn each metering rod 180° and lift them from the hanger. Do not lose the two, metering rod discs.

4. Remove the top cover, lifting straight up so as to avoid damaging the floats, vacuum piston, or plunger assembly. Be sure the cover gasket is free of the bowl before lifting the cover. Mark the floats before removing them from the cover, to avoid unnecessary bending during assembly adjustments.

5. Remove the secondary float needle, seat, and gasket, and group together.

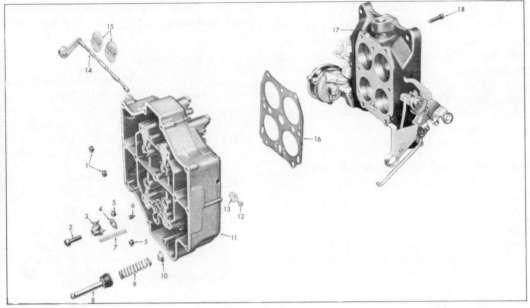

WCFB throttle body parts

1. Secondary jets
2. Pump jet cluster attaching screw
3. Pump jet cluster
4. Cluster gasket
5. Metering rod jets
6. Pump discharge needle
7. Vacuum piston spring
8. Pump plunger assembly

9. Pump plunger return spring
10. Pump inlet ball retainer
11. Carburetor body
12. Screw
13. Auxiliary throttle valve cam
14. Auxiliary throttle valve shaft
    and weight assembly

15. Auxiliary throttle valves
16. Carburetor body gasket
17. Throttle flange
18. Throttle flange attaching
    screw

Remove the pump plunger assembly and spring and soak the lether pump plunger in gasoline or kerosine to prevent it from drying out. Turn the vacuum piston ¼ turn to disconnect and remove the piston link.

6. At this time, check the fuel in the bowl for contamination. Sweep the bottom of the bowl with a magnet while the fuel is still present. This will pick up iron oxide dust or metallic particles. Water contamination will appear as milky globules at the bottom of the bowl.

7. Invert the carburetor body and remove the pump jet cluster and gasket. Tap out the pump discharge needle. Attach a 5/16 in. six-point socket to a six-inch extension and pry the pump inlet ball retainer and check ball from the bottom of the pump cylinder well.

8. Remove the primary metering rod jets from the pump side of the carburetor. Remove the secondary main jets but do not mix them as their orifices are not the same size. Check the low speed jets to see that they are angled slightly on installa-

tion. The anti-percolator plugs and bushings and main discharge nozzles are a press fit and should not be removed.

9. Separate the throttle flange and carburetor body. Remove the idle-mixture screws and springs, throttle-lever adjusting screw, washer, and spring. Remove the fast-idle cam assembly and lockout arm. Remove the primary/secondary throttle valve connector rod. Back out the primary throttle shaft screw and washer and remove the throttle levers. Dislodge the secondary throttle return spring. Remove the primary and secondary-throttle valves and shafts. It will be necessary to file the staked ends of the throttle valve securing screws before they can be removed. Remove the choke housing and baffle.

10. Clean and inspect the disassembled components. Use a carburetor cleaning solution to wash everything but the coil housing assembly and pump plunger. Clean the choke housing assembly in gasoline. Reassembly is the reverse of this procedure.

CARTER AFB CARBURETOR

The Carter AFB (aluminum four-barrel) carburetor is a high performance option found on the 327 cubic inch Corvette engine from 1963–1965. It is a four-throat downdraft type and offers improved flow rates over the standard carburetor. A clean air system reduces contamination of the choke vacuum circuit and linkage, and subsequent malfunctioning.

Idle Speed and Mixture Adjustment

Idle speed and mixture are adjusted with the engine thoroughly warmed and idling and with the aid of a tachometer and vacuum gauge attached to the engine. With the choke fully off, adjust the idle-speed adjustment screw to give 475 rpm (450 for automatic transmission models in Drive). Adjust each idle-mixture screw until peak steady vacuum is achieved at the specified rpm.

Automatic Choke Adjustment

The automatic choke is correctly adjusted when the scribe mark on the coil housing is aligned with the center notch in the choke housing for Powerglide models and one notch lean with synchromesh.

Float Adjustments

Remove the metering rods and the bowl cover. Align the float by sighting down its side to determine if it is parallel with the outer edge of the air horn. Bend to adjust. The float level is adjusted with the air horn inverted and the air horn

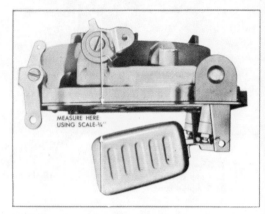

AFB float drop adjustment

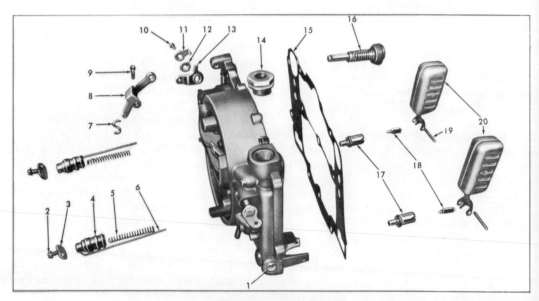

AFB bowl cover parts

1. Bowl cover assembl,	8. Pump lever	15. Cover gasket
2. Screw	9. Pump lever pivot screw	16. Pump plunger assembly
3. Piston cover plate	10. Screw	17. Float needle seat
4. Power piston	11. Choke shaft outer lever	18. Float needle
5. Spring	12. Washer (spacer)	19. Float hinge
6. Metering rod	13. Choke shaft kick lever	20. Float
7. Pump link	14. Fuel inlet fitting	

gasket in place. Clearance between each float (at the outer end) and the air horn gasket should be 5/16 in. Bend to adjust.

The float drop is adjusted by holding the air horn in the upright position and bending the float arm until the vertical distance from the air horn gasket to the outer end of each float measures ¾ in.

Intermediate Choke Rod Adjustment

The intermediate choke rod adjustment begins with the removal of the choke coil housing assembly, gasket and baffle plate. Position a 0.026 in. wire gauge between the bottom of the slot in the piston and the top of the slot in the choke piston housing. Close the choke piston against the gauge and secure it with a rubber band. Now bend the intermediate choke rod so that the distance between the top edge of the choke valve and the air horn divider measures 0.070 in.

Accelerator Pump Adjustment

The first step in adjusting the accelerator pump is to push aside the fast-idle cam and seat the throttle valves firmly. Bend the pump rod at the lower angle to obtain a ½ in. measurement between the air horn and the top of the plunger shaft.

Unloader, Closing Shoe, and Secondary Throttle Adjustment

To adjust the unloader, hold the throttle wide open and bend the unloader tang to obtain a 3/16 in. clearance between the upper edge of the choke valve and inner wall of the air horn.

Clearance between the positive closing shoes on the primary and secondary throttle valves is checked with the valves closed. Bend the secondary closing as required to obtain a clearance of 0.20 in.

The secondary throttle opening is governed by the pick-up lever on the primary throttle shaft. It has two points of contact with the loose lever on the primary shaft. If the contact points do not simultaneously engage, bend the pick-up lever to obtain proper engagement. The primary and secondary throttle valve opening must be synchronized.

Disassembly and Assembly

1. Remove the pump rod and intermediate choke rod. Remove the outer lever and washer from the choke shaft, then remove the inner lever and fast-idle rod as an assembly. Remove the step-up position cover plates, piston, and step-up rod and spring. Lightly tap the fuel inlet fitting. Before removing it, remove its gasket and strainer then carefully lift the top cover to protect the floats and pump plunger from damage.

2. Remove the float lever pins, floats, float needles, seats, and gaskets. Keep separate to avoid unnecessary adjustment. Remove the pump plunger lever, S link, plunger, and cover gasket.

3. Do not remove the choke valve and shaft(s) unless there is obvious shaft binding or damage to the valve.

4. Remove the accelerator-pump lower spring and, after checking the fuel for contamination, drain the bowl. Sweep a magnet around the bottom of the bowl while fuel is still present to capture iron oxide dust or metal particles which may damage the needle seats. Water contamination will appear as milky globules at the bottom of the fuel bowl.

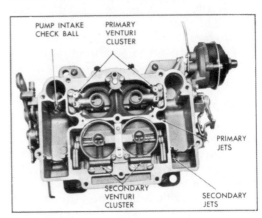

AFB main body components

5. Remove the choke housing cover, gasket, and baffle. Remove the O-ring seal from the vacuum opening in the mounting boss. Remove the choke piston, levers, pump cluster and gasket, and pump discharge needle. Remove the venturi cluster. The venturi assemblies are dissimilar and cannot be assembled in the wrong location. Primary venturi gaskets differ from secondary.

6. Remove the secondary auxiliary valves, idle-mixture screws and springs, and all four metering jets. Metering rods are used in the primary metering jets and

these jets are visibly larger than their secondary counterparts. Remove the pump intake check valve and seat assembly.

7. Wash all parts except the choke coil housing and the pump plunger in carburetor cleaning solution. Clean the choke housing in gasoline.

8. Reassembly is the reversal of this procedure.

ROCHESTER 4MV QUADRAJET

The Rochester 4MV is a four-throat unit which serves as standard carburetor on the 327, 350, 427, and 454 cu in. engines. The 4MV is designed as an all-purpose carburetor. Its primary throats feature small bores and a triple venturi configuration for better fuel control and corresponding gas mileage at idle and normal operational speeds. The secondary throats are quite a bit larger and are designed to meet the greater air flow demands of harder driving.

The float chamber is centrally located and has a pressure-balanced float valve which allows the use of a small, single float. This combination greatly reduces erratic fuel delivery during acceleration. The 4MV is used in combination with a temperature-sensing choke coil mounted on the intake manifold.

Idle Speed and Mixture Adjustment

Attach a tachometer and a vacuum gauge to the engine, disconnect the vacuum advance, and bring the engine to operating temperature. Adjust the idle-speed adjustment screw to obtain the specified engine idle rpm. Adjust each idle-mixture adjustment screw until the smoothest idle is reached at the highest steady vacuum reading.

Float Adjustment

Remove the top cover and gasket, and use an adjustable T-scale to measure the distance from the top of the float bowl gasket surface to the top of the float at a point 3/16 in. back from the toe of the float. Bend the float tang to specifications.

Accelerator Pump Adjustment

Close the throttle valves and position the pump rod in the specified hole of the pump lever. Use an adjustable T-scale to measure from the top of the choke valve wall, nearest the vent stack, to the top of the pump stem. Bend the pump lever to obtain the specified distance.

Idle Vent Adjustment

Close the vent valve and open the primary throttle until the vent valve arm touches the bi-metallic strip next to the valve. Measure the distance between the top of the choke valve wall and the top of the pump stem. Bend to adjust.

Fast Idle Adjustment

Close the primary throttles and position the cam follower above the high step of the fast-idle cam. Turn the fast-idle screw clockwise until it touches the lever then turn it down three full turns.

Choke Rod Adjustment

Position the cam follower on the second step of the fast-idle cam, touching the high step. Close the choke valve and gauge the clearance between the lower edge of the valve and the body. Bend choke rod to obtain the specified clearance.

Air Valve Dashpot Adjustment

Seat the vacuum break diaphragm and gauge the clearance between the dashpot rod and the end of the slot in the air valve lever. Bend rod to adjust.

Vacuum Break Adjustment

Close the choke valve and secure it with a rubber band. Place the cam follower on the highest step of the fast-idle cam and position the break diaphragm stem against its seat with the vacuum link at the end of the slot. Bend the tang so that the measurement between the lower edge of the choke valve and the air horn meets specifications.

Unloader Adjustment

Close the choke valve and secure it with a rubber band placed on the vacuum break lever. Completely open the primary throttle and measure the distance between the air horn and the lower edge of the throttle valve. Bend the fast-idle lever tang to achieve specifications.

Secondary Lockout Adjustment

Completely open the choke valve and rotate the vacuum break lever clockwise. Bend the lever if the measurement between the lever and the secondary throttle shaft exceeds specifications. Close the choke and gauge the distance between the lever and secondary throttle shaft pin. Bend the lever to adjust.

Air Valve Spring Adjustment

Remove all spring tension by loosening the locking screw and backing out the spring adjusting screw. Close the air valve and turn in the adjusting screw until the torsion spring touches the pin on the shaft then turn it the additional turns specified. Secure the locking screw.

Secondary Opening Adjustment

With the primary throttle valves open and the actuating link touching the secondary lever, the bottom of the link should be in the center of the secondary lever slot and clearance between the tang and link should be 0.070 in.

Secondary Closing Adjustment

With the curb idle-speed set to specified rpm and the cam follower free of the fast-idle cam, there should be 0.020 in. clearance between the actuation link and the front of the secondary lever slot. The tang must touch the tang on the primary shaft's actuating lever. Bend to adjust.

Disassembly and Assembly

1. Remove the idle vent valve, and choke rod, then disconnect the accelerator pump rod from the pump lever. Back out the nine retaining screws and separate the top cover from the carburetor body. Lift the cover straight up so that the two, main well air-bleed tubes will not be damaged. These tubes are pressed into the top cover and should not be removed.

2. Completely open the secondary air valves and extract the secondary metering rods. Remove the choke valve and shaft, then the accelerator pump lever roll pin and lever. Do not disturb the calibrated air valves and shaft.

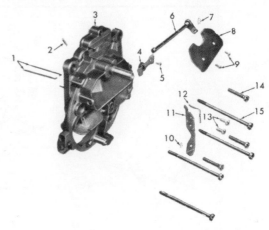

Quadrajet top cover

3. Remove the accelerator pump plunger and the float bowl gaskets. Remove the accelerator pump spring and the plastic filler over the float valve. Grasp the metering rod hanger with needle nose pliers and withdraw the hanger, power piston, and primary metering rods, then rotate and slip the rods from the power piston.

4. Remove the float retaining pin and slide the float assembly forward and up to free. Remove the float needle and seat assembly, discarding the gasket. Remove the primary metering jets but leave the secondary metering discs in place. Remove the accelerator pump check ball retainer and ball.

5. Remove the secondary float bowl baffle and the vacuum break assembly hose. Remove the choke assembly and the secondary lock-out link. Remove the vacuum break lever rod and the vacuum break assembly. Remove the fast-idle cam, lower choke rod, and actuating lever found inside the float bowl. Remove the inlet fuel filter and spring, then remove the attaching screws and separate the bowl from the throttle plate.

6. Rotate the pump rod free of the primary throttle lever and remove the idle mixture screws and springs.

7. Clean the carburetor parts in a cold, immersion type cleaner. Do not put the vacuum break assembly, pump plungers, diaphragms, or plastic parts in the cleaner.

8. Clean and blow dry with compressed air, then reassemble by reversing the disassembly procedure.

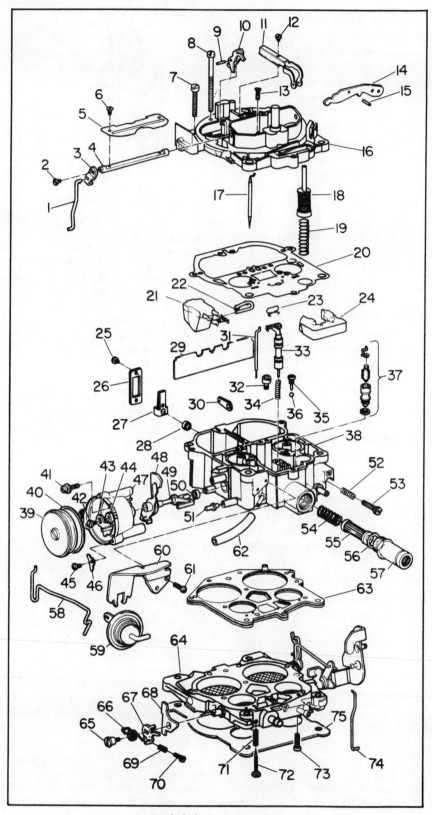

Exploded view of Quadrajet

C.E.C. Valve Maintenance— 1971 Quadrajet

The Rochester 4MV Quadrajet has a number of revisions for 1971 which include: calibration changes, greater capacity accelerator pump, increase in the size of the vacuum break diaphragm restriction to 0.020 in., a beefed-up, choke-closing assist spring, removal of the wide open kick lever from the choke unloader mechanism and its replacement with a tang on the fast-idle lever that contacts the fast-idle cam and forces the choke valve to admit more air under flooded engine conditions, and the adaption of a combination emission control valve (C.E.C. valve). This valve increases the idle speed during high gear overrun and helps to control normally unburned hydrocarbons. The mixture is set at the factory and the idle-mixture screws are capped to prevent adjustment in the field.

When disassembling the carburetor, remove the C.E.C. valve from the carburetor but leave the valve bracket attached to the carburetor. Do not immerse the C.E.C. valve in carburetor cleaner. Disassembly practices differ in the 1971 4MV due to calibration changes. Of primary importance is the revised procedure for removing the power piston. Do not use pliers but press the piston down and release it. Do not remove the idle mixture screws.

If it should be necessary to replace the idle-mixture adjustment screws, carefully bottom the old screws and count the turns so that the replacement screws will retain the same mixture.

If the throttle body is replaced it will be necessary to adjust the idle-mixture screws. Before making the adjustment, read and follow the instructions on the inner fender tune-up sticker on each 1971 and later Corvette. Lightly bottom

1. Choke rod
2. Choke lever screw
3. Choke lever
4. Choke shaft
5. Choke valve
6. Choke valve screw
7. Short air horn screw
8. Long air horn screw
9. Roll pin
10. Lever
11. Secondary metering rod holder
12. Secondary metering rod holder screw
13. Air horn screw
14. Pump actuating lever
15. Pump lever roll pin
16. Air horn assembly
17. Seconary metering rod
18. Pump assembly
19. Pump return spring
20. Air horn gasket
21. Float assembly
22. Float assembly hinge pin
23. Primary metering rod retainer spring
24. Float bowl
25. Idle compensator cover screw
26. Idle compensator cover
27. Idle compensator
28. Idle compensator seal
29. Float bowl baffle
30. Choke rod lever
31. Primary metering rod
32. Primary main metering jet
33. Power piston assembly
34. Power piston spring
35. Pump discharge ball retainer
36. Pump discharge ball
37. Needle and seat assembly, gasket, and pull clip
38. Float bowl assembly

39. Thermostatic cover and coil assembly
40. Thermostatic cover gasket
41. Choke housing-to-bowl screw
42. Choke coil lever screw
43. Choke coil lever
44. Intermediate choke shaft
45. Stat cover screw
46. Stat cover retainer
47. Choke housing
48. Fast idle cam
49. Inter choke shaft lever assembly
50. Intermediate choke shaft seal
51. Choke housing-to-bowl seal
52. Idle adjust screw spring
53. Idle adjusting screw
54. Filter relief spring
55. Fuel inlet filter
56. Filter nut gasket
57. Fuel inlet filter nut
58. Vacuum break rod
59. Vacuum break diaphragm assembly
60. Vacuum break control bracket
61. Bracket attaching screw
62. Vacuum control hose
63. Throttle body-to-bowl gasket
64. Throttle body assembly
65. Cam and fast idle lever screw
66. Fast idle lever spring
67. Fast idle lever
68. Cam follower lever
69. Fast idle screw spring
70. Fast idle adjusting screw
71. Idle mixture needle spring
72. Idle mixture needle
73. Throttle body-to-bowl attaching screw
74. Pump rod
75. Flange gasket

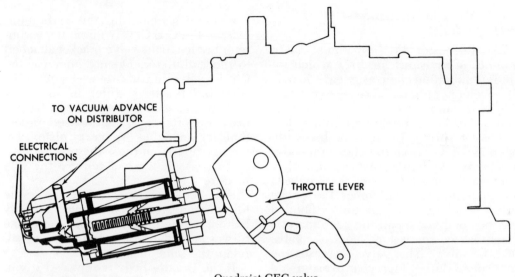

TO VACUUM ADVANCE
ON DISTRIBUTOR

ELECTRICAL
CONNECTIONS

THROTTLE LEVER

Quadrajet CEC valve

the mixture screws and back out four turns. Set the idle-speed adjusting screw to obtain the specified initial idle speed, then make equal adjustments to the mixture screws until the required carbon monoxide level is reached in the exhaust gas. Adjust the idle-speed screw until the final idle setting is achieved. Install the idle-mixture screws' limiter caps and reconnect the distributor vacuum hose and the fuel tank vapor hose.

An alternate method is available if access to exhaust gas analyzing equipment is not practical. Follow the same procedure until the mixture adjustment stage. Adjust the mixture screws equally leaner until the final idle speed is achieved. Install the limiter caps, vacuum hose, and tank vapor hose.

HOLLEY 2300 AND 2300C CARBURETORS

The Holley 2300 and 2300C are used as the three, two-barrel high performance option on the 427 engine from 1967 through 1969. This configuration uses one 2300C as the primary carburetor and two 2300 models as the two secondary units. The two models differ in that the C model contains the choke, power, and accelerator pump systems while the straight 2300 does not. The C model is operated through conventional linkage while the two secondaries are vacuum actuated.

Idle Adjustment

Adjust the idle-speed screw until it touches the throttle lever. Add one and ½

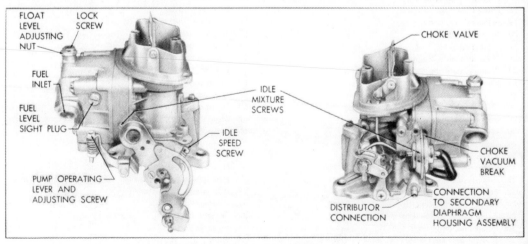

FLOAT LEVEL ADJUSTING NUT

LOCK SCREW

CHOKE VALVE

FUEL INLET

FUEL LEVEL SIGHT PLUG

PUMP OPERATING LEVER AND ADJUSTING SCREW

IDLE MIXTURE SCREWS

IDLE SPEED SCREW

CHOKE VACUUM BREAK

CONNECTION TO SECONDARY DIAPHRAGM HOUSING ASSEMBLY

DISTRIBUTOR CONNECTION

Holley 2300C primary carburetor

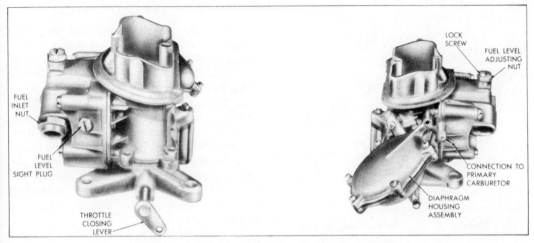

Holley 2300 secondary carburetor

turns to obtain the preliminary adjustment.

Fast-idle adjustment on the primary carburetor is made as follows: crack the throttle, and with the choke closed, place the fast-idle lever against the top step of the fast-idle cam. Bend the fast-idle lever so that the specified opening of the throttle plate on the idle transfer slot of the carburetor is achieved.

Float Level Adjustment

Position the car on a flat, level surface and start the engine. Remove the sight plugs and check to see that the fuel level reaches the bottom threads of the sight plug port. A plus or minus tolerance of 1/32 in. is acceptable. To change the level, loosen the fuel inlet-needle locking screw and adjust the nut. Clockwise lowers the fuel level and counterclockwise raises it. Turn the nut 1/16 of a turn for each 1/16 in. desired change. Open the primary throttle slightly to assure a stabilized adjusting condition on the secondaries. There is no required float drop adjustment.

Accelerator Pump Adjustment—Primary Carb

Secure the throttle plate fully open and depress the pump lever, fully. Gauge the distance between the pump lever arm and the spring adjusting nut. Turn the nut or screw to adjust. The slightest movement of the throttle lever will actuate the correctly adjusted pump lever.

Vacuum Break Adjustment—Primary Carb

Secure the choke valve closed and restrain the vacuum break against its stop. Bend the break rod to achieve the specified measurement between the lower edge of the choke valve and the body.

Choke Unloader Adjustment—Primary Carb

Fully open the throttle valve and secure it. Close the choke valve against the throttle shaft unloader tang and bend the choke rod to obtain the specified measurement between the lower edge of the choke valve and the body.

Disassembly and Assembly

PRIMARY CARBURETOR

1. Remove the fuel bowl, metering body, and splash shield. Disconnect the vacuum break hose, remove the throttle body attachment screws, and separate the throttle body from the primary carburetor body.

2. Remove the fuel inlet baffle, float hinge screws, and the brass float. Remove the needle and seat assembly lock screw, then back out the adjusting nut and remove the seat assembly.

3. Remove the sight plug and gasket, fuel inlet fitting, filter, spring and gasket. Remove the accelerator pump cover, diaphragm, and spring.

4. Check the accelerator pump inlet ball. If damage is evident, replace the bowl assembly.

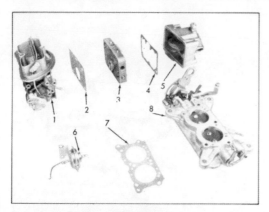

Primary carburetor components

1. Carburetor body	5. Fuel bowl assembly
2. Metering body gasket	6. Vacuum break
3. Metering body	7. Throttle body gasket
4. Fuel bowl gasket	8. Throttle body

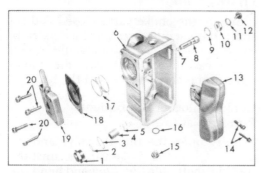

Primary carburetor float bowl; secondary has no accelerator pump

1. Nut—fuel inlet	11. Gasket—inlet
2. Gasket—fuel filter	lockscrew
3. Gasket—inlet nut	12. Screw—inlet lock
4. Fuel filter	13. Float assembly
5. Spring fuel filter	14. Screw—float hinge
6. Fuel bowl	15. Fuel level sight plug
7. Seal—inlet needle	16. Gasket—sight plug
and seat assembly	17. Spring—pump
8. Inlet needle and seat	diaphragm
assembly	18. Pump diaphragm
9. Gasket—inlet	19. Cover assembly—
adjusting nut	pump diaphragm
10. Nut—inlet	20. Screw—pump
adjusting	diaphragm cover

5. Remove the main metering jets, power valve, vacuum fitting, and the idle-mixture needles and screws.

6. Remove the choke vacuum break, choke lever and fast-idle cam. Remove the accelerator pump discharge nozzle and its check valve.

7. Reverse the above procedure to assemble.

SECONDARY CARBURETORS

1. Remove the fuel bowl and metering block. Disconnect the secondary diaphragm housing from the throttle lever and separate the housing from the carburetor body.

2. Remove the throttle body attaching screws and separate the throttle body from the main body. Remove the fuel inlet baffle hinge screws and plastic float.

3. Remove the needle and seat assembly, sight plug, fuel inlet fitting, filter, and spring. Remove the metering body plate and gaskets. Remove the diaphragm cover and diaphragm.

4. Reverse this procedure to reassemble.

HOLLY 4150, 4160 SERIES CARBURETORS

Holley four-barrel carburetors first appeared on the Corvette in 1964. The 4160 used is an end-inlet carburetor, while the 4150 carburetors used have been both end and center-inlet designs. The secondary metering body on the 4150 carburetor is similar to the primary metering body. The 4160 secondary metering body is a cast body and a plate attached to the main body by six screws. The center-inlet 4150 has been utilized on the higher performance versions of the Corvette. In 1971, the Holley carburetor has revised calibration and a C.E.C. valve. Holley part numbers are located on the carburetor air horn.

Idle-Speed and Mixture Adjustment

This adjustment is made with the vacuum advance connected. Lightly bottom the mixture screws and back out each one turn for an initial adjustment. Bring the engine to operating temperature, with the choke fully open and the carburetor operating at the curb idle speed.

Set the idle-speed screw to obtain the specified idle-speed then adjust the mixture screws evenly until the highest steady vacuum reading is reached. Readjust the idle-speed and the mixture screws until the peak steady vacuum reading at specified rmp is reached. Late model carburetors with limiter caps on the idle mixture screws should not be adjusted or tampered with.

Choke Adjustment

The early model 4150 uses a bi-metallic choke mounted on the carburetor. It is correctly set when the cover scribe mark aligns with the specified notch mark. The later model 4150 and 4160 employ a remotely located choke. To adjust, disconnect the choke rod at the choke lever and secure the choke lever closed. Bend the rod so that when the rod is depressed to the contact stop, the top is even with the bottom of the hole in the choke lever.

Float Level Adjustment

Position the car on a flat, level surface and start the engine. Remove the sight plugs and check to see that the fuel level reaches the bottom threads of the sight plug port. A plus or minus tolerance of $1/32$ in. is acceptable. To change the level, loosen the fuel-inlet needle locking screw and adjust the nut. Clockwise lowers the fuel level and counterclockwise raises it. Turn the nut $1/16$ of a turn for each $1/16$ in. desired change. Open the primary throttle slightly to assure a stabilized adjusting condition on the secondaries. There is no required float drop adjustment.

Holley float level adjustment

Fast-Idle Adjustment

EARLY 4150

Bring the engine to normal operating temperature with the air cleaner off. Open the throttle. Place the fast-idle cam on its high step and close the throttle. Adjust the fast-idle screw to reach the specified idle speed.

LATE MODEL 4150 AND 4160

Open the throttle and place the choke plate fast-idle lever against the top step of the fast-idle cam. Bend the fast-idle lever to achieve the specified throttle plate opening.

Choke Unloader Adjustment

Adjustment should be made with the engine not running. Fully open and secure the throttle plate. Force the choke valve toward a closed position, so that contact is made with the unloader tang. Bend the choke rod to gain the specified clearance between the main body and the lower edge of the choke valve.

Accelerator Pump Adjustment

Turn off the engine. Block open the throttle and push down the pump lever. Clearance between the pump lever arm and the spring adjusting nut should be 0.015 in. minimum. Turn the screw or nut to adjust this clearance.

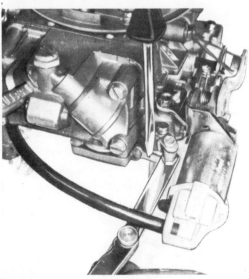

Holley accelerator pump adjustment

Secondary Throttle Valve Adjustment

LATE MODEL 4150 AND 4160

Close the throttle plates then turn the adjustment screw until it contacts the throttle lever. Advance the screw ½ turn more.

Air Vent Valve Adjustment

LATE MODEL 4150 AND 4160

Close the throttle valves and open the choke valve so that the throttle arm is free of the idle screw. Bend the air vent valve rod to obtain the specified clearance between the choke valve and seat. Advance the idle-speed screw until it touches the throttle lever then advance it 1½ turns.

Vacuum Break Adjustment

LATE MODEL 4150 AND 4160 HOLLEY

Secure the choke valve closed and the vacuum break against the stop. Bend the vacuum break link to gain the specified clearance between the main body and the lower edge of the choke valve.

C.E.C. Valve Adjustment

1971 4150 HOLLEY

This adjustment is made only when it has been necessary to remove the throttle plate, overhaul the carburetor, or replace the solenoid. To adjust, warm the engine and place the transmission in Neutral for manual transmissions or Drive for automatic transmissions. If so equipped, turn off the air conditioner. Disconnect the vapor-canister fuel tank hose and remove and plug the distributor vacuum hose. Extend the C.E.C. valve plunger until it touches the throttle lever and then adjust its length until the specified idle speed is reached.

Disassembly and Assembly

Disassembly and assembly are similar for the 4150 and 4160 series carburetors although there are minor differences from model to model. The following is a generalized disassembly and assembly procedure for all Corvette, four-barrel Holley carburetors.

1. Remove the primary and secondary fuel bowls, metering bodies, plates, splash shields, and fuel tubes.

2. Disconnect the secondary throttle-operating rod from the throttle lever. Remove the secondary throttle-operating assembly and gasket from the main body of the carburetor.

3. Remove the float hinge pin re-

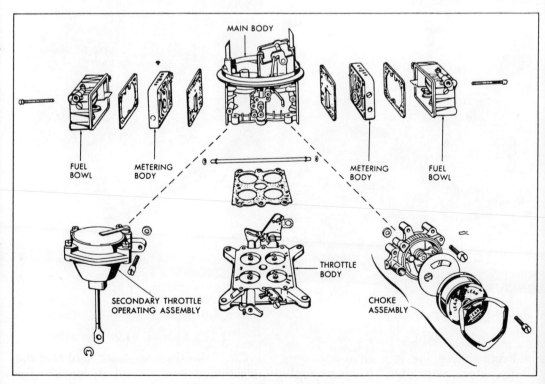

Exploded view of Holley 4150

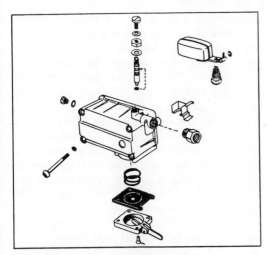

Exploded view of Holley 4150 bowl

tainer and remove the float and spring from the bowl. If so equipped, remove the inlet baffle.

4. Loosen the inlet needle and seat lock screw and remove the assembly. Remove the sight plug and gasket.

5. Remove the inlet fitting(s), gaskets, fuel filter, and spring.

6. On the primary bowl: remove the air vent assembly (except early 4150); remove the pump diaphragm screws and lift the pump housing, diaphragm, and spring from the fuel bowl; check that the pump inlet ball can move freely. Replace the bowl assembly if ball movement is restricted or if either the ball or passage are damaged.

7. To disassemble the metering body (all except 4160 secondary): remove the main metering jets.

CAUTION: *Use a jet wrench or very wide screwdriver to prevent damaging the jets.*

Use a one-inch, twelve-point socket to remove the power valves. On the primary side, remove the idle mixture screws and seals.

8. On the 4160 secondary: remove the plate and gasket from the metering body dowel pins.

9. On the early model 4150: remove the choke housing, retainer, and gasket. Remove the choke housing shaft, fast-idle cam, and choke piston.

10. On late model 4150 and 4160 carburetors: remove the choke vacuum break disconnecting link, fast-idle cam, and choke lever.

11. Remove the discharge nozzle, invert the carburetor, and shake the discharge needle out.

12. Replace gaskets, seals, and small parts with those provided in the rebuilding kit. Reverse the disassembly procedure to assemble the carburetor.

FUEL INJECTION

The Rochester fuel injection system was a performance option on 1963 through 1965 327 cubic inch engines. It delivers a constantly regulated air/fuel flow regardless of the engine requirements and eliminates carburetion difficulties caused by cornering or braking. While the fuel injection system is more complex than the ordinary carburetor, it is not beyond the repair capabilities of the average owner/mechanic—provided he adheres to procedure and specification recommendations.

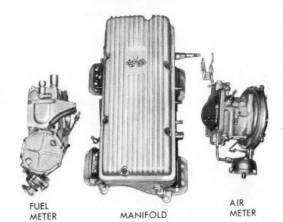

FUEL METER   MANIFOLD   AIR METER

Three major components of the fuel injection system

The first hurdle is understanding the design of the fuel injector and this is best done by thinking of the unit as three separate systems, interlocked to accomplish a common function. The first system is the air meter and this simultaneously furnishes the fuel meter with an assessment of the load demands of the engine and feeds air to the intake manifold. The intake manifold is designed to ram charge the air as it distributes it to the cylinders. The fuel meter evaluates the air meter signal and furnishes the correct amount of fuel to the nozzles where it is injected into the engine.

Description and Operation

AIR METER

The 1963–1964 air meter consists of three sub-components: the throttle valve, cold enrichment valve and diffuser cone assembly, and the meter housing. The 1965 air meter was modified to the extent that a choke piston was added and the choke valve stop was relocated in the diffuser cone. This allows an initial choke opening of 10° which increases to 30° after an initial cold start. The throttle valve regulates the flow of air into the manifold and is mechanically actuated by the accelerator pedal. The diffuser cone, suspended in the bore of the air meter inlet, functions as an annular venturi and accelerates the air flow between the cone and the meter housing. The air meter houses the previously mentioned components plus the idle and main venturi signal systems.

The main venturi vacuum signals are generated at the venturi as the incoming air rushes over an annular opening formed between the air meter body and

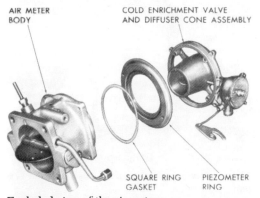

AIR METER
BODY

COLD ENRICHMENT VALVE
AND DIFFUSER CONE ASSEMBLY

SQUARE RING   PIEZOMETER
GASKET   RING

Exploded view of the air meter

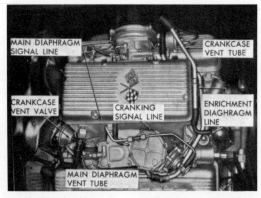

MAIN DIAPHRAGM
SIGNAL LINE

CRANKCASE
VENT TUBE

CRANKCASE
VENT VALVE

CRANKING
SIGNAL LINE

ENRICHMENT
DIAPHRAGM
LINE

MAIN DIAPHRAGM
VENT TUBE

Fuel injection lines

piezometer ring. They are then transmitted through a tube to the main control diaphragm in the fuel meter. The venturi vacuum signal measures the flow of air into the engine and automatically controls the air/fuel ratio. The one exception to this is at idle speeds.

Idle air requirements are handled differently by the fuel injection method. Approximately 40% of the idle-speed air flow enters the engine through the nozzle block air connections tapped into the air meter body. Part of the remaining 60% flows past the throttle valve which is preset against a fixed stop. The remainder enters through the idle air, by-pass passage that is controlled by the large, idle-speed adjusting screw. Idle speed is adjusted by turning this screw in or out.

FUEL METER

The fuel meter's float-controlled fuel reservoir is basically the same as that found in conventional carburetion. The fuel meter receives fuel from the regular engine fuel pump. The incoming fuel is routed through a 10 micron filter before entering the main reservoir of the fuel meter, where the high pressure gear pump picks it up. This, high pressure, spur-gear type pump is completely submerged in the lower part of the fuel meter main reservoir. A distributor-powered, flexible shaft drives the pump at ½ engine speed. Fuel pressures span a range of near zero to 200 psi, according to engine speed. Fuel not used by the engine reenters the fuel meter through a fuel control system. The 1965 fuel meter contains a vent screen and baffle which helps to stabilize the air/fuel mixture.

FUEL CONTROL SYSTEM

A fuel control system regulates fuel pressure (flow) from the fuel pump to the nozzles. This flow is controlled by the amount of fuel that is spilled or recirculated from the high pressure pump, through the nozzle block, back to the fuel meter spill ports. This is accomplished by a three-piece spill plunger or disc that is located between the gear pump and the nozzles.

When high fuel flow is required, it moves downward, closing the spill ports to the fuel meter reservoir and concentrating the flow to the nozzle circuits.

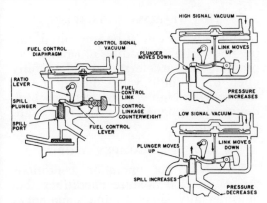

Fuel control linkage

Correspondingly, the spill plunger or disc must be raised to allow the spill ports to be exposed when a low fuel flow is required. This causes the main output of the gear pump to by-pass the nozzle circuits and reenter the meter reservoir through the now-opened spill ports.

The spill plunger is not mechanically controlled by the accelerator pedal. Fuel control is accomplished by a precisely counterbalanced linkage system sensitive to fuel pressure and diaphragm vacuum. Thus the slightest change in venturi vacuum signal on the main control diaphragm will activate the linkage. One end of the fuel control lever rests against the spill plunger head while the other end connects by a link to the main control diaphragm. The control lever pivots on the roller end of an arm called the ratio lever. When the increased vacuum above the diaphragm forces the control lever upward, the lever pivots on the ratio lever's roller and pushes the spill plunger or disc downward. This closes the spill ports and steps up fuel flow to the nozzles. When decreased vacuum above the diaphragm reverses the pivot action, fuel pressure forces the spill plunger upward and permits the spill ports to by-pass fuel into the reservoir, thus fuel flow to the nozzles is reduced.

The diaphragm vacuum-to-fuel pressure ratio, and subsequent fuel/air ratio, is regulated by the position of the ratio lever. As the ratio lever changes position, the mechanical advantage of the linkage system also changes, thus providing the correct fuel/air ratio for each driving condition. As long as engine manifold vacuum exceeds 8 in. Hg (mercury), the ratio lever remains at the economy stop and

fuel flow follows the dictates of the main control diaphragm vacuum. A sudden decrease in manifold vacuum moves the ratio lever to the power stop. The resulting increase in the mechanical advantage of the linkage system closes the spill ports and increases full flow to the nozzles.

STARTING SYSTEM

Cold engine starting conditions require richer fuel/air mixtures to compensate for poor fuel evaporation. The absence of an accelerator pump prevents the driver from providing extra fuel by pumping the accelerator pedal. The correct method is to depress the pedal once and then release. This pre-sets the throttle for starting by the fast-idle cam. The vacuum signal generated at cranking rpm is very low and must be boosted. This boost is provided by a spring-loaded, open-cranking signal valve located at the enrichment diaphragm housing. This open valve allows the manifold cranking vacuum to react directly on, and lift, the main control diaphragm. This closes the spill valve. In addition, the spring-loaded enrichment diaphragm holds the ratio lever at the rich or power stop, thus providing maximum fuel flow to the nozzles. As soon as the engine starts, manifold vacuum overcomes the springs in the cranking signal valve and enrichment diaphragm, and the regular idle system is brought into operation.

The vacuum-controlled, cranking-signal valve circuit was eliminated on 1965 model injectors and replaced by a solenoid-controlled, by-pass fuel circuit. This system delivers the entire output engine fuel pump to the fuel distributor via a by-pass line. The fuel is then routed through a check valve and finally arrives at the individual nozzles. The control solenoid is energized when the ignition switch is held in the start position and the accelerator pedal is depressed less than ⅓ of its travel. Depressing the accelerator pedal further trips a micro-switch on the throttle linkage and stops fuel delivery to the by-pass circuit.

IDLE SYSTEM

Correct injector operation at idle speed is highly dependent upon the generation of a strong venturi signal and its subsequent transmittal to the control diaphragm. To ensure this signal during cold engine idle, the fast-idle cam holds the throttle valve cracked open. This increases the velocity of air flowing through the venturi which in turn strengthens the venturi vacuum signal being transported to the main control diaphragm. The electrically heated choke valve remains closed during initial cold engine operation, and this requires the entire air flow to pass through the venturi. This rerouting of the air flow generates a usable venturi signal even at relatively low engine speeds. Intake manifold vacuum acts directly on the enrichment diaphragm. The diaphragm's response movement adjusts the ratio lever to the economy stop as soon as manifold vacuum is sufficient to overcome the diaphragm spring. As the electric heating element senses a rise in engine temperature, it relaxes the thermostat and permits the choke valve to open. Air flow through the venturi decreases and the signal generated here drops. The idle signal system now becomes the more dominant signal.

Fuel control during warm engine idle is a result of main control diaphragm response to the idle circuit signal. With the ratio lever already positioned at the economy stop, air now enters through the idle air circuit and the nozzle blocks.

ACCELERATION

Acceleration is instantaneous at normal driving speeds. Opening the throttle valve increases both air flow and the venturi signal at the main diaphragm. The momentary drop in manifold vacuum causes the ratio lever to move to the power stop position. A calibrated restriction in the main control signal circuit stabilizes the idle signal and adds this to the total signal as long as it is present.

RATIO LEVER—POWER STOP

The air/fuel ratio requirements for power are basically the same as those necessary for acceleration. The drop in manifold vacuum, caused by a wide-open throttle condition, moves the ratio lever to the power stop. The open throttle also provides a stronger venturi signal through the increased air flow.

HOT STARTING/UNLOADING

Rich mixtures must be prevented during hot starting/unloading situations. Depressing the accelerator pedal to fully open the throttle valve during staring will prevent high vacuum from reaching the cranking signal valve and will facilitate starting.

HOT IDLE COMPENSATOR

Extremely hot operation conditions can cause rich mixture conditions that detrimentally affect engine smoothness and idling. To remedy this, a thermostatically controlled valve on the top side of the air meter throttle valve allows additional air to bleed into the manifold and restore the idle mixture to a correct ratio.

Idle Speed and Fuel Adjustments

Idle speed and fuel adjustments require pre-setting of the idle-speed and

Idle speed adjustment

Idle mixture adjustment

idle-fuel adjusting screws 1½ turns out from their fully closed position. Start the engine and adjust the idle-speed screw until 800–850 rpm is obtained. Adjust the idle-fuel screw until the smoothest engine idle is attained. Should the two idle-adjusting screws become completely out of phase, purge the system or stop the engine and repeat the entire preceding procedure.

Fast Idle-Speed and Cold Enrichment Adjustments

Adjust the fast idle-speed by bending the enrichment linkage until clearance between the fast-idle cam and the adjusting screw resembles the illustration. With the engine stopped, crack the throttle valve and manually close the cold enrichment valve. Release the throttle linkage and check to see that the fast-idle is now positioned for cold engine operation. Release the cold enrichment valve, warm the engine, and adjust the fast-idle screw to obtain 2200 rpm. Make the cold enrichment adjustment by setting the cold enrichment cover to 3 notches lean. Be sure that the valve linkage operates freely.

Ratio Lever Stop Settings

This series of adjustments requires the use of a manometer. Attach the manometer in a convenient place on the vehicle and use the two-position bracket so that the most vertical position may be obtained. After the unit has been leveled by means of the leveling vial, open both water manometer valves and see if a zero reading exists. If not, adjust the oil leveling screw. If this fails to zero the indicator, add red oil (specific gravity 0.826). Back off the leveling screw for this procedure.

Remove both hose adapters on the mercury (Hg) manometer and plugs located in the adapters. Install the tee fitting in the most easily accessible fuel nozzle circuit. Attach the fuel pressure line to the tee fitting and the mercury manometer. Check the fuel trap inlet to see that it is properly positioned in the line. Clamp the venturi signal line to the cranking signal valve line and the water manometer. Check the clamp to be sure it is tightly closed on the line. If it isn't, high vacuum during engine cranking will cause the red oil to be lost. Replace the main diaphragm vent tube with the large

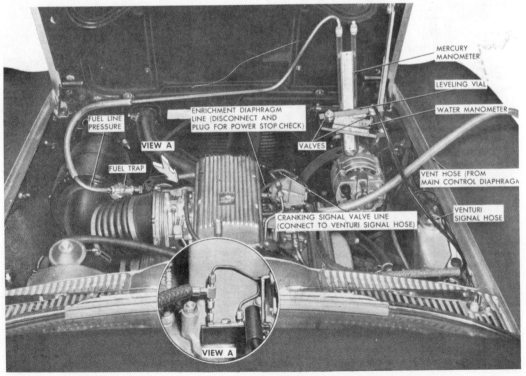

Manometer installation

rubber tube. Adjust the scale of the mercury manometer to read zero inches. Recheck the manometer leveling vial and make any necessary adjustments. This completes the installation.

The economy stop adjustment procedure begins with a visual check of the unit for physical defects. With the engine warmed up, check to see that the unit is operating on the economy stop. Some injectors may be difficult to start with the cranking-signal valve line disconnected. The line may be reconnected during the initial starting procedure.

Increase engine rpm until a 0.5 in. signal is registered on the water manometer. Check the mercury manometer and record its reading. Decrease the engine rpm and repeat the above procedure. Average three readings for best accuracy. To adjust, loosen the locknut and turn the economy stop screw in or out until the mercury manometer reads 0.8 in. (±0.1 in.) when the water manometer reads 0.5 in.

Economy and power stop adjusting screws

The power stop readings are obtained with the manometer hooked up as in the previous procedure. Disconnect and plug the vacuum line going to the enrichment diaphragm and the injection unit will operate only on the power stop. Do not prolong this operation or spark plug fouling will result.

Increase the engine rpm until a 0.5 in. signal is reached on the water manometer and check and record the mercury manometer reading. Reduce engine speed and repeat the above operation. Average

three readings for the best results. Check the enrichment diaphragm to see that it is not bottoming in the housing. To adjust the power stop, loosen the locknut and turn the adjusting screw until a reading of 1.2 in. (±0.1 in.) is reached on the mercury manometer when the water manometer reads 0.5 in.

Removal and Installation

1. Disconnect the washer vacuum line, accelerator linkage, electric choke lead wire, and the bellcrank return spring.

2. Loosen the flexible hose clamp and slide the hose from the air meter adapter.

3. Disconnect the fuel line at the filter and the drive cable coupling at the distributor by sliding the cable into the

Removing fuel pressure lines

pump housing to disengage it from the distributor, and then pulling it clear. Don't lose the fiber washer on the end of the cable.

4. Remove the engine/manifold adapter-plate retaining nuts and lift the assembly from the engine.

5. Install a ⅜ in. x 2 in. bolt and nut in each manifold outer mounting-hole to allow the unit to be placed upright on a workbench without damaging the nozzles.

6. Reverse the above procedure to install.

Disassembly and Assembly

1. The first step in disassembly is to separate the fuel injection unit into its three main components: fuel meter, air meter, and manifold.

2. Separate the air meter from the injector unit by disconnecting the bellcrank from the pivot shaft and leaving it attached to the air meter. Disconnect the main control signal tube at both ends and remove. Remove the retaining nuts and washers and carefully lift the air meter while simultaneously disconnecting the rubber, nozzle balance tube elbow at the air meter.

3. Disconnect the enrichment diaphragm tube at both ends, disengaging the tube at the manifold end first. Disconnect the main control diaphragm vent tube at tboth ends. Invert the injector and drain the fuel reservoir through the cover vent, then disconnect the fuel pressure lines. Remove the lower retaining screws, the single upper bolt, and the short vent tube. Discard the rubber O-ring at the fuel meter end of the fuel line. Remove the fuel meter from the injector unit.

Fuel pump piston and valve assembly

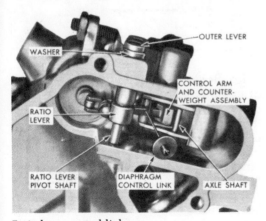

Ratio lever control linkage

4. Disassemble the air meter by removing the air cleaner adapter, fast-idle cam pivot screw, diffuser cone assembly, and piezometer ring from the air meter.

5. Remove the idle-speed and idle-fuel adjusting screws. The throttle valve need not be removed unless shaft binding exists.

6. Disassemble the fuel meter by re-

moving the diaphragm cover and shield. Carefully remove the diaphragm retaining nut and diaphragm from the control link. The control link must be kept from rotating to prevent damaging the control link.

7. Remove the nylon splash shield, the fuel bowl cover attaching screws and carefully lift the cover, upper support bracket, and gasket from the meter body. Do not bend the control link. Start the link into the slot, then pry the opposite side upward and turn the shield over the link.

8. Remove the fuel pump, enrichment housing, and cranking signal valve. Remove the spill plunger cover and filter, spill plunger and sleeve assembly from the fuel meter bore. If the spill plunger separates from the sleeve, use a hooked wire to pull the sleeve out.

9. Remove the ratio lever and shaft. Rotate the control arm and coun-

Fuel injection pump

1. Inlet housing cover	7. Drive pin	13. Main housing
2. Thrust washer	8. Driveshaft	14. Discharge valve (5)
3. Drive plate	9. Inlet piston (5)	15. Valve spring (5)
4. Thrust washer	10. Inlet valve (5)	16. O-ring seal
5. Wobble plate	11. Valve spring (5)	17. O-ring seal
6. Bearing plate	12. Valve retainer (5)	18. Discharge housing

terweights on the axle and remove the axle. Remove the control arm and counterweight assembly from the meter body. This will also remove the lead sealing ball on the outer end of the axle shaft.

10. The fuel pump is secured to the fuel meter by 5 screws. Remove these, noting that the shortest screw is positioned in the 9 o'clock position. With pump separated from the fuel meter, scribe reassembly marks on the pump housing.

11. Remove the cover attaching screws and the cover. Hand pressure is sufficient to pull the drive shaft from the pump drive gear and housing. Use a suitable driver to remove the drive shaft seal from the pump housing. Bear in mind, the fuel meter contains 48 parts in addition to screws. Be careful. Reassembly is the reverse of this procedure.

12. Nozzles may be disassembled for cleaning but care should be taken to ensure correct reassembly. Never clean

nozzle orifices with wire. If a nozzle is dirty, replace it. Should more than one nozzle be found exceptionally dirty, replace the fuel meter filter. Replace nozzles only as complete assemblies and according to the following chart:

Nozzle Code	Part Number
W17 or 18	7017323
X18 or 19	7017324
Y19 or 20	7017325

13. Begin disassembly by carefully disconnecting and lifting the fuel lines out of the way. Disconnect either the throttle bell crank or fuel pump drive cable when removing nozzles in their vicinity. Remove the nozzles and nozzle blocks as complete assemblies. Invert the blocks and remove the individual nozzles. Carefully remove the old nozzle gaskets. Disassemble the unit by securing the nozzle body and inserting a drift punch in the head to turn it. Avoid damaging, losing, or mixing parts. Remember: the nozzle orifice discs are assembled with the bright side toward the engine. After cleaning or replacing nozzle assemblies, reinstall them in the nozzle block, using new gaskets. Check to see that the nozzle gaskets remain in position during reinstallation and that the nozzles are properly placed in the nozzle

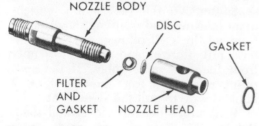

Nozzle assembly

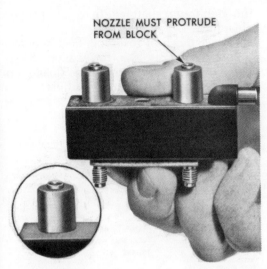

NOZZLE MUST PROTRUDE
FROM BLOCK

Nozzle block assembly

shields. Reassembly is the reversal of this procedure.

14. A fuel nozzle spray-pattern check should be made whenever a complete nozzle cleaning is made. Drive the gear pump with an electric drill while applying oral vacuum at the main control diaphragm. The latter ensures that all fuel is routed through the nozzle circuit. The spray pattern is correct when each bank of nozzles appears as a single spray when viewed from the end of the assembly.

15. Spill plunger assemblies are basically the same for all fuel injection units. After removing the assembly from the fuel meter, lubricate with fuel, and check the valve action. Clean or replace the assembly as required.

16. Reassembly of the air meter is the reversal of the disassembly procedure. At

this time, check for throttle shaft binding. If such a condition exists, attempt to remedy by soaking in solvent. If the throttle shaft still binds, disconnect the throttle shaft from the linkage, remove the throttle plate screws, and file the burrs on the shaft. Remove the shaft, clean, rebush and then reassemble. During reassembly, preset the idle-speed and idle-fuel adjusting screws 1½ turns out from the bottom.

17. Fuel meter reassembly is the reversal of the disassembly procedure. When installing the main control diaphragm, keep in mind that the slots in the diaphragm should readily align with the cover attaching screw holes located in the bowl cover. Repeat the reassembly steps until the diaphragm holes line u naturally. Do not force this alignment. . the diaphragm seemed tight when removed, it is defective. The replacement

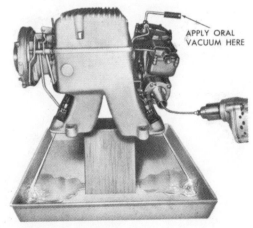

APPLY ORAL
VACUUM HERE

Checking spray pattern

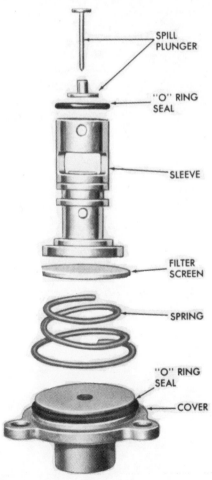

SPILL
PLUNGER

"O" RING
SEAL

SLEEVE

FILTER
SCREEN

SPRING

"O" RING
SEAL

COVER

Spill plunger assembly

diaphragm should not be installed in the same condition. At this time check the clearance between the housing and the enrichment diaphragm. A minimum of 0.040 in. is required to prevent interference during power stop operation. Adjust the diaphragm shaft length to gain proper clearance.

Check the fuel reservoir float settings before replacing the top cover. Float level should be $2^9/_{32}$ in. while float drop should be $2^{27}/_{32}$ in. Bend to adjust.

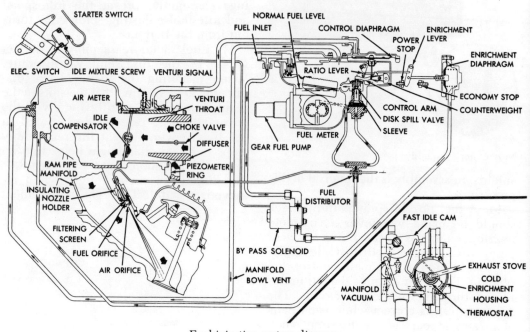

Fuel injection system diagram

Carburetor Specifications

Year	Application	Carburetor Model	Float Level (in.)	Float Drop (in.)	Pump Rod (in.)	Automatic Choke Setting	Main Metering Jet (in.)		Metering Rod (in.)		Throttle Bore (in.)		Fast Idle (rpm)
							Prim	Sec	Prim	Sec	Prim	Sec	
1963–65	250 hp	Carter WCFB	$7/32$①	$3/4$	$1/2$	index	0.086	0.0635	0.042	0.067	$1\%_{16}$	$1\%_{16}$	1750
	300, 340 hp	Carter AFB	$7/32$	$3/4$	$1/2$	1 lean	0.104	0.0689	0.060	0.069	$1\%_{16}$	$1^{11}/_{16}$	1750
	365, 350 hp	Holley 4150	②	—	—	1 lean	0.065	0.076	—	—	$1\%_{16}$	$1\%_{16}$	2300
1966	300, 350 hp	Holley 4160	②	—	0.015	½–1 rod dia interf	0.065	0.076	—	—	$1\%_{16}$	$1\%_{16}$	2200
	350 hp	Holley 4150	②	—	0.015	½–1 rod dia interf	0.067	0.074	—	—	$1\%_{16}$	$1\%_{16}$	2200
	390 hp③	Rochester 4MV	$9/32$	—	$13/32$ inner hole	½–1 rod dia interf	0.071	—	—	—	1%	2%	2000
	390 hp	Holley 4160	②	—	0.015	½–1 rod dia interf	0.065	0.076	—	—	$1\%_{16}$	$1\%_{16}$	2000
	425 hp	Holley 4150	②	—	0.015	½–1 rod dia interf	0.073 0.070	0.076	—	—	$1^{11}/_{16}$	$1^{11}/_{16}$	2000
1967	300, 350 hp	Holley 4160	②	—	0.015	½–1 rod dia interf	0.065 ④	0.076	—	—	$1\%_{16}$	$1\%_{16}$	2000
	390 hp	Holley 4160	②	—	0.015	½–1 rod dia interf	0.065 ⑤	0.073	—	—	$1\%_{16}$	$1\%_{16}$	2200
	400, 435 hp⑥	Holley 2300C	②	—	0.015	½–1 rod dia interf	0.064 ⑦	—	—	—	1%	—	2200

Carburetor Specifications (cont.)

Year	Application	Carburetor Model	Float Level (in.)	Float Drop (in.)	Pump Rod (in.)	Automatic Choke Setting	Main Metering Jet (in.)		Metering Rod (in.)		Throttle Bore (in.)		Fast Idle (rpm)
							Prim	Sec	Prim	Sec	Prim	Sec	
1967	400, 435 hp⑥	Holley 2300	②	—	0.015	—	0.076	—	—	—	1¾	—	—
	430 hp	Holley 4150	②	—	0.015	½–1 rod dia interf	0.069	0.076	—	—	1 11/16	1 11/16	2200
1968	300 hp	Rochester	9/32	—	9/32	1 rod dia interf	0.071	—	NA	27/32	1⅜	2¼	2400
	350 hp	Rochester	9/32	—	9/32	1 rod dia interf	0.071	—	NA	27/32	1⅜	2¼	2400
	390 hp	Rochester	3/16	—	9/32	1 rod dia interf	0.071	—	NA	27/32	1⅜	2¼	2400
	400 hp⑥	Holley 2300C	②	—	0.015	½–1 rod dia interf	0.064 ⑦	—	—	—	1½	—	2200
	435 hp	Holley 2300	②	—	0.015	½–1 rod dia interf	0.076	—	—	—	1¾	—	—
	430 hp	Holley 4150	②	—	0.015	½–1 rod dia interf	0.069	0.076	—	—	1 11/16	1 11/16	2200
1969	300 hp	Rochester 4MV	7/32	—	5/16	⑧	0.067	—	NA	NA	1⅜	2¼	2400
	350 hp	Rochester 4MV	¼	—	5/16	⑧	0.071	—	NA	NA	1⅜	2¼	2400
	390 hp	Rochester 4MV	¼	—	5/16	⑧	0.071	—	NA	NA	1⅜	2¼	2400
	400, 435 hp⑥	Holley 2300C	②	—	0.015	⑧	0.063 ⑨	—	—	—	1½	—	2200

Year	hp	Carburetor											
1969		Holley 2300	②	—	0.015	—	0.076	—	—	—	1 3/4	—	—
	430 hp	Holley 4150	②	—	0.015	⑧	0.082L 0.078R	0.080L 0.082R	—	—	1 3/4	1 3/4	2200
1970	300 hp	Rochester 4MV	¼	—	5/16	⑧	0.076	—	NA	NA	1 3/8	2 1/4	2400
	350 hp	Rochester 4MV	¼	—	5/16	⑧	0.078	—	NA	NA	1 3/8	2 1/4	2400
	370 hp	Holley 4150	②	—	0.015	⑧	0.068	0.076	—	—	1 9/16	1 9/16	2200
	390 hp	Rochester 4MV	¼	—	5/16	⑧	0.078	—	NA	NA	1 3/8	2 1/4	—
	460 hp	Holley 4150	②	—	0.015	⑧	0.070	0.076	—	—	1 9/16	1 9/16	2200
1971	270 hp	Rochester 4MV	¼	—	NA	0.100	0.074	—	NA	NA	1 3/8	2 1/4	—
	330 hp	Holley 4150	②	—	0.015	⑧	0.070	0.076	—	—	1 11/16	1 11/16	2200
	365 hp	Rochester 4MV	¼	—	NA	0.100	0.074	—	NA	NA	1 3/8	2 1/4	—
	425 hp	Holley 4150	②	—	0.015	⑧	0.070	0.076	—	—	1 11/16	1 11/16	2200
1972	200 hp	Rochester 4MV	¼	—	3/8	0.100	0.074	—	NA	NA	1 3/8	2 1/4	1350 man, 2200 auto
	255 hp	Holley 4150	②	—	0.015	⑨	0.068	0.073	—	—	1 11/16	1 11/16	2350
	270 hp	Rochester 4MV	¼	—	3/8	0.100	0.078	—	NA	NA	1 3/8	2 1/4	1350 man, 1500 auto

Carburetor Specifications (cont.)

Year	Application	Carburetor Model	Float Level (in.)	Float Drop (in.)	Pump Rod (in.)	Automatic Choke Setting	Main Metering Jet (in.)		Metering Rod (in.)		Throttle Bore (in.)		Fast Idle (rpm)
							Prim	Sec	Prim	Sec	Prim	Sec	
1973	All	Rochester 4MV	$7/32$	—	$13/32$	0.100	NA	NA	NA	NA	$1\frac{3}{8}$	$2\frac{1}{4}$	1300 man, 1600 auto
1974	All	Rochester 4MV	$\frac{1}{4}$	—	$13/32$	0.43	NA	NA	NA	NA	$1\frac{3}{8}$	$2\frac{1}{4}$	1300 man, 1600 auto
1975	All	Rochester 4MC	$15/32$	—	$9/32$	0.43	NA	NA	NA	NA	$1\frac{3}{8}$	$2\frac{1}{4}$	1300 man, 1600 auto
1976	All	Rochester 4MC	$15/32$	—	$9/32$	0.43	NA	NA	NA	NA	$1\frac{3}{8}$	$2\frac{1}{4}$	1300 man, 1600 auto

NA Not available
L Left-side
R Right-side
① Primary floats, ¼ in. for secondaries

② Fuel level at sight plug = ± $\frac{1}{32}$ in.
③ Equipped with A.I.R.
④ 0.063 with A.I.R.
⑤ 0.067 with A.I.R.

⑥ Three two-barrel carburetors
⑦ 0.062 for 400 hp with auto trans
⑧ Top of rod even with bottom of hole
⑨ 0.061 for 400 hp with auto trans

Fuel Injection Specifications

		1963	Early 1964 [1]	Late 1964 [2]	1965
Fuel pressure @ 0.5 H_2O (± Hg)	Power Stop	1.2	1.9	1.9	1.9
	Economy Stop	0.8	1.0	1.0	1.0
Fast idle speed (rpm-engine hot)		2000	2200	2200	2600
Float level (in.)		$2\frac{9}{32}$	$2\frac{9}{32}$	$2\frac{9}{32}$	$2\frac{9}{32}$
Float drop (in.)		$2\frac{27}{32}$	$2\frac{27}{32}$	$2\frac{27}{32}$	$2\frac{27}{32}$
Vacuum to apply—Enrichment Diaphragm (in. Hg)	Economy Stop	9	6	6	6
	Travel Center	NA	4	4	4
	Power Stop	3	2	2	2
Minimum Enrichment Diaphragm Clearance (in.)		0.040	0.010	0.010	0.010
Cold Enrichment Setting		Index	3 notches lean	3 notches lean	Index
Maximum vacuum to apply—Cranking signal valve (in. Hg)		1	1	——	——
Vacuum to apply—Main signal diaphragm (in. H_2O)		½	½	½	½

[1] Part No. 7017375-R
[2] Part No. 7017380

Chapter 5

Chassis Electrical

Heater Blower

Removal and Installation

1963–1967

1. It is not necessary to drain the cooling system to remove the heater blower. Remove the radiator expansion-tank re-taining straps and move the tank from the work area.

2. Disconnect the ground cable from the battery.

3. Remove the blower motor leads.

4. Mark the blower motor mounting plate and blower motor assembly for correct reassembly.

5. Remove the five retaining screws and remove the blower assembly.

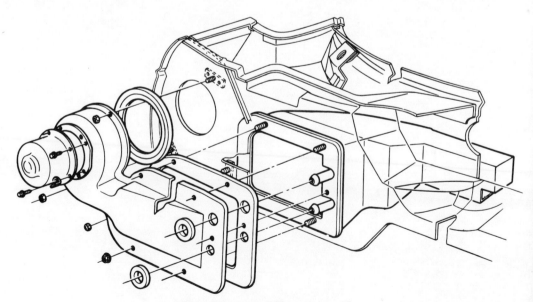

1963–67 heater and blower assembly

6. Reverse the removal procedure to reinstall, being careful to reposition the blower according to the marks previously made.

1968–1976

1. Disconnect the ground cable from the battery.

2. If so equipped, remove the radiator expansion-tank retaining screws and move the tank out of the way.

3. Remove the blower motor leads.

4. Remove the case mounting screws and remove the blower assembly. Gentle pry on the flange, should the sealer hold the motor in place.

5. Use the reverse procedure to install the motor.

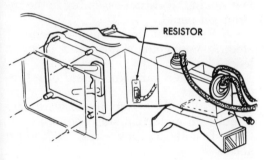

1968 heater and defroster assembly

Heater Assembly

Removal and Installation

1963–1967

1. Drain the radiator, remove the radiator expansion-tank retaining straps, and move it from the work area.

2. Remove the battery.

3. Remove the water hoses from the heater assembly.

4. Remove the seven stud nuts attaching the blower and an inlet assembly to the firewall. Remove the assembly.

5. Remove the glove compartment and panels on both sides of the console.

6. As a precaution, place a plastic sheet or other waterproof covering over the passenger-side carpet.

7. Remove the two control cables from the instrument panel.

8. Disconnect the wire leads from the lower switch and the resistor.

9. Carefully remove the heater assembly from under the dashboard.

10. Remove the four, core cover retaining screws.

11. Loosen the four screws holding the core retaining yokes and the core to the retainer cover.

12. Remove the rear cover and core.

13. To install, reverse this procedure.

1968–1976

1. Disconnect the battery ground cable.

2. Drain the cooling system and remove and plug the water hoses from the heater connections.

3. Remove the air-distributor duct stud nuts on the firewall.

4. Remove the right instrument panel pad, right-hand dashboard braces, center dash console duct, and the floor outlet duct.

5. Remove the radio and center dashboard console.

6. Pull the distributor duct from the firewall and remove the resistor wires when clearance is sufficient.

7. Remove the heater-core retaining springs and remove the core.

8. Installation is the reverse of removal. If core-to-case sealer was damaged during removal, replace with new sealer.

Radio

Removal and Installation

1963–1967

1. Remove both console side panels and trim strip(s).

2. Remove the radio knobs, washers, bezels, and nuts.

3. Disconnect the antenna lead-in, the radio-to-electrical harness, and radio-to-speaker connectors.

4. Remove the one attaching bolt located on the lower, right side of the radio.

5. Turn the radio on its side and remove it from the left side of the console.

1968–71 COUPE

1. Disconnect battery.

2. Remove right and left door sill plates and kick pads.

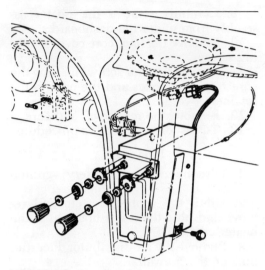

1963–67 radio installation

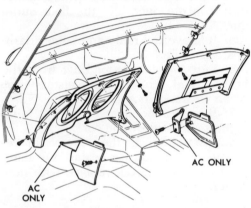

AC ONLY

AC
ONLY

1968–71 instrument panels and lower trim assemblies

3. Disconnect right and left side radio-to-speaker connectors.

4. Remove right side dash pad.

5. Remove right and left console forward trim pads.

6. Remove bolt and remove the heater floor outlet duct by pulling it through left hand opening.

7. From front of console, tape radio push buttons in depressed position. From rear of console, disconnect electrical connector, brace and antenna lead-in.

8. Remove radio knobs and bezel retaining nuts. Push radio assembly forward and remove from rear through right side opening.

9. Install by reversing procedure above.

1969–71 Convertible

1. Disconnect battery.

2. Remove right instrument panel pad.

3. Disconnect speaker connectors.

4. Remove wiper switch trim plate screws to gain access to switch connector and remove connector and trim plate from cluster assembly.

5. Unclip and remove right and left console forward trim pads and remove forwardmost screw on right and left side of console.

6. Inserting a flexible drive socket between the console and metal horseshoe brace, remove the nuts from the two studs on the lower edge of the console cluster. Remove the remaining screws that retain the cluster assembly to the instrument panel.

7. From rear of console, disconnect electric connector, brace and antenna lead-in.

8. Remove radio knobs and bezel retaining nuts.

9. Pull radio assembly forward and remove through right side opening.

10. Install by reversing procedure above.

1972–76

1. Disconnect the negative battery cable and remove the right instrument panel pad.

2. Disconnect the radio speaker connectors.

3. Remove the wiper switch trim plate screws and tip the plate forward to gain access to the switch connector. Remove the switch connector and trim plate from the dash.

4. Unclip and remove the right and left forward console trim pads. Remove the forwardmost screw on the left and right sides of the console.

5. Working with a flexible drive socket between the console and the metal horseshoe brace, remove the nuts from the studs on the lower edge of the console cluster.

6. Remove the remaining console attaching screws and disconnect the radio electrical connectors, antenna wire and radio brace from the rear of the console. Remove the radio knobs and nuts.

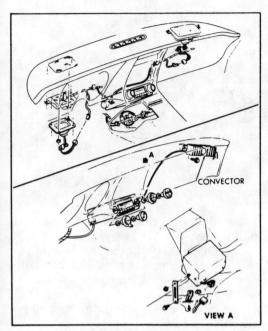

CONVECTOR

VIEW A

1974 radio and speaker installation

7. Pull the top of the console rearward and separate the radio from the console and remove it from the right side opening.

NOTE: *The center instrument cluster trim panel is designed to collapse under impact. Do not deflect the panel to gain access to the radio. Also, the remotely located radio heat sink should be removed with the radio when servicing is required.*

Instrument Cluster

Removal and Installation

1963–1967

All instruments are contained in one cluster.

1. Disconnect the negative battery cable. Remove the instrument panel harness from the lower steering column switch and disconnect the switch.

2. Remove the steering wheel cap and the center nut and washer.

3. Pull off the steering wheel with a suitable puller.

4. Remove the steering column escutcheon screws and the nuts from the column support U-bolt.

5. Loosen the lower column clamp at the firewall.

6. Loosen the lower, spring stop-clamp and slide the stop and spring down on the shaft.

7. Paint or mark the steering shaft and coupling with chalk. Remove the upper coupling clamp bolt.

8. Pull the jacket and steering shaft assembly from the coupling and very carefully pull it out through the dash, at the same time sliding the lower spring stop, spring, bearing, and seat off the steering shaft.

9. Disconnect the tachometer drive cable, cowl-vent control cable brackets, and headlight motor switch from the instrument cluster.

10. Disconnect the parking brake lever support bracket from the cowl crossmember.

11. Pull the headlight switch on. Reach under the instrument cluster and push in the detent pin on the switch; remove the knob and shaft.

12. Screw out the retaining nut with a wide bladed screwdriver. Remove the bezel and switch assembly from the instrument cluster. Disconnect the wiring connector from the switch.

13. Remove the lock cylinder from the ignition switch by turning it to the "Lock" position and inserting a wire in the small cylinder face hole. Push the wire in while turning the ignition key counterclockwise, until the lock cylinder can be removed.

14. Carefully remove ignition-switch escutcheon nut using a screwdriver held in the escutcheon slot and tapping it with a small hammer.

15. Remove the ignition switch from the instrument cluster and remove all wiring connectors. Unsnap the two lockings tangs with a screwdriver and unplug the ignition connector. Disconnect the ignition switch lamp support.

16. Disconnect the oil pressure line and the instrument and lamp lead wires. Disconnect the trip odometer cable.

17. Remove the cluster retaining screws and pull the cluster slightly forward for access to the speedometer and

tachometer cables and the remaining wires.

18. Remove cluster. All instruments are now easily accessible for service. Installation uses a reverse of the removal procedure.

1968–1976

1. To service instruments other than the speedometer and tachometer, follow radio removal procedures. Small instruments are easily removed, after the center cluster is removed from the console.

2. To remove the driver's-side instrument cluster, first disconnect the negative battery cable.

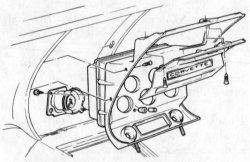

1968–71 center instrument and radio cluster

3. Lower the steering column.

4. Remove retaining screws and washers at the door opening, dash top, and leftside of the center panel.

5. Unclip and remove the left, front console trim-panel.

6. Pull the cluster slightly forward for access to speedometer and tachometer cables, headlight switch connectors, and lamp wires.

7. Remove the cluster. Speedometer and tachometer may now be serviced.

8. Install using a reversal of the removal procedure.

Windshield Wiper Motor

Removal and Installation
1963–1967

1. Remove the negative cable from the battery.

2. Remove distributor and left-side ignition shields. Remove the left-side,

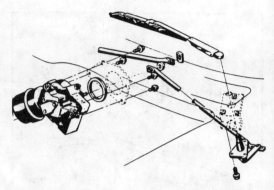

1963–67 windshield wiper motor and linkage

spark plug wire bracket and position out of the way.

3. Disconnect the ballast resistor on the firewall, then remove washer inlet and outlet hoses at the pump valve assembly.

4. Remove the distributor cap and position one side.

5. Disconnect washer pump and wiper-motor lead wires.

6. Remove the glove compartment.

7. Ensure that the wipers and motor are parked, then remove the wiper linkage retaining clip and disconnect both linkage and spacer from the crank arm.

8. Remove the wiper motor-to-firewall bolts and remove the motor.

9. To install, have an assistant aid in positioning and mount the wiper motor to the firewall. Ensure that the motor is in the parked position.

10. Position the left linkage, spacer, and right linkage on the crank arm and install the retaining clip in the groove in the crank arm.

11. Install remaining parts in a reverse order of removal.

12. Connect battery and test wipers and washers.

1968–1976

1. Ensure that the wiper motor is in the Park position.

2. Disconnect washer hoses and wire leads from the motor.

3. Remove the plenum chamber grille.

4. Remove the crank arm-to-motor retaining nut.

5. Remove the ignition shilding and distributor cap.

6. Remove the three, motor retaining screws or nuts and remove the motor.

7. Check gaskets and replace if neces-

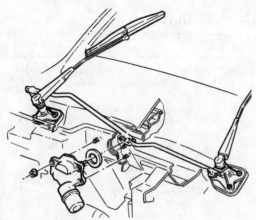

1968–76 windshield wiper motor and linkage

sary. Ensure that the motor is in Park position.

8. Reverse removal steps to install.

Seat Belts

WARNING SYSTEM

1972–73

The seat belt warning system consists of lap belt retractor switches, a pressure-sensitive switch underneath the right-hand front passenger's seat, a warning lamp and a buzzer.

On manual transmission-equipped cars, the circuit is wired through the ignition switch, the parking brake warning light switch, and a relay, which is located between the instrument cluster wiring and the switch on the parking brake. A diode is used to prevent feedback into the parking brake warning circuit.

On cars having automatic transmissions, the seat belt warning circuit is wired through the ignition switch and the combination back-up lamp/neutral safety switch.

With the ignition key in the "RUN" position, a weight of 40–50 lbs on the driver's or passenger's seat pressure-sensitive switch) energizes the circuit when the parking brake is released (M/T) or the gear selector placed in a forward drive range (A/T).

A warning light will glow and a buzzer will sound with the circuit energized, unless the seat belts are withdrawn from the retractors and fastened over the laps of the two outboard front seat occupants.

SEAT BELTS/STARTER INTERLOCK SYSTEM

As required by law, all 1974 and some 1975 Chevrolet passenger cars cannot be started until the front seat occupants are seated and have fastened their seat belts. If the proper sequence is not followed, e.g., the occupants fasten their seat belts and then sit on them, the engine cannot be started.

If, after the car is started, the seat belts are unfastened, a warning buzzer and light will be activated in a similar manner to that described for 1972–73 models.

The shoulder harness and lap belt are permanently fastened together, so that they both must be worn. The shoulder harness uses an inertia-lock reel to allow freedom of movement under normal driving conditions.

NOTE: *This type of reel locks up when the car decelerates rapidly, as during a crash.*

The lap belts use the same ratchet-type retractors that the 1972–73 models use.

The switches for the interlock system have been removed from the lap belt retractors and placed in the belt buckles. The seat sensors remain the same as those used in 1972–73.

For ease of service, the car may be started from outside, by reaching in and turning the key, but without depressing the seat sensors.

In case of system failure or for service, an override switch is located under the hood. This is a "one start" switch and it must be reset each time it is used.

Disabling the Interlock System

Since the requirement for the interlock system was dropped during the 1975 model year, these systems may now be legally disabled. The seat warning light is still required.

1. Disconnect the battery ground cable.

2. Locate the interlock harness connector under the left-side of the instrument panel on or near the fuse block. It has orange, yellow, and green leads.

3. Cut and tape the ends of the green wire on the body side of the connector.

4. Remove the buzzer from the fuse block or connector.

Light Bulb Specifications

Year	Usage	Number	Year	Usage	Number
1963	Headlamp (outer)	4002	1969–	(inner)—high beam only	4001
	Headlamp (inner)	4001	72	Parking lamp and directional	
	Parking lamp and directional	1034		signal	1157NA
	signal			Tail, stop and directional signal	1157
	Tail, stop, and turn signal			Backing lamp	1156
	lamps	1034		Instrument illumination lamps	1895
	Directional signal indicator			Temperature indicator	194
	lamps	1816		Oil pressure indicator	194
	High beam indicator lamp	53		Generator indicator	194
	Lighter lamp	53		Hi-beam indicator	1895
	Ignition switch lamp	53		Directional indicator	1895
	Instrument panel lamps	1816		Cigarette lighter lamp	1445
	Courtesy and/or dome lamps	90		Warning lamps	
	License plate lamp	67		Door ajar	1895
	Radio lamp	1816		Headlamps up	1895
	Clock lamp	1816		Seat belts	1895
	Parking brake alarm lamp	257		Heater or A/C control panel	1816
	Headlamp position warning			Glove box lamps	1895
	lamp	257		Dome and courtesy lamps	
				Cartridge type	211
1964	Headlamp (outer)	4002L		Bayonet type	90
	Headlamp (inner)	4001L		Seat separator-courtesy lamp	212
	Parking lamp and directional			Side marker-front	194
	signal	1157		Side marker-rear	194
	Tail, stop, and turn signal			License plate lamp	97
	lamps	1157		All tape players and FM radios	1893
	Directional signal indicator			Tape player lens illumination	
	lamps	1816		lamp	216
	High beam indicator lamp	1445		Stereo indicator lamp	2182D
	Lighter lamp	1445		Brake alarm lamp	1895
	Ignition lamp	1445		Luggage compartment lamp	1003
	Instrument panel lamps	1816		Map lamp (mirror)	563
	Courtesy and/or dome lamps	90			
	License plate lamp	1155	1973	AC and heater controls	1816
	Radio lamp	1816		Alternator light	—
	Clock lamp	1816		Back-up	1156
	Parking brake alarm lamp	257		Brake system warning	1895
	Headlamp position warning			Cargo	1895
	lamp	257		Cigar lighter	1445
				Clock	1895
1965–	Headlamp (outer)	4002		Courtesy	631
68	Headlamp (inner)	4001		Dome	90
	Parking and front directional,			Door ajar	1895
	tail and stop and rear			Gearshift indicator	1895
	directional	1157		Glove box	—
	Back-up lamp	1156		Hi-beam indicator	1895
	Instrument lamps, panel com-			Head lamps-UP	1895
	partment, temperature, oil			Instrument and speedometer	1895
	pressure, generator, hi-beam			License	67
	indicator, clock lamp	1895		Map	563
	A.T. quadrant, directional			Oil pressure	—
	signal, ignition lock, heater			Park and directional	1157NA
	control panel	1145		Radio	1893
	Dome lamp	1004		Radio stereo	564
	License plate lamp	1155		Sealed beam	
	Radio dial lamp	1893		High	4001
	Brake alarm lamp	257		Low-High	4002
				Seat belt indicator	1895
1969–	Headlamp			Side marker	
72	(outer)—high beam	4002		front	168
	(outer)—low beam	4002		rear	168
				Tail and stop	1157

Light Bulb Specifications (cont.)

Year	Usage	Number	Year	Usage	Number
1973	Trunk/engine	93	1974	Washer fluid level	168
	Turn signal indicators	1895		Wiper washer control	1445
	Temperature indicators	——			
	Washer fluid level	——	1975	AC and heater controls	1816
	Washer and wiper switch	1445		Alternator light	——
				Back-up	1156
1974	AC and heater controls	1816		Brake system warning	1895
	Alternator light	——		Cargo	——
	Back-up	1156		Clock	1895
	Brake system warning	1895		Cigarette lighter	1445
	Cargo	1895		Courtesy	631
	Cigarette lighter	1445		Dome	212
	Clock	1895		Door ajar	1895
	Courtesy	631		Gearshift indicator	1895
	Dome	212		Glove box	1895
	Door ajar	1895		High-beam indicator	——
	Gearshift indicator	1895		Headlamp-UP	1895
	Glove box	——		Instrument and speedometer	1895
	High-beam indicator	1895		License	168
	Head light door-UP	1895		Map	563
	Instrument and speedometer	1895		Oil pressure	——
	License	168		Park and directional	1157
	Map	563		Radio	1893
	Oil pressure	——		Radio stereo	564
	Park and directional	1157NA		Sealed beam	
	Radio	1893		High	5001
	Radio stereo	564		Low-High	4000
	Sealed beam			Seat belt indicator	1895
	High	5001		Side marker	
	Low-High	4000		front	168
	Seat belt indicator	1895		rear	168
	Side marker			Tail and stop	1157
	front	168		Trunk/engine	93
	rear	168		Turn signal indicators	1895
	Tail and stop	1157		Temperature indicators	——
	Trunk/engine	93		Washer fluid level	168
	Turn signal indicators	1895		Wiper washer control	1445
	Temperature indicators	——			

Fuses, Circuit Breakers, and Fusible Links

Year	Circuit	Type
1963–66	Headlamp circuit	15 amp circuit breaker
	Headlamp motors and power windows	40 amp circuit breaker
	Instrument, clock, and radio lamps	4 amp fuse
	Taillights	10 amp fuse
	Radio	2½ amp fuse
	Heater	10 amp fuse
	Stop, license, courtesy, and dome lamps	15 amp fuse (1963, 20 amp)
	Parking brake alarm, back-up lamp, and gas gauge	10 amp fuse
	Air conditioning	30 amp fuse
	AC high blower speed	30 amp fuse (in-line)
1967	Back-up lamp and gauges	10 amp fuse
	Heater and air conditioning	25 amp fuse
	Radio and wipers	20 amp fuse
	Instrument lamps	4 amp fuse
	Stop and taillights	20 amp fuse

Fuses, Circuit Breakers, and Fusible Links (cont.)

Year	Circuit	Type
1967	Clock, lighter, courtesy lamps, and flasher	20 amp fuse
	AC high blower speed	30 amp fuse
	Solenoid Bat terminal	14 gauge fusible link
	Horn relay	16 gauge fusible link
	Voltage regulator No. 3 terminal	20 gauge fusible link
	Voltage circuit (both sides of meter)	20 gauge fusible link
	Headlamp circuit	15 amp circuit breaker
	Headlamp motors and power windows	40 amp circuit breaker
1968–69	Headlamp circuit breaker	15 amp circuit breaker
	Power window circuit	30 amp circuit breaker
	Wiper/washer	25 amp fuse
	Back-up lights and turn signals	20 amp fuse
	Heater and air conditioning	25 amp fuse
	Radio and power windows	10 amp fuse
	Tail and side marker lamps	20 amp fuse
	Instrument lamps	5 amp fuse
	Gauges	10 amp fuse
	Stop light and flasher	20 amp fuse
	Clock, lighter, courtesy and dome lamps	20 amp fuse
	AC high blower speed	30 amp fuse (in-line)
	Solenoid Bat terminal	14 gauge fusible link
	Horn relay	16 gauge fusible link
	Voltage regulator No. 3 terminal	20 gauge fusible link
	Ammeter circuit (both sides of meter)	20 gauge fusible link
1970	Headlamp circuit	15 amp circuit breaker
	Power window circuit	30 amp circuit breaker
	Wiper/washer	25 amp fuse
	Back-up lights, turn signal, heater	25 amp fuse
	Air conditioning and TCS solenoid	25 amp fuse
	Radio and power windows	10 amp fuse
	Taillights and side marker lights	20 amp fuse
	Instrument lamps	5 amp fuse
	Gauges	20 amp fuse
	Clock, lighter, courtesy and dome lights	20 amp fuse
	AC high blower speed	30 amp fuse (in-line)
	Solenoid Bat terminal	14 gauge fusible link
	Horn relay	16 gauge fusible link
	Voltage regulator No. 3 terminal	20 gauge fusible link
	Ammeter circuit (both sides of meter)	20 gauge fusible link
1971–72	Headlamp circuit	15 amp circuit breaker
	Power window circuit	30 amp circuit breaker
	Radio, TCS system, and power windows	10 amp fuse
	Wiper/washer	25 amp fuse
	Stop lights and flasher	20 amp fuse
	Heater and air conditioning	25 amp fuse
	Directional signals, back-up lights, and AC blocking relay	20 amp fuse
	Instrument lamps	5 amp fuse
	Gauges	10 amp fuse
	Clock lighter, courtesy and dome lights	25 amp fuse
	Anti-diesel control and anti-theft alarm	25 amp fuse
	Tail, side marker, and back-up lights	20 amp fuse
	AC high blower speed	30 amp fuse (in-line)
	Solenoid Bat terminal	14 gauge fusible link
	Horn relay	16 gauge fuisble link
	Voltage regulator No. 3 terminal	20 gauge fusible link
	Ammeter circuit (both sides of meter)	20 gauge fusible link

Fuses, Circuit Breakers, and Fusible Links (cont.)

Year	Circuit	Type
1973–76	Headlamp circuit	circuit breaker
	Power window circuit	30 amp circuit breaker
	Back-up lamps and turn signals	
	Power window relay	25 amp AGC fuse
	Heater/air conditioning	25 amp 3AG fuse
	Radio, automatic trans, downshift switch, TCS solenoid, rear defogger	20 amp AGC fuse
	Rear window defogger (low speed)	3 amp AGC fuse (in-line)
	Instrument lamps	5 amp AGC fuse
	Taillamps (side marker and parking lamps)	20 amp SFE fuse
	Clock, lighter, courtesy, anti-theft alarm	20 amp SFE fuse
	Stop/hazard warning, key warning buzzer	20 amp SFE fuse
	Gauges/telltale lamps, seat belt buzzer lamp	10 amp AGC fuse
	High blower speed (air conditioning)	30 amp AGC fuse (in-line)
	Wipers/washers	25 amp AGC fuse

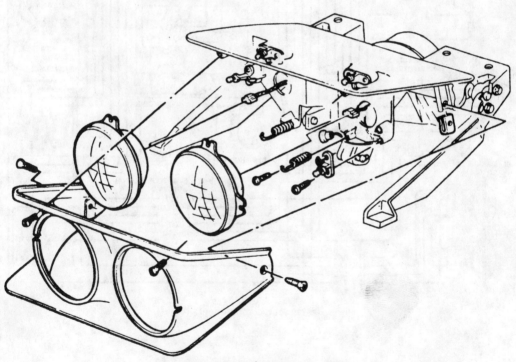

1968–76 headlight mounting

Wiring Diagrams

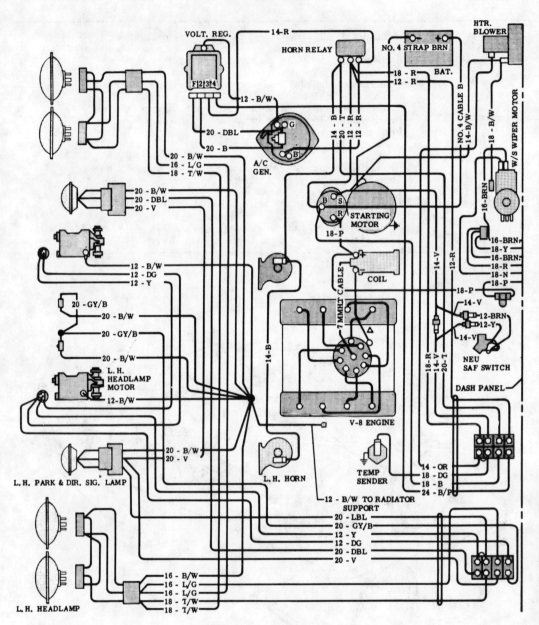

1963 engine compartment

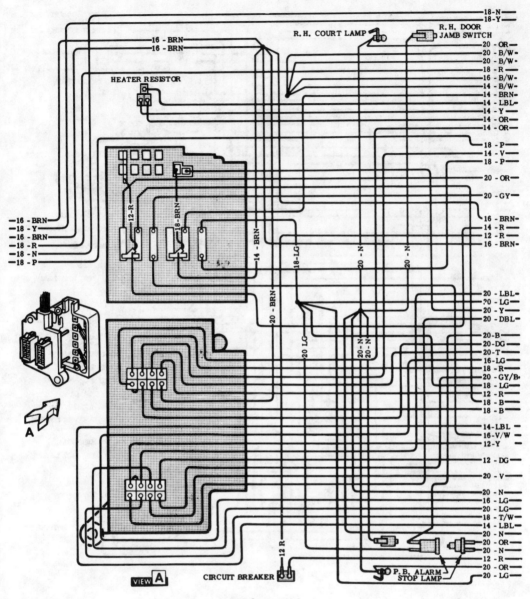

1963 fuse panel

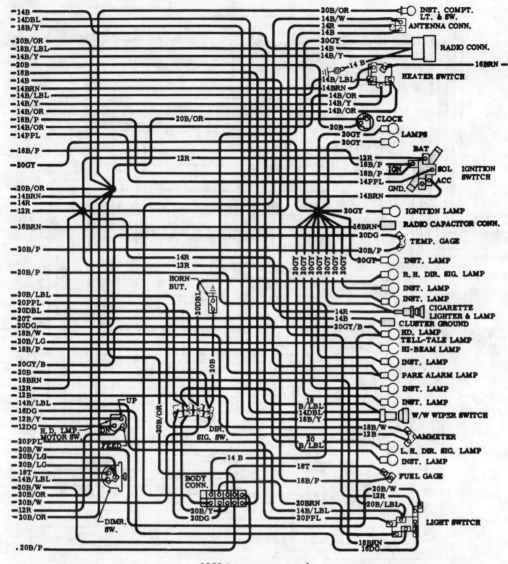

1963 instrument panel

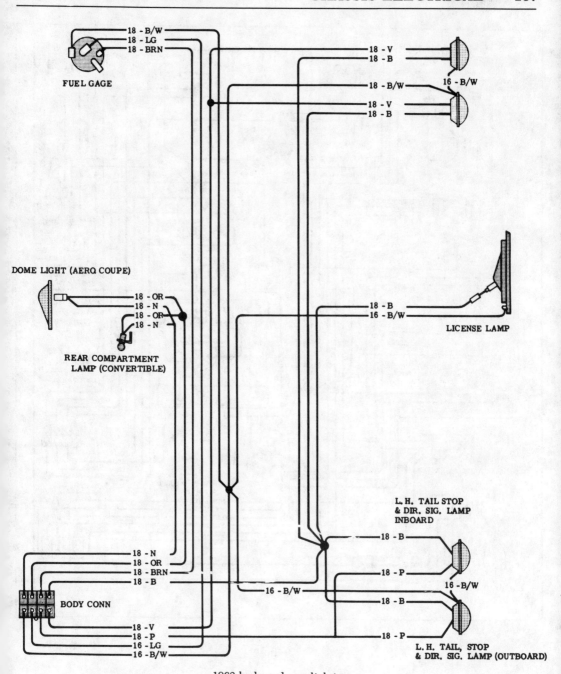

1963 body and rear lighting

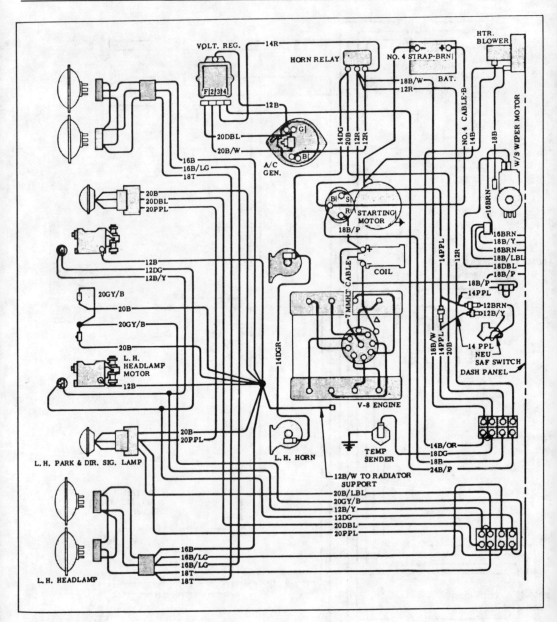

1964 engine compartment

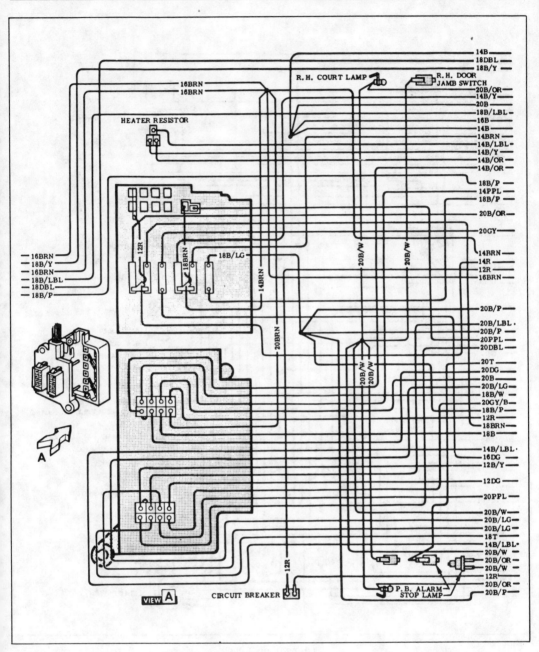

1964 fuse panel

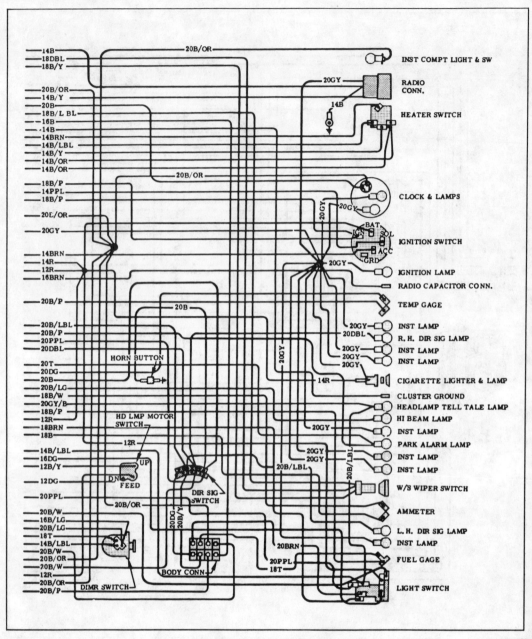

1964 instrument panel

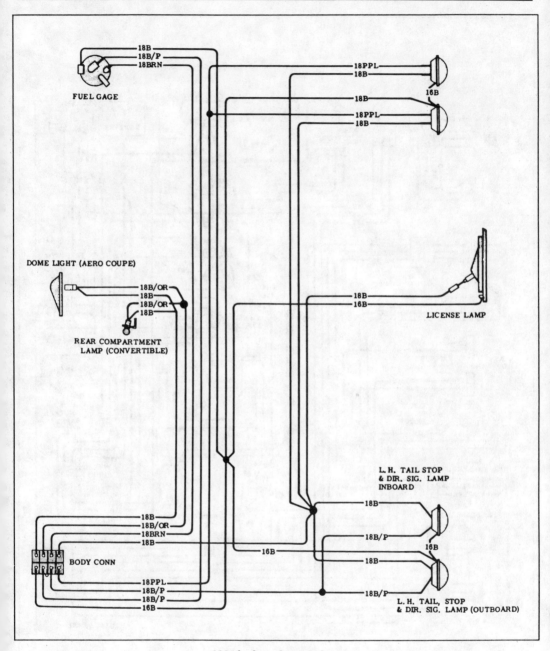

1964 body and rear lighting

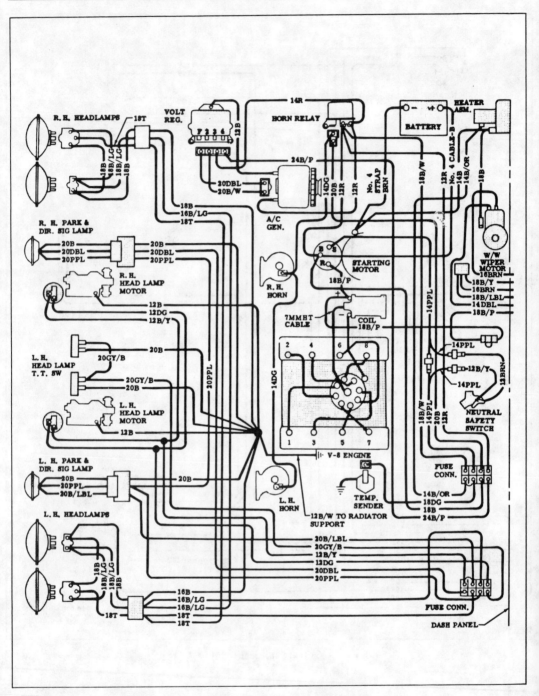

1965 engine compartment

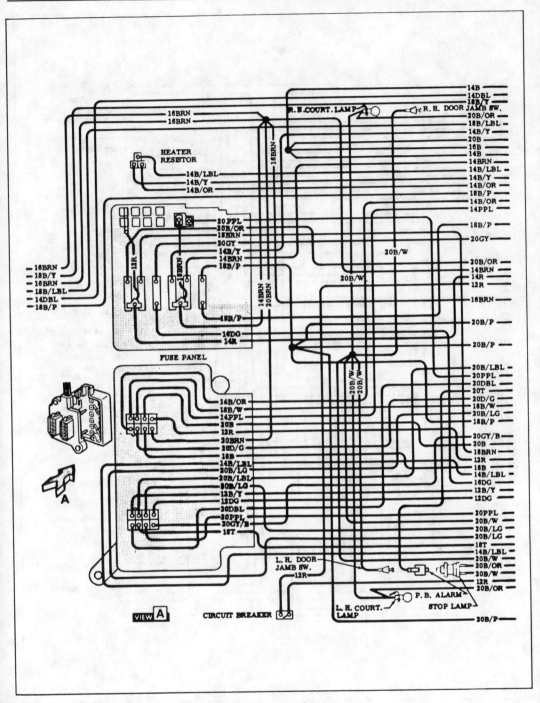

1965 fuse panel

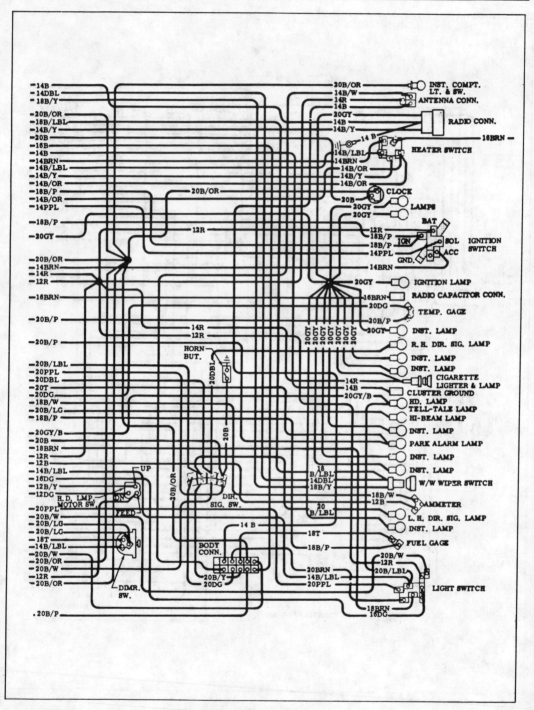

1965 instrument panel

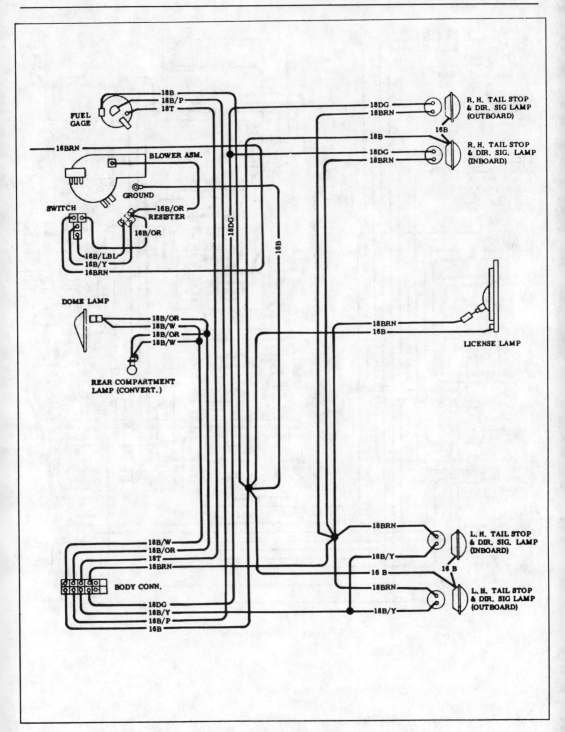

FUEL GAGE

18B
18B/P
18T

18DG
18BRN

R. H. TAIL STOP & DIR. SIG LAMP (OUTBOARD)

16B

18B

16BRN

BLOWER ASM.

18DG
18BRN

R. H. TAIL STOP & DIR. SIG. LAMP (INBOARD)

GROUND

SWITCH

16B/OR
RESETER

16B/OR

18DG

16B

18B/LBL
18B/Y
16BRN

DOME LAMP

18B/OR
18B/W

18B/OR
18B/W

18BRN
16B

LICENSE LAMP

REAR COMPARTMENT LAMP (CONVERT.)

18BRN

L. H. TAIL STOP & DIR. SIG. LAMP (INBOARD)

18B/Y

16B

18B/W
18B/OR
18T
18BRN

16 B

18BRN

L. H. TAIL STOP & DIR. SIG LAMP (OUTBOARD)

BODY CONN.

18DG
18B/Y
18B/P
16B

18B/Y

1965 body and rear lighting

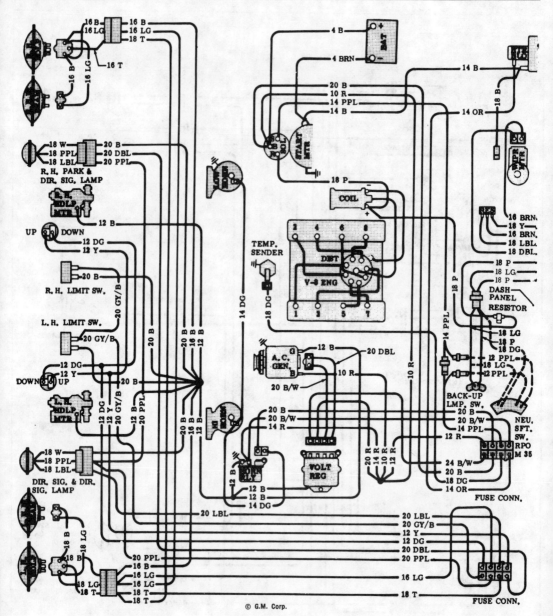

1966 engine compartment

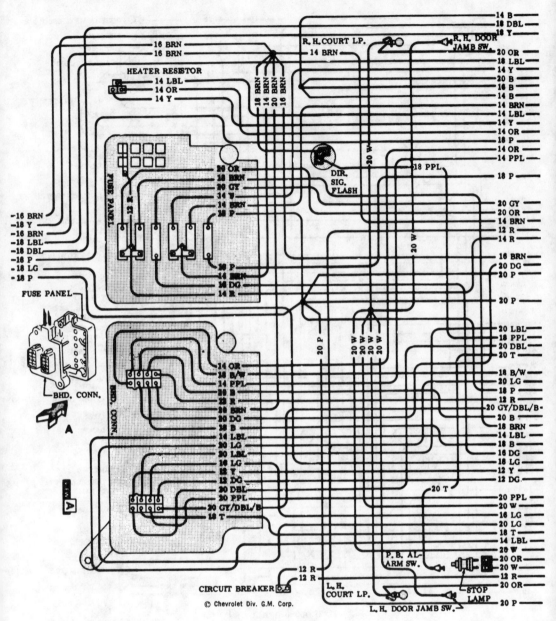

1966 fuse panel

R. H. COURT LP.
R. H. DOOR JAMB SW.

HEATER RESISTOR

DIR. SIG. FLASH

FUSE PANEL

BHD. CONN.

A

BED. CONN.

A

CIRCUIT BREAKER

© Chevrolet Div. G.M. Corp.

P. B. ALARM SW.

L. H. COURT LP.

L. H. DOOR JAMB SW.

STOP LAMP

14 B
18 DBL
18 Y
16 BRN
16 BRN
14 BRN
20 OR
18 LBL
14 Y
20 B
16 B
14 B
14 BRN
14 LBL
14 Y
14 OR
18 P
14 OR
14 PPL
18 P
18 PPL
20 GY
20 OR
14 BRN
12 R
14 R
16 BRN
20 DG
20 P
20 P
20 LBL
18 PPL
20 DBL
20 T
18 B/W
20 LG
18 P
12 R
20 GY/DBL/B
20 B
18 BRN
14 LBL
18 B
16 DG
18 LG
12 Y
12 DG
20 PPL
20 W
16 LG
20 LG
18 T
14 LBL
20 W
20 OR
20 W
12 R
20 OR
20 P

14 LBL
14 OR
14 Y

16 BRN
18 Y
16 BRN
18 LBL
18 DBL
18 P
18 LG
18 P

14 OR
18 B/W
14 PPL
18 B
12 R
20 BRN
20 DG
18 B
14 LBL
20 LG
20 LBL
14 LG
18 Y
12 DG
20 DBL
20 PPL
20 GY/DBL/B
18 T

12 R
12 R

20 T

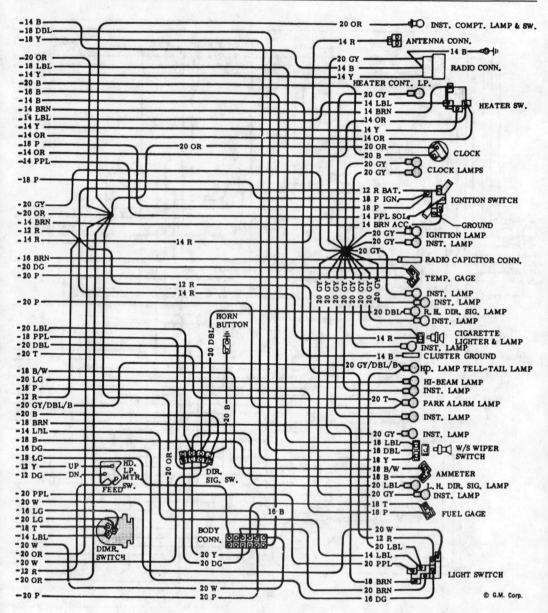

1966 instrument panel

© G.M. Corp.

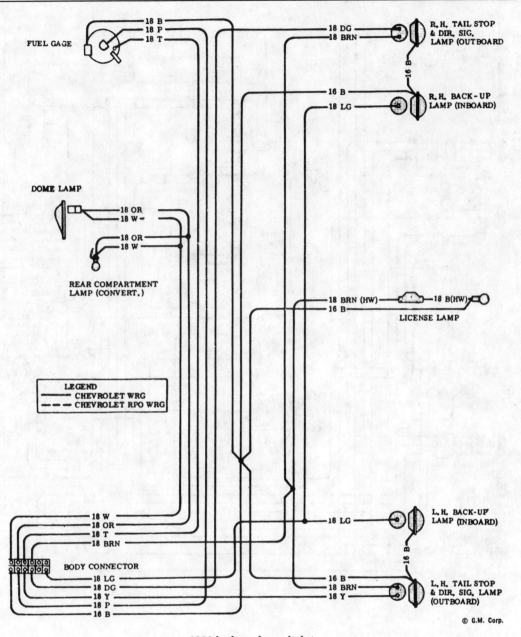

1966 body and rear lighting

© G.M. Corp.

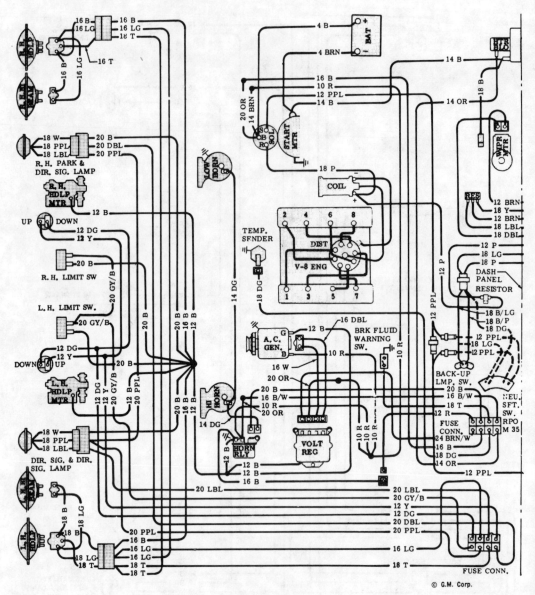

1967 engine compartment

© G.M. Corp.

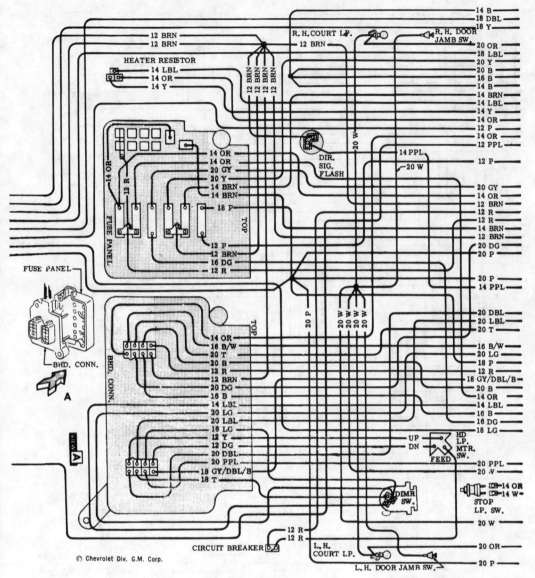

1967 fuse panel

© Chevrolet Div. G.M. Corp.

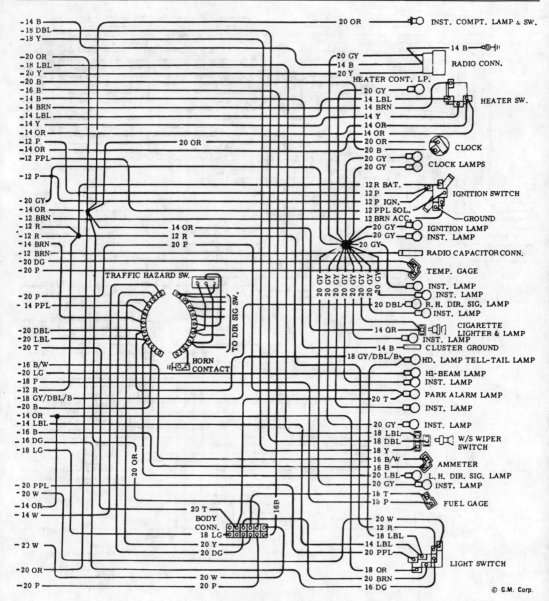

1967 instrument panel

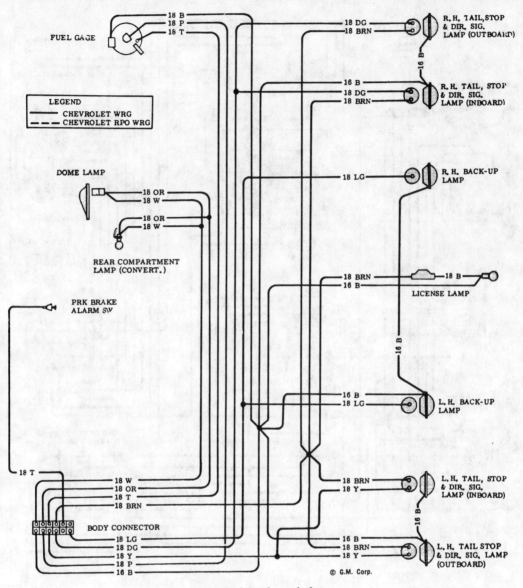

1967 body and rear lighting

FUEL GAGE

18 B
18 P
18 T

R. H. TAIL, STOP & DIR. SIG. LAMP (OUTBOARD)

18 DG
18 BRN

16 B

R. H. TAIL, STOP & DIR. SIG. LAMP (INBOARD)

16 B
18 DG
18 BRN

LEGEND
——— CHEVROLET WRG
– – – CHEVROLET RPO WRG

DOME LAMP

18 OR
18 W

R. H. BACK-UP LAMP

18 LG

18 OR
18 W

REAR COMPARTMENT LAMP (CONVERT.)

18 BRN
16 B

LICENSE LAMP

18 B

16 B

PRK BRAKE ALARM SW

L. H. BACK-UP LAMP

16 B
18 LG

18 T

18 W
18 OR
18 T
18 BRN

L. H. TAIL, STOP & DIR. SIG. LAMP (INBOARD)

18 BRN
18 Y

16 B

BODY CONNECTOR

18 LG
18 DG
18 Y
18 P
16 B

L. H. TAIL STOP & DIR. SIG. LAMP (OUTBOARD)

16 B
18 BRN
18 Y

© G.M. Corp.

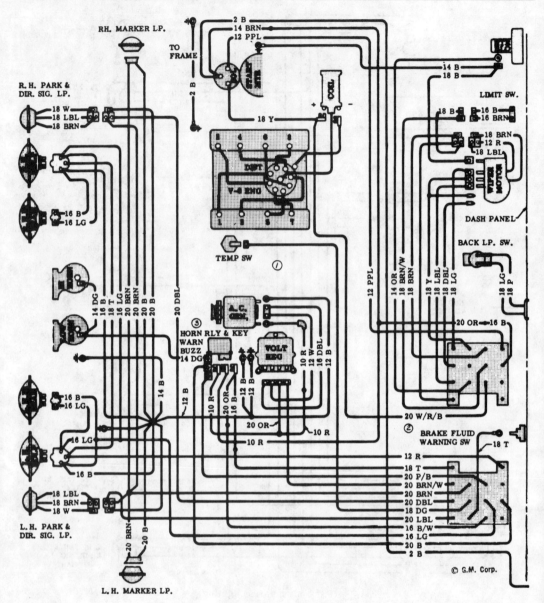

RH. MARKER LP.

TO FRAME

R.H. PARK & DIR. SIG. LP.

L.H. PARK & DIR. SIG. LP.

L.H. MARKER LP.

LIMIT SW.

DASH PANEL

BACK LP. SW.

HORN RLY & KEY WARN BUZZ

VOLT REG

TEMP SW

BRAKE FLUID WARNING SW

© G.M. Corp.

1968 engine compartment

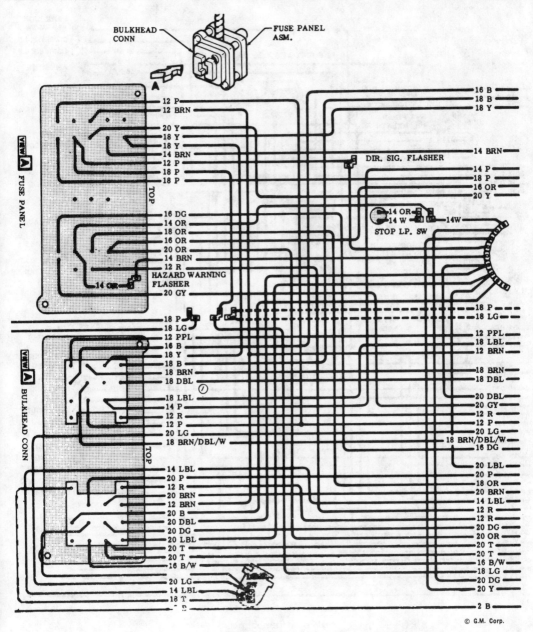

1968 fuse panel

© G.M. Corp.

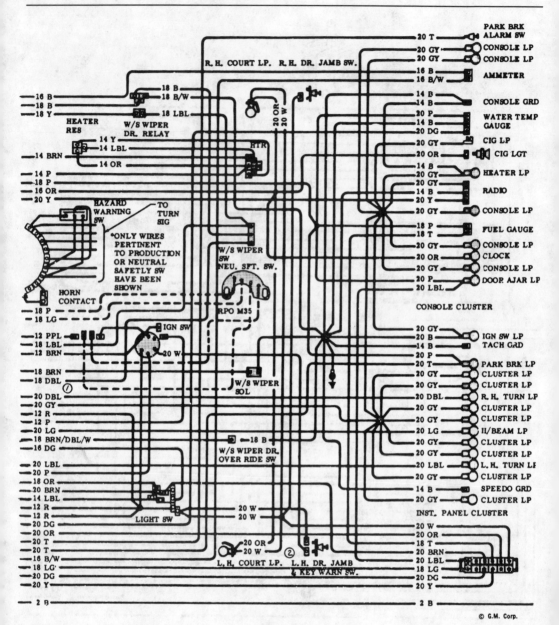

1968 instrument panel

© G.M. Corp.

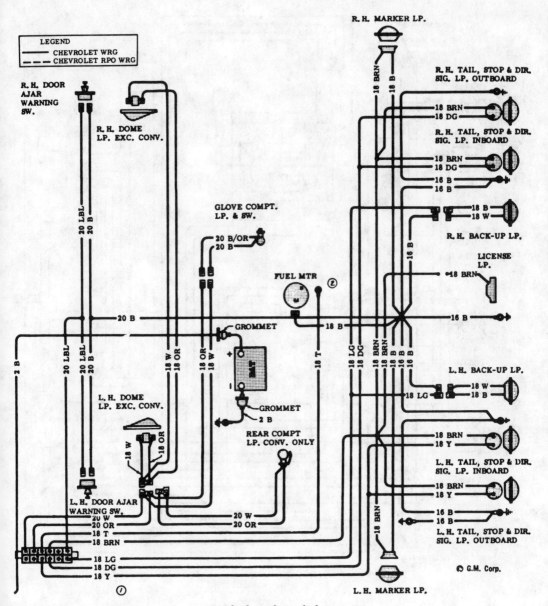

1968 body and rear lighting

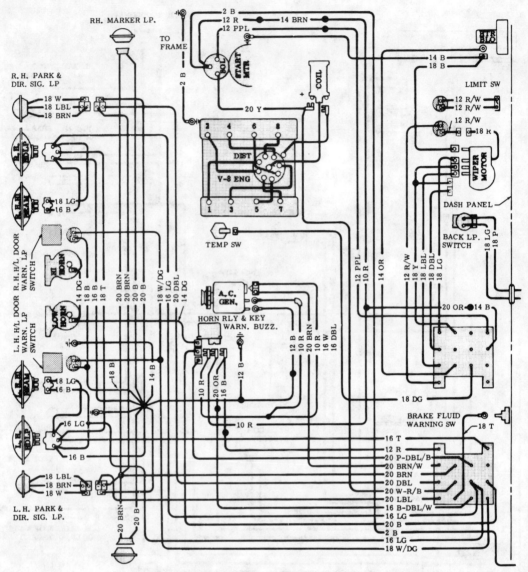

1969 engine compartment

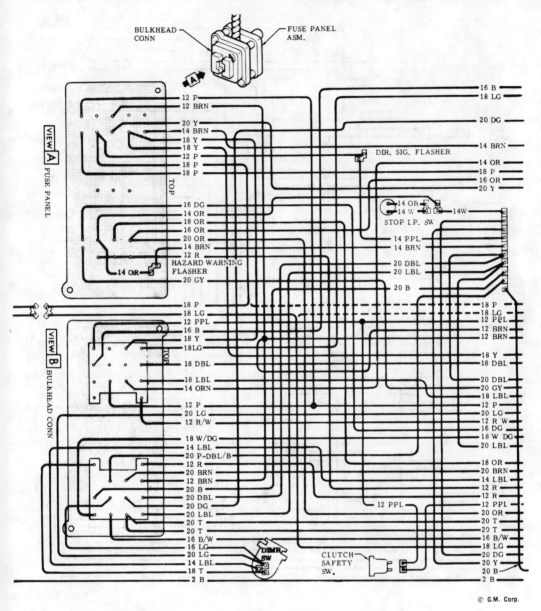

1969 fuse panel

© G.M. Corp.

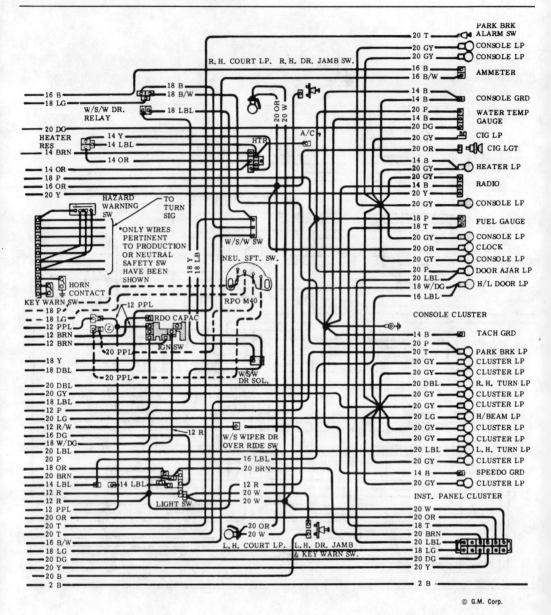

1969 instrument panel

© G.M. Corp.

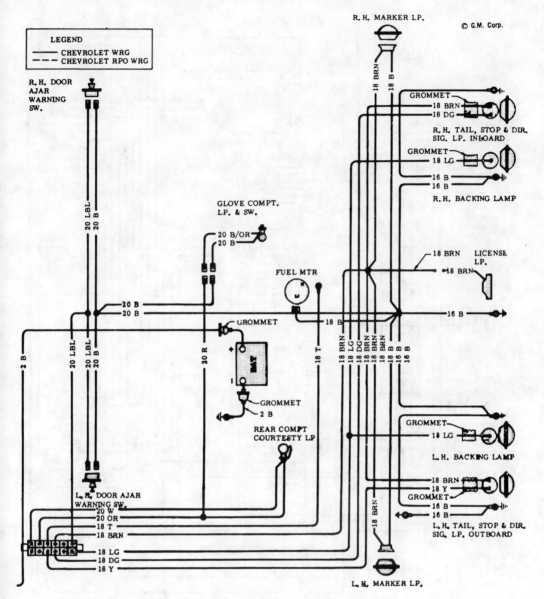

1969 body and rear lighting

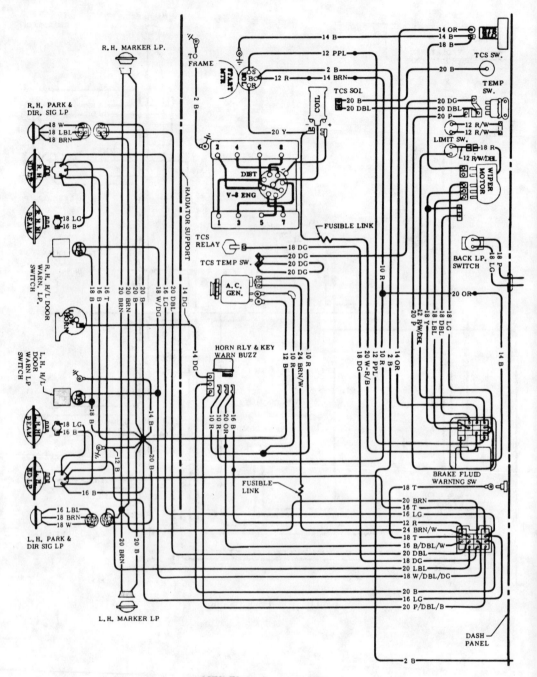

1970–71 engine compartment

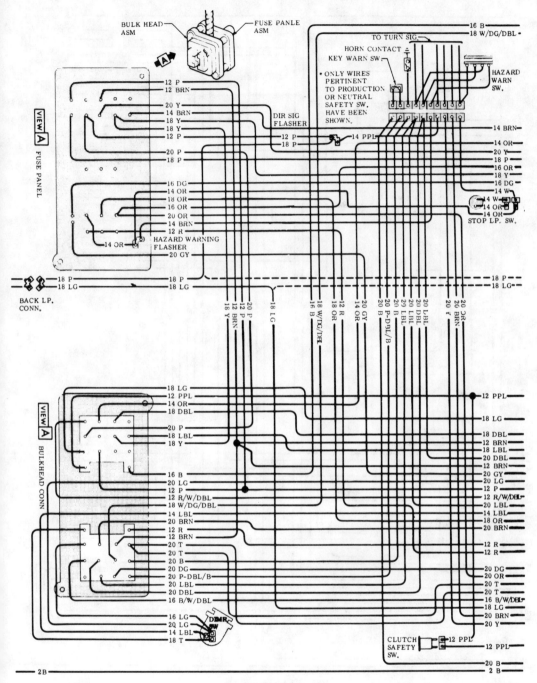

1970–71 fuse panel

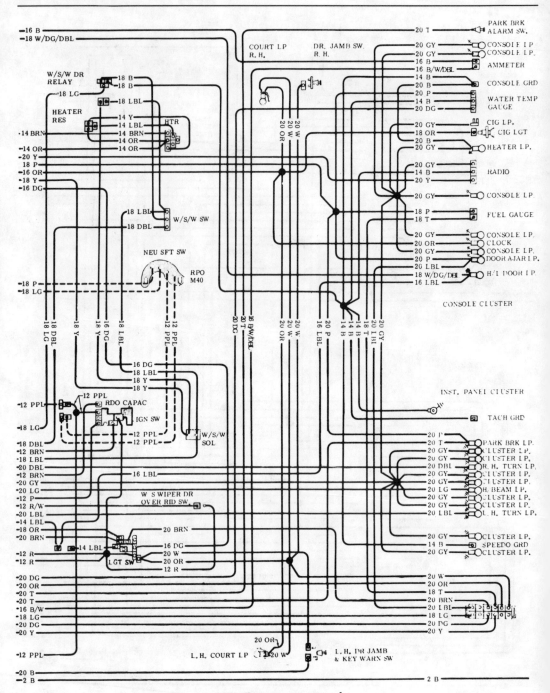

1970–71 instrument panel

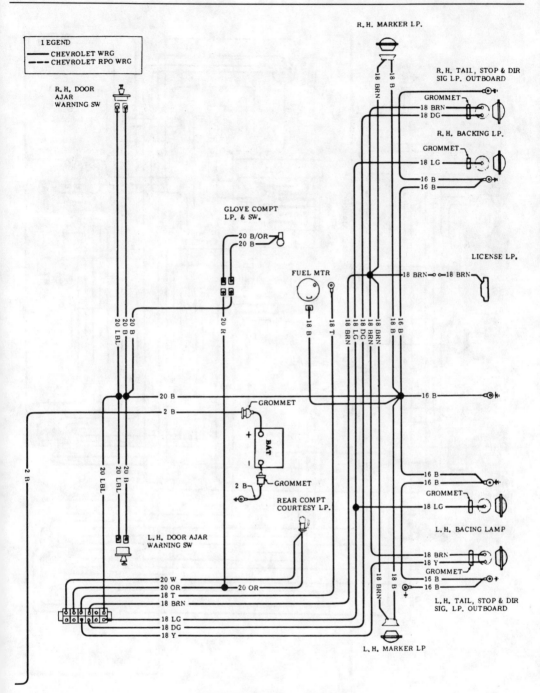

1970–71 body and rear lighting

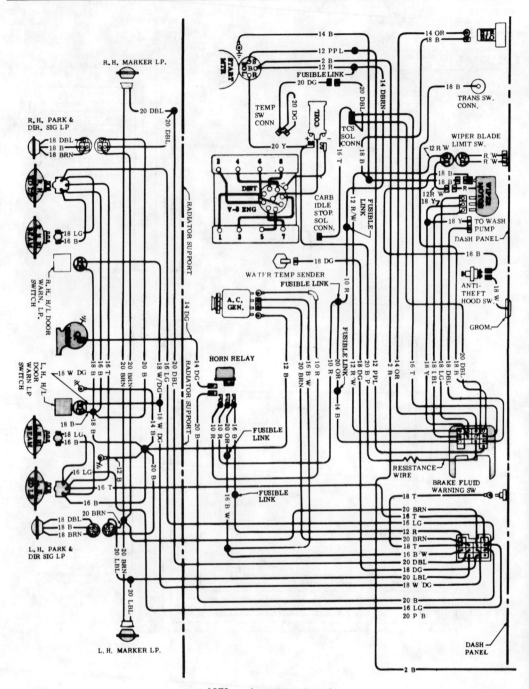

1972 engine compartment

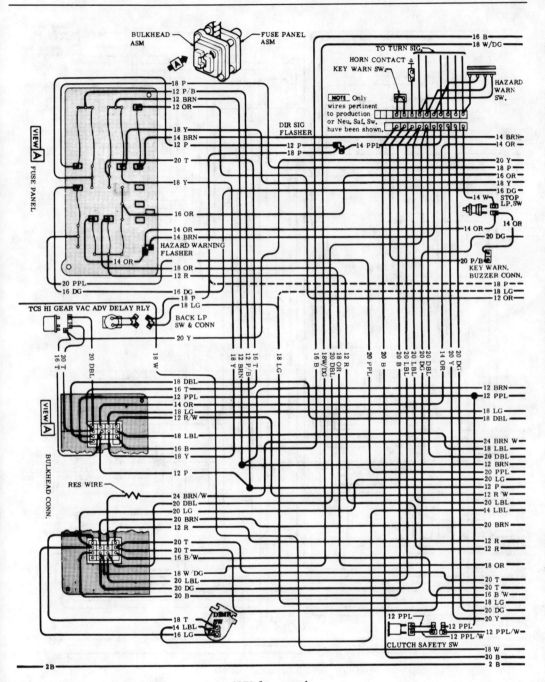

1972 fuse panel

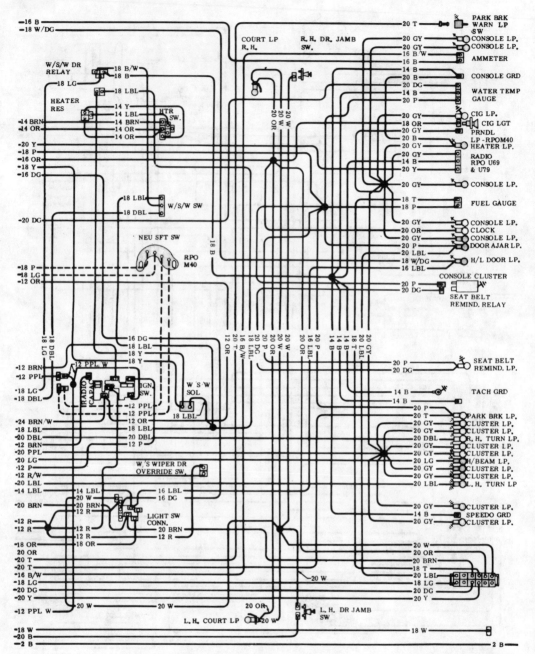

1972 instrument panel

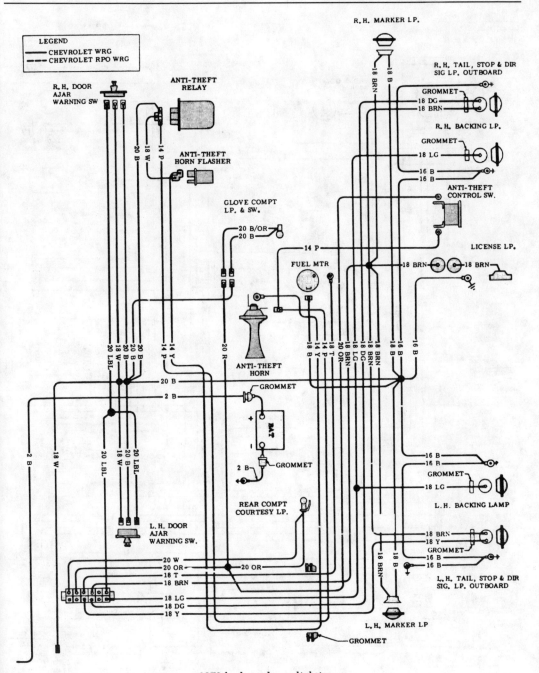

1972 body and rear lighting

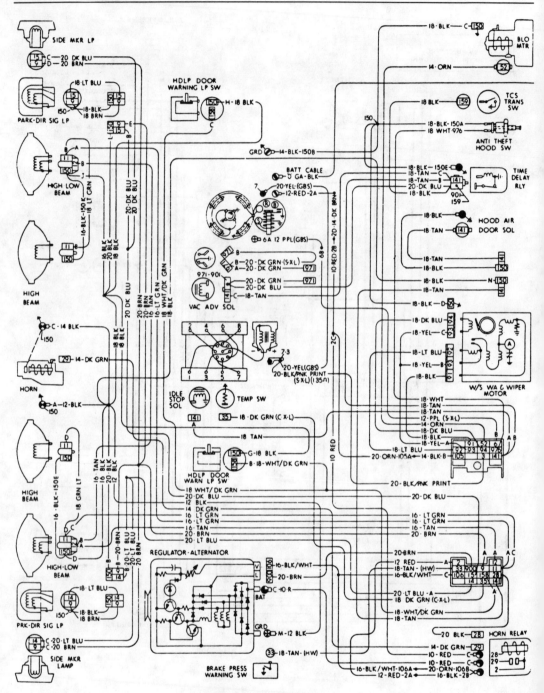

1973 engine compartment

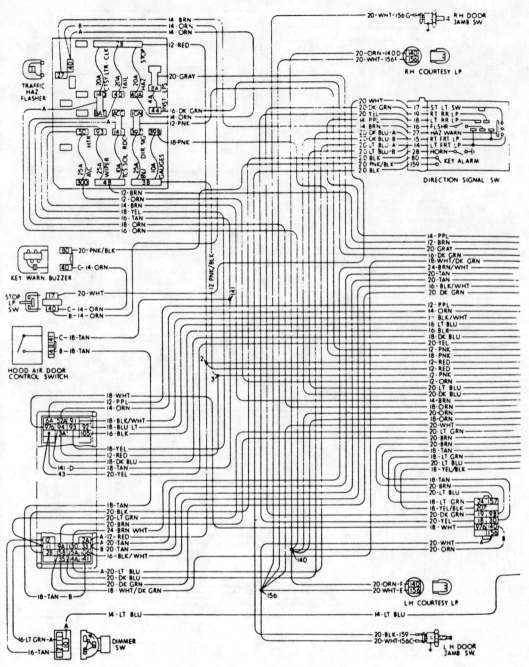

1973 center section

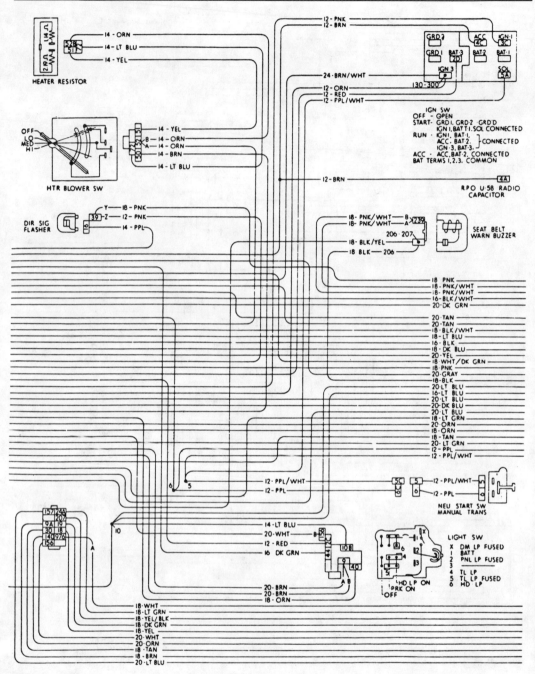

1973 center section

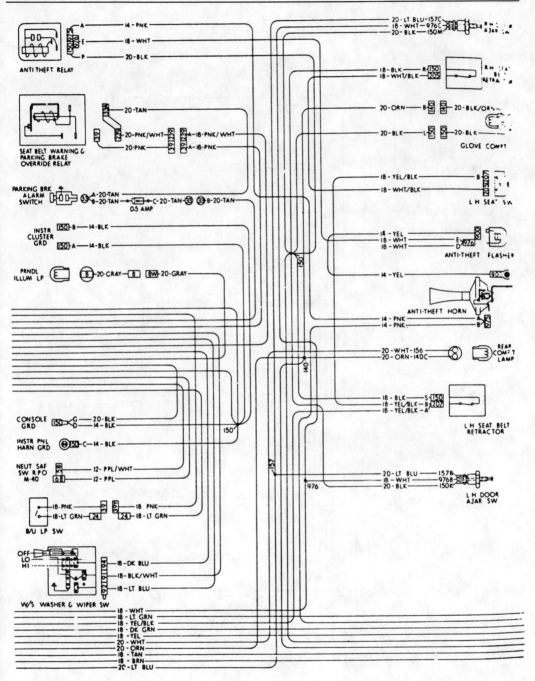

1973 rear body

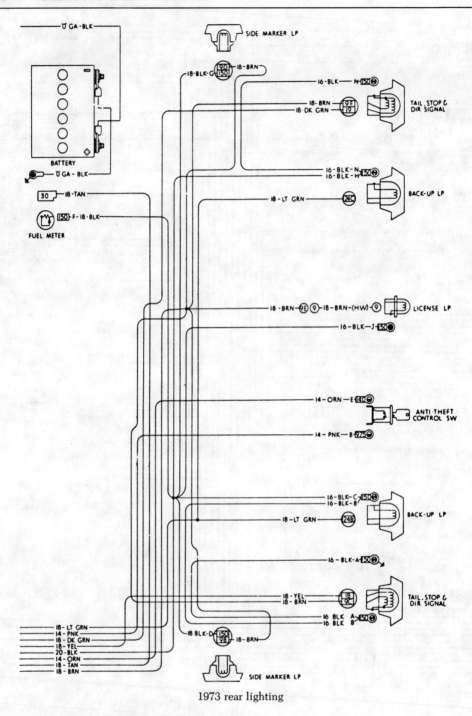

1973 rear lighting

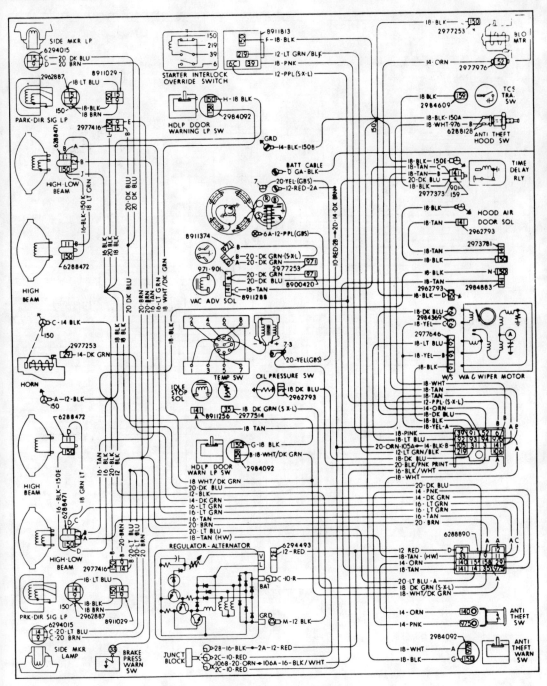

1974 engine compartment

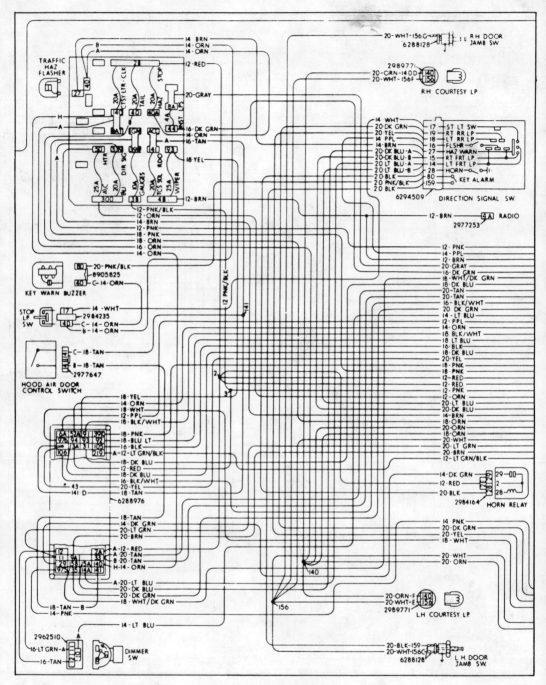

1974 instrument panel

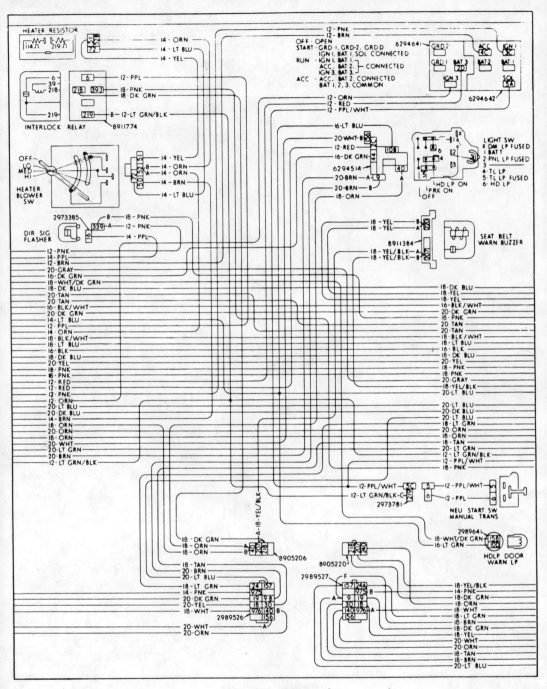

1974 instrument panel

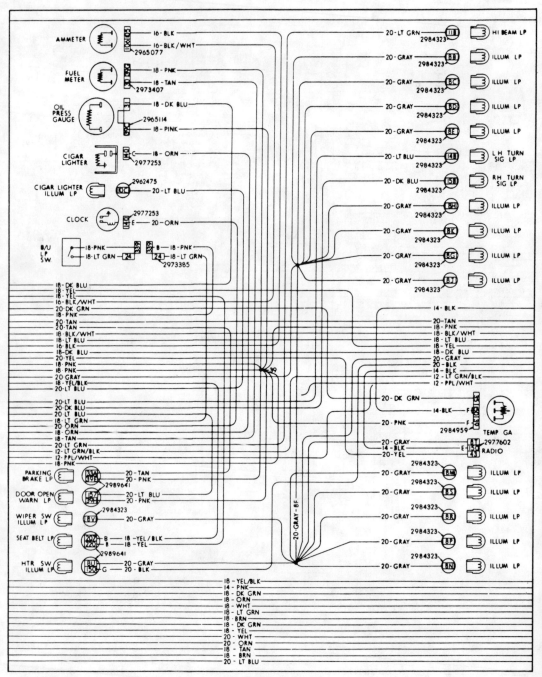

1974 instrument cluster

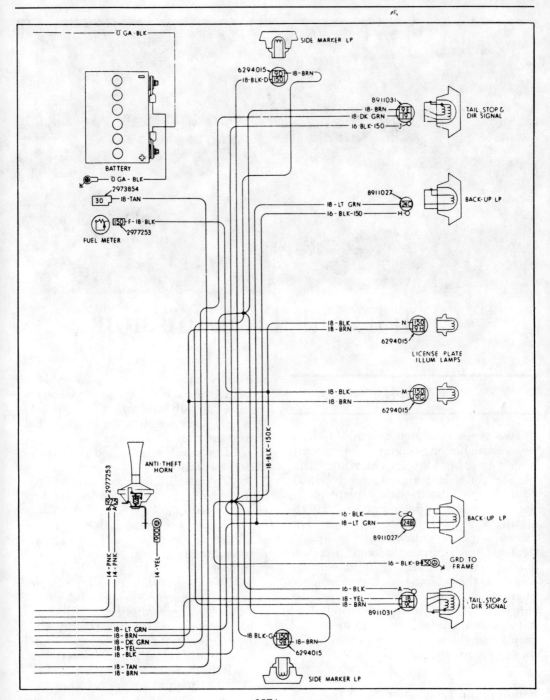

1974 rear

Chapter 6

Clutch and Transmission

Clutch

Two types of clutch assemblies have been available on Stingray. The standard clutch is a bent-finger, centrifugal diaphragm unit first introduced in 1963. This design permits heavy plate loads, yet allows low pedal effort without resorting to center booster springs. The second type of clutch is a dual-plate, bent-finger diaphragm model that was available in 1969 and 1970. It was optional on the 427/454 high performance engines and requires a 14 in. diameter ring gear. The throwout bearing used with both models is 1¼ in. in overall length and should not be replaced by the longer 1⅞ in. unit.

Removal and Installation

1. Remove the transmission from the car as previously outlined.
2. Disconnect the clutch-fork push rod and spring.
3. Remove the bell housing.
4. Install a clutch pilot tool (wooden versions available at most automotive parts stores) to hold the clutch plate during removal.
5. The flywheel and clutch cover are marked with x's for correct assembly, if these are not visible, scribe new marks.
6. Gradually loosen the clutch-to-flywheel bolts one turn at a time until all spring pressure is released.
7. Remove the bolts and remove the clutch assembly.
8. To install, crank the engine over by hand until the x-mark on the flywheel is on the bottom.
9. Position the clutch disc and pressure plate in the same relative location as removed and support with the clutch pilot tool.

NOTE: *The clutch disc is installed with the damper springs and slinger toward the transmission.*

10. Rotate the clutch assembly until the x-marks on the flywheel and clutch assembly align. Align the cover bolt holes with those in the flywheel.
11. Install bolts in every other hole and tighten down evenly. Install the remaining bolts.
12. Remove the clutch pilot tool.
13. Lubricate the ball socket on the clutch fork and reinstall on the ball stud.
14. Pack the recess on the inside of the throwout bearing collar and the throwout groove with graphite grease.
15. Install the bell housing.
16. Install the throwout bearing on the fork.

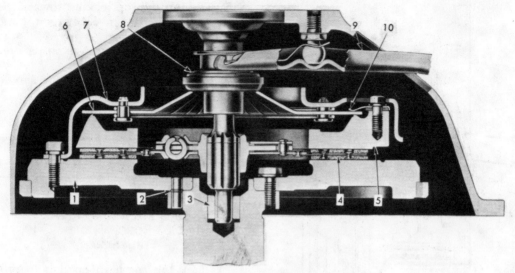

Cutaway of single disc clutch

1. Flywheel	5. Pressure plate	9. Fork
2. Dowel hole	6. Diaphragm spring	10. Retracting spring
3. Pilot bushing	7. Cover	
4. Driven disc	8. Throwout bearing	

17. Install the transmission as previously outlined.

18. Connect the fork push rod and spring.

19. Adjust the free pedal play and check the clutch release position.

Pedal Repositioning

Earlier Corvette clutch linkage includes a provision for a second clutch setting which reduces total pedal travel approximately 1½ in. The reduced travel will make the release faster and permit faster gear shifting.

1. Remove the clutch return spring at the cross-shaft and the pedal push rod at the pedal.

2. Loosen the pedal bracket lower bolt, remove the upper bolt, and rotate the bracket so that it will align with the extra upper bolt hole. Install the upper bolt.

3. Disconnect the pedal push rod at the cross-shaft and turn it ½ turn. Reconnect the push rod at the cross-shaft.

4. Tighten the bracket bolts and connect the pedal push rod.

Clutch Adjustment

1963–74

1. Disconnect the spring between the clutch push rod and cross shaft lever.

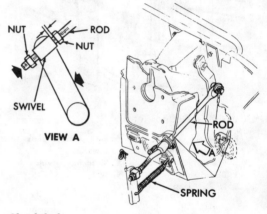

Clutch linkage

2. While holding the clutch pedal against the stop, loosen the two locknuts enough to allow the adjusting rod to move against the clutch fork until the throwout bearing lightly touches the pressure plate springs.

3. Turn the upper nut against the swivel and then back it off 4½ turns. Tighten the bottom locknut to lock the swivel against the top nut.

4. Reinstall the return spring. Pedal free travel, the distance the pedal can be moved before the throwout bearing contacts the pressure plate spring, should be:

1963–64 Corvette—¾–1 in.
1965–71 Corvette—1¼–2 in.

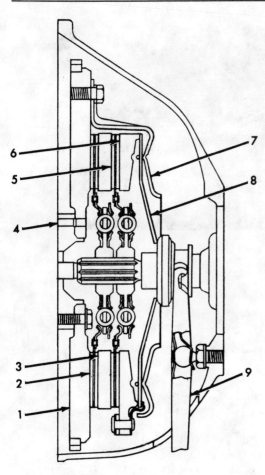

Cutaway of dual disc clutch

1. Flywheel
2. Front driven disc
3. Front pressure plate
4. Dowel hole
5. Rear driven disc

6. Rear pressure plate
7. Cover
8. Retracting spring
9. Fork

1969–70 Corvette with HD clutch—2–2½ in.
1972 Corvette—1¼–1¾ in.
1973 Corvette—1¼–1½ in.
1974 Corvette—1–1½ in.

1975–76

1. Disconnect the return spring between the floor and the cross shaft.
2. Push the clutch lever and shaft assembly until the clutch pedal is tightly against the rubber stop under the dash.
3. Loosen the two locknuts on the shaft.
4. Push the shaft until the throwout bearing just touches the pressure plate spring.

5. Tighten the top locknut toward the swivel until the distance between it and the swivel is 0.4 in.
6. Tighten the bottom locknut against the swivel.
7. Check pedal free travel. It should be 1–1½ in.

Manual Transmission

Removal and Installation

1963–1965 MUNCIE THREE-SPEED
AND 1963 BORG-WARNER T–10,
FOUR-SPEED

1. Jack the car high enough to provide working clearance.
2. Disconnect the speedometer cable from the transmission.
3. Disconnect the shift linkage from the shift rods on the transmission. Remove the shift lever assembly and linkage.
4. Remove the driveshaft as described in the drivshaft section of Chapter 7.
5. Support the engine at the rear of the oil pan with a jack.
6. Remove the left and right exhaust pipes.
7. Remove the transmission tailshaft-to-crossmember attaching bracket.
8. Remove the two, top transmission-to-bell housing bolts and replace them with two guide pins; these may be fabricated from studs. This will prevent damaging the clutch disc.
9. Remove the bottom two bolts and slide the transmission straight back on the guide pin until the input shaft is clear of the clutch splines.
10. Move the transmission back to clear the bell housing. Tilt the forward end of the transmission down and withdraw from the car.
11. To install, insert a guide pin in the upper right bell housing bolt hole.
12. Raise the transmission and support it on the guide pin.
13. Rotate the transmission and engage the input shaft with the clutch disc. Slide the transmission forward until it bottoms against the clutch housing.

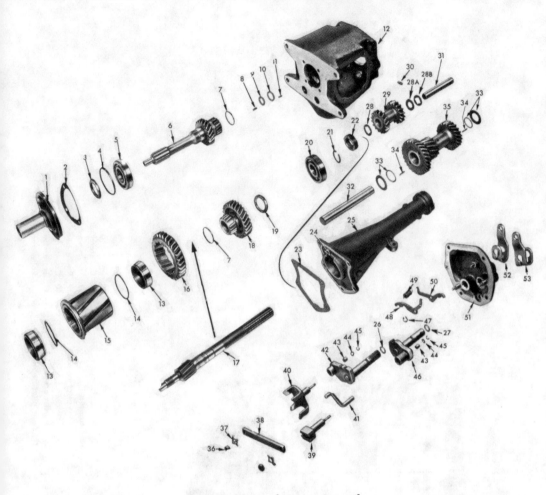

Exploded view of Muncie 3-speed

1. Clutch gear bearing retainer
2. Bearing retainer gasket
3. Bearing nut and oil slinger
4. Bearing snap-ring
5. Clutch gear bearing
6. Clutch gear
7. Energizing spring
8. Front pilot bearing roller
9. Thrust washer
10. Thrust washer
11. Rear pilot bearing rollers
12. Transmission case
13. Synchronizer ring
14. Snap-ring
15. Second and third speed clutch
16. First and Reverse sliding gear
17. Mainshaft
18. Second speed gear
19. Thrust washer
20. Mainshaft rear bearing

21. Snap-ring
22. Speedometer drive gear
23. Case extension gasket
24. Rear bearing snap-ring
25. Case extension
26. First and Reverse shifter shaft O-ring
27. Second and Third shifter shaft O-ring
28. Thrust washer
28a. Thrust bearing
28b. Thrust bearing washer
29. Reverse idler gear
30. Reverse idler shaft pin
31. Reverse idler shaft
32. Countershaft
33. Countergear and roller thrust washers
34. Bearing roller
35. Countergear
36. Shifter interlock retainer stud nut

37. Shifter interlock retainer stud nut lock
38. Shifter interlock retainer
39. Second and Third shifter fork
40. First and Reverse shifter fork
41. Shifter interlock shaft
42. First and Reverse shifter shaft and plate assembly
43. Shifter fork spacer
44. Shifter fork washer
45. Shifter fork retainer
46. Second and Third shifter shaft and plate assembly
47. Detent cam retainer
48. First and Reverse detent cam
49. Detent cam spring
50. Second and Third detent cam
51. Side cover
52. First and Reverse shifter lever (outer)
53. Second and Third shifter lever (outer)

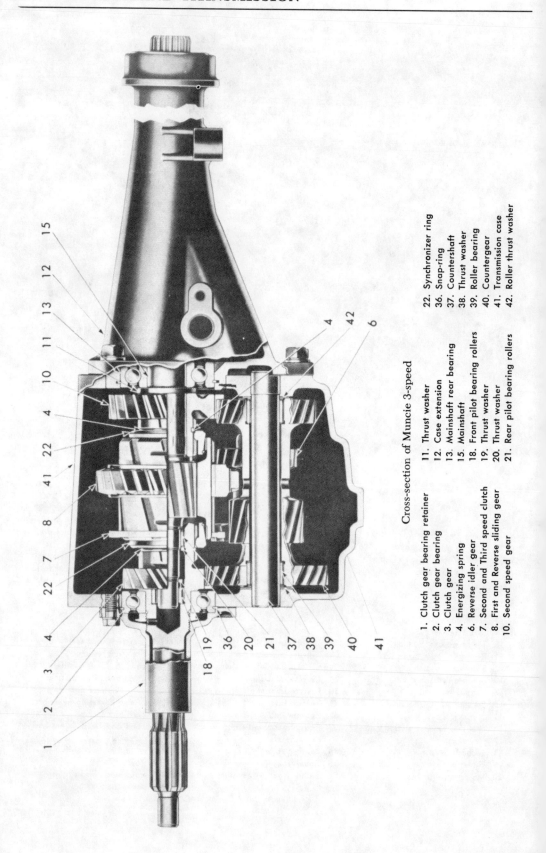

Cross-section of Muncie 3-speed

1. Clutch gear bearing retainer
2. Clutch gear bearing
3. Clutch gear
4. Energizing spring
6. Reverse idler gear
7. Second and Third speed clutch
8. First and Reverse sliding gear
10. Second speed gear

11. Thrust washer
12. Case extension
13. Mainshaft rear bearing
15. Mainshaft
18. Front pilot bearing rollers
19. Thrust washer
20. Thrust washer
21. Rear pilot bearing rollers

22. Synchronizer ring
36. Snap-ring
37. Countershaft
38. Thrust washer
39. Roller bearing
40. Countergear
41. Transmission case
42. Roller thrust washer

14. Install the two, bottom transmission-to-bell housing bolts. Remove the guide pin, and install the top two bolts. Torque all four bolts to 40–50 ft lbs.

15. Position the tailshaft mount-to-frame crossmember bracket and install the bolts hand tight. Install the bracket-to-extension mount bolts.

16. Tighten the support bracket-to-frame retaining bolts. Remove the jack from under the oil pan and tighten the bracket-to-extension mount bolts.

17. Install the driveshaft.

18. Install the speedometer cable to the transmission.

19. Install the shift lever assembly onto the transmission and connect the shift linkage.

20. Refill the transmission with lubricant. Check and adjust the shift pattern, if necessary.

1963–76 FOUR-SPEED AND 1966–69 THREE-SPEED

1. Disconnect the negative cable from the battery.

2. Disassemble the shift lever. Unscrew the ball from the lever, lift out the "T" handle return spring and "T" handle, and remove the anti-rattle bushings. On 1968 and later cars, remove the console trim plate.

3. Jack the car high enough to provide working clearance.

4. Remove the driveshaft as described in the driveshaft section of Chapter 7.

5. Remove the exhaust pipe heat deflectors and remove the left and right exhaust pipes. On a large block engine it is necessary to remove the forward stud on each manifold.

6. Remove the two, rear-mount, cushion-to-bracket attaching bolts. Support the rear of the oil pan with a jack to take off the load from the rear mount cushion.

CAUTION: *Place a board between the oil pan and jack to prevent damage.*

7. Remove the three, transmission mount bracket-to-crossmember bolts and remove the bracket.

8. Remove the two, mount pad-to-transmission bolts and remove the rubber mount cushion and the exhaust pipe.

9. Disconnect the shift linkage by removing the shift levers at the transmission side cover.

10. Disconnect the speedometer cable at the tailshaft. Disconnect the TCS switch wiring, on cars so equipped.

11. Remove the two, shift lever-and-bracket bolts; lower and remove the assembly.

12. Remove the four, transmission-to-bell housing bolts and lower left extension bolt on later models.

13. Pull the transmission rearward until it clears the bell housing. Turn the transmission to the left while pulling to the rear.

14. Slowly lower the rear of the engine until the tachometer drive cable on the distributor just clears the horizontal ledge across the front of the firewall.

CAUTION: *The tachometer cable can be easily damaged.*

15. Slide the transmission rearward out from the clutch. Lower the front end of the transmission and remove it from the car.

16. Perform the above steps in reverse order to install the transmission.

Overhaul

1963–65 MUNCIE THREE-SPEED

Disassembly

1. Remove the transmission side cover and gasket.

2. Unbolt the transmission extension and slide the extension and mainshaft assembly from the main case.

3. Turn the mainshaft and second/third gear clutch gear until the clutch teeth and splines align then remove first and reverse gear from the clutch sleeve, and withdraw them separately through the side cover opening.

4. Carefully shake out the pilot bearing, roller bearings from the clutch gear.

5. Four screws hold the clutch gear bearing retainer. Remove the screws and the retainer, observing that the uneven screw spacing prevents incorrect reassembly.

6. Place a soft steel drift punch against the front end of the countershaft and remove it by driving it front to rear and lowering the counter gear to the bottom of the case.

7. Remove the clutch gear and bearing through the rear of the case by tapping the shaft with a soft hammer after the bearing snap-ring has been removed.

8. Withdraw the counter gear, roller bearings, and thrust washers, then drive the idler shaft lockpin into the shaft. This frees the idler shaft for removal.

9. Tap the idler shaft from the rear so that it drives out the plug in front of it. Do not rotate the shaft during removal or the lockpin may fall between the idler gear bushings.

10. Extract the reverse idler gear, thrust washer, bearing, and bearing washer. Expand the bearing snap-ring and tap the rear of the mainshaft with a soft hammer to remove it along with the speedometer drive gear, second gear, and its bearing from the case extension.

Mainshaft Disassembly and Assembly

1. Press the speedometer gear off.

2. Expand the snap-ring and press the rear bearing off.

3. Slide off the second gear thrust washer and gear.

4. Clean all parts with solvent and check for excessive wear or damage.

5. Lubricate the second gear with oil and position it on the mainshaft.

6. Place the thrust washer against it so that the oil grooves face the gear.

7. Position the replacement bearing on the shaft so that the groove in the outside diameter of bearing faces the gear.

8. Bearing end play is adjusted by the selection of different thickness snap-rings. Select one of the four available that restricts end play to no more than 0.004 in.

9. Install the speedometer drive gear on the end of the shaft and press on so that the gear's rear face is separated from the bearing by $1^7/_{16}$ in.

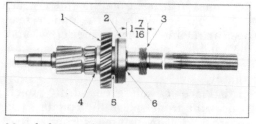

Mainshaft assembly

1. Second speed gear
2. Rear bearing
3. Speedometer drive gear
4. Energizing spring
5. Thrust washer
6. Snap-ring

Clutch Gear Bearing Replacement

1. Secure the clutch gear in a vise with soft jaws and remove the retainer nut and oil slinger. This nut and slinger assembly is staked into place and has left-hand threads.

2. Remove the gear from the vise and position it in the transmission case with the snap-ring installed on the bearing.

3. Position the case in an arbor press and press the shaft from the bearing. Tap the bearing from the case.

4. Clean all parts in solvent and check for excessive wear or damage.

5. Start the replacement bearing onto the shaft then press into correct position with an arbor press. The bearing is correctly placed when the locating ring groove is toward the front of the gear-shaft.

6. Install the retaining nut/oil slinger on the clutch gearshaft and securely tighten. Stake it into the hole in the shaft being careful not to damage the threads of the shaft.

Clutch Sleeve and Synchronizer Ring Repair

1. Remove the first/reverse sliding gear and rotate the clutch sleeve synchronizer ring until its ends can be seen through the clutch sleeve slot. Expand the synchronizer ring retainer into the clutch sleeve counterbore and slide the ring from the sleeve.

2. Check the synchronizer cones for wear or excessive looseness in the clutch sleeve. Damaged cones will necessitate the replacement of the sleeve assembly and both synchronizer rings.

3. Check the rings for smoothness. Place them over the cones and check for excessive rocking. Rocking indicates poor contact between the surfaces and will cause poor synchronizing action during shifting.

4. Place the synchronizer retainers in the clutch sleeve counterbores. Lubricate each synchronizer ring with light engine oil, expand the retainers and slip the rings into position. Check to see that the retainers are correctly seated in their grooves and will not interfere with the free rotation of the rings.

5. Install the first/reverse gear on the clutch sleeve.

6. The energizing springs for the synchronizers have one end that is slightly offset. When the springs are correctly installed in their respective grooves in the clutch gear and second gear, the offset end is positioned between the third and fourth tooth of either of the two banks of teeth. This prevents the spring from spinning in its groove.

7. These springs do not normally require replacement. Should it become necessary, they may be slid from the gear with any thin bladed instrument.

Reverse Idler Assembly

1. Lubricate the thrust washer and needle thrust bearing with grease and install them on the gear in the following sequence: needle bearing nearest chamfered gear teeth, larger washer next to the bearing, and smaller washer at the opposite end.

2. Flood the bushings with gear oil.

3. Position the idler gear assembly in the case with the thrust bearing at the rear. Insert the idler shaft and position it so that the lockpin hole in the shaft aligns with the hole in the case. Check to see that both are at the correct angle.

4. Install a new lockpin. Coat it with sealer and drive it in until it is positioned $1/16$ in. beyond flush, then peen the hole. Pin fit must be exact or an oil leak will result at this point.

5. Install a replacement idler shaft expansion plug in the case.

Counter Gear and Clutch Gear Assembly

1. Install 25 roller bearings in each end of the counter gear. Coat the bearings and the area with cup grease to prevent their dislodgement during assembly.

2. Grease the bearing thrust washers and counter gear thrust washers and position one of each at the ends of the counter gear.

3. Lay the counter gear on the inside floor of the transmission case.

4. Coat the mainshaft pilot hole in the clutch gear with cup grease and install its roller bearings. Position the first group of 14 rollers and the small inside diameter spacer, followed by the large inside diameter spacer and the second group of 24

rollers. Handle the clutch gear carefully to avoid losing the roller bearings.

5. Position the clutch gear in the case and tap the outer race of the clutch gear bearing with a brass drift. Drive the assembly straight until the locating ring groove on the bearing is outside the case front.

6. Slip the snap-ring on the bearing and drive the clutch gear backwards until the snap-ring seats against the case.

7. Install the clutch gear bearing retainer and gasket so that the oil slot in the retainer aligns with the oil slot in the front race of the transmission. The gasket should not extend beyond the retainer's edge.

8. Torque the retainer screws to 12–15 ft lbs. Use sealer to ensure that the screws are securely locked.

9. Coat the countershaft with gear oil and position it in the rear of the case.

10. Align the shaft with the counter gear and drive the shaft into place.

11. Rotate the countershaft until the flat on the shaft is one the bottom horizon of the shaft. This is necessary to permit the transmission extension to be attached to the case. The front end of the shaft should align with the hole in the front of the case, when the shaft is driven in until the flat is flush with the back of the case.

Clutch Sleeve Assembly

1. Position the first and reverse gears on the clutch assembly and place both pieces through the side opening of the case, front end first.

2. Position the assembly on the gear with the lug of the synchronizing ring aligned with the synchronizing slot of the clutch gear.

Mainshaft Assembly

1. Insert the mainshaft assembly into the transmission case extension and position the clutch gear rear roller spacer on the mainshaft so that the chamfered inside diameter faces the rear.

2. Position the transmission case gasket and align the synchronizer ring lugs with the mainshaft slots. The ring lugs should slide freely in the gear slots.

3. Check the clutch gear rollers for correct positioning then push the shaft into the clutch sleeve and seat the transmis-

sion case extension against the main case body.

Dip the threads of the lower extension bolt with sealer and install it with the other bolts. Torque all bolts to 40–50 ft lbs.

1963 BORG-WARNER, T-10 FOUR-SPEED

The Borg-Warner T-10 was used as the optional four-speed transmission until mid-year 1963 when it was replaced by the Muncie four-speed. Except for the larger gears of the Muncie, there are only minor differences between the two transmissions. Identification may be made by the shape of the side cover; the T-10 has a round-bottomed side cover and the Muncie has a straight-bottomed side cover. Beginning in mid-year 1974, a heavier duty T-10 was reintroduced as the standard Corvette four-speed.

Disassembly

1. Remove the side cover and unbolt and remove the front bearing retainer and gasket.
2. Move the individual selector levers until two gears are simultaneously selected and the transmission is locked. Remove the main, drive-gear retaining nut.
3. Return the selector levers to neutral and drive out the reverse shifter lever lockpin.
4. Disengage the reverse shifter fork by sliding the shifter shaft about ⅛ in. from the boss.
5. Remove the transmission-extension retaining bolts and slide the extension away until the idler gear restricts further movement.
6. Angle the extension to the left to permit the reverse fork to clear the reverse gear, then separate the extension from the main case.

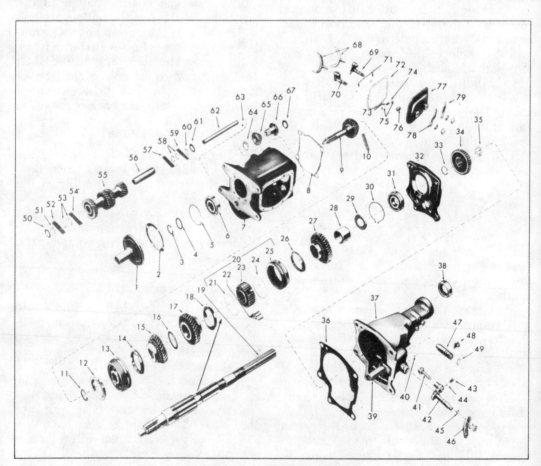

Exploded view of Borg-Warner T-10

7. Remove the reverse idler gear, flat thrust washer, shaft, and roll spring pin. A gear puller is required to remove the speedometer gear.

8. Remove reverse gear.

9. Position the third/fourth gear synchronizer sleeve forward then tap the rear bearing retainer with a soft hammer to remove it and the mainshaft from the case.

10. Extract the main, drive-gear roller bearings and withdraw the fourth-gear synchronizer blocker ring.

11. Pull the front portion of the reverse idler gear and its thrust washer from the case.

12. Press the main drive gear loose from the front bearing then tap the bearing from inside the case to remove it and its front snap-ring.

13. Press the counter gear shaft from the front of the case and remove the counter gear and its two washers. Carefully remove the roller bearings, spacers, and roller spacer from the counter gear.

14. Expand and remove the front snap-ring from the mainshaft then slide the third and fourth-gear clutch assembly, and the third gear and synchronizer ring from the shaft.

15. Expand the rear bearing retainer ring, then press the mainshaft free of the retainer.

16. Expand and remove the mainshaft rear snap-ring and, with the second gear supported, press the rear of the mainshaft. This will remove the rear bearing, first gear and sleeve, first gear synchronizer ring, first/second gear synchronizer ring, and the second gear.

17. Clean the transmission case exterior and interior with suitable solvent and check for cracks or other damage. Clean the front and rear bearings in cleaning solvent and blow dry with compressed air. Avoid spinning the bearings. Lubricate the bearings with light engine oil and set them aside.

18. Clean and inspect all roller bearings and replace if necessary. Clean and

1. Bearing retainer	28. First speed gear	54. Bearing rollers (20)
2. Gasket	bushing	55. Countergear
3. Snap-ring	29. First speed gear thrust	56. Countergear roller
4. Spacer washer	washer	spacer
5. Bearing snap-ring	30. Rear bearing snap-ring	57. Bearing rollers (20)
6. Main drive gear bearing	31. Rear bearing	58. Spacers
7. Transmission case	32. Rear bearing retainer	59. Bearing rollers (20)
8. Rear bearing retainer	33. Snap-ring	60. Spacers
gasket	34. Reverse gear	61. Tanged washer
9. Main drive gear	35. Speedometer drive	62. Countershaft
10. Bearing rollers (14)	gear	63. Countershaft woodruff
11. Snap-ring (.086" to .088")	35A. Special snap-ring	key
12. Fourth speed gear	36. Rear bearing retainer-to-	64. Reverse idler front
synchronizing ring	case extension gasket	Thrust washer (flat)
13. Third and Fourth speed	37. Case extension	65. Reverse idler gear
clutch sliding sleeve	38. Rear oil seal	(front)
14. Third speed	39. Reverse idler shaft	66. Reverse idler gear
synchronizing ring	40. Reverse shifter shaft	(rear)
15. Third speed gear	lockpin	67. Tanged thrust washer
16. Second and Third speed	41. Reverse shift fork	68. Forward speed shift forks
gear thrust washer	42. Reverse shifter shaft	69. First and Second speed
(needle roller bearing)	and detent plate	gear shifter shaft and
17. Second speed gear	43. Reverse shifter shaft	detent plate
18. Second speed gear	ball detent spring	70. Third and Fourth speed
synchronizing ring	44. Reverse shifter shaft	gear shifter shaft and
19. Mainshaft	detent ball	detent plate
20. First and Second speed	45. Reverse shifter shaft	71. O-ring seals
clutch assembly	O-ring seal	72. Gasket
21. Clutch key spring	46. Reverse shifter lever	73. Interlock pin
22. Clutch keys	47. Speedometer driven	74. Interlock spring
23. Clutch hub	gear and fitting	75. Detent balls
24. Clutch key spring	48. Retainer and bolt	76. Interlock sleeve
25. First and Second speed	49. O-ring seal	77. Transmission side cover
clutch sliding sleeve	50. Tanged washer	78. Third and Fourth speed
26. First speed gear	51. Spacer	shifter lever
synchronizing ring	52. Bearing rollers (20)	79. First and Second speed
27. First speed gear	53. Spacer	shifter lever

check all gears. It is good practice to mag-naflux the gears if such facilities are available.

Reverse Idler Shaft Replacement

1. Drive the reverse idler shaft lockpin into the boss until it falls into the shaft clearance hole.
2. Pry the welch plug out of the end of the shaft and press the shaft from the extension.
3. Align the lockpin hole in the shaft with the hole in the boss.
4. Install the idler shaft and tap the pin in place to lock the shaft.

Reverse Shifter Shaft and
Seal Replacement

1. Remove the shift fork.
2. Cautiously tap the shifter shaft into the case allowing the ball detent to drop into the case.
3. Remove the shaft and ball detent spring.
4. Place the ball detent spring into the detent spring hole and start the reverse shifter shaft into the hole in the boss.
5. Put the detent ball on the spring and while holding the ball down, push the new shaft into place and turn until ball drops into place.
NOTE: *Don't drive the shifter shaft lockpin into position until the extension has been installed on the transmission case.*

Clutch Key and Spring Replacement

Clutch hubs and sliding sleeves are selectively fit assemblies and must be kept together as originally assembled. Keys and springs may be replaced.
1. Remove the hub from the sliding sleeve. Remove the keys and springs when they fall free.
2. Replace one spring on each side of the hub so that the tanged end of each spring falls into the same keyway in the hub.
3. Put the keys in position and, while holding them in place, slide the hub into the sleeve.

Mainshaft Assembly

1. Assemble the first and second gear clutch assembly onto the mainshaft from the rear. Press the first gear bushing on the shaft.

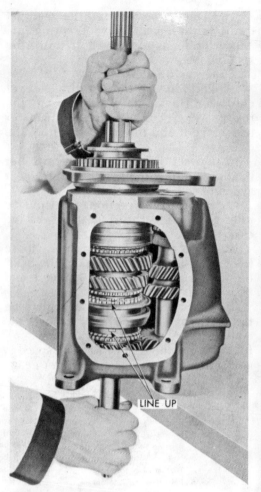

T-10 mainshaft assembly

2. Install the first-gear synchronizing ring with the notches in the ring matching the keys in the hub.
3. Install the first speed gear (with the hub toward the front) and thrust washer.
4. Press the rear bearing on the shaft with the snap-ring groove facing frontward. The bearing should abut the shoulder on the mainshaft.
5. Select a snap-ring (0.087 in., 0.093 in., or 0.099 in.) that will give a maximum distance of 0 to 0.005 in. between it and the rear face of the bearing when installed on the groove behind the rear bearing. Use all new snap-rings when reassembling the transmission.
6. Install the second-gear synchronizing ring from the front of the mainshaft, so that the notches in the ring match the keys in the hub.
7. Install the second speed gear with

the hub facing the back of the transmission and install the second and third-speed-gear thrust washer.

8. Install the third speed gear with the hub facing to the front. Install the third speed gear synchronizing ring with the notches facing frontward.

9. Install the third and fourth gear clutch assembly with the taper facing frontward. Make sure the keys in the hub match the notches in the third-gear synchronizing ring.

10. Install a snap-ring in the mainshaft groove in front of the third and fourth-gear clutch assembly.

11. If there is no end-play, the snap-ring thickness should be checked. It should be 0.087 in.

12. Install the rear bearing retainer. Expand the snap-ring in the plate to allow it to drop around the rear bearing and press on the end of the mainshaft until the snap-ring engages the groove in the rear bearing.

13. Install the reverse gear with the shift collar facing to the rear.

14. Press the speedometer drive gear onto the mainshaft. The distance from the center of the gear to the flat surface of the rear bearing retainer should be 4½ in.

Countergear Assembly

1. Install the roller spacer.

2. Install twenty rollers in either end of the countergear, two 0.050 in. spacers, twenty more rollers, and then one 0.050 in. spacer.

NOTE: *When installing rollers, use heavy grease to retain them.*

Transmission Assembly

1. With the transmission on its side and the side cover opening up, install the tanged, countergear thrust washers. Use heavy grease to retain them and make sure that the tangs are resting in the case notches.

2. Install the countergear in the bottom of the transmission case. Be careful not to displace the tanged thrust washers.

3. Press the bearing onto the main drive gear with the snap-ring groove facing the front. Make sure that the bearing fully seats against the gear shoulder.

4. Install the clutch bearing retaining nut on the clutch gearshaft and tighten.

Stake the retaining-nut oil slinger into the hole with a center punch.

5. Install the main drive gear and bearing assembly through the side cover opening and position in the case front bore. If necessary, tap it into place with a plastic hammer. Install a snap-ring into the front bearing groove.

6. Stand the transmission case on its front face. Mesh the countergear with the main drive gear. Make sure that the thrust washers stay in place. Install the woodruff key into the countershaft end. Press the shaft until the end is flush with the rear face of the transmission case.

7. Attach a dial indicator to the side of the transmission case so the feeler can extend and contact the countergear. Measure the end-play, which should not be more than 0.025 in.

8. Install the fourteen roller bearings into the main drive gear. Use heavy grease to hold the bearings in position.

9 Coat the front surface of the rear bearing retainer with grease and install the gasket.

10. Install the fourth-gear synchronizing ring on the main drive gear with the notches facing toward the rear of the transmission.

11. Place the reverse, idler-gear thrust washer on the machined face of the cast ear in the case for the reverse idler shaft. Position the front reverse idler gear on top of the thrust washer, with the hub facing toward the rear of the case.

12. Lower the mainshaft into the transmission case. Be sure that the fourth gear synchronizer notches match the keys in the clutch assembly.

13. Insert the rear, reverse idler-gear from the back of the case. Engage the splines with the portion of the gear within the case.

14. Grease the rear of the rear bearing retainer and install the gasket.

15. Install the remaining thrust washer into place on the reverse idler shaft. Be sure that the tang on the thrust washer is in the notch in the idler thrust face of the extension.

16. Put the two clutches into neutral position. Pull the reverse shifter shaft to the left side of the extension and turn the shaft to bring the reverse shift fork as far forward as possible.

17. Start the extension onto the trans-

mission case, while slowly pushing in on the shifter shaft to engage the shift fork with the reverse-gear shift collar.

18. When the fork engages, turn the shifter shaft to move the reverse gear backward allowing the extension to slide onto the transmission case.

19. Install the five retaining bolts and tighten to 35–45 ft lbs.

20. Move the reverse shifter shaft to line up the groove in the shaft with the holes in the boss and tap in the lockpin. Install the shifter lever.

21. Install the main, drive-gear bearing retainer, gasket, and four retaining bolts using sealer on the bolts. Torque the bolts to 15–20 ft lbs.

22. Install a shift fork in each clutch sleeve.

23. Position both clutches in neutral and install the side cover and bolts. Tighten the bolts evenly to avoid distortion. Apply sealer to the lower right bolt.

1963–74 MUNCIE FOUR-SPEED

Use the disassembly, reverse shifter-shaft replacement, and clutch key and spring replacement procedures given for the T-10 four-speed. Mainshaft and transmission assembly procedures are outlined below.

Reverse Idler

The reverse, idler-gear bushings are not serviced separately. The bushings are first pressed into place, then peened to secure, and drilled. The correct clearance between the bushings and the shaft is 0.003 in.–0.005 in.

Mainshaft Assembly

1. Assembly of the mainshaft begins from the rear with the placement of the second gear on the shaft so that the gear hub faces the rear of the shaft.

2. Assemble the first/second gear synchronizer clutch to the mainshaft with the clutch sleeve taper facing the rear of the shaft.

3. Position a synchronizer ring on both sides of the clutch assembly and align their keyways with the clutch keys.

4. Cut a suitable length of 1¾ in. inside diameter pipe and use it to press the first gear sleeve onto the mainshaft.

5. Use a suitable length of 1⅝ in. in-side diameter pipe to assemble the first gear, hub first, onto the mainshaft.

6. Again use the pipe to press on the rear bearing. This bearing is correctly positioned when the snap-ring groove faces the front of the transmission and the bearing is fully seated.

7. The maximum clearance between the snap-ring and the rear bearing face is 0.005 in. Snap-ring sizes of 0.087 in., 0.090 in., 0.093 in., and 0.096 in. are available for adjustment.

8. Install the third gear and its synchronizer ring, so that the gear hub and the ring notches face forward.

9. Third/fourth gear clutch assembly follows, and both its sleeve taper and hub face forward. Align the third-gear synchronizer-ring notches to the hub keys.

Measuring countergear end-play

Aligning Fourth gear synchronizer ring notches with clutch keys

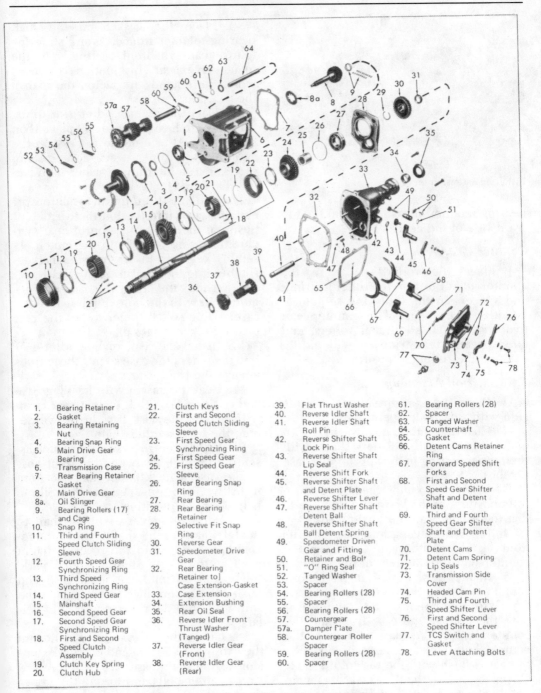

Exploded view of Muncie 4-speed

1.	Bearing Retainer	21.	Clutch Keys	39.	Flat Thrust Washer	61.	Bearing Rollers (28)
2.	Gasket	22.	First and Second	40.	Reverse Idler Shaft	62.	Spacer
3.	Bearing Retaining		Speed Clutch Sliding	41.	Reverse Idler Shaft	63.	Tanged Washer
	Nut		Sleeve		Roll Pin	64.	Countershaft
4.	Bearing Snap Ring	23.	First Speed Gear	42.	Reverse Shifter Shaft	65.	Gasket
5.	Main Drive Gear		Synchronizing Ring		Lock Pin	66.	Detent Cams Retainer
	Bearing	24.	First Speed Gear	43.	Reverse Shifter Shaft		Ring
6.	Transmission Case	25.	First Speed Gear		Lip Seal	67.	Forward Speed Shift
7.	Rear Bearing Retainer		Sleeve	44.	Reverse Shift Fork		Forks
	Gasket	26.	Rear Bearing Snap	45.	Reverse Shifter Shaft	68.	First and Second
8.	Main Drive Gear		Ring		and Detent Plate		Speed Gear Shifter
8a.	Oil Slinger	27.	Rear Bearing	46.	Reverse Shifter Lever		Shaft and Detent
9.	Bearing Rollers (17)	28.	Rear Bearing	47.	Reverse Shifter Shaft		Plate
	and Cage		Retainer		Detent Ball	69.	Third and Fourth
10.	Snap Ring	29.	Selective Fit Snap	48.	Reverse Shifter Shaft		Speed Gear Shifter
11.	Third and Fourth		Ring		Ball Detent Spring		Shaft and Detent
	Speed Clutch Sliding	30.	Reverse Gear	49.	Speedometer Driven		Plate
	Sleeve	31.	Speedometer Drive		Gear and Fitting	70.	Detent Cams
12.	Fourth Speed Gear		Gear	50.	Retainer and Bolt	71.	Detent Cam Spring
	Synchronizing Ring	32.	Rear Bearing	51.	"O" Ring Seal	72.	Lip Seals
13.	Third Speed		Retainer to)	52.	Tanged Washer	73.	Transmission Side
	Synchronizing Ring		Case Extension-Gasket	53.	Spacer		Cover
14.	Third Speed Gear	33.	Case Extension	54.	Bearing Rollers (28)	74.	Headed Cam Pin
15.	Mainshaft	34.	Extension Bushing	55.	Spacer	75.	Third and Fourth
16.	Second Speed Gear	35.	Rear Oil Seal	56.	Bearing Rollers (28)		Speed Shifter Lever
17.	Second Speed Gear	36.	Reverse Idler Front	57.	Countergear	76.	First and Second
	Synchronizing Ring		Thrust Washer	57a.	Damper Plate		Speed Shifter Lever
18.	First and Second		(Tanged)	58.	Countergear Roller	77.	TCS Switch and
	Speed Clutch	37.	Reverse Idler Gear		Spacer		Gasket
	Assembly		(Front)	59.	Bearing Rollers (28)	78.	Lever Attaching Bolts
19.	Clutch Key Spring	38.	Reverse Idler Gear	60.	Spacer		
20.	Clutch Hub		(Rear)				

10. Spread the snap-ring into the mainshaft groove so that it is in front of the third/fourth gear clutch assembly and behind the spline teeth.

11. Attach the rear bearing retainer by expanding the snap-ring in the plate until it slips over the rear bearing, then press the end of the mainshaft until the ring seats in the rear bearing groove.

12. Slide on the reverse gear with its shift collar facing rearward.

13. Press the speedometer gear onto the mainshaft and position it 4⅞ in. (6 in. for Saginaw) from the flat surface of the

Installing extension on case

bearing retainer, measuring from the forward side of the gear.

Counter Gear Assembly

1. Place the roller spacer in the counter gear. Position the roller bearings and spacers in the following sequence: 20 rollers in each end of the counter gear, two spacers, 20 additional rollers, and one spacer. Heavy grease will aid in keeping the rollers in position.

Transmission Assembly

1. Place the transmission case on its side with side plate opening up.
2. Coat the counter gear washers with heavy grease and position them with their tangs resting in the appropriate case notches.
3. Insert the countergear and carefully position in the bottom of the case so that the washers are not dislodged.
4. Lift the transmission case onto its front face then lubricate and start the countershaft into the rear of the case.
5. Rotate the shaft until its flat is horizontal and facing the bottom of the case. Check for alignment of the counter gear with the hole in the case front and the countershaft in the rear, then press the countershaft into the case, stopping when the flat is flush with the rear of the case. Check to see that the thrust washers were not displaced during installation.
6. Use a dial indicator to measure the counter-gear end play. A measurement of more than 0.025 in. warrants installation of new thrust washers.
7. Coat the 17 roller bearings with heavy grease and install them and their cage in the main drive gear.
8. Insert the gear and pilot bushings through the side cover opening and position them in the transmission front bore.

9. Place the gasket on the rear, bearing-retainer front face and slide the fourth-gear synchronizer ring onto the main drive gear. Installation is correct when the notches are facing the rear of the transmission.
10. Coat the reverse, idler-gear thrust washer with heavy grease and place it on the machined face of the ear cast in the case. Set the front, reverse idler-gear in place next to the thrust washer; hub facing rearward.
11. Slide the third/fourth synchronizer clutch sleeve into the fourth-gear detent position, then align the fourth gear synchronizer ring notches to the clutch assembly keys and insert the mainshaft assembly into the transmission case.
12. Align the rear, bearing-retainer guide pin with the hole in the rear of the case. Use a soft hammer to tap the rear bearing retainer into place.
13. Install the rear, reverse idler-gear into the rear of the case so that the splines engage the front gear.
14. Coat the gasket with heavy grease and position it on the retainer rear face.
15. Slide the last flat thrust washer onto the reverse idler shaft.
16. Install the reverse, idler-shaft assembly into the gears and the front boss of the case. Check to see that the front thrust washer is engaged and the roll pin is in a vertical position.
17. Slide the reverse shifter shaft to the left and turn the shaft to move the reverse shift fork into the reverse detent position (forward). Simultaneously slide the extension onto the main case and push the shifter shaft in to engage the shift fork with the reverse-gear shift collar.
18. Guide the reverse idler shaft into the extension housing and join the extension to the main case. Insert the extension retainer bolts and torque the upper three to 15–24 ft lbs and the lower three to 25–35 ft lbs.
19. Align the shifter shaft groove with the holes in the boss, tap in the lockpin, and install the shift lever.
20. Position the bearing, snap-ring groove forward, onto the main drive gear and press the bearing into the case so that several threads of the drive-gear retaining nut are exposed.
21. Shift the transmission into two

gears simultaneously to lock it, and install the main, drive-gear retainer nut on the gear shaft. Check to see that the bearing seats against the gear shoulder and torque the retainer nut to 40 ft lbs. Stake the nut into the main, drive-gear shaft hole.

22. Bolt on the main, drive-gear bearing retainer and torque to 18–26 ft lbs.

23. Position the third/fourth, sliding clutch sleeve into neutral and the first/second sleeve into second gear. Rotate the side cover third/fourth selector lever into Neutral and the first/second gear selector lever into second gear.

24. Carefully align and install the side cover. Torque the bolts to 14–22 ft lbs.

1966–72 SAGINAW 4-SPEED

Disassembly

1. Remove the side cover and shift forks after draining the transmission.

2. Remove the clutch gear bearing retainer. Remove the bearing-to-gear stem snap-ring, and pull out on the clutch gear until a screwdriver can be inserted between the bearing, large snap-ring, and case to pry the bearing off.

NOTE: *The clutch gear bearing is a slip-fit on the gear and in the case. Removal of the bearing will provide clearance for clutch gear and mainshaft removal.*

3. Remove the rear extension attaching bolts and remove the clutch gear, mainshaft, and extension as an assembly.

4. Spread the snap-ring which holds the mainshaft rear bearing and remove the extension case.

5. Remove the countershaft and its woodruff key by driving out of the rear of the case with a pipe or an old countershaft. Remove the countergear assembly and bearings.

6. Using a long drift, drive the reverse idler shaft and woodruff key through the rear of the case.

7. Expand and remove the third and fourth speed sliding clutch hub snap-ring from the mainshaft. Remove the clutch assembly, third gear blocker ring, and third speed gear from the front of the mainshaft.

8. Press in the speedometer gear retaining clip and slide the gear off the

mainshaft. Remove the rear bearing snap-ring from its groove in the mainshaft.

9. With first gear supported on press plates, press first gear, thrust washer, spring washer, rear bearing, and snap-ring from the rear of the mainshaft.

CAUTION: *Be careful to center the gear, washers, bearings, and snap-ring when pressing rear bearing.*

10. Expand and remove the first and second sliding clutch hub snap-ring from the mainshaft and remove the clutch assembly, second speed blocker ring, and second speed gear from the rear of the mainshaft.

After thoroughly cleaning all parts and the transmission case, inspect and replace all damaged or worn parts. When checking the bearings, do not spin them at high speeds. Clean and rotate the bearings by hand to detech roughness and unevenness. Spinning can damage balls and races.

Mainshaft Assembly

Install the following parts with the front of the mainshaft facing up:

1. Install the third speed gear with the clutching teeth up, the rear face of the gear will abut with the mainshaft flange.

Removing extension, mainshaft, and clutch gear

2. Install a blocking ring, clutching teeth down, over the third speed gear synchronizing surface.

NOTE: *All four blocker rings are the same.*

3. Press the third and fourth synchronizer assembly, fork slot down, onto the mainshaft splines until it bottoms.

CAUTION: *The blocker ring notches must align with the synchronizer assembly keys.*

4. Install the synchronizer nub-to-mainshaft snap-ring. (Both synchronizer snap-rings are the same.)

Install the following parts with the rear of the mainshaft up.

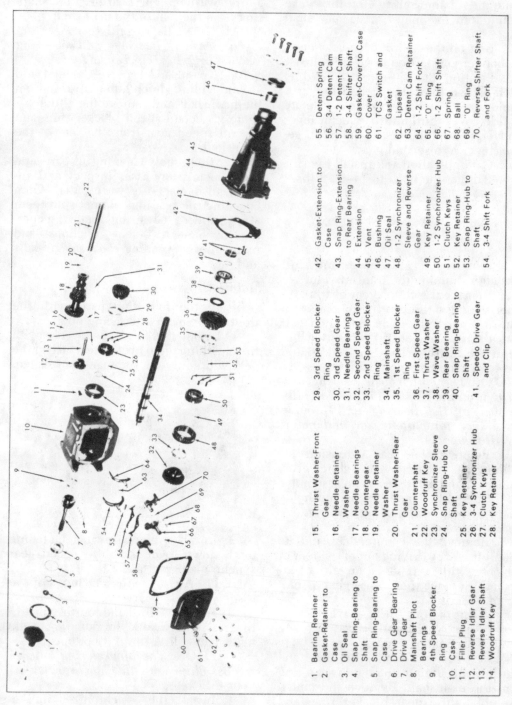

Exploded view of Saginaw 4-speed

1. Bearing Retainer
2. Gasket-Retainer to Case
3. Oil Seal
4. Snap Ring-Bearing to Shaft
5. Snap Ring-Bearing to Case
6. Drive Gear Bearing
7. Drive Gear
8. Mainshaft Pilot Bearings
9. 4th Speed Blocker Ring
10. Case
11. Filler Plug
12. Reverse Idler Gear
13. Reverse Idler Shaft
14. Woodruff Key
15. Thrust Washer-Front Gear
16. Needle Retainer Washer
17. Needle Bearings
18. Countergear
19. Needle Retainer Washer
20. Thrust Washer-Rear Gear
21. Countershaft
22. Woodruff Key
23. Synchronizer Sleeve
24. Snap Ring-Hub to Shaft
25. Key Retainer
26. 3-4 Synchronizer Hub
27. Clutch Keys
28. Key Retainer
29. 3rd Speed Blocker Ring
30. 3rd Speed Gear
31. Needle Bearings
32. Second Speed Gear
33. 2nd Speed Blocker Ring
34. Mainshaft
35. 1st Speed Blocker Ring
36. First Speed Gear
37. Thrust Washer
38. Wave Washer
39. Rear Bearing
40. Snap Ring-Bearing to Shaft
41. Speedo Drive Gear and Clip
42. Gasket-Extension to Case
43. Snap Ring-Extension to Rear Bearing
44. Extension
45. Vent
46. Bushing
47. Oil Seal
48. 1-2 Synchronizer Sleeve and Reverse Gear
49. Key Retainer
50. 1-2 Synchronizer Hub
51. Clutch Keys
52. Key Retainer
53. Snap Ring-Hub to Shaft
54. 3-4 Shift Fork
55. Detent Spring
56. 3-4 Detent Cam
57. 1-2 Detent Cam
58. 3-4 Shifter Shaft
59. Gasket-Cover to Case
60. Cover
61. TCS Switch and Gasket
62. Lipseal
63. Detent Cam Retainer
64. 1-2 Shift Fork
65. "O" Ring
66. 1-2 Shift Shaft
67. Spring
68. Ball
69. "O" Ring
70. Reverse Shifter Shaft and Fork

Removing reverse idler shaft

5. Install the second speed gear with the clutching teeth up, the front face of the gear will abut with the flange on the mainshaft.

6. Install a blocking ring, clutching teeth down, over the second speed gear synchronizing surface.

7. Press the first and second synchronizer assembly fork slot down, onto the mainshaft.

CAUTION: *The blocker ring notches must align with the synchronizer assembly keys.*

8. Install the synchronizer hub-to-mainshaft snap-ring.

9. Install a blocker ring with the notches down so they align with the first/second synchronizer assembly keys.

10. Install first gear with the clutching teeth down. Install the first gear thrust washer and spring washer.

11. Press the rear ball bearing, snap-

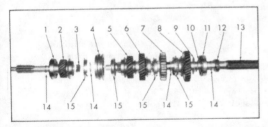

Mainshaft and clutch gear

1. Clutch gear bearing	8. First speed gear
2. Clutch gear	9. Thrust washer
3. Mainshaft pilot bearings	10. Spring washer
	11. Rear bearing
4. 3-4 synchronizer assembly	12. Speedometer drive gear
5. Third speed gear	13. Mainshaft
6. Second speed gear	14. Snap-ring
7. 1-2 synchronizer and reverse gear assembly	15. Synchronizing blocker ring

ring slot down, onto the mainshaft. Install the snap-ring. Install the speedometer gear and clip.

Transmission Assembly

1. Using a dummy countergear shaft, load a row of roller bearings (27) and a bearing thrust washer at each end of the countergear. Grease can be used to hold the bearings in place.

2. Position the countergear assembly into the case through the rear opening. Place a tanged thrust washer at each end of the countergear.

3. Install the countergear shaft and woodruff key from the rear of the case. Make sure that the shaft engages both thrust washers and that the tangs align with their notches in the case.

4. Install the reverse idler gear and shaft and woodruff key. Install the extension-to-rear bearing snap-ring.

5. Install the fourteen mainshaft pilot bearings into the clutch opening and install the fourth speed blocker ring onto the clutching surface of the clutch gear (clutching teeth toward the gear).

6. Assemble the clutch gear, pilot bearings, and fourth speed blocker ring unit over the front of the mainshaft. Do not assemble the bearing to the gear at this point.

CAUTION: *Ensure that the blocker ring notches line up with third/fourth synchronizer assembly keys.*

7. Install the extension-to-case gasket and secure with grease. Insert the clutch gear, mainshaft, and extension into the case as a unit. Install the extension-to-case bolts (apply sealer to the bottom bolt) and torque to 45 ft lbs.

8. Install the outer snap-ring on the front bearing and place the bearing over the stem of the clutch gear and into the case bore.

9. Install the snap-ring to the clutch gear stem. Install the clutch gear bearing retainer and gasket to the case, with the retainer oil return hole at the bottom.

10. Place the synchronizer sleeves into neutral positions and install the cover, gasket, and fork assemblies to the case. Insure that the forks align with their synchronizer sleeve grooves. Torque the cover bolts to 22 ft lbs.

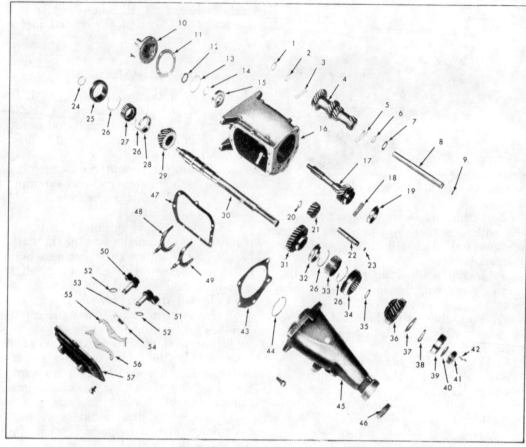

Exploded view of Saginaw 3-speed

1. Thrust washer—front	21. Reverse idler gear	41. Speedometer drive gear
2. Bearing washer	22. Reverse idler shaft	42. Clip
3. Needle bearings	23. Woodruff key	43. Gasket
4. Countergear	24. Snap-ring—hub-to-shaft	44. Snap-ring—rear bearing-to-extension
5. Needle bearings	25. 2-3 synchronizer sleeve	
6. Bearing washer	26. Synchronizer key spring	45. Extension
7. Thrust washer—rear	27. 2-3 synchronizer hub assembly	46. Oil seal
8. Countershaft	28. Second speed blocker ring	47. Gasket
9. Woodruff key	29. Second speed gear	48. 2-3 shift fork
10. Bearing retainer	30. Mainshaft	49. First and Reverse shift fork
11. Gasket	31. First speed gear	50. 2-3 shifter shaft assembly
12. Oil seal	32. First speed blocker ring	51. First and Reverse shifter shaft assembly
13. Snap-ring—bearing-to-case	33. 1-2 synchronizer hub assembly	
14. Snap-ring—bearing-to-gear	34. 1-2 synchronizer sleeve	52. O-ring seal
15. Clutch gear bearing	35. Snap-ring—hub-to-shaft	53. E-ring
16. Case	36. Reverse gear	54. Spring
17. Clutch gear	37. Thrust washer	55. Second and Third detent cam
18. Pilot bearings	38. Spring washer	56. First and Reverse detent cam
19. Third speed blocker ring	39. Rear bearing	57. Side cover
20. Retainer E-ring	40. Snap-ring—bearing-to-shaft	

1966–69 SAGINAW THREE-SPEED

Transmission Disassembly

1. Remove side cover assembly and shift forks.

2. Remove clutch gear bearing retainer.

3. Remove clutch gear bearing to gear stem snap-ring. Pull clutch gear outward until a screwdriver can be inserted between bearing and case. Remove clutch gear bearing.

4. Remove speedometer driven gear and extension bolts.

5. Remove reverse idler shaft snapring. Slide reverse idler gear forward on shaft.

6. Remove mainshaft and extension assembly.

7. Remove clutch gear and third speed blocker ring from inside case. Remove 14 roller bearings from clutch gear.

8. Expand the snap-ring which retains the mainshaft rear bearing. Remove the extension.

9. Using a dummy shaft, drive the countershaft and key out the rear of the case. Remove the gear, two tanged thrust washers, and dummy shaft. Remove bearing washer and 27 roller bearings from each end of counter gear.

10. Use a long drift to drive the reverse idler shaft and key through the rear of the case.

11. Remove reverse idler gear and tanged steel thrust washer.

Mainshaft Disassembly

1. Remove second and third-speed, sliding, clutch hub snap-ring from mainshaft. Remove clutch assembly, second-speed blocker ring, and second gear from front of mainshaft.

2. Depress speedometer drive-gear retaining clip. Remove gear. Some units have a metal speedometer drive-gear which must be pulled off.

3. Remove rear bearing snap-ring.

4. Support reverse gear. Press on rear of mainshaft. Remove reverse gear, thrust washer, spring washer, rear bearing, and snap-ring. When pressing off the rear bearing, be careful not to cock the bearing on the shaft.

5. Remove first and reverse sliding clutch hub snap-ring. Remove clutch assembly, first-speed blocker ring, and first gear.

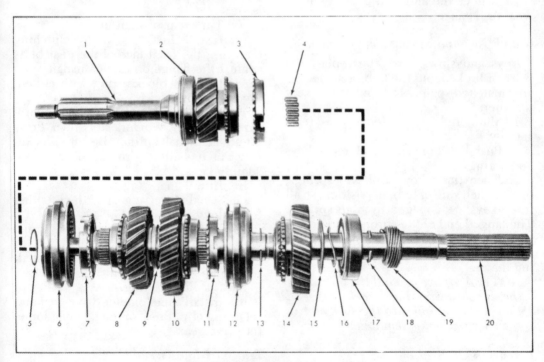

Clutch gear and mainshaft assembly

1. Clutch gear	8. Second speed gear
2. Clutch gear bearing	9. Shoulder (part of mainshaft)
3. Third speed blocker ring	10. First speed gear
4. Mainshaft pilot bearings (14)	11. First speed blocker ring
5. Snap-ring	12. First speed synchronizer assembly
6. 2-3 synchronizer assembly	13. Snap-ring
7. Second speed blocker ring	

14. Reverse gear
15. Reverse gear thrust washer
16. Spring washer
17. Rear bearing
18. Snap-ring
19. Speedometer drive gear and clip
20. Mainshaft

Cleaning and Inspection

1. Wash all parts and the transmission case in solvent.

2. Check the case front and rear faces for burrs, and remove with a fine file.

3. Examine the bearing bores for damages and replace the case if necessary.

4. Clean the front and rear bearings. Lubricate them with light oil and slowly rotate to check for roughness.

CAUTION: *Never spin dry bearings.*

5. Check the bearing rollers for wear and replace if worn.

6. Examine the countershaft and reverse idler shaft for wear or damage, and replace if necessary.

7. Replace all worn washers and snap-rings.

8. Check all the gears for wear, chips, or cracks. If the reverse gear bushing is worn or damaged, replace the entire gear.

9. Check that both clutch sleeves slide freely on their hubs.

10. Check the anti-lash plate teeth for wear or damage.

Clutch Key and Spring Replacement

Keys and springs may be replaced if worn or broken, but the hubs and sleeves are matched pairs and must be kept together.

1. Mark hub and sleeve for reassembly.

2. Push hub from sleeve. Remove keys and springs.

3. Place three keys and two springs, one on each side of hub, in position, so all three keys are engaged by both springs. The tanged end of the springs should not be installed into the same key.

4. Slide the sleeve onto the hub, aligning the marks.

NOTE: *A groove around the outside of the synchronizer hub marks the end that must be opposite the fork slot in the sleeve when assembled.*

Extension Oil Seal and Bushing Replacement

1. Remove seal.

2. Using bushing remover and installer tool, or other suitable tool, drive bushing into extension housing.

3. Drive new bushing in from the rear, Lubricate inside of bushing and seal. Install new oil seal with extension-seal installer tool or other suitable tool.

Clutch Bearing Retainer Oil Seal Replacement

1. Pry old seal out.

2. Install new seal using seal installer or suitable tool. Seat seal in bore.

Mainshaft Assembly

1. Turn front of mainshaft up.

2. Install second gear with clutching teeth up; the rear face of the gear butts against the flange on the mainshaft.

3. Install a blocker ring with clutching teeth down. All three blocker rings are the same.

4. Install second and third-speed synchronizer assembly with fork slot down. Press it onto mainshaft splines. Both synchronizer assemblies are the same. Be sure that blocker ring notches align with synchronizer assembly keys.

5. Install synchronizer snap-ring. Both synchronizer snap-rings are the same.

6. Turn rear of shaft up.

7. Install first gear with clutching teeth up; the front face of the gear butts against the flange on the mainshaft.

8. Install a blocker ring with clutching teeth down.

9. Install first and reverse synchronizer assembly with fork slot down. Press it onto mainshaft splines. Be sure blocker ring notches align with synchronizer assembly keys.

10. Install snap-ring.

11. Install reverse gear with clutching teeth down.

12. Install steel, reverse-gear thrust washer and spring washer.

13. Press rear ball bearing onto shaft with snap-ring slot down.

14. Install snap-ring.

15. Install speedometer drive gear and retaining clip. Press on metal speedometer drive-gear.

Transmission Assembly

1. Using dummy shaft, load a row of 27 roller bearings and a thrust washer at each end of countergear. Hold in place with grease.

2. Place countergear assembly into case through rear. Place a tangled thrust washer, tang away from gear, at each end.

Install countershaft and key, making sure that tangs align with notches in case.

3. Install reverse, idler-gear thrust washer, gear, and shaft with key from rear of case. Be sure thrust washer is between gear and rear of case with tang toward notch in case.

4. Expand snap-ring in extension. Assemble extension over rear of mainshaft and onto rear bearing. Seat snap-ring in rear bearing groove.

5. Install 14 mainshaft pilot bearings into clutch gear cavity. Assemble third-speed blocker ring onto clutch gear, clutching surface with teeth toward gear.

6. Place clutch gear, pilot bearings, and third-speed blocker-ring assembly over front of mainshaft assembly. Be sure blocker rings align with keys in second/third synchronizer assembly.

7. Stick extension gasket to case with grease. Install clutch gear, mainshaft, and extension together. Be sure clutch gear engages teeth of countergear anti-lash plate. Torque extension bolts to 45 ft lbs.

8. Place bearing over stem of clutch gear and into front case bore. Install front bearing to clutch gear snap-ring.

9. Install clutch-gear bearing retainer and gasket. The retainer oil-return hole must be at the bottom. Torque retainer bolts to 10 ft lbs.

10. Install reverse, idler gearshaft E-ring.

11. Shift synchronizer sleeves to neutral positions. Install cover, gasket, and forks, aligning forks with synchronizer sleeve grooves. Torque side cover bolts to 10 ft lbs.

12. Install speedometer driven gear.

Linkage Adjustment

1963 MUNCIE THREE-SPEED

1. Position both transmission side-cover selector fork levers and the shift lever in Neutral.

2. Attach rod to lever then adjust the clevis on its opposite end until the clevis pin will freely enter the side cover lever.

3. Insert the pin and secure it with a cotter pin.

4. Position the shift lever so that it activates the first and reverse lever, but still remains in Neutral.

5. Attach the first/reverse shift rod to the shift lever, adjust the clevis as done

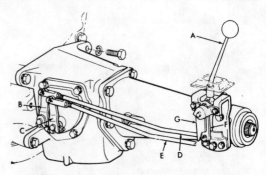

1963–64 3-speed linkage

A. Shift lever
B. 2-3 fork lever
C. First/Reverse fork lever
D. 2-3 shift rod
E. First/Reverse shift rod
F. 2-3 shift lever
G. First/Reverse shift lever

with the other shift rod, and secure it to selector lever.

6. Tighten the locknuts on both shift rod clevis fittings, and check the shift pattern for correct operation.

1964–68 THREE-SPEED

1. Set the side cover selector levers in Neutral and position the shift lever in Neutral and lock it in place with a 5/16 in. (early models) or 41/64 in. (late models) locating pin.

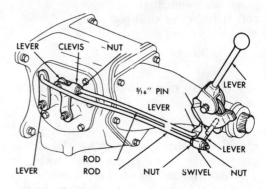

1965–68 3-speed linkage

2. Attach the first and reverse rod as with earlier transmissions and secure it.

3. Attach the second/third shift rod and attach it in the same manner.

4. Secure the locknuts on the clevis of each rod then withdraw the locating pin and check the shift pattern.

1969 THREE-SPEED WITH BACKDRIVE

1. Place the ignition switch in the "off" position and the side cover selector levers in Neutral.

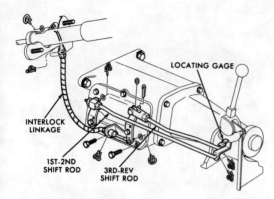

1969 3-speed linkage

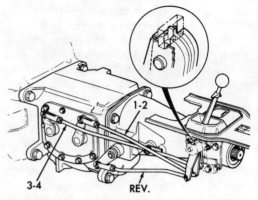

Borg-Warner T-10 linkage

2. Position the shift lever in Neutral and secure it with a $^{41}/_{64}$ in. locating gauge, between the shift lever notch and the linkage bracket.

3. Adjust the clevis of each rod so that they freely enter the attachment locations on their respective ends. Secure the locknuts, remove the gauge, and shift the transmission into Reverse.

4. Loosen the bracket assembly on the dash and allow any tension in the backdrive cable to position the bracket.

5. Secure the bracket and switch the key from "off" to "lock." Binding of the key will necessitate readjustment of the interlock mechanism.

6. Check the shift pattern.

1963 BORG-WARNER, T-10 FOUR-SPEED

The illustrated wooden gauge, if made, will greatly aid in shift linkage adjustment.

1. Put the shift lever in Neutral, install the block gauge, and remove the clevis pin from the clevis of each shift rod.

2. Adjust the threaded clevis until the clevis pin freely enters the holes in the clevis and the selector levers.

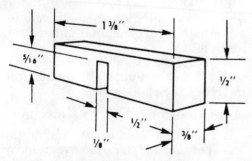

Borg-Warner T-10 adjustment gauge

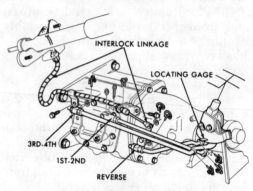

Muncie 4-speed linkage with interlock

3. Secure the pins and lock the clevis securing nuts.

Remove the gauge block and check the shift pattern. Minor adjustment of the rods may be necessary to remove all traces of shifting roughness.

1963–68 MUNCIE FOUR-SPEED

1. Position the individual selector levers and the shift lever in Neutral.

2. Construct a block gauge $^1/_8$ in. thick by $^{41}/_{64}$ in. wide and install it in the shift lever bracket assembly.

3. Attach the first/second shift rod to the lever. Hold the lever against the gauge block and adjust the threaded swivel on the shift rod until the clevis pin freely enters the clevis hold and the hole in selector lever. Secure the locking nuts.

4. Repeat the procedure and attach the reverse rod to the selector lever, and the bracket lever. Repeat again to adjust the third/fourth rod.

5. Remove the block gauge, check the pattern for correct shifting, and adjust, if necessary, to correct minor shifting difficulties.

6. An alternate clevis pin hole is placed on each selector lever below the regular pattern hole. This lower placement of the shift rods will tighten the pattern and permit shorter shift lever movement for a faster shift. Bear in mind, however, that this adjustment will increase the shifting effort.

1969–76 FOUR-SPEED WITH INTERLOCK

1. Switch the ignition to "off" and loosen the locknuts on the shift rod swivels.

2. Place the individual selector levers in Neutral, then put the shift lever in Neutral and insert the gauge block in the bracket assembly, lever adjustment slot.

3. Adjust the shift rods to remove all slack then tighten the swivel locknuts.

4. Remove the gauge block and check the pattern for correctness of shifting.

5. Turn the ignition switch through "off" and "lock." If binding is present, shift the transmission into Reverse and loosen the bolts that secure the interlock bracket to the dash.

6. Allow the cable tension to reposition the bracket. Tighten the securing bolts and check the operation of the ignition switch.

Automatic Transmission

Removal and Installation

1963–67 POWERGLIDE

1. Disconnect the battery ground cable and remove the ball end from the shift lever.

2. Jack the car to the desired working height.

3. Remove the driveshaft as outlined in the driveshaft section of Chapter 7.

4. Remove the left and right exhaust pipes.

5. Remove the two bolts that hold the rear mount rubber cushion to the rear bracket.

6. Support the engine at the oil pan with a jack. Place a board between the oil pan and jack pad to prevent damaging the pan.

7. Remove the three, transmission

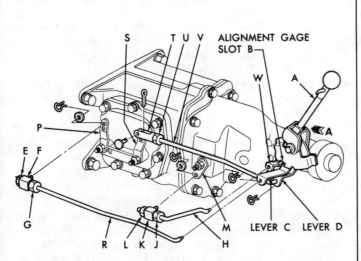

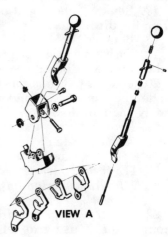

Muncie 4-speed linkage

mount-to-crossmember bolts, and remove the mount bracket.

8. Remove the two bolts from the pad to transmission case, and remove the rubber cushion and exhaust pipe bracket (except 1963 models on which the bracket would have been removed when the exhaust pipes were removed).

9. On 1964 and later models, disconnect the oil cooler lines at the transmission and swing them out of the way.

10. Remove the underpan.

11. Remove the converter-to-flywheel bolts, and mark or scribe the converter/flywheel relationship for assembly.

NOTE: *The lighter side of the converter is marked with a blue paint stripe which should be aligned with the white paint stripe on the flywheel outer rim to keep the assembly in balance.*

12. Disconnect the vacuum modulator line and speedometer cable at the transmission.

13. Disconnect the shift linkage from the control lever, and remove the shift lever.

14. Remove the throttle valve linkage and shift control linkage, and disconnect the neutral safety switch linkage.

15. Remove the neutral safety switch from the transmission.

16. Remove the transmission output shaft yoke and insert a plug to prevent transmission fluid from escaping.

17. Remove the ignition shielding from the distributor.

18. Remove the dipstick and tube.

19. Disconnect the vacuum modulator tube at the distributor advance line tee.

20. Place a transmission jack or hoist under the transmission and secure with a safety chain or line.

21. Remove the transmission converter housing-to-engine bolts and slowly pull the transmission rearward.

NOTE: *If the converter does not move with the transmission, pry it out from the flywheel.*

22. Install a strap or wire across the front of the housing to retain the converter.

23. Tilt the front of the transmission down and to the right while lowering. Remove the transmission from the vehicle.

24. To install the transmission, reverse the preceding steps.

25. Transmission case-to-flywheel housing bolt torque and converter-to-flywheel bolt torque is 35 ft lbs.

1968–76 TURBO HYDRA-MATIC

1. Disconnect the battery ground cable and release the parking brake.

2. Jack the car to the desired working height.

3. Remove the left and right exhaust pipes; forward exhaust manifold bolts must be removed first on large block engines.

4. Remove the driveshaft as outlined in the driveshaft section of Chapter 7.

5. Disconnect the speedometer cable, electrical lead to case connector, vacuum line modulator, and oil cooler lines.

6. Disconnect the shift linkage.

7. Support the transmission with a jack.

8. Disconnect the rear transmission mount from the frame crossmember.

9. Remove the two bolts at each end of the transmission crossmember and the thru-bolts on the inside of the frame and parking brake pulley.

10. Remove the detent, solenoid connector wire at the transmission.

11. Remove the converter underpan.

12. Remove the converter-to-flywheel bolts.

13. Lower the transmission so that the jack is just barely supporting it, and remove the transmission-to-engine bolts and the fluid tube.

14. Raise the engine back up to its normal position, then slide it rearward and down from the car.

CAUTION: *Be sure to keep the rear of the transmission lower than the front, or the converter may fall out.*

15. Installation is the reverse of removal, with the exception of the following procedure. Before installing the flex plate-to-converter bolts, be sure that the weld nuts on the converter are flush with the flex plate and that the converter rotates freely. Hand-tighten all three bolts, then torque them to 33 ft lbs.

16. Transmission-to-engine mounting bolt torque is 28 ft lbs. The torque on the rear mount-to-transmission bolts and rear

mount-to-crossmember bolts is 40 ft lbs. Torque the crossmember-to-frame bolts to 25 ft lbs.

Shift Linkage Adjustment

1963–67 POWERGLIDE

All Powerglides are adjusted in the same manner, although the shift pattern was changed in 1965 from the staggered pattern of 1963–64 to a straight pattern.

1. Disconnect the control rod from the shift lever.

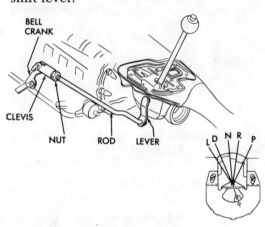

Powerglide shift linkage

2. Position both the shift lever and the control rod bell crank in Park, then loosen the clevis locknut and rotate the rod until it freely enters the shift lever.

3. Secure the rod to the shift lever and lock the clevis nut.

1968–72

1. Disconnect the pushrod at the transmission lever.

2. With the transmission lever in Drive detent and the selector lever in Drive, rotate the push-rod until the hole lines up with the lever pin.

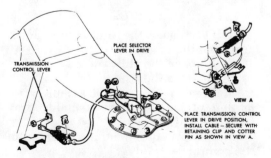

1968–72 Turbo Hydra-Matic shift linkage

3. Install the pushrod on the pin and install the retainer clip.

4. Check operation of the linkage in all positions.

1973–76

1. Loosen the nut on the transmission lever so that the pin can move in the slot. Remove the console cover.

2. Move the transmission lever counter-clockwise to the L1 position and then clockwise five detents to Park.

3. Place the shift lever in Park and insert a 0.40 in. spacer in front of the pawl.

4. Tighten the nut on the transmission lever to 20 ft lbs.

5. Turn the ignition switch to Lock with the shift lever in Park.

6. Remove the cotter pin and washer from the backdrive cable at the column lever. Disconnect the cable.

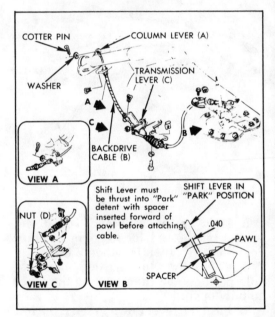

1973–76 Turbo Hydra-Matic shift linkage

7. Working under the dash, remove the two nuts at the steering column-to-dash bracket.

8. Turn the lock tube lever counterclockwise (when viewed from the front of the column) to remove any free-play from the column.

9. Move the bracket until the cable eye passes freely over the retaining pin on the bracket.

10. While holding the bracket in place,

have an assistant tighten the bracket retaining nuts.

11. Install the cotter pin and washer to retain the cable to the lever retaining pin.

Throttle Valve Adjustment

1963–67 POWERGLIDE

1. Fully open the lever and pull the rod forward until it contacts the internal transmission stop.

2. Adjust the swivel on the rod until the rod freely enters the lever, and then lengthen three full turns.

3. Secure the swivel then remove the toe panel carpeting.

4. Fully depress the accelerator pedal until the carburetor lever contacts the firewall.

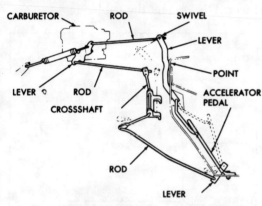

Throttle valve adjustment

5. Hold in position and adjust the swivel on the rod for freedom of entry into the lever, then lengthen 2 turns.

6. Check by returning the linkage to idle position and then rotating the lever to fully open.

7. Push the lever down to see if the rod deflects. If it does, or if the lever fails to open fully, repeat the adjustment.

Detent Switch Adjustment

1968–72 TURBO HYDRA-MATIC 400

The detent switch is located on the carburetor.

1. Pull the detent switch driver rearward until the hole in the switch body aligns with the hole in the driver.

2. Insert a 0.092 in. pin through the aligned holes to a depth of 0.10 in. to hold the driver in position.

3. Loosen the switch mounting bolt.

4. With the throttle held in wide open position, move the switch forward until the driver contacts the accelerator lever.

5. Tighten the mounting bolt and remove the pin.

1973–76 TURBO HYDRA-MATIC 400

The switch is located over the accelerator pedal. After installing a new switch, adjustment is made by pressing the plunger in. This presets the switch and it will self-adjust the first time the pedal is fully depressed.

Neutral Safety Switch Adjustment

1963–65 POWERGLIDE

Adjustment is made by varying the length of the bellcrank-to-switch control rod. One end of the rod has a swivel to allow adjustment.

1966–67 POWERGLIDE AND 1968–71 TURBO HYDRA-MATIC 400

In all models the adjustment is made with the shift lever in Drive position. Loosen the switch mounting screws. Align the slot in the contact support with the hole in the switch and insert a $3/32$ in. pin to hold the support in place.

The shift control lever must be disconnected from the control rod and the shift control knob removed. Then remove the trim plate to get at the switch. Proceed as described in the first paragraph above, then place the contact support drive slot over the drive tang. Tighten the switch mounting screws, then remove the pin. Reinstall the shift control lever and trim plate.

1972

1. Disconnect the shift control lever arm from the control rod.

2. Remove the shift knob.

3. Remove the trim plate.

4. Remove the control assembly retaining screws and lift the assembly away from the seal.

5. Remove the neutral switch from the control assembly.

To install:

6. On early 1972 models put the

shifter into Drive or Neutral on later models.

7. Align the hole in the contact support with the hole in the switch and insert a 3/32 in. pin to hold the support in place.

8. Place the contact support drive slot over the drive tang and tighten the switch mounting screws. Remove the pin.

9. Install the control assembly mounting screws. Connect the switch wiring and check the switch operation.

10. Install the trim plate and shift knob.

11. Connect the shift lever arm to the transmission control rod.

1973–76

Use the procedure outlined previously except that during installation, the shift lever is positioned in Drive. It is only necessary to use the 3/32 in. pin for alignment when the original switch pin has been sheared off.

Low Band Adjustment

1963–67 POWERGLIDE

Low band adjustment should be performed at 12,000 mile intervals, or if slipping is encountered.

1. Place the selector lever in Neutral.

2. Jack the car up to the required working height.

3. Remove the cap from the adjusting screw.

4. Lower the left exhaust pipe for clearance.

5. Loosen the adjusting screw ¼ turn and hold with a wrench

6. Using an in. lb torque wrench, adjust the band to 70 in. lb and back-off exactly four turns for a band in use over 6,000 miles and three turns for one in use less than 6,000 miles.

NOTE: *The locknut must be held at exactly ¼ turn loose during the adjustment. The number of back-off turns must be exactly as stated here.*

7. Tighten the locknut to 15 ft lbs.

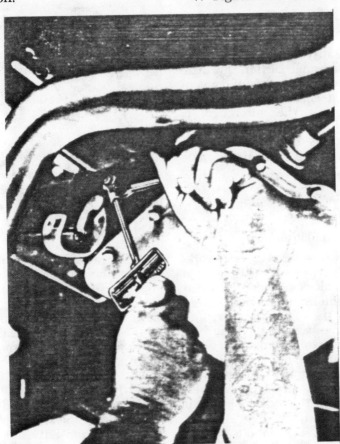

Powerglide low band adjustment

Chapter 7

Drive Train

Driveline

The Stingray driveline consists of the driveshaft, differential carrier, and axle driveshafts. The driveshaft is of conventional tubular design with a universal joint at each end. The differential is mounted directly to a suspension crossmember. Power is transmitted to the wheels through universal-jointed axle driveshafts.

DRIVESHAFT AND UNIVERSAL JOINTS

Removal and Installation

1. Jack the car to a convenient working height.

2. Wedge a block of wood between the top of the differential carrier and the car floor to keep the carrier from twisting on its rubber mounts when the front support bracket is disconnected.

3. Loosen and remove the carrier support-bracket front bolt. Remove the two rubber biscuits and large washer. Discard and replace the rubber biscuits if they show any deterioration.

4. Remove the two side bolts or front thru-bolt on later models from the carrier support bracket. Loosen, but do not re-

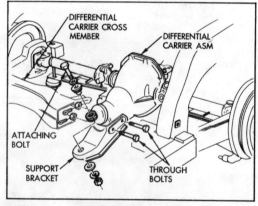

Differential and axle driveshaft mounting

move, the rear thru-bolt and swivel the bracket down and away.

5. Remove the U-bolts from both ends of the driveshaft.

6. Push the front yoke into the transmission and remove the driveshaft by pulling it down and to the rear.

7. Check the universal joints and replace damaged or worn units. Grease both universal joints before reinstalling them.

8. Install the driveshaft and attach to the transmission yoke and carrier flange.

9. Install the front bolt biscuits and flat washer and raise the bracket to the crossmember.

NOTE: *At this point it may be neces-*

238

sary to install a jack under the carrier. This will aid in lining up the side-bracket bolt holes and compressing the rubber biscuits.

10. Install the front crossmember bolt and nut. Install the side bolts. Front bolt torque is 30 ft lbs. Torque the two side bolts to 45–55 and the long thru-bolt to 40–60 ft lbs.

NOTE: *The carrier support bracket bolts frequently work loose, causing vibration and rear axle hop. Periodic torquing of these four bolts will eliminate this problem.*

Universal Joint Overhaul

Except for early Stingrays, Corvettes are equipped with lubed-for-life universal joints without grease fittings. Whenever universal joints are removed from the car, they should be checked and re-greased.

1. Remove the joints from the driveshaft. These can sometimes be tapped out, but stubborn joints must be pressed out.

2. Remove the bearing cups and seals, being careful not to lose any rollers.

3. Inspect the cups and trunnion ends for damage or wear. Ensure that all bearing rollers are present. Replace the rubber seals.

4. Clean the cups and rollers. Repack the cup with grease and reassemble the joint.

AXLE DRIVESHAFT

Removal and Installation

1. Jack the rear of the car up.

2. Disconnect the inside trunnion from the carrier yoke.

3. On the outer end, bend down the french locktabs and wire-brush the bolts.

4. Scratch a mark on the camber adjusting cam and the bracket to permit realignment.

5. Loosen the camber adjustment nut and turn the cam so that the eccentric end points inward. Doing this will push the trailing arm out and give more room for driveshaft removal.

6. Remove the driveshaft, outside end first.

7. To install, position the inside end of the driveshaft in the carrier yoke and as-

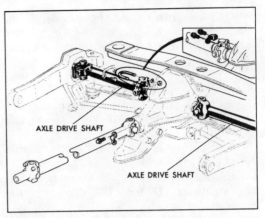

Axle driveshaft installation

semble U-bolts or clamp and bolts. Torque the bolts to 14–18 ft lbs.

NOTE: *When removing and installing both axle driveshafts, be certain to position the carrier side yokes so that the trunnion seats are at 90° angles to each other.*

8. Install the outside end of the driveshaft into the spindle drive flange. Install the french locks and bolts. Torque the bolts to 70–90 ft lbs and bend the locktabs up.

9. Realign the camber adjusting cam and bracket. Torque the nut to 15–22 ft lbs.

Differential Carrier

Removal and Installation

1. Remove the transverse spring end-link bolts using the procedures for spring removal.

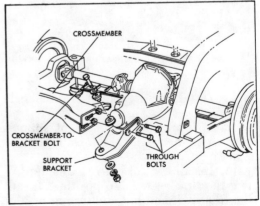

Differential carrier support bracket mounting

2. Disconnect the axle driveshafts at the carrier. Disconnect the front carrier support bracket from the frame and the carrier and remove.

3. Remove the driveshaft as previously described.

4. Mark the camber cam/bolt for proper indexing with the strut rod bracket and loosen the cam bolts.

5. Remove the bracket-to-carrier bolts and lower the bracket.

6. Remove the cam bolts and swing the struts up. Loosen the carrier cover bolts and gradually drain the fluid.

7. Remove the bolts, slide the carrier back and down, and remove.

8. Before reinstalling the carrier, clean the inside of the cover and grease the gasket surface. Install a new gasket on the cover.

9. Fabricate two aligning studs by cutting the heads off from two ¼ in.–13 x 1¼ in. bolts and slotting the unthreaded end. Install the two studs into two lower bolt holes, one to a side.

10. Using the studs as support, position the carrier to align the carrier-to-cover bolt holes. Install the bolts and tighten to 35–55 ft lbs.

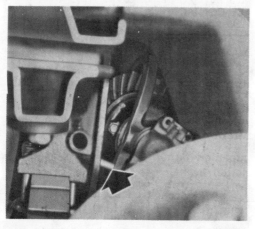

Differential carrier installation utilizing locating studs

11. Install the driveshaft as previously outlined.

12. Position the carrier front support bracket on the carrier and install the thru-bolt.

13. Install the rubber biscuits and rotate the bracket up into position. Install the front bolt and nut and torque to 30 ft lbs. Install the two side bolts in the

bracket and torque to 45–55 ft lbs. Torque the thru-bolt to 40–60 ft lbs.

14. Assemble the axle drive shafts to the carrier side yokes. Torque the bolts to 14–18 ft lbs.

15. Connect the strut rods to the bracket and install the bracket to the carrier. Torque the four bolts to 15–22 ft lbs. Adjust the camber cams with reference to the marks previously scribed on the cams and bracket. Tighten cam nuts to 15–22 ft lbs.

16. Install the spring end links as described under spring removal.

17. Remove the filler plug and fill the differential with the correct gear lubricant.

DIFFERENTIAL

Overhaul

1. Mount the carrier in a secure position.

2. Expand the side-gear yoke snap-rings and remove the yokes.

3. Reference-mark the differential bearing caps and remove them.

4. Carefully slide the differential assembly from the carrier case.

5. Reference-mark the bearing shims and remove them.

6. Remove the companion flange nut, then remove the flange.

7. Pry out the seal with a screwdriver.

8. Remove the front pinion bearing and pry out the side gear yoke seals.

9. Select a 1¾ in. outside diameter pipe of sufficient length and drive the yoke bearings from their bores.

10. Back out the pinion pin locking screw and remove the pinion pin, differential pinions, and side gears. Do not remove the ring gear unless replacement of it, or of the differential bearings is necessary.

11. If the pinion bearing is being replaced, use a brass drift to tap out the old cups. Drive the front and rear replacement cups into the case and seat them against their respective carrier shoulders.

12. Press out the rear pinion-bearing inner race and roller assembly and discard the shim.

13. Clean all parts in solvent. Check the gears for chipping, cracking, and excessive wear. Check all bearings for scoring, pitting, and unusual wear. Closely

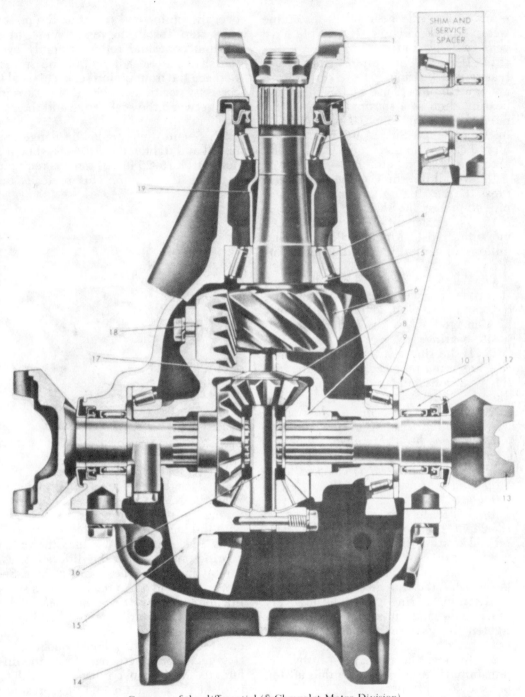

Cutaway of the differential (© Chevrolet Motor Division)

1. Companion Flange	8. Differential Side Gear	14. Carrier Cover
2. Pinion Seal	9. Differential Bearing	15. Differential Case
3. Front Pinion Bearing	10. Differential Bearing Shim	16. Differential Pinion Shaft
4. Rear Pinion Bearing	11. Yoke Bearing	17. Thrust Washer
5. Pinion Shim	12. Yoke Bearing Seal	18. Ring Gear
6. Pinion	13. Side Gear Yoke	19. Pinion Bearing Spacer
7. Differential Pinion		

examine the side gear yokes for spline wear and yoke arching. If possible have gears and yokes magnafluxed.

14. If the ring and pinion, front and/or rear pinion bearings on the carrier case are being replaced, use a 0.027 in. pinion bearing shim as a starting figure. Shims range from 0.021 in. to 0.036 in. in 0.003 in. increments. Shims are notched for identification: no notch on 0.021 in.; one notch on 0.024 in., etc.

15. Install the shim on the pinion and press the bearing on the pinion using a pipe to protect the shaft.

16. To replace differential bearing, remove the old bearing(s) with a bearing puller and carefully drive on new bearing(s).

17. When replacing both bearings, stand the side with the installed bearing on a protective plug, so the bearing won't be damaged when driving on the opposite bearing.

18. If the ring gear or the differential case are being replaced, remove the ten, ring gear bolts and tap the ring gear from the case.

NOTE: *The ring gear should not be bolted to the differential case until the bearing has been shimmed to give the correct preload. Inaccurate readings will result if preload is checked with the ring gear mounted to the differential case.*

19. Fabricate five guide pins from ⅜ in.–24 x 1½ in. bolts by cutting the heads off and slotting the ends.

20. Clean the differential case ring-gear flange and ring-gear mounting surface. Install the ring gear on the case.

21. Insert a ring gear bolt in every other hole and gradually and evenly tighten the gear so it is flush with the case.

22. Remove the guide pins, install the remaining five bolts, and torque all ten bolts to 40–60 ft lbs.

23. If replacing the side-gear yoke bearings, start the bearings into their carrier bores. Drive the bearings in to a firm seating.

24. Install new seals after the bearings.

25. To assemble the pinion, grease the pinion bearings and position the pinion gear in the carrier.

26. Put a new pinion bearing spacer over the pinion and seat it on the pinion shaft step. Install the replacement, front bearing cone and roller assembly over the shaft and seat it against the spacer. Replace the front pinion seal. This seal is correctly positioned when there is a ⅛ in. gap between the seal flange and the carrier.

27. Secure the companion flange and install and tighten the flange washer and nut until a 15–25 in. lbs force is required to rotate the pinion. This preloads the bearing.

Checking bearing preload

28. To set the differential bearing preload, place the side gears and pinions inside the case, insert the pinion pin through the pinion bores, and secure with the locking screw.

29. Place the cups over the differential bearings and position the differential assembly into the carrier bearing bores. Select an 0.080 in. shim thickness as a starting point, and insert one shim behind the outer cup of each differential bearing.

30. Mount a dial indicator on the rear cover flange with its pointer touching the ring-gear mounting flange. Press the differential in and move it back and forth to indicate the amount of end-play present.

31. Add 0.008 in.–0.010 in. to the indicated end-play to determine the required thickness shim needed to obtain the correct preload. Shims are available in sizes from 0.064 in. to 0.94 in., in increments of 0.002 in.

32. To make the backlash adjustment, return the bearing caps to their original positions and tighten, but don't torque, the cap bolts.

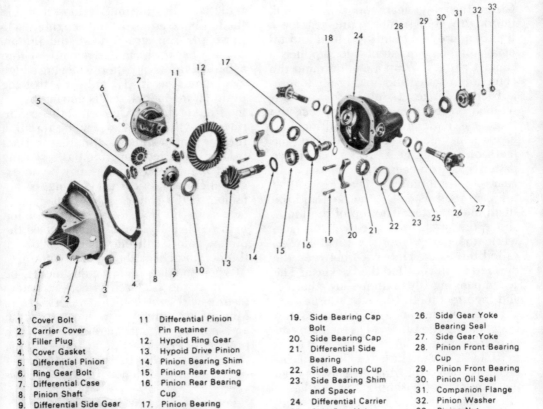

1. Cover Bolt	11 Differential Pinion	19. Side Bearing Cap	26. Side Gear Yoke
2. Carrier Cover	Pin Retainer	Bolt	Bearing Seal
3. Filler Plug	12. Hypoid Ring Gear	20. Side Bearing Cap	27. Side Gear Yoke
4. Cover Gasket	13. Hypoid Drive Pinion	21. Differential Side	28. Pinion Front Bearing
5. Differential Pinion	14. Pinion Bearing Shim	Bearing	Cup
6. Ring Gear Bolt	15. Pinion Rear Bearing	22. Side Bearing Cup	29. Pinion Front Bearing
7. Differential Case	16. Pinion Rear Bearing	23. Side Bearing Shim	30. Pinion Oil Seal
8. Pinion Shaft	Cup	and Spacer	31. Companion Flange
9. Differential Side Gear	17. Pinion Bearing	24. Differential Carrier	32. Pinion Washer
10. Side Gear Thrust	Spacer	25. Side Gear Yoke	33. Pinion Nut
Washer	18. Side Gear Yoke Snap	Bearing	
	Ring		

Exploded view of the differential

33. Attach a dial indicator to the carrier case and position the pointer on a ring gear tooth. Check the backlash; if between 0.003 in. and 0.010 in., it is correct. If backlash exceeds these limits, install varying size shims behind the bearings to move the ring gear toward or away from the pinion.

34. Maintain the same, combined-total shim thickness as original. Example: 0.002 in. plus 0.004 in. equals 0.006 in.; 0.003 in. plus 0.003 in. equals 0.006 in.

35. When correct backlash is obtained, torque the bearing caps to 50–60 ft lbs.

36. Install the side gear yokes and snap-rings.

Ring Gear and Pinion Contact Pattern Test

To prevent noisy gears, a ring-gear and pinion-tooth contact pattern test must be made before the differential assembly is installed. Allowable variations in the car-rier of the rear pinion may cause the pinion to be too far in or out, even when the pinion is properly shimmed. Mount the carrier assembly in the holding fixture.

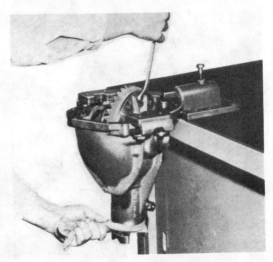

Establishing ring and pinion contact pattern

Clean the ring gear and pinion teeth thoroughly, then paint the ring gear teeth lightly and evenly with red lead and oil of a suitable consistency to produce a contact pattern. Wrap a cloth around the companion flange and hold firmly to form a friction brake. Using a 9/16 in. box wrench on the ring gear bolts, rock the ring gear back and forth, shifting bolt heads to develop a contact pattern on the teeth of the ring gear. To analyze these patterns; it is necessary to understand gear tooth terminology. The large end of the gear tooth is called the heel and the small end, the toe. The top of the tooth, above the pitch line, is called the face, while the part below the pitch line is called the flank. The space between the meshed teeth is called the backlash. The accompanying illustration shows correct and incorrect tooth contact patterns.

The ideal clearance for quietness and long bearing life is provided by tooth pattern (A). A pattern showing toe contact as in (B) indicates too little backlash. To correct this, move the ring gear away from the pinion by loosening the left-hand, differential adjusting nut and tightening the right-hand adjusting nut. Make this adjustment one notch at a time, repeating the pattern, checking with red lead, and continuing the adjustment until the tooth contact pattern appears as in (A). Backlash must stay within specified limits.

A pattern showing heel contact (C) indicates too much backlash. Correction of this condition is similar to that made for (B), differing in that the right-hand, differential adjusting nut is loosened and the left-hand adjusting nut is tightened to move the ring gear toward the pinion. Again, backlash must remain within specified limits. A pattern showing a high face contact as in (D) indicates that the pinion is too far out, that is, too far toward the front of the car. To correct this condition, it will be necessary to install a thicker pinion-shim. A shim that is 0.003 in. thicker is recommended as a starting point. Continued changes may be necessary before the correct setting is obtained. If the pattern shows a flank contact, as in (E), it indicates that the pinion is in too far. To correct this, replace the pinion shim with one that is 0.003 in. thinner and check the contact pattern.

When making pinion adjustments, be sure that the backlash is correct before testing with red lead for tooth pattern. Moving the pinion in reduces backlash and moving it out increases it. When proper tooth contact is achieved, wipe the red lead from the gears and carrier with a cloth moistened in cleaning solvent.

Pour a generous amount of rear axle lubricant on the gear and bearing and turn the gears, working the lubricant into all surfaces.

Companion Flange Oil Seal Replacement

1. Place the vehicle on jack stands so that the wheels clear the ground.

2. Position a wood block between the floor and carrier upper surface to prevent

TOE CONTACT

FACE CONTACT

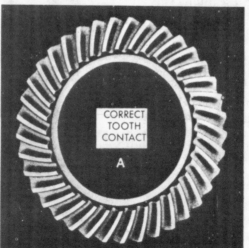
CORRECT TOOTH CONTACT

HEEL CONTACT

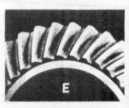
FLANK CONTACT

Pinion and ring gear tooth contact patterns

the differential carrier from twisting when the forward mounting bracket is disconnected.

3. Remove the carrier front-mounting bracket bolt from the frame crossmember.

4. Remove the front bolts, or bolt on late models, but only loosen the rear bolt.

5. Rotate the bracket out of the way.

6. Remove the driveshaft as outlined earlier in this chapter.

7. Mark the companion flange nut and the pinion so that alignment and subsequent correct bearing preload will not be lost.

8. Immobilize the flange and remove the flange nut and washer.

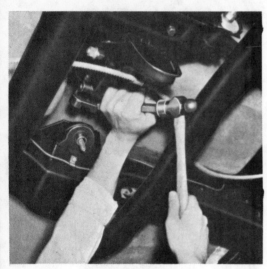

Removing companion flange

9. Use a soft, brass drift punch to drive the companion flange from the carrier and pry out the seal with a screwdriver.

10. Inspect the companion flange for excessive spline wear and the deflector for looseness. Replace the deflector, if necessary, and stake in place.

11. Coat the outside diameter of the replacement seal with sealing compound and install the seal. Position the seal with a ⅛ in. gap between the flange and the carrier.

12. Grease the companion flange splines and tap the flange into place. Start the companion flange washer and nut and tighten until the reference marks align.

13. Install the driveshaft and the carrier front mounting bracket.

14. Torque the front bolts 45–55 ft lbs and the rear, 40–60 ft lbs. Insert the crossmember mounting nut and tighten to 20–30 ft lbs torque.

POSITRACTION DIFFERENTIAL

Overhaul

1. Remove the ring gear, the side bearings, and the differential, pinion-shaft locking screw, then drive the pinion shaft from the case.

2. Insert a punch through the observation hole in the positraction case and tap the preload spring retainer a sufficient distance through the case opening to permit the placement of a ¼ in. bolt in each of the retainer's two front springs. Secure each bolt with a nut.

3. When the bolts have been installed, drive the retainer another distance sufficient to attach a C-clamp and two pieces of bar stock as shown.

4. Compress the C-clamp sufficiently to withdraw the retainer and spring assembly from the case.

5. Secure the retainer in a vise and withdraw the bolts. Release the vise and clamp pressure evenly until all spring tension is absent.

6. Extract the pinion thrust washers from behind the pinion gears, then rotate the gears, first one way then the other, to permit their removal.

7. Use a soft punch to tap the side gear, clutch pack, shims and guides from the case.

8. Separate the clutch pack assembly from the side gear but keep each pack with its original side gear.

9. Check the discs and clutch plates for excessive wear or signs of overheating. If damage is present on any plate or disc, the entire clutch pack must be replaced as an assembly.

10. Check the preload springs for distortions or other damage. Compress the springs and replace any that seem to lack sufficient tension to preload the clutch pack. Check the spring-retainer corresponding mating of the two halves.

11. Coat each clutch plate and disc with positraction lubricant. Starting with a clutch plate, stack the plates and discs onto the side gear in an alternating sequence. The stacking should also end with a clutch plate.

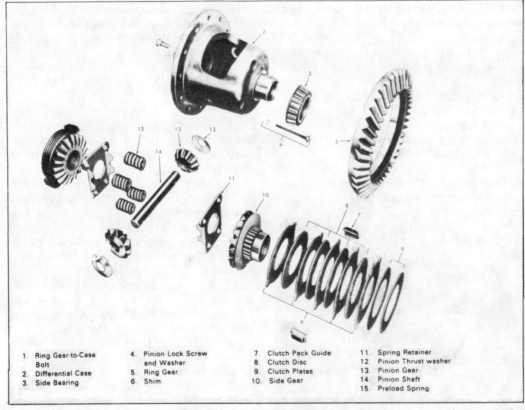

1. Ring Gear-to-Case Bolt
2. Differential Case
3. Side Bearing
4. Pinion Lock Screw and Washer
5. Ring Gear
6. Shim
7. Clutch Pack Guide
8. Clutch Disc
9. Clutch Plates
10. Side Gear
11. Spring Retainer
12. Pinion Thrust washer
13. Pinion Gear
14. Pinion Shaft
15. Preload Spring

Exploded view of Positraction differential

12. Attach clutch pack guides to the plate lugs and check to see that the lugs and teeth engage each other. If the old shims are not usable, replace them with new ones of equal thickness and slide them over the side gear hub.

13. When both side gears have been assembled, install one of the complete build-ups into the differential case.

14. Place the pinion gears and thrust washers over the side gears and insert the pinion shaft into the case and through the gears.

15. Attach a dial indicator to the case and position its pointer against the pinion gear. Use a screwdriver to compress the clutch pack, then move the pinion gear to obtain a tooth gear tolerance of 0.001 in. to 0.006 in. Change shim thickness to achieve a clearance within these tolerances.

16. Withdraw the side gear assembly and repeat the tooth clearance check for its counterpart on the opposite side of the differential case.

17. Remove the pinion shaft, gears, and thrust washers, and install the re-maining side gear assembly. Reverse the pinion gear removal procedure to install the pinion gears and washers.

18. Assemble the spring retainer and secure it in a vise. Attach the C-clamp and the ¼ in. bolts and compressing nuts.

19. Insert the spring pack between the side gears and release the C-clamp and bar stock pieces.

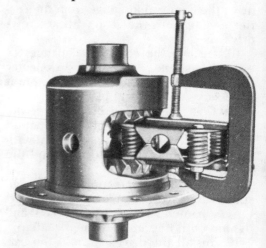

Spring pack installation

20. Force the spring pack into the case until the unity of the assembly is assured, then remove the nuts and bolts from the springs and tap the spring pack into correct position.

21. Install the pinion shaft and locking screw; torquing the latter to specifications. Check spring retainer to side gear alignment and make necessary adjustments.

22. Install the side bearings and ring gear, then position the differential in the carrier and make the necessary bearing and backlash adjustments.

23. To test the positraction operation, place the car on stands so that the wheels are clear of the ground and remove one wheel. Install a special three-prong adapter to the axle shaft flange and thread a ½ in.–13 bolt into the center of the adapter.

24. Secure the wheel and tire assembly on the opposite side of the vehicle so that it will not rotate, then measure the amount of torque required to turn the opposite axle shaft. Torque on new cars should be 70 ft lbs and no less than 40 ft lbs on used units.

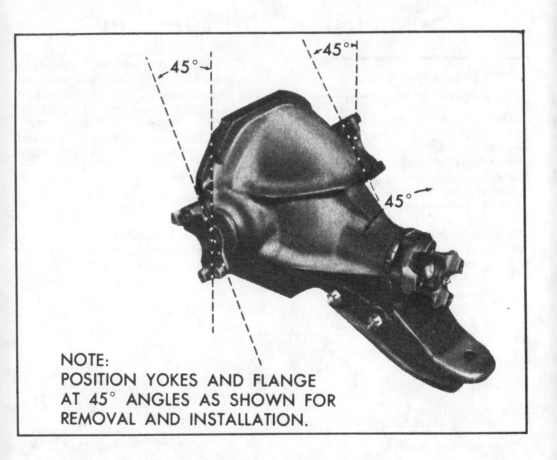

NOTE:
POSITION YOKES AND FLANGE
AT 45° ANGLES AS SHOWN FOR
REMOVAL AND INSTALLATION.

Chapter 8

Suspension and Steering

Front Suspension

The Corvette Stingray front suspension is an unequal length arm, independent design. Springing action is provided by coil springs. Ball joints connect the steering knuckles to the control arms. The upper and lower control arms have their cross-shafts bolted to fixed frame members. The upper arm cross-shaft has shims to provide the means for setting caster and camber. The front shock absorbers have their bottom ends attached

to the lower control arm while the upper end extends through the frame member. The shock absorbers are double action and fit inside the front coil springs. A stabilizer bar connects the lower control arms to the front frame rails. Tapered roller bearings are used in the front wheels.

SPRINGS

Removal and Installation
CAUTION: *Great care should be exercised when removing springs, as the*

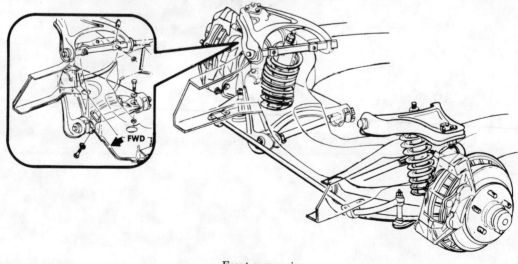

Front suspension

compressed force of a coil spring is potentially very dangerous.

1. Support the car so that the control arms hang loosely.

2. Remove the wheel and tire, stabilizer bar, and shock absorber.

3. Loosen the lower ball joint-to-steering knuckle nut and the two, lower control arms, cross-shaft bushing bolts.

4. Wrap a safety chain around the lower arm and the coil spring.

5. Install a floor jack under the spring and slightly compress the spring.

6. Disconnect the lower ball joint from the steering knuckle.

7. Very slowly and carefully, lower the control arm and release the spring. It may be necessary to pry the spring out of the tower.

8. To install, position the spring on the control arm and jack up the arm.

9. Install the ball joint on the steering knuckle, and remaining components in a reverse order.

SHOCK ABSORBERS

Corvette Stingray shock absorbers are the sealed, hydraulic type with no provision for adding fluid or making adjustments. They should be replaced when evidence of faulty operation is discovered.

Removal and Installation

1. To remove, raise the vehicle and hold the upper stem of the shock absorber with an open-end wrench. This prevents the stem from turning and allows the removal of the retaining nut, washer, and rubber grommet.

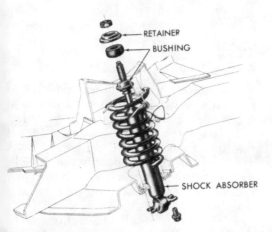

Shock absorber mounting

2. Remove the two bolts that fasten the lower pivot point of the shock absorber to the lower control arm and slip the shock absorber free.

3. Reverse the procedure to install the replacement shock absorbers.

BALL JOINTS

Erratic front suspension behavior or alignment difficulties suggest possible excessive ball-joint wear. To check, raise the vehicle so that the front suspension hangs freely and remove the wheel and tire assembly. Check the upper ball joint by supporting the lower control arm and by separating the upper ball-joint stud from the steering knuckle. With the steering knuckle and hub hanging freely, install the retaining nut on the ball joint stud and note the torque required to rotate the ball joint with a torque wrench. A ball joint in good condition will require a torque of 2–10 ft lbs. Less than 2 ft lbs torque indicates excessive wear and warrants replacement of the ball joint.

To test the lower, control-arm ball joint, support the lower control arm so that the wheel hub hangs freely. Measure between the tip of the ball joint stud and the tip of the grease fitting found on the top side of the ball joint. Now position the support under the wheel hub and repeat the measurement. A difference in measurement of more than $1/16$ in. dictates replacement of the lower ball joint.

Removal and Installation

Replacement of the ball joints may be done without removing the control arms from the vehicle.

1. Raise the vehicle and remove the wheel and tire. Be sure that the lift is positioned so that the front suspension will hang freely.

2. Remove the stabilizer link from the lower control arm, then disconnect the top ball joint from the steering knuckle and let the knuckle and the wheel hub hang unsupported.

3. The ball joint assembly is riveted to the control arm. Use a suitable cold chisel and knock the heads off the rivets and remove the ball joint.

4. Clean the mounting surface on the control arm and check for signs of cracks or other damage.

5. Measure the thread diameter of the

kit-supplied mounting bolts and drill out the control arm rivet holes to the appropriate size.

6. Install the replacement ball joint assembly and torque the new securing bolts to 15–25 ft lbs.

7. Lift the lower control arm so that the upper ball joint stud can be rejoined to the steering knuckle. Torque the retaining nut to 42–47 ft lbs and install a new cotter pin.

8. To replace the lower ball joint, support the lower control arm, disconnect the lower ball joint from the steering knuckle and lift the knuckle and wheel hub out of the way.

NOTE: *Removal of the spring is not necessary so long as the lower control arm is adequately supported.*

9. The lower ball joint assembly is also riveted to the control arm surface. Chisel it free as with the upper ball joint.

10. Replace the joint as previously described, then reconnect the lower ball joint stud to the steering knuckle.

NOTE: *It may be necessary to install grease fittings on the replacement ball joints if none are provided.*

STEERING KNUCKLE

Removal and Installation

1. Raise and support the vehicle on the lower control arm.

2. Remove the wheel and tire, brake drum or disc caliper, and hub and bearing assembly.

3. On drum brakes, remove the backing plate from the steering knuckle and wire it to the frame. Do not disconnect the brake hose.

4. Remove the upper and lower ball joint stud-retaining nuts and rap the steering knuckle free of the upper and lower control arms.

5. Reverse the procedure to replace the steering knuckle.

6. Torque the upper stud nut to 50 ft lbs, and the lower stud nut to 90 ft lbs.

UPPER AND LOWER CONTROL ARMS

Shaft Removal and Installation

1. To remove the lower, control arm shaft, remove the front coil spring as previously described.

2. Count the shims at each end of the cross-shaft, then unbolt it from the frame and remove the control arm.

3. Remove the bolts, washers, and collars from both ends of the shaft, then screw in a $7/16$ in. x 20 capscrew into one end of the shaft.

4. Support the control arm in a press and press on the capscrew until the bushing is forced from the arm.

5. Unscrew the capscrew and repeat the procedure on the other end on the cross-shaft.

6. Position the replacement cross-shaft and/or bushings in the control arm and start the bushings into the arm.

7. Place the assembly in a press, put a spacer over the bushing, and press into place.

8. Repeat the procedure for the other end, then install the collar and lockwasher but loosely thread in the bolts.

9. Reverse the removal procedure to install the spring and lower control arm. After the arm is installed, lower the vehicle to the floor and tighten the cross-shaft bushing bolts to 45–55 ft lbs.

10. The procedure for replacing the upper, control arm shaft is the same as for the lower control arm shaft, except a $3/8$ in.–24 capscrew is used to remove the bushings. Torque the bushing bolts to 35–40 ft lbs.

Control Arm Removal and Installation

The upper and lower control arms are removed by combining the operations for replacing the upper and lower cross-shafts and the operations for replacing the steering knuckle.

STABILIZER BAR

Removal and Installation

The stabilizer bar is rubber-mounted to the frame in two locations and attaches to the lower control arms through two links.

1. Raise the vehicle and disconnect the links from the stabilizer bar.

2. Unbolt the rubber frame attachments and remove the bar from the car.

3. Reverse the procedure to install the stabilizer.

4. Hand-tighten all connections until the bar and links are fully assembled.

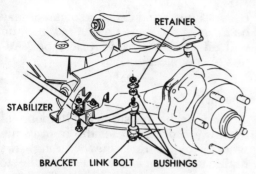

Stabilizer mounting

5. Tighten all connections, lower the vehicle, and bounce it a few times.

6. Raise the car and tighten all connections with a wrench.

WHEEL HUB

Removal and Installation

1. To remove the wheel hub, snap off the wheel covers and loosen the lug nuts, then raise and secure the vehicle.

2. Remove the lug nuts, wheel and tire, and brake drum or disc brake caliper.

3. Insert a wood spacer between the

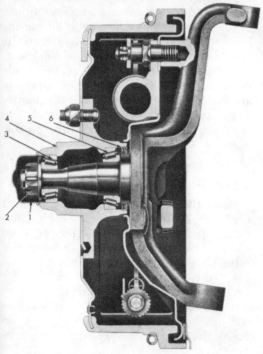

Hub cross-section

brake calipers, on disc brake vehicles, and secure the assembly out of the way.

4. Pry off the grease cap and extract the cotter pin from the spindle nut. Back off the spindle nut and washer, and remove the hub—on drum-equipped models—and the hub and disc on all others. Be careful not to drop the bearings as the hub comes off.

Bearing Replacement

1. Disassembly of the hub removed the outer roller bearing assembly. The inner roller bearing remains in the hub, held in place by the inner bearing lip seal.

2. Pry out this seal, discard it, and remove the inner roller bearing assembly.

3. Select a suitable brass drift punch and insert it through the inner opening of the bearing hub so that it catches on the notches behind the outer bearing race.

4. Drive the bearing from the hub. Insert the punch through the outer hub opening and repeat the procedure to remove the inner race.

NOTE: *It is good practice to replace bearing roller assemblies when replacing bearing races.*

5. Thoroughly clean the hub assembly then position the replacement inner bearing to its bore and drive it into place.

6. Use a driver for this operation, a suitable socket spacer, or even the old race—positioned over the replacement—and hammer it into its seat. Be sure the race is properly seated, then repeat the operation on the outer race.

7. Lightly coat the inside of the hub and the spindle with grease, then insert the inner roller bearing assembly and install the inner seal.

8. Position the hub or hub and disc assembly over the spindle and slide the outer bearing into its race.

9. Hold the assembly in position to prevent the hub from slipping and forcing out the outer roller bearing, and install the washer and nut, and hand-tighten.

10. Assemble the backing plate and drum assembly on 1963–1964 models. On 1965 and later models, remove the spacer block from the caliper and position the caliper to the caliper bracket, over the

disc. Insert the mounting bolts and torque them to 70 ft lbs.

11. Install the wheel and tire assembly and torque the lug nuts to 75 ft lbs.

12. Rotate the wheel and make the bearing adjustment. Install a new cotter pin, tap on the grease cap and replace the wheel cover.

ADJUSTMENTS

Caster

Caster is the measured angle between a true vertical line passing through the center of the wheel and a line drawn through the center of the upper and lower ball joints. Adjustments to the caster angle are made by the insertion of shims between the upper control arm pivot shaft and the frame bracket. Moving shims front to rear will decrease positive caster. Insertion and removal of a $1/32$ in. shim will effect a $1/4°$ caster change. Adjust caster to specifications.

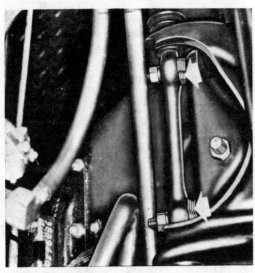

Caster and camber shim location

Camber

Camber is the measurement in degrees of the outward or inward tilt of the top of the wheel and tire in relation to the true vertical. Tilting of the top of the tire away from the centerline of the vehicle is called positive camber. Tilting toward the vehicle centerline is negative camber. Camber adjustment is made by adding or removing shims equally at both bolts. Camber and caster adjustment may be made at the same time. A $1/32$ in. shim will effect a $1/6°$ change in camber. Adjust to specifications.

Toe-In

Toe-in is the measurement in inches of the inward departure of the front of the wheels from a line drawn through the horizontal center of the wheel, parallel to the centerline of the vehicle. Toe-in is expressed as the difference in measurement between the extreme front of the wheel pair and the extreme rear of the wheel pair.

Two methods of setting toe-in may be employed. In the first, position the steering gear on high point and mark the 12 o'clock position on the steering shaft, with the wheel in the straight-ahead position. Loosen both tie-rod clamp bolts and adjust each evenly to obtain the total toe-in specified. Secure the inner tie-rod clamp protrusions forward to 90° down to prevent interference with the stabilizer link bolt.

If a tram gauge is available, position the front wheels straight-ahead. Loosen the tie-rod clamp on one end and adjust the one rod to the total specified toe-in. Loosen the other tie-rod clamp and rotate both rods the same amount in the same direction to put the steering gear on high point and the wheel positioned straight-ahead. Secure the inner tie-rod clamps with the bolts down and horizontal. Secure the outer bolts vertical and to the rear.

Wheel Bearing Adjustment

Raise the front end of the vehicle until the wheels clear the ground. Pry off the dust cap and extract the cotter pin from the end of the spindle. Slowly rotate the wheel and torque the spindle nut to 12 ft lbs. Turn the spindle nut back one flat and install a new cotter pin. If this one-flat turn back does not align a slot and cotter pin hole, continue to turn back no more than ½ flat to achieve the alignment.

Spin the wheel to check for free rolling, then reinstall the dust cap and repeat the adjustment on the other front wheel.

Wheel Alignment Specifications

| Year | Caster | | Camber | | Toe-in (in.) | Kingpin Inclination (deg) |
	Range (deg)	Pref Setting (deg)	Range (deg)	Pref Setting (deg)		
1963–66	1P to 2P②	1½P	¼P to 1¼P③	¾P	7⁄32 to 11⁄32①	6½ to 7½
1967	½P to 1½P	1P	¼P to 1¼P③	¾P	3⁄16 to 5⁄16①	6½ to 7½
1968–69	½P to 1½P④	1P	½P to 1¼P⑤	¾P	3⁄16 to 5⁄16⑤	6½ to 7½
1970	½P to 1½P④	1P	½P to 1¼P⑤	¾P	3⁄16 to 5⁄16⑤	6½ to 7½
1971–73	0 to 2P⑥	1P	0 to 1½P⑤	¾P	3⁄16 to 5⁄16⑤	6½ to 7½
1974–75	½P to 1½P⑥	1P	¼P to 1¼P⑤	¾P	3⁄32 to 5⁄32⑤⑦	7¾

① Rear wheels ¹⁄16–³⁄16
② 1966—½P to 1½P
③ Rear wheels—½° ± ½°
④ W/pwr steering: 1¾P to 2¾P
⑤ Rear wheel alignment: camber ⅞N to ⅛N; toe-in ¹⁄32–³⁄32
⑥ Power steering—1¼P to 3¼P
⑦ 1975 toe-in—¹⁄32–³⁄32
N Negative
P Positive

Rear Suspension

The Stingray rear suspension is a three-link independent system. Longitudinal location is provided by control arms which pivot at the front on bolts through the frame step-up. The lower link is a strut rod which also serves as a camber rod with adjustment permitted by an eccentric cam on the inner end. The universal-jointed axle driveshafts double as the upper locating links. Shock absorbers attach to the frame at the top and attach to the spindle/camber rod strut at the bottom. Springing is provided by a 9-leaf (7 on heavy duty, 10 on all 1975–76 models), transverse spring bolted to the rear cover of the differential carrier. 6½ in. rubber-cushioned link bolts locate the spring ends to the control arms.

SPRING

Removal and Installaion

1. Jack the rear of the car up high enough to provide working clearance.

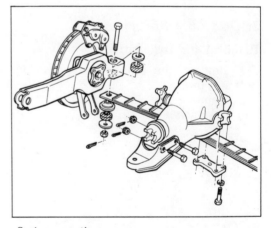

Spring mounting

2. Position a floor jack under the link bolt on one side. Raise the jack until the spring is compressed tightly, and install a ¼ in., or larger, chain around the suspension crossmember and the spring. Use a C-clamp to hold the chain to the spring.

3. Lower the jack to permit access to the link bolt, and then remove the link bolt nut, cushions, and retainers.

4. Raise the spring again and remove the chain and C-clamp.

5. Slowly lower the spring until all tension is released.

6. Perform the same steps on the other side.

7. Remove the four, spring pad bolts and plate.

8. Withdraw the spring over the exhaust pipes and down from the car.

9. To install, position the spring on the bottom carrier mounting pad with the center bolt aligned with the hole in the mounting pad.

10. Install the center clamp and the four mounting bolts. Tighten the bolts to 55–75 ft lbs.

11. Jack one end of the spring and secure with chain as in the removal procedure.

12. Lower the jack and position the control arm for the link bolt installation. Install the link bolt, rubber cushions, and retainers. Install the castellated nut on the link bolt and secure with a cotter pin.

13. Raise the spring and remove the C-clamp and chain.

14. Repeat the above operation on the other side.

15. Lower the car.

SHOCK ABSORBERS

Removal and Installation

1. Remove the upper shock absorber bolt and nut.

2. Remove the lower mounting nut and lockwasher.

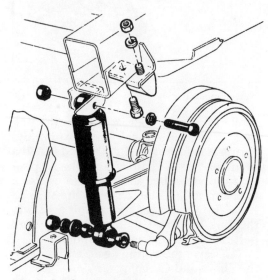

Shock absorber mounting

3. Slide the upper eye of the shock absorber out of the frame bracket.

4. Pull the lower eye off the strut rod shaft and remove the rubber grommets.

5. To install, position the upper shock absorber eye in the frame mounting bracket and install the bolt, lockwasher, and nut.

6. Install the inner rubber grommet and then the shock absorber eye on the strut rod shaft. Install the outer grommet, washer, lockwasher, and nut.

7. Torque the upper nut to 40–60 ft lbs and the lower nut to 50–60 ft lbs.

STRUT ROD AND BRACKET

Removal and Installation

1. Jack the rear of the car high enough to allow working clearance.

2. Disconnect the lower shock absorber eye from the strut rod shaft.

3. Remove the strut rod shaft cotter pin and nut. Drive the shaft out of the spindle support.

CAUTION: *The strut rod shaft is often very hard to remove; take care not to distort either the shaft or the spindle support in the removal process.*

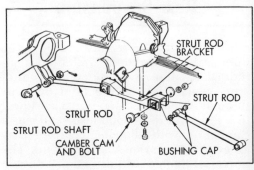

Strut rod mounting

4. Scribe the camber adjusting cam-to-bracket relationship for correct relocation.

5. Loosen the cam adjusting bolt and nut.

6. Remove the four bracket-to-carrier bolts, and lower the bracket.

7. Remove the cam, bolt, and nut. Remove the strut from the bracket and remove the bushing caps.

8. Inspect the strut rod bushings and replace if necessary.

9. Install the inside bushing caps and slip the strut rod into the bracket.

10. Install the cam and bolt assemblies, and align the previously scribed marks. Hand-tighten the adjustment nut.

11. Raise the bracket assembly and install the four bracket-to-carrier bolts. Torque the bolts to 15–22 ft lbs.

12. Raise the outer end of the strut rod into the spindle support. Install the strut rod shaft through the spindle support and strut rod.

NOTE: *The strut rod shaft has a flat side which should line up with the matching flat in the spindle support.*

13. Replace the shock absorber lower eye on the strut rod shaft. Torque the nut to 50–60 ft lbs.

14. Lower the car and then tighten the camber cam nut to 55–70 ft lbs. Tighten the strut rod shaft nut to 80 ft lbs and install a new cotter pin.

ADJUSTMENTS

Camber

The rear wheel camber adjustment is made by rotating the eccentric cam and bolt assembly that connects the strut rod to the differential carrier bracket. Loosen the locknut and turn the eccentric cam bolt until the correct wheel camber angle is obtained. Secure the locknut and torque to 55–70 ft lbs.

Adjusting camber

Toe-In

Rear wheel toe-in is adjusted by the placement of shims of different thickness on both sides of the control arm pivot bushings. These shims are available in 1/64 in., 1/32 in., 1/8 in., and 1/4 in. sizes. To make this adjustment, remove the pivot

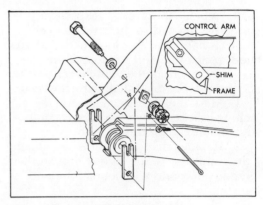

Toe-in adjustment shim location

bolt and position the torque arm so that the correct toe-in specifications are achieved. Insert shims in the gap nearest the car centerline between the bushing and the frame inner wall. Use shims of only the thickness required to bridge the gap. Do not overshim or force the shims during the adjusting. Insert shims in the outside gap until solidarity is reached between the pivot bushing and the frame walls. Insert the bolt, torque the nut to 50 ft lbs, and install a cotter pin.

WHEEL BEARINGS

Adjustment

The spindle bearings are of a tapered, roller design and require an end-play of 0.001 in. to 0.008 in. To measure end-play, lift the rear wheels clear of the ground and disconnect the axle drive-shaft from the spindle. There is insufficient clearance to drop the axle drive-

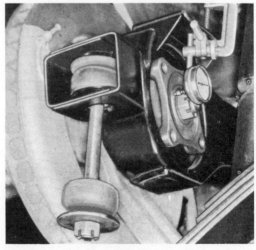

Checking spindle bearing play

shaft when the rear suspension is correctly adjusted so the strut rod eccentric cam/bolt must be loosened and rotated so that the strut rod forces the trailing arm away from the vehicle centerline and permits the driveshaft to be lowered.

1. Mark the eccentric cam and the attaching bracket so that the correct camber adjustment can be returned to.

2. Remove the rear wheels and attach a dial indicator to the torque arm so that its indicator point will contact the end of the spindle.

3. Move the disc in and out and observe the dial indicator reading. If the reading exceeds the 0.001 in. to 0.008 in. tolerances, the bearings must be adjusted.

4. Set the handbrake and remove the drive spindle nut.

5. Release the brake and remove the brake drum or caliper and disc as described in Chapter 9.

6. Remove the spindle flange then reinstall the nut until it is flush with the end of the spindle. Use a puller to withdraw the spindle from its support.

7. Remove the spindle-support dust deflector and pry out the inner seal. Remove the inner bearing race, roller assembly, shim, and bearing spacer from the spindle support.

8. Check the size of the old shim and, if the dial indicator reading exceeded 0.008 in., replace it with one that is thinner by the required amount to bring end-play within allowable tolerances. A dial indicator reading of less than 0.001 in. requires a shim thick enough to move the end-play beyond the 0.001 in. minimum.

NOTE: *Shims are available in 0.003 in. increments and range in thickness from 0.097 in. to 1.48 in.*

9. Insert the spindle bearing and seal in the spindle support and install the bearing spacer and shim.

10. Place the inner race and roller assembly on the spindle and a suitable spacer to aid in pressing the bearing into position.

11. Start the nut onto the spindle and against the press spacer. Tighten the nut and press the bearing in a sufficient amount to permit the installation of the spindle drive flange.

12. Remove the spindle nut and washer and discard the nut. Use a new replacement for reassembly.

13. Tap the replacement inner seal in place, install the dust deflector, drive flange, spindle washer, and nut. Torque the nut to 100 ft lbs and install a new cotter pin.

Replacement

OUTER BEARING

1. With the wheel spindle removed, attach a bearing puller around the bearing and secure the tool and spindle in a press, and remove the bearing from the spindle.

2. Remove the outer seal and replace if necessary.

3. Position the replacement seal on the spindle before installing the bearing assembly.

4. Pack the replacement bearing with a high melting point grease and place it on the spindle, large end facing the spindle shoulder.

5. Support the spindle and press the bearing into position. Install the reassembled spindle to the spindle support.

Steering

The Stingray steering system is a recirculating ball, relay type. A pitman arm

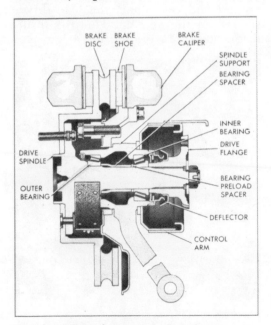

Wheel spindle and support cross-section

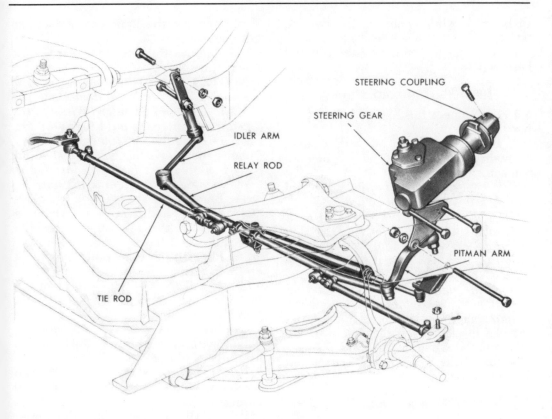

Steering linkage

connects the steering gear to the relay rod by way of a pivoted joint. The opposite end of this transverse relay rod attaches to a frame-mounted idler arm by way of another pivoting joint. These joints are the adjustable ball and socket type.

Two adjustable tie-rods join each steering arm to the relay rod through self-adjusting ball and socket joints. The steering arms have two tie-rod end holes drilled in them to provide a road steering ratio of: 19.6:1 or 20.2:1 on ealier models; a faster ratio of 17:1 or 17.6:1 on later models. This adjustment is made by disconnecting the tie-rod ends from one steering arm hole and moving to the other. The latest models (1969–1976) have Function Locking Energy Absorbing steering columns. With this design, the mast jacket and steering shaft are designed to collapse during conditions generated by a front end collision.

The collapsible mast jacket has ball bearings embedded in plastic and pressed between the upper and lower jackets. A predetermined load will collapse the assembly. The steering shaft collapses under predetermined loads, shearing the plastic pins. Additionally, these columns contain an anti-theft ignition switch and ignition lock system. This system prevents the removal of the ignition key unless the automatic transmission is in Park or the manual transmission is in Reverse, and the key is in the "Lock" position. In this position, a rod and lock plate mechanism lock the steering wheel and shift lever.

STEERING WHEEL

Removal and Installation

1963–67 STANDARD WHEEL

1. Disconnect the battery ground cable.
2. Pry off the horn cap with a small screwdriver.
3. Remove the steering shaft nut and washer.
4. Install a wheel puller in the two threaded holes provided. Remove the steering wheel.
5. To install, align the wheel in a straight, up-and-down position.
6. Install the washer and nut on the

shaft, and while holding the wheel, tighten the nut to 35–40 ft lbs.

7. Reinstall the contact assembly and horn cap.

1968–76 STANDARD WHEEL

1. Disconnect the battery ground cable.

2. Pry the horn cap off with a small screwdriver and remove the upper horn contact.

3. Remove the six steering wheel retaining screws and remove the wheel.

NOTE: *To remove the wheel for turn signal switch service, follow Steps 3–6 of the "1963–67 Standard Wheel" procedure. Tighten the nut to 30 ft lbs. On 1975–76 models, it is necessary to remove the snap-ring from the steering shaft first. Don't forget to install the snap-ring after tightening the nut.*

4. To install, attach the wheel to the hub with the six screws.

5. Install the upper horn contact and the horn cap.

1965–67 TELESCOPING WHEEL

1. Disconnect the battery ground cable.

2. Pry off the horn cap with a small screwdriver and remove the horn contact assembly.

3. Remove the lock screw-to-lock knob retaining screws, and remove the lock screw, lock knob, and the spacer.

4. Remove the six steering wheel-to-hub screws and remove the wheel.

5. Replace the steering wheel on the hub and install the six retaining screws.

6. Install the spacer on the steering wheel and position the lock knob.

7. The lock screw installs through the lock knob, is turned into the shaft, and adjusted to the lock position.

8. Attach the spacer to the steering wheel. Put the lock knob in lock position and attach it to the lock screw with two screws.

9. Remove the three, spacer retaining screws and install the horn contact to the spacer and the steering wheel with three screws.

10. Install the horn cap.

1968–76 TELESCOPING WHEEL

1. Disconnect the battery ground cable.

2. Remove the horn cap and upper horn contact.

3. Remove the shim, star screw, lock lever, and spacer.

NOTE: *To remove the wheel for turn signal switch service, follow Steps 3–6 of the "1963–67 Standard Wheel" procedure. Tighten the nut to 30 ft lbs. On 1975–76 models, it is necessary to remove the snap-ring from the steering shaft first. Don't forget to install the snap-ring after tightening the nut.*

4. Remove the six, steering wheel retaining screws and remove the wheel.

5. Replace the steering wheel on the hub and install the six retaining screws.

6. Position the spacer and lock lever on the steering wheel.

7. Install the star screw through the lock lever, turn it into the shaft, and put it into lock position.

8. Install the spacer to the steering wheel with three screws. Position the lock lever in "Lock."

9. Attach the star screw with two screws and remove the three, spacer retaining screws.

10. Install the shims and the upper horn contact.

11. Install the horn cap.

TURN SIGNAL SWITCH

Replacement

1963

The 1963 turn signal switch is mounted on the lower part of the steering column. The switch is operated by a cable from the signal housing located under the steering wheel.

1. Remove the screws holding the switch case to the mast jacket.

2. Remove the control cable from the spring clip at the switch.

3. Loosen the cable-to-switch retaining screw.

4. Disconnect the switch wire.

5. Put the column lever in neutral.

6. Move the switch slide so that it is in the center of the slot on the switch.

7. Install the cable into the spring clip without disturbing the switch slide. Fasten the cable with the screw.

8. Install the switch on the column.

1964–66

1. Remove the steering wheel as previously outlined.

2. Remove the terminal wires from the connector and remove the mast jacket harness cover.

3. Remove the turn signal lever and the three switch retaining screws.

4. Remove the retainer plate, switch housing, and the switch from the mast jacket. Pull each wire separately through the mast jacket slot to prevent damaging the harness.

5. Transfer the wiring harness to the replacement switch and install the components using a reverse of the removal procedure.

1967–68

1. Remove the steering wheel as previously outlined.

2. From under the dash, disconnect the switch harness connector from the chassis harness.

3. Remove the preload spring and the cancelling cam.

4. Remove the turn signal lever. Push the flasher knob in and remove it by unscrewing.

5. Remove the lower trim cover.

6. Remove the retaining ring and the thrust and wave washers from the top of the steering shaft. Cut the wiring above the connector.

7. Unscrew the switch, and slide it, the cover, and the upper bearing housing out of the column. Pull the wire through the column protector and escutcheon.

8. Install the new switch by assembling it and the upper bearing housing into the switch cover, and then working the wire down through the escutcheon and column protector until the switch can be positioned on the mast jacket.

9. Install the switch and remaining components in a reverse order of removal.

1969–76

1. Remove the steering wheel as previously outlined.

2. Loosen the three cover screws and lift the cover off the shaft.

3. Position the special lockplate compressing tool (J-23131 1969–70 or J-23653 1971–75) on the end of the steering shaft and compress the lockplate by turning the shaft nut clockwise. Pry the wire snap-ring out of the shaft groove.

4. Remove the tool and lift the lockplate off the shaft.

5. Slip the cancelling cam, upper bearing pre-load spring, and thrust washer off the shaft.

6. Remove the turn signal lever. Push the flasher knob in and unscrew it.

7. Pull the switch connector out of the mast jacket and tape the upper part to facilitate switch removal. On tilt wheels, place the turn signal and shifter housing in Low position and remove the harness cover.

8. Remove the three switch mounting screws. Remove the switch by pulling it straight up while guiding the wiring harness cover through the column.

9. Install the replacement switch by working the connector and cover down through the housing and under the bracket. On tilt models, the connector is worked down through the housing, under the bracket, and then the cover is installed on the harness.

10. Install the switch mounting screws and the connector on the mast jacket bracket. Install the column-to-dash trim plate.

11. Install the flasher knob and the turn signal lever.

12. With the turn signal lever in neutral and the flasher knob out, slide the thrust washer, upper bearing pre-load spring, and cancelling cam onto the shaft.

13. Position the lockplate on the shaft and press it down until a new snap-ring can be inserted in the shaft groove.

14. Install the cover and the steering wheel.

TILT-TELESCOPE 1969–76

1. Remove the steering wheel as previously outlined and press off the hub with a puller.

2. Remove the steering column/dash trim cover.

3. Remove the C-ring plastic retainer, if so equipped.

4. Install the special lockplate compressing tool (J-23131 1969–70 or J-23653 1971–75) over the steering shaft. Position a 5/16 in. nut under each tool leg and reinstall the star screw to prevent the shaft from moving.

5. Compress the lockplate by turning the shaft nut clockwise until the C-ring can be removed.

6. Remove the tool and lift out the lockplate, horn contact carrier, and the upper bearing preload spring.

NOTE: *1969 Corvette assembly order is: horn control carrier, lockplate, and upper bearing preload spring.*

7. Pull the switch connector out of the mast jacket and tape the upper part to facilitate switch removal.

8. Remove the turn signal lever. Push the flasher in and unscrew it.

9. Position the turn signal and shifter housing in Low position. Remove the switch by pulling it straight up while guiding the wiring harness out of the housing.

10. Install the replacement switch by working the harness connector down through the housing and under the mounting bracket.

11. Install the harness cover and clip the connector to the mast jacket.

12. Install the switch mounting screws, signal lever, and the flasher knob.

13. With the turn signal lever in neutral and the flasher knob out, install the upper bearing pre-load spring, horn contact carrier, and lockplate onto the shaft. Horn contact carrier is last on 1969 models.

14. Position the tool as in Step 4 and compress the plate far enough to allow the C-ring to be installed.

15. Remove the tool. Install the plastic C-ring retainer.

16. Install the column/dash trim cover. Install the steering wheel.

STEERING GEAR

Removal and Installation

1. Remove the retaining nuts, lockwashers, and bolts from the steering gear.

2. Remove the pitman arm nut and washer, and remove the pitman arm with a puller after marking the arm-to-shaft position.

3. Remove the steering gear-to-frame retaining bolts, and remove the steering gear.

4. To install, position the steering gear so that the coupling mates correctly with the end of the steering shaft.

5. Install the retaining bolts, washers, and nuts. Ensure that the coupling reinforcement bottoms on the worm-shaft so that the coupling bolt goes through the cut-out in the worm-shaft.

6. Install the steering coupling retaining nuts and lockwashers.

7. Install the pitman arm, aligning the previously scribed marks.

Adjustment

Mark the pitman arm and sector shaft with alignment references, then back off the retaining nut and remove the pitman arm. Slacken the locknut and rotate the pitman-shaft lash adjuster screw several turns in a counterclockwise direction to remove the worn bearing preload. Rotate the wheel in either direction until it reaches its stop, then turn it back one turn. Do this gently to avoid damaging the ball guides while the relay is disconnected. Attach a spring gauge and measure the amount of pull at the wheel rim necessary to keep the steering wheel in motion. This is normally between ⅜ and ¾ pounds. Measurements that exceed these tolerances indicate a need to adjust the worm bearings. Do so by loosening the locknut on the worm bearing adjuster screw and turning the screw clockwise until all end-play is removed from the worm. Check the wheel rim pull again and if satisfactory, secure the locknut.

Now turn the steering wheel slowly from one stop to the other and count the turns of the wheel. Turn the wheel back half the number of turns and rotate the lash adjuster screw clockwise to remove all lash in the gear teeth. Check the wheel rim pull again as the rim moves through the center position. Pull should be ⅞ to 1½ pounds. When all adjustments are made, attach the pitman arm to the sector shaft.

STEERING LINKAGE

The Corvette has two tie-rods. Each rod is a three-piece assembly made up of the rod itself and two tie-rod ends. The ends screw onto the rod and are clamped in place. Right and left-hand threads are used to assist toe-in and centering adjustments. The ends are self-adjusting and, with the exception of periodic lubrication, require no servicing.

Adjustments

Relay Arm Ball Joint

1. Remove the cotter pin and adjust the end plug slot clockwise until the inside springs are bottomed.

Steering ratio adjustment

2. Turn the plug ¾ turn counterclockwise and reinsert the cotter pin.

STEERING RATIO

1. Two-position steering arms permit an adjustment for quicker steering. Do not make this adjustment on Corvettes equipped with power steering, as frame interference will result.

2. Disconnect the tie-rod ball joint stud from the steering arm.

3. Insert the stud in the forward hole for a quick steering ratio, or the rear hole for a slower ratio.

4. Install the nut and cotter pin. Repeat this operation on the opposite side.

5. Reset the toe-in after a steering ratio adjustment.

POWER STEERING GEAR

The optional power steering on the Corvette is of the linkage assist type. The steering gear and linkage is identical to that used on manual steering cars. All procedures for the manual gear apply to the power steering gear. A belt-driven pump supplies hydraulic pressure to a sensing valve, and then on demand to a power cylinder on the linkage, which provides the power assist to the linkage.

POWER STEERING PUMP

Removal and Installation

1. Remove the hoses at the pump, and tape the ends to prevent dirt from entering.

2. Plug the pump fittings to keep the fluid in the pump.

3. Loosen the bracket retaining nuts and remove the drive belt.

4. Withdraw the bracket-to-pump bolts and remove the pump from the car. On large block Corvettes, the alternator drive belt must be removed first.

5. Place the pump on the bracket and install the attaching pieces hand-tight.

6. Install the hoses and tighten the fittings.

7. Refill the pump reservoir. Turn the pulley backward to bleed the pump.

8. Install the belt over the pulley and tighten to the correct tension.

9. Bleed the hydraulic system.

Chapter 9

Brakes

1963–64 Corvettes are equipped with four-wheel drum brakes. These are hydraulically operated, self-adjusting, and feature double-piston wheel cylinders. Three brake options were available with the drum system. Power brakes featured a Moraine vacuum assist master cylinder and were the first power brakes ever offered on the Corvette. The second option was the standard drums (honed to a 20 micro-inch finish and equipped with special heat resistant springs) and metallic linings for more fade resistance. The third option was intended for heavy-duty or competition usage. These cerametallic linings were larger and the drums were finned and scooped.

In 1965, the four-wheel disc brake system was introduced. This system includes a fixed caliper, rotating vented disc, and four-piston pad actuation. A heavy-duty, optional disc brake system is available for special purposes. A different front caliper, brake pad, and brake line pressure regulator are used. Heavy-duty brake calipers are easily recognized by

the two, pad retaining pins instead of the standard brake's single pin.

Drum Brakes

MASTER CYLINDER

Removal and Installation

1. Disconnect the hydraulic lines from the cylinder. Plug the lines to keep dirt out of the lines and master cylinder.

2. Remove the clevis pin and clip from the brake pedal arm.

3. Remove the main cylinder-to-firewall nuts and lockwashers, and remove the master cylinder.

4. Install the master cylinder on the firewall studs. Install the lockwashers, and tighten the nuts.

5. Insert the clevis pin through the clevis and the brake pedal and secure with a cotter pin.

6. Install the hydraulic lines to the master cylinder.

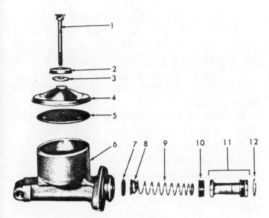

Exploded view of 1963–64 master cylinder

1. Thumbscrew	7. Valve seat
2. Vent cover	8. Valve assembly
3. Flat washer	9. Spring
4. Reservoir cover	10. Primary cup
5. Gasket	11. Secondary cup and piston
6. Body	12. Lockring

7. Refill the cylinder with brake fluid and bleed the lines.

8. Adjust the brake pedal as necessary.

Overhaul

NOTE: *Overhaul of the main cylinder portion of power brake master cylinders is the same as that for manual master cylinders.*

1. Secure the master cylinder in a vise and remove the push rod assembly and the protective boot. This exposes the lock ring which, when removed, allows extraction of the piston stop, secondary cup, and piston.

2. Remove the cylinder end plug and push out the primary cup, spring, valve assembly, and seat.

3. Wash the component parts with clean alcohol only, and be sure that all traces of gasoline or kerosene are removed. Gasoline will cause premature deterioration of the cylinder's rubber parts.

4. Carefully inspect the washed metal parts and the cylinder bore. A corroded cylinder must be replaced. Discoloration or stains should be removed with crocus cloth. When doing so, wrap the cloth around a finger and rotate the cylinder around the supported cloth. Do not polish the bore lengthwise as this can cause a fluid leak.

5. Check the piston-to-cylinder clearance with a feeler gauge. Clearance should be between 0.001 in. and 0.005 in.

6. To reassemble, moisten the cylinder bore with clean brake fluid and replace the valve seat, valve assembly, and spring.

NOTE: *Be sure that the valve and seat are properly installed before proceeding. An incorrectly assembled check valve will distort and fail to provide a check valve seal, which will result in a reduction of brake pedal travel and a corresponding loss of actual braking.*

7. Moisten the primary cup with clean brake fluid and install it, flat side out, and seated over the spring. The primary cup is distinguished by a brass support ring at its base.

8. Dip the secondary cup in clean brake fluid and slip it over the end of the piston.

9. Insert the completed assembly, with the bleeder brake end of the piston installed first. Secure the parts with the piston stop and the snap-ring, and install the end plug.

10. Attach the rubber boot and push rod, and replace the cylinder on the firewall.

11. Attach the brake pedal clevis and adjust the push rod-to-piston clearance. Correct adjustment calls for a barely perceptible free pedal before piston/push rod contact.

WHEEL CYLINDERS

Overhaul

Wheel cylinder overhaul procedures are similar to those for the master cylinder. Overhaul kits containing the necessary replacements are readily available. When rebuilding and installing the wheel cylinders, avoid introducing contaminants into the system. Piston-to-cylinder clearance should be 0.003 in. to 0.006 in. and is checked in the same manner as for the master cylinder. Cleaning and honing procedures are the same.

To reassemble, moisten the pistons and cups with clean brake fluid and position the spring in the center of the cylinder. Install the rubber cups—flat side out—followed by the pistons—flat side in. Complete the assembly with the push rods and protective boots. The front wheel cylinder housings are secured to

Exploded view of wheel cylinder

1. Pushrod boot
2. Piston
3. Piston cup
4. Housing
5. Fluid inlet
6. Spring
7. Piston cup
8. Piston
9. Pushrod boot

the backing plate by a threaded anchor pin. Torque the pin to 65 ft lbs.

Brake Bleeding

The hydraulic brake system must be bled any time one of the lines is disconnected or air enters the system. This may be done manually or by the pressure method. Correct bleeding sequence is: left rear wheel cylinder, right rear, right front, left front.

PRESSURE BLEEDING

1. Clean the top of the master cylinder, remove the cover, and attach the pressure bleeding adapter.
2. Check the pressure bleeder reservoir for correct pressure and fluid level, then open the release valve.
3. Fasten a bleeder hose to the wheel cylinder bleeder nipple and submerge the free end of the hose in a transparent receptacle. The receptacle should contain enough brake fluid to cover the open end of the hose.
4. Open the wheel cylinder bleeder nipple and allow the fluid to flow until all bubbles disappear and an uncontaminated flow exists.
5. Close the nipple, remove the bleeder hose and repeat the procedure on the other wheel cylinders according to the bleeding sequence.

MANUAL BLEEDING

An alternative to the pressure method of bleeding requires two people to perform: one to depress the brake pedal and the other to open the bleeder nipples.
1. Observe the cleaning operation of the pressure method, then remove the cover and fill the reservoir.
2. Attach a bleeder hose and clear container as before.

3. Have the assistant depress the brake pedal to the floor, and then pause until fluid flow ceases and the bleeder nipple is closed.
4. Allow the pedal to return and repeat the procedure until a steady, bubble-free flow is seen.
5. Secure the nipple and move to the other wheels in the correct sequence.
6. Periodically check the master cylinder for an adequate supply of fluid. If the reservoir runs dry, air will enter the system and bleeding will have to be done again.

BRAKE DRUMS

Removal and Installation

1. Jack the car so wheels are off the ground.
2. Remove the wheel or wheels where brake drums are to be removed.
3. Pull the brake drum off—it may be necessary to gently tap the rear edges of the drum to start it off the studs.
4. If extreme resistance to removal is encountered, it will be necessary to retract the adjusting screw. Knock out the access hole in the brake drum and turn the adjuster to retract the linings.
5. Install brake drums after adjusting the linings.
6. Install the drums in the same position on the hub or axle shaft as removed.

BRAKE SHOES

Adjustment

Rotate the star wheel adjuster until a slight drag is felt between the shoes and drum, then back off 1¼ turns on the adjuster. Backing the car and firmly braking will allow the self-adjustment feature to complete the adjustment.

Removal and Installation

1. Support the car on jackstands, slacken the parking brake cable and remove the rear wheels, rear brake drums, and front drums and hub assemblies.
2. Free the brake shoe return springs, actuator pull-back spring, hold-down pins and springs, and actuator assembly.
3. On rear wheels, disconnect the adjusting mechanism and spring, and remove the primary shoe.

Freeing hold-down pins and springs

4. Disconnect the parking brake lever from the secondary shoe and remove the shoe. Front wheel shoes may be removed simultaneously.

5. Clean and inspect all parts. Scored or out-of-round drums should be reconditioned or replaced.

6. Check wheel bearings, oil seals, wheel cylinders, and rear axle seals; repacking or replacing as needed.

7. Inspect the replacement shoes for nicks or burrs, lubricate the backing plate contact points, brake cable and levers, and adjusting screws, then reassemble.

8. Be sure that the left and right-hand adjusting screws are not mixed. The star wheel should be nearest the secondary shoe when properly installed.

9. Reverse the procedure for reassembly. When completed, make an initial adjustment as described under adjustments.

METALLIC BRAKES

Maintenance procedures for the metallic lining-only option are the same as those for standard brakes. Do not substitute these linings in standard drums, unless they have been honed to a 20 micro-inch finish and equipped with the special heat resistant springs.

The oversize metallic lining and finned drum option requires attention to the following maintenance deviations: The adjusting screw uses a solid film lubricant, and should not be cleaned with

solvent or lubricated. The final brake adjustment also differs for this option in that the self-adjustment feature actuates when firm pedal application is made while the car is moving forward. Maintenance procedures require these linings to be broken in. Make an initial adjustment then use moderate pedal pressure to make six to eight stops from approximately 30 mph. Follow this with six to eight stops from approximately 60 mph; making each stop at a one-mile interval.

PARKING BRAKE

Adjustment

The rear brakes do double duty as both wheel brakes and parking brakes. Such an arrangement makes proper adjustment of the parking brakes dependent upon proper adjustment of the wheel brakes. With the wheel brakes correctly adjusted, remove the idler return spring and loosen the locknut on the convex side of the rear brake cable equalizer. Next, tighten the adjustment nut against the concave side of the equalizer until a 16 lb strand tension is achieved in the forward brake cable. Tighten the locknut and attach the idler return spring.

Disc Brakes

MASTER CYLINDER

The early disc brake master cylinder is serviced in the same manner as the drum brake master cylinder. The later master cylinder is the dual reservoir type. This offers a separate brake circuit for the front and rear wheel pairs and prevents total loss of braking should one circuit fail.

This master cylinder is actually two complete master cylinders contained in a single housing, with the front reservoir controlling the front brake pairs and the rear reservoir, the rear brake pairs. The heavy-duty option includes a pressure regulator switch in the rear brake line just below the master cylinder.

Two dual master cylinders have been used on the Corvette and are easily identified by referring to the following chart.

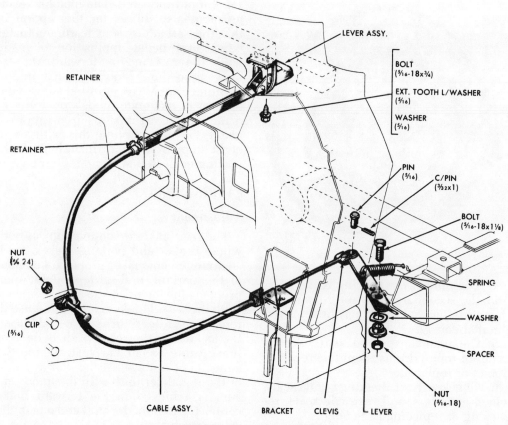

1963–64 parking brake assembly

Manufacturer	Brake Type	Main Cylinder Code	Secondary Piston
Delco Moraine	Manual-Disc Power-Disc	DC	5 rings/ grooves
	Power-Disc	PG	1 ring/ groove

Be absolutely certain that replacement parts are identified as identical to those being replaced when overhauling the dual master cylinder. The displacement capability of the master cylinder is dependent upon the length of the secondary piston.

Overhaul

1. Remove the unit from the vehicle using the same general procedure as described for conventional master cylinders.

2. Remove the mounting gasket and boot, and the main cover; purge the unit of its fluid.

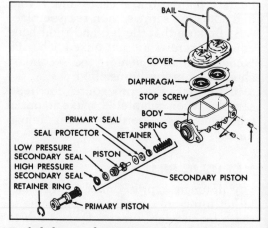

Exploded view of 1967–76 master cylinder

3. Secure the cylinder in a vise and remove the push rod retainer and the secondary piston stop bolt found inside the forward reservoir.

4. Compress the retaining ring and extract it along with the primary piston assembly.

5. Blow compressed air into the pis-

ton stop screw hole to force the secondary piston, spring, and its retainer from the bore of the cylinder. An alternate method uses a piece of wire, hooked on one end, to snag and extract the secondary piston.

6. Check the brass tube-fitting inserts and if they are damaged, remove them. Leave undamaged inserts in place.

7. If replacement is necessary, thread a 6–32 x ⅝ in. self-tapping screw into the insert. Hook the head of the screw with a claw hammer and pry the insert free.

8. An alternate way to remove the inserts is to first drill the outlet holes to ¹³/₆₄ in. and thread them with a ¼ in.–20 tap. Position a thick washer over the hole to serve as a spacer then thread a ¼ in.–20 x ¾ in. hex head bolt into the insert and tighten the bolt until the insert is freed.

9. Use denatured alcohol and compressed air to clean the component parts. Slight rust may be removed with fine crocus cloth.

10. Replace the brass tube inserts at this time by positioning them in their holes and threading a brake line tube nut into the outlet hole. Turn down the nut until the insert is seated.

11. Check the piston assemblies for correct identification and, when satisfied, position the replacement secondary seals in the twin grooves of the secondary piston.

12. The outside seal is correctly placed when its lips face the piston's flat end. The lips of the inner seal face the piston compensating holes.

13. Slip the primary seal and its protector over the end of the secondary piston opposite the secondary seals. The flat side of this seal should face the piston's compensating hole flange.

14. Replace the primary piston assembly with the assembled component found in the overhaul kit.

15. Moisten the cylinder bore and the secondary piston's inner and outer seals with new brake fluid. Assemble the secondary piston spring to its retainer and position them over the end of the piston with the retainer inside the lips of the primary seal.

16. Insert the combined spring and piston assembly into the cylinder and use a small wooden dowel or pencil to seat the spring against the end of the bore.

17. Moisten the primary piston seals with new brake fluid and push it, push rod receptacle end out, into the cylinder.

18. Keep the piston pushed in and snap the retaining ring into place.

19. Relax the pressure on the pistons and allow them to seek their static positions.

20. Replace the secondary piston stop screw and torque it to 25–40 in. lbs.

21. Replace the reservoir diaphragm and cover.

BRAKE PADS

Replacement

1. Drain ⅔ of the brake fluid from the master cylinder.

NOTE: *The insertion of the thicker replacement brakes will push the caliper pistons back into their bores and the resulting hydraulic action will cause a full master cylinder to overflow.*

2. Raise and support the car and remove the wheels.

Brake pad replacement

3. Extract and discard the cotter pin found on the inside end of the brake pad retaining pin(s) (two retaining pins on heavy duty brakes).

4. Withdraw the retaining pin(s) and remove the pads.

5. Force the caliper pistons into their bores and insert the replacement pads.

6. Replace the retaining pins and secure them with new 3/32 in. x 5/8 in. plated cotter pins.

7. Refill the master cylinder and bleed the system if necessary.

CALIPERS

Removal and Overhaul

1. With the vehicle securely raised and its wheels removed, disconnect the front caliper's brake hose at its support bracket and the rear unit's line from the inside caliper.

2. Tape the open end of each line to prevent dirt from entering.

3. Pull the cotter pins, retaining pins, and brake pads, and unbolt the caliper from its mounting bracket.

4. Remove the two large bolts and split the caliper case.

5. Remove the fluid transfer hole's O-rings.

6. The pistons are retained by ring-like boots. To remove them, fully depress the pistons and, with a screwdriver, lever the boots from their seats. Remove the pistons, springs, and seals.

7. Clean all parts with a non-mineral based solvent and compressed air, and replace the rubber parts with those in the brake service kit.

8. Inspect the piston bores for damage or corrosion. Polish corroded bores with crocus cloth and, if this is not enough, replace the caliper.

9. Maintain the proper tolerances by referring to the following chart.

Caliper Piston-to-Bore Clearance

3/8 in. bore	0.0035–0.009
7/8 in. bore	0.0045–0.010

10. Reverse the disassembly procedure to reassemble.

NOTE: *Remember, when positioning the piston seal on the piston, that it goes in the groove nearest the piston's flat end with the lap facing the largest end. If placement is correct, the seal lips will be in the groove and not extend over the groove's step.*

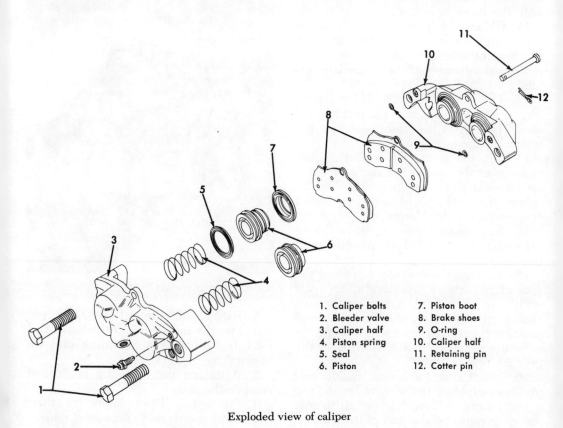

1. Caliper bolts	7. Piston boot
2. Bleeder valve	8. Brake shoes
3. Caliper half	9. O-ring
4. Piston spring	10. Caliper half
5. Seal	11. Retaining pin
6. Piston	12. Cotter pin

Exploded view of caliper

DISC

Removal and Maintenance

Braking performance is greatly affected by the disc run-out. Lateral run-out must not exceed 0.002 in. total. Discs should not be refinished to a thickness of less than 1.215 in.

Checking disc run-out

Should it become necessary to replace the disc, the rivets that attach the disc to its hub must be drilled out. The replacement disc does not have to be riveted to the hub as the lug nuts adequately secure both.

PARKING BRAKE

Adjustment

The parking brake is a conventional drum brake located in the rear wheel disc. Adjustments are similar to those for a regular drum brake.

1. Block the front wheels. Jack the rear wheels off the ground and remove the wheels. Release the handbrake.
2. Rotate the disc until the adjusting screw can be seen through the hole in the disc.
3. Loosen the parking brake cables at the equalizer until they go slack. Insert a screwdriver and adjust with an up-and-down motion.
4. Tighten the adjuster until the disc cannot move, then back off six to eight notches.

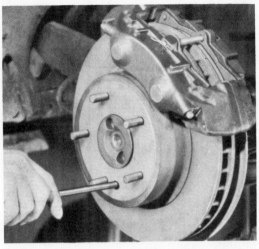

Parking brake adjustment on disc brake model

5. Apply the parking brake to the fourth notch. Tighten the cables at the equalizer to give a light drag with the wheel mounted.
6. Release the parking brake and check for a no drag condition.

Brake Shoe Removal and Replacement

1. Jack the car up and remove the wheel and tire.
2. Remove the brake caliper as previously outlined. Do not disconnect the brake line, but remove the line clip from the control arm and hang the caliper above the disc with wire.
3. Drill the disc retaining rivets out and remove the disc from the axle hub.
4. Insert a screwdriver into the adjusting hole and turn the screw several times to expand the shoes.
5. Push the brake shoes forward until the front shoe hold-down spring can be seen through the adjusting hole.
6. Insert a pair of needle-nosed pliers through the hole and grasp the hold-down pin. Depress the spring with a screwdriver inserted from the side and turn the pin 90° to free the spring and retainer. Remove the spring and retainer.
7. Repeat this operation on the rear brake shoe.
8. Retract the shoes by turning the adjuster screw. Pull the shoes from the adjuster and remove the adjuster and spring.
9. Separate the shoes at the anchor pin and lift the shoes up and out of the housing, while allowing the straight part

of the return spring to go between the outer tip of the anchor pin and the axle flange plate.

10. Lightly lubricate the backing plate shoe contact surfaces, anchor pin, and adjusting screw threads.

11. Install the return spring on the replacement shoes and position the shoes on the anchor pin.

12. Install the adjuster spring and adjuster. Turn the adjuster screw to expand the shoes.

13. Turn the axle shaft flange so that the adjustment hole aligns with the front hold-down spring pin.

14. Push the shoe forward and over the hold-down pin.

15. Install the spring and retainer over the hold-down pin and using needle-nosed pliers again, and a screwdriver as in Step 6, depress the spring and twist the pin 90°.

16. Repeat the above step on the rear shoe. Another pair of needle-nosed pliers will have to be utilized to hold the pin in position, as head of this pin is not accessible.

17. Turn the adjuster screw to retract the shoes.

18. Install the brake disc onto the studs, making sure that the adjustment holes in the disc and flange align.

19. Install the caliper as previously outlined.

20. Adjust the parking brake as previously described.

21. Install the tire and wheel and lower the car.

22. After installation of new parking brake linings, the shoes should be burnished. At a speed of 50 mph, apply the parking brakes until a slight drag is felt. Keep the brakes on for approximately 50–60 seconds.

Brake Specifications

	Brake Cylinder Bore				
		Wheel Cylinder Diameter (in.)		Drum or Disc Diameter (in.)	
Year	Master Cylinder (in.)	Front	Rear	Front	Rear
1963–64	1.0①	1³⁄₁₆	1.0	11.00	11.00
1965–76	1.0	1⅞	1⅜	11.75 (Disc)	11.75 (Disc)

① Metallic brakes—⅞

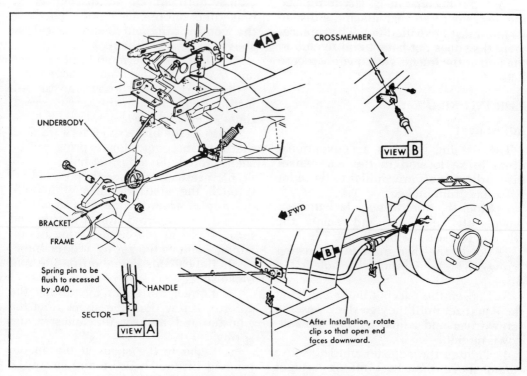

Disc brake parking brake cable assembly

Chapter 10

Body

Doors

Removal and Installation

1963–67

1. Remove window cranks, armrest (1963–64), door lock control (top reflects on 1963–64), and door control knob.
2. Remove the door trim panel by carefully prying it off.
3. Scribe the door hinge position on the body.

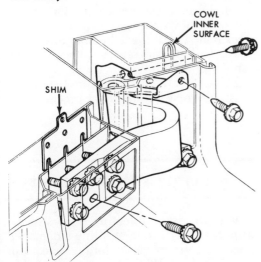

COWL INNER SURFACE

SHIM

1963–67 door hinge

4. Remove the hinge bolts, while an assistant supports the door. On cars with electric windows, disconnect the wiring.
5. Remove the door, noting the position and number of any hinge shims.
6. To install, position the hinges on the previously scribed mark and hand-tighten the bolts. Remember to install any shims under the hinges.
7. Check for proper door closing and adjust the hinge bolt positioning in the slotted holes.
8. The door lock striker position is movable, should further adjustment be necessary.

1968–76

1. Remove the window crank and door lock control.
2. Remove the retaining screws and remove the door panel by carefully prying it off.
3. Remove the door lock handle screw and slide the handle off.
4. Peel the inside plastic cover off the door.
5. Remove the hinge access cover.
6. Remove the door threshold plate, the side kick panel, and the radio speaker.
7. Remove the air intake ducts, lower

mast jacket cover, and the instrument panel pad and/or dash panel pad.

8. Disconnect and remove the wiring between the hinge pillar and door on cars with electric windows.

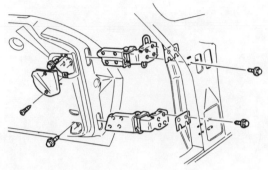

1968–72 door hinge

9. Scribe the door hinge position and remove the door. An assistant should be used to hold the door during removal. Note the location and number of hinge shims.

10. To install, position the hinges on the previously scribed mark and hand-tighten the bolts. Remember to install any shims under the proper hinges.

11. Check for proper door closing, and if necessary adjust hinge bolt position in the dotted holes.

12. The door lock strike is movable for further adjustment.

Engine Hood

Removal and Installation

1. Scribe the hinge positioning and the prop mounting location on the hood.

2. While an assistant supports the hood, loosen and remove the hinge and prop bracket bolts.

3. Lift hood off the car.

4. To install the hood, position the hinges on the previously scribed lines and screw bolts in hand-tight.

5. Adjust the hinge bolt positioning for correct opening and closing, then tighten the hinge bolts.

6. Install and tighten the prop to the hood.

Fuel Tank

Removal and Installation

1. Disconnect the battery ground cable.

2. Remove the fuel line and drain the tank.

3. Remove the spare tire compartment.

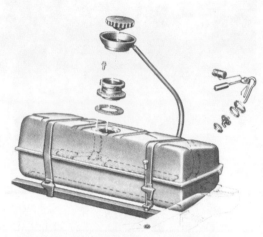

1963–67 fuel tank assembly

4. Remove the exhaust pipe-to-tailpipe U-bolts at the crossmember.

5. Remove the tailpipe extensions.

6. Disconnect the muffler brackets and drop the entire assembly out of the way.

7. Remove the two retaining straps from the tank.

8. Disconnect fuel gauge wiring.

9. Remove the gas cap and rubber neck boot. Disconnect the filler drain line.

10. Unbolt and remove the frame gas tank support.

11. Lower the tank and turn to remove.

12. Reverse the removal procedure to install.

Fiberglass Body Repair

The process of effecting repairs to the Stingray body is one of filling a damaged area with either glass cloth and resin or plastic solder. While this may appear to be an over-simplification, it is interesting to note that the factory interpretations of body damage are restricted to the two general categories of minor and major. Repair kits, appropriate to the definitions, are made available accordingly.

Minor repairs are made with the Plastic Solder Repair Kit. Proper use of the materials contained in this kit will produce an easy, quick, and lasting repair of small cracks and holes, as well as surface imperfections.

Major repairs are required for large holes, torn panels, and separated joints. Such repairs require the adhesive qualities of the resin and the reinforcing qualities of the glass fibers found in the Resin Repair Kit. This kit contains resin, hardener, thixatrope, fiberglass cloth, mixing utensils, and protective creams.

The cream protects the skin from a noncontagious form of dermatitis known as occupational, or contact dermatitis. Improvements in resin formulas have virtually eliminated this problem but the creams are still included in the kit for those who may be sensitive to the resins

Mixing plastic solder

Applying hardener/resin to fiberglass cloth

or dust. While the creams are not generally required when using the plastic solder kit, their application is recommended whenever the materials in the resin kit are used. To obtain maximum benefit from them, it is necessary to first wash, then dry the hands thoroughly. Next, squeeze about ½ in. of no. 71 cream into the cuticle, between the fingers, and around the wrists, spreading it evenly and lightly until it disappears. Apply a second coat and then set the cream by holding both hands under cold running water. When the cream has set, apply the no. 55 cream over the no. 71 cream in the same manner. Do not rub your hands together when rinsing in water.

In working with fiberglass, remember that the materials being used are potentially harmful to the careless worker. The resin mixture should be removed from the hands as soon as possible and imperatively before the mixture starts to gel. This gel condition may be observed by the action of the material. To ensure complete removal of resin, apply lacquer thinner followed by a careful washing in soap and water. Minor skin irritation from glass and powdered, cured resin can be minimized by washing in cold water. Avoid getting the resin material on clothing.

Minute particles of glass fibers are potentially harmful if inhaled into the lungs, so always use respirators when grinding. It is also advisable to use a belt sander with a vacuum attachment to control dust. As an added safeguard, always work with resin mixtures in well-ventilated areas to reduce the effects of toxic fumes.

An important point to remember, when working on the Corvette body, is to always use materials that are comparable to those being repaired. Repair kits, conforming to original equipment specifications, may be ordered from dealers. Keep the work area, materials, and tools clean and dry, as dirt or moisture can adversely affect the chemical reactions in fiberglass repair.

Prior to making repairs, look for hidden damage such as hairline cracks and other breakage. This is best accomplished by applying pressure around the obviously damaged area. Check for minor damage around exhaust pipes, grille, and other points of wear. Detection at this point can prevent additional repairs at a later date.

Minor Repairs

Minor repairs are those necessary to correct surface imperfections. These are best made by using the materials found in the Plastic Solder Kit. To properly utilize this kit, it is necessary to first remove the exterior finish from the damaged area with paint remover or a power sander. After checking for additional damage, mix the Plastic Solder materials according to kit directions and apply the finished mixture with a putty knife or rubber squeegee. Work into the damaged area, building it up to the desired contour. It may be necessary to use several ½ in. layers for deep filling and on vertical surfaces. Complete the repair in the usual manner of grinding, sanding and painting.

Major Repairs

The procedure used for making major repairs is basic for repairing any fiberglass panel or component and is made using the Resin Repair Kit.

Check for hidden damage as previously outlined. When the initial inspection has been made, use paint remover to strip the finish from the damaged area and look for additional breakage.

With the second inspection completed, the actual repair work is begun by first grinding the damaged area so that it forms a "V" at the broken or cracked portion. Shape the sides of the "V" to a shallow pitch so that it will provide a maximum bonding surface.

If the rear of the damaged area is accessible, clean behind it to allow the use of resin-saturated glass cloth laminates on both sides of the damage. Cut fiberglass cloth to size, using a minimum of five layers for the average repair.

Mix resin and hardener, one part hardener to four parts resin. Thicken the material if needed, by adding thixatrope. Cleanliness must be observed at all times during the operation. Make certain that all containers are clean and dry and that resin and hardener cans are kept closed when not in use. Also do not use waxed cups for mixing or allow resin to enter hardener can or vice versa.

Prepare the laminates by saturating the layers of fiberglass cloth with the resin mixture. Apply the laminates to the panel, making certain that all wrinkles are smoothed out and the general contour of the area is followed.

With the laminates in place, use heat lamps to cure the repaired area. Place the lamps no closer than 12 in. away from the repair and allow at least 15–20 minutes curing time. Trim the repair to shape when the gel stage is reached. When the laminates have cured, complete the normal finishing procedures. Small pits or surface irregularities can be covered with plastic solder.

Specific Repairs

SCRATCHES, SPOT REFINISHING

Minor scrapes and scratches will normally require nothing more than a paint refinishing job. For scratches that have gone through to the plastic remove all paint from the area around the scratch with lacquer removing solvent. Next, feather-sand the area, first with no. 220 wet or dry paper. Cutting too deeply into the fiberglass mat during the sanding process will make it necessary to change the repair procedure to that suggested for dents and pits.

Use a surface preparatory solvent or its equivalent for initial clean-up of the repair area, then follow with a tack rag. Use non-staining type masking tape on the body to mask and protect surrounding areas when painting. Complete the refinishing as outlined in the paint refinishing portion of this chapter.

DENTS OR PITS AND CRACKED GLAZE COAT

A heavy glancing blow to the Corvette body will usually result in a large pit or indentation in the panel. The following repair procedure for this type of damage may also be used to remedy cracks in the glaze or finish coat of the paint, however, it should only be used to effect a plastic build-up when the damaged area is neither extensive nor pierced.

To begin this repair, first use lacquer thinner or its equivalent to remove the paint. Next provide a good bonding surface by scuffing the area surrounding the damage. Use the preparatory solvent for the initial clean-up of the repair area, then finish with a tack rag.

Fill surface imperfections with plastic solder, then feather-sand the repaired area with no. 220 sandpaper and finish-sand with no. 320. Complete refinishing as outlined in this chapter.

HOLES

Due to the strength of reinforced plastic, this type of damage is not common. Grind or file away all cracked or splintered material around the hole and bevel the edges to a 30° angle. Use lacquer solvent to remove the exterior paint. Completely remove all dirt, deadener, and paint from the underside of the damaged panel for a 4 in. area around the hole, then scuff the plastic surface on both sides of the panel, using no. 80–d sandpaper.

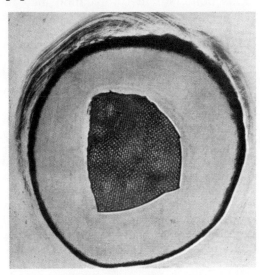

Back-up laminates under damage

Cut two pieces of glass cloth that are large enough to overlap the hole. These pieces will be used for back-up lamination. If the damaged panel is rather thick, an appropriate number of laminates should be tailored to the approximate shape of the hole and used for build-up. The amount of resin needed for the back-up inserts will be determined by the size of the damaged area. Use two back-up laminations on the underside of the panel and complete the repair procedure.

Use plastic solder for final filling. Block-sand the plastic fill with no. 80–d sandpaper and finish-sand with no. 220

and no 320 wet or dry sandpaper. Prepare the area for paint refinishing.

CRACKS

It should be noted that the best results will be obtained when the ambient temperature is at least 70° F to 75° F. Begin the repair by removing the broken portion of the panel, cutting along the break line with a hacksaw blade. Use lacquer remover or its equivalent to remove the paint from a distance, 2–3 in. from the fracture on the underside of both portions of the panel. Scuff the area clean.

Grind or file away all cracked and fractured material along the break. Bevel the edges of the fracture at a 30° angle using a file or grinder and scuff the plastic surfaces along the edge of the break. Align the fractured panels with C-clamps, leaving ⅛ in. clearance for alignment.

Cut a strip of fiberglass cloth to a size sufficient to overlap the fracture by 1–2 in. on all sides. Prepare the plastic mixture, according to resin repair kit directions and saturate the glass fiber cloth with the mixture. Squeeze the excess mixture from the cloth. Using excessive amounts of plastic should be avoided since the strength of the patch is directly proportional to the glass fiber content of the patch.

Should a low spot exist, prepare another plastic mixture, mixing resin and hardener thoroughly. Add short fibers cut from glass cloth to this mixture to give it a putty-like consistency. Using a spatula, liberally apply the plastic mixture to the fracture and the surrounding area, depositing enough material build-up to allow for sanding and filing.

When the patch has hardened, shape it to conform with the general contour of the panel by filing or grinding. Avoid gouging the repair or the surrounding area. Fill any imperfections that appear with plastic solder. When the fill has sufficiently hardened, finish-sand the surface and paint.

CRACK AT PANEL JUNCTION

A minimum of time and effort is required to repair a crack at the junction of two panels. First step is to provide a good bonding strip by cutting all splintered material from the crack and sanding the adjacent area. Fill the crack with plastic solder. When the patch has hardened, sand the area to match the contour of the surrounding panel.

PANEL REPLACEMENT

In cases of extensive damage it is often advisable to install a replacement panel. Such repair panels are available for this purpose. The complete panel may be installed or sections may be cut from it to accommodate the necessary repair. Proper alignment should be checked prior to plastic application by fitting the panel and installing all attaching parts. When availability of the correct panel has been assured, you may then cut out the damaged section with a hacksaw blade. Remove dirt, deadener, and paint from the underside of the old panel for a distance of 2–3 in. back from the attaching line. Bevel the mating edges at a 30° so that a single "V" butt joint will be formed on the exterior surface when the pieces are joined. Perform any necessary reshaping to assure a close fit of the replacement section.

Cut two back-up pieces of glass fiber cloth of a sufficient size to run the entire length of the joint and overlap the junction line on either side by 2–3 in. Align the replacement section and clamp in place, forming a closed "V" butt joint at the panel junction. In cases where panels cannot be clamped, use 3/16 in. bolts with large washers on inner and outer panels, or straps and sheet metal screws.

Prepare a sufficient amount of liquid plastic in an un-waxed paper cup, as outlined in resin repair procedures. Saturate the back-up plies of cloth, then use a squeegee to remove any excess plastic from the cloth. Place the saturated plies on the underside of the damaged panels and, if necessary, use paper to hold them in place until the plastic gels. For fill purposes on exterior surfaces, use glass cloth or another plastic mixture of resin, hardener and ½ in. lengths of cut glass fiber mixed to a putty-like consistency. Use the saturated glass cloth or reinforced plastic material to fill the "V" groove; building the area with sufficient material to allow for finish operations. When the patch has hardened, file or sand the patch to the general body contour using no. 80–d. Finish-sand and prepare for painting.

PAINT REFINISHING

Lacquer preparations and painting procedures for the Stingray plastic body are the same as for metal bodies. To facilitate paint matching, it is easier to refinish panels to the nearest break line. Wipe the entire work area with a clean cloth soaked with the preparatory solvent to remove all traces of wax, polish and grease, then wipe surface dry with a second clean cloth. The old paint finish may be removed by sanding with coarse sandpaper or using solvent. Use no. 220 wet or dry sandpaper for initial feather-sanding or paint edges and finish with no. 440 wet or dry paper.

To obtain the best results, always feather-sand from the outside of the paint break toward the center so as to eliminate the possibility of low spots in the paint. This done, surface preparation may be carried out using first, the preparatory solvent and then a tack rag to thoroughly clean the surface. Avoid touching the surface with bare hands from this point on, as skin oil deposited on the surface of the panel may adversely affect the adhesion of the paint to the body.

With surface preparation completed, spray the bare plastic and feathered areas with a mixture of one part primer-surfacer to two parts thinner. Apply two or more medium coats and allow each to flash or dull before applying each succeeding coat. Allow at least one hour between the application of the final coat and the beginning of sanding operations. Best results will be obtained if no. 320 wet or dry sandpaper is used. If dry sanding is preferred, then no. 360 paper is called for.

Should pinpoint imperfections become evident at this time, knife them out with putty and allow ½ hours for drying. Finish-sand when dry. These small pits in the plastic may be filled before the primer-surfacer is applied. Following sanding operations, wipe clean and fill the imperfections with plastic solder. This material is faster than body glazing compounds when they are used on the Corvette, although both are acceptable. In fact, most glazing putty failures are due to insufficient drying time for the putty or excessively heavy applications.

When the surface imperfections have been removed, dust the repaired area and spray with one coat of make-ready sealer, reduced one part to one and a half parts thinner. To ensure maximum sealing, allow at least 30 minutes to dry. The surface may be scuffed lightly with no. 440 sandpaper to remove nibs, then dusted and tack-wiped. Spray the primed surface in three or four wet, double-color coats. Let each coat flash before spraying the succeeding coat.

Allow a minimum of four hours for drying, preferably overnight; then hand-rub with rubbing compound or machine polish using machine compound no. 14. Complete the final finishing by hand or machine polishing with liquid polish or dry-buff with a polishing disc or lamb's wool bonnet. Allow thirty days before waxing to ensure hardening of the lacquer and dispersal of trapped solvents.

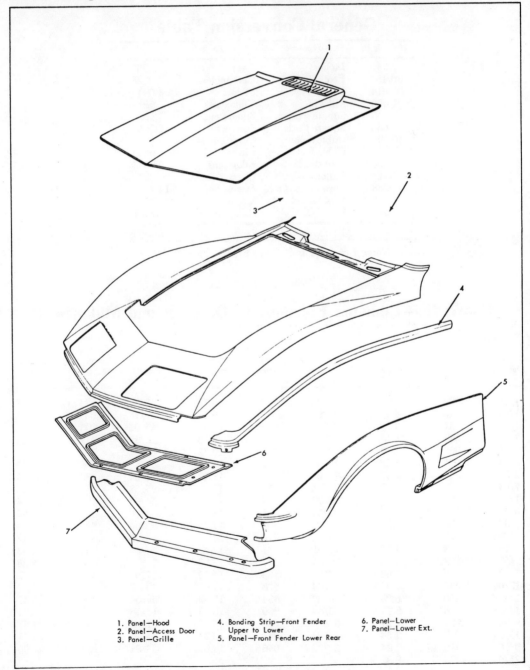

1. Panel—Hood
2. Panel—Access Door
3. Panel—Grille
4. Bonding Strip—Front Fender Upper to Lower
5. Panel—Front Fender Lower Rear
6. Panel—Lower
7. Panel—Lower Ext.

1973–75 front body panels

Appendix

General Conversion Table

Multiply by	To convert	To	
2.54	Inches	Centimeters	.3937
30.48	Feet	Centimeters	.0328
.914	Yards	Meters	1.094
1.609	Miles	Kilometers	.621
.645	Square inches	Square cm.	.155
.836	Square yards	Square meters	1.196
16.39	Cubic inches	Cubic cm.	.061
28.3	Cubic feet	Liters	.0353
.4536	Pounds	Kilograms	2.2045
4.226	Gallons	Liters	.264
.068	Lbs./sq. in. (psi)	Atmospheres	14.7
.138	Foot pounds	Kg. m.	7.23
1.014	H.P. (DIN)	H.P. (SAE)	.9861
——	To obtain	From	Multiply by

Note: 1 cm. equals 10 mm.; 1 mm. equals .0394″.

Conversion—Common Fractions to Decimals and Millimeters

INCHES			INCHES			INCHES		
Common Fractions	Decimal Fractions	Millimeters (approx.)	Common Fractions	Decimal Fractions	Millimeters (approx.)	Common Fractions	Decimal Fractions	Millimeters (approx.)
1/128	.008	0.20	11/32	.344	8.73	43/64	.672	17.07
1/64	.016	0.40	23/64	.359	9.13	11/16	.688	17.46
1/32	.031	0.79	3/8	.375	9.53	45/64	.703	17.86
3/64	.047	1.19	25/64	.391	9.92	23/32	.719	18.26
1/16	.063	1.59	13/32	.406	10.32	47/64	.734	18.65
5/64	.078	1.98	27/64	.422	10.72	3/4	.750	19.05
3/32	.094	2.38	7/16	.438	11.11	49/64	.766	19.45
7/64	.109	2.78	29/64	.453	11.51	25/32	.781	19.84
1/8	.125	3.18	15/32	.469	11.91	51/64	.797	20.24
9/64	.141	3.57	31/64	.484	12.30	13/16	.813	20.64
5/32	.156	3.97	1/2	.500	12.70	53/64	.828	21.03
11/64	.172	4.37	33/64	.516	13.10	27/32	.844	21.43
3/16	.188	4.76	17/32	.531	13.49	55/64	.859	21.83
13/64	.203	5.16	35/64	.547	13.89	7/8	.875	22.23
7/32	.219	5.56	9/16	.563	14.29	57/64	.891	22.62
15/64	.234	5.95	37/64	.578	14.68	29/32	.906	23.02
1/4	.250	6.35	19/32	.594	15.08	59/64	.922	23.42
17/64	.266	6.75	39/64	.609	15.48	15/16	.938	23.81
9/32	.281	7.14	5/8	.625	15.88	61/64	.953	24.21
19/64	.297	7.54	41/64	.641	16.27	31/32	.969	24.61
5/16	.313	7.94	21/32	.656	16.67	63/64	.984	25.00
21/64	.328	8.33						

Conversion—Millimeters to Decimal Inches

mm	inches	mm	inches	mm	inches	mm	inches	mm	inches
1	.039 370	31	1.220 470	61	2.401 570	91	3.582 670	210	8.267 700
2	.078 740	32	1.259 840	62	2.440 940	92	3.622 040	220	8.661 400
3	.118 110	33	1.299 210	63	2.480 310	93	3.661 410	230	9.055 100
4	.157 480	34	1.338 580	64	2.519 680	94	3.700 780	240	9.448 800
5	.196 850	35	1.377 949	65	2.559 050	95	3.740 150	250	9.842 500
6	.236 220	36	1.417 319	66	2.598 420	96	3.779 520	260	10.236 200
7	.275 590	37	1.456 689	67	2.637 790	97	3.818 890	270	10.629 900
8	.314 960	38	1.496 050	68	2.677 160	98	3.858 260	280	11.032 600
9	.354 330	39	1.535 430	69	2.716 530	99	3.897 630	290	11.417 300
10	.393 700	40	1.574 800	70	2.755 900	100	3.937 000	300	11.811 000
11	.433 070	41	1.614 170	71	2.795 270	105	4.133 848	310	12.204 700
12	.472 440	42	1.653 540	72	2.834 640	110	4.330 700	320	12.598 400
13	.511 810	43	1.692 910	73	2.874 010	115	4.527 550	330	12.992 100
14	.551 180	44	1.732 280	74	2.913 380	120	4.724 400	340	13.385 800
15	.590 550	45	1.771 650	75	2.952 750	125	4.921 250	350	13.779 500
16	.629 920	46	1.811 020	76	2.992 120	130	5.118 100	360	14.173 200
17	.669 290	47	1.850 390	77	3.031 490	135	5.314 950	370	14.566 900
18	.708 660	48	1.889 760	78	3.070 860	140	5.511 800	380	14.960 600
19	.748 030	49	1.929 130	79	3.110 230	145	5.708 650	390	15.354 300
20	.787 400	50	1.968 500	80	3.149 600	150	5.905 500	400	15.748 000
21	.826 770	51	2.007 870	81	3.188 970	155	6.102 350	500	19.685 000
22	.866 140	52	2.047 240	82	3.228 340	160	6.299 200	600	23.622 000
23	.905 510	53	2.086 610	83	3.267 710	165	6.496 050	700	27.559 000
24	.944 880	54	2.125 980	84	3.307 080	170	6.692 900	800	31.496 000
25	.984 250	55	2.165 350	85	3.346 450	175	6.889 750	900	35.433 000
26	1.023 620	56	2.204 720	86	3.385 820	180	7.086 600	1000	39.370 000
27	1.062 990	57	2.244 090	87	3.425 190	185	7.283 450	2000	78.740 000
28	1.102 360	58	2.283 460	88	3.464 560	190	7.480 300	3000	118.110 000
29	1.141 730	59	2.322 830	89	3.503 903	195	7.677 150	4000	157.480 000
30	1.181 100	60	2.362 200	90	3.543 300	200	7.874 000	5000	196.850 000

To change decimal millimeters to decimal inches, position the decimal point where desired on either side of the millimeter measurement shown and reset the inches decimal by the same number of digits in the same direction. For example, to convert 0.001 mm into decimal inches, reset the decimal behind the 1 mm (shown on the chart) to 0.001; change the decimal inch equivalent (0.039″ shown) to 0.000039″.

Tap Drill Sizes

Screw & Tap Size	National Fine or S.A.E. Threads Per Inch	Use Drill Number	Screw & Tap Size	National Coarse or U.S.S. Threads Per Inch	Use Drill Number
No. 5	44	37	No. 5	40	39
No. 6	40	33	No. 6	32	36
No. 8	36	29	No. 8	32	29
No. 10	32	21	No. 10	24	25
No. 12	28	15	No. 12	24	17
$\frac{1}{4}$	28	3	$\frac{1}{4}$	20	8
$\frac{5}{16}$	24	1	$\frac{5}{16}$	18	F
$\frac{3}{8}$	24	Q	$\frac{3}{8}$	16	$\frac{5}{16}$
$\frac{7}{16}$	20	W	$\frac{7}{16}$	14	U
$\frac{1}{2}$	20	$\frac{29}{64}$	$\frac{1}{2}$	13	$\frac{27}{64}$
$\frac{9}{16}$	18	$\frac{33}{64}$	$\frac{9}{16}$	12	$\frac{31}{64}$
$\frac{5}{8}$	18	$\frac{37}{64}$	$\frac{5}{8}$	11	$\frac{17}{32}$
$\frac{3}{4}$	16	$\frac{11}{16}$	$\frac{3}{4}$	10	$\frac{21}{32}$
$\frac{7}{8}$	14	$\frac{13}{16}$	$\frac{7}{8}$	9	$\frac{49}{64}$
$1\frac{1}{8}$	12	$1\frac{3}{64}$	1	8	$\frac{7}{8}$
$1\frac{1}{4}$	12	$1\frac{11}{64}$	$1\frac{1}{8}$	7	$\frac{63}{64}$
$1\frac{1}{2}$	12	$1\frac{27}{64}$	$1\frac{1}{4}$	7	$1\frac{7}{64}$
			$1\frac{1}{2}$	6	$1\frac{11}{32}$

Decimal Equivalent Size of the Number Drills

Drill No.	Decimal Equivalent	Drill No.	Decimal Equivalent	Drill No.	Decimal Equivalent
80	.0135	53	.0595	26	.1470
79	.0145	52	.0635	25	.1495
78	.0160	51	.0670	24	.1520
77	.0180	50	.0700	23	.1540
76	.0200	49	.0730	22	.1570
75	.0210	48	.0760	21	.1590
74	.0225	47	.0785	20	.1610
73	.0240	46	.0810	19	.1660
72	.0250	45	.0820	18	.1695
71	.0260	44	.0860	17	.1730
70	.0280	43	.0890	16	.1770
69	.0292	42	.0935	15	.1800
68	.0310	41	.0960	14	.1820
67	.0320	40	.0980	13	.1850
66	.0330	39	.0995	12	.1890
65	.0350	38	.1015	11	.1910
64	.0360	37	.1040	10	.1935
63	.0370	36	.1065	9	.1960
62	.0380	35	.1100	8	.1990
61	.0390	34	.1110	7	.2010
60	.0400	33	.1130	6	.2040
59	.0410	32	.1160	5	.2055
58	.0420	31	.1200	4	.2090
57	.0430	30	.1285	3	.2130
56	.0465	29	.1360	2	.2210
55	.0520	28	.1405	1	.2280
54	.0550	27	.1440		

Decimal Equivalent Size of the Letter Drills

Letter Drill	Decimal Equivalent	Letter Drill	Decimal Equivalent	Letter Drill	Decimal Equivalent
A	.234	J	.277	S	.348
B	.238	K	.281	T	.358
C	.242	L	.290	U	.368
D	.246	M	.295	V	.377
E	.250	N	.302	W	.386
F	.257	O	.316	X	.397
G	.261	P	.323	Y	.404
H	.266	Q	.332	Z	.413
I	.272	R	.339		

ANTI-FREEZE CHART

Temperatures Shown in Degrees Fahrenheit
+32 is Freezing

Cooling System Capacity Quarts	Quarts of **ETHYLENE GLYCOL** Needed for Protection to Temperatures Shown Below													
	1	2	3	4	5	6	7	8	9	10	11	12	13	14
10	+24°	+16°	+ 4°	−12°	−34°	−62°								
11	+25	+18	+ 8	− 6	−23	−47								
12	+26	+19	+10	0	−15	−34	−57°							
13	+27	+21	+13	+ 3	− 9	−25	−45							
14			+15	+ 6	− 5	−18	−34							
15			+16	+ 8	0	−12	−26							
16			+17	+10	+ 2	− 8	−19	−34	−52°					
17			+18	+12	+ 5	− 4	−14	−27	−42					
18			+19	+14	+ 7	0	−10	−21	−34	−50°				
19			+20	+15	+ 9	+ 2	− 7	−16	−28	−42				
20				+16	+10	+ 4	− 3	−12	−22	−34	−48°			
21				+17	+12	+ 6	0	− 9	−17	−28	−41			
22				+18	+13	+ 8	+ 2	− 6	−14	−23	−34	−47°		
23				+19	+14	+ 9	+ 4	− 3	−10	−19	−29	−40		
24				+19	+15	+10	+ 5	0	− 8	−15	−23	−34	−46°	
25				+20	+16	+12	+ 7	+ 1	− 5	−12	−20	−29	−40	−50°
26					+17	+13	+ 8	+ 3	− 3	− 9	−16	−25	−34	−44
27					+18	+14	+ 9	+ 5	− 1	− 7	−13	−21	−29	−39
28					+18	+15	+10	+ 6	+ 1	− 5	−11	−18	−25	−34
29					+19	+16	+12	+ 7	+ 2	− 3	− 8	−15	−22	−29
30					+20	+17	+13	+ 8	+ 4	− 1	− 6	−12	−18	−25

For capacities over 30 quarts divide true capacity by 3. Find quarts Anti-Freeze for the ⅓ and multiply by 3 for quarts to add.

For capacities under 10 quarts multiply true capacity by 3. Find quarts Anti-Freeze for the tripled volume and divide by 3 for quarts to add.

To Increase the Freezing Protection of Anti-Freeze Solutions Already Installed

Cooling System Capacity Quarts	Number of Quarts of **ETHYLENE GLYCOL** Anti-Freeze Required to Increase Protection												
	From +20°F. to					From +10°F. to				From 0°F. to			
	0°	−10°	−20°	−30°	−40°	0°	−10°	−20°	−30°	−40°	−10°	−20°	−30°	−40°
10	1¾	2¼	3	3½	3¾	¾	1½	2¼	2¾	3¼	¾	1½	2	2½
12	2	2¾	3½	4	4½	1	1¾	2½	3¼	3¾	1	1¾	2½	3¼
14	2¼	3¼	4	4¾	5½	1¼	2	3	3¾	4½	1	2	3	3½
16	2½	3½	4½	5¼	6	1¼	2½	3½	4¼	5¼	1¼	2¼	3¼	4
18	3	4	5	6	7	1½	2¾	4	5	5¾	1½	2½	3¾	4¾
20	3¼	4½	5¾	6¾	7½	1¾	3	4¼	5½	6½	1½	2¾	4¼	5¼
22	3½	5	6¼	7¼	8¼	1¾	3¼	4¾	6	7¼	1¾	3¼	4½	5½
24	4	5½	7	8	9	2	3½	5	6½	7½	1¾	3½	5	6
26	4¼	6	7½	8¾	10	2	4	5½	7	8¼	2	3¾	5½	6¾
28	4½	6¼	8	9½	10½	2¼	4¼	6	7½	9	2	4	5¾	7¼
30	5	6¾	8½	10	11½	2½	4½	6½	8	9½	2¼	4¼	6¼	7¾

Test radiator solution with proper hydrometer. Determine from the table the number of quarts of solution to be drawn off from a full cooling system and replace with undiluted anti-freeze, to give the desired increased protection. For example, to increase protection of a 22-quart cooling system containing Ethylene Glycol (permanent type) anti-freeze, from +20°F. to −20°F. will require the replacement of 6¼ quarts of solution with undiluted anti-freeze.